PLAY IN A COVID FRAME

Play in a Covid Frame

Everyday Pandemic Creativity in a Time of Isolation

Edited by Anna Beresin and Julia Bishop

https://www.openbookpublishers.com

ISBN Paperback: 978-1-80064-891-3
ISBN Hardback: 978-1-80064-892-0
ISBN Digital (PDF): 978-1-80064-893-7
ISBN Digital ebook (EPUB): 978-1-80064-894-4
ISBN XML: 978-1-80064-896-8
ISBN HTML: 978-1-80064-897-5
DOI: 10.11647/OBP.0326

Cover photo by Volodymyr Hryshchenko on Unsplash, https://unsplash.com/photos/7JAyy7jLTAk.

Cover design by Jeevanjot Kaur Nagpal

The game would commence by him batting a sensory ball that loosely resembles the virus pictures we see everywhere onto the trampoline [...]. If the ball hit them once, they would 'self-isolate' at the edge of the trampoline, counting to 10. This could happen 3 times, but once the ball hit you a fourth time, dramatic coughing would begin, then they would fall over and 'die'.

Rebecca Oberg (quoted in Beresin 2020)

Contents

List of Figures and Recordings

Introduction

Anna Beresin and Julia Bishop

Teddy bears in windows.
LEGO ventilators.
Corona Tag. . .

Play in a Covid Frame documents everyday pandemic creativity, a record of how children, youth, adults and communities improvised expressively in different places around the world. What emerges is an exploration of the complicated bio-social cultural process of play as framed by the novel coronavirus SARS-CoV-2 and its phases of lockdown and quarantine from 2020–2022. Our book mainly emphasizes the play of children during this time, although we recognize that play remains important for health throughout the lifespan. For many during the pandemic, access to play became both a public health and an educational crisis associated with extreme isolation. For some, the pandemic offered new opportunities for play.

There are books explaining Covid-19 to young children and books explaining the basic idea that play is important for those who care for children in general. There are studies of how Covid has affected children in health care settings and schools, and how children have been affected behaviourally by loss or by lockdown (Kara and Koo 2021; Alabdulkarim et al. 2021; Sama et al. 2020). There are graphic novels and poetry collections about Covid and picture books with titles like *Momma Can I Sleep with You Tonight? Helping Children Cope with the Impact of COVID-19*. Everyone on this planet of nearly eight billion people has been affected by the loss of face-to-face social time, the removal of public encounters, the increase in uncertainty and the strangeness of the unknown trajectory of the virus. For some, it has been particularly devastating, with multiple losses of life, income and housing. According to the World Health Organization, a study published in *The Lancet* estimated 1.5 million children have lost a parent, custodial grandparent or other caregiver because of Covid between March 2020 and April 2021 (Hillis et al. 2021). Many traditional avenues of mourning or comforting the ill face-to-face had become impossible. Mental health referrals for children in the editors' home countries of the US and UK have sky-rocketed (Abramson 2022; Weedy 2021). What we have very little knowledge about is *how* children, youth, families and communities have coped creatively and how Covid has appeared in children's play cultures. What happens improvisationally when people are cut off from their normal social networks and the spaces they typically inhabit? How have we used the riskiness of play to help deal with the pandemic's unknowns?

The title *Play in a Covid Frame* references the notion that play is always rooted in some sort of frame. In fact, all knowledge is framed by specific moments in time and geography and is seen through particular lenses. In the following chapters, we find that play in its complexity has been illuminated by Covid, and that children and families have adapted in both traditional and innovative ways. For some in crisis, play may disappear entirely, but for many, play has been a key to emotional and social survival. The sociologist Erving Goffman saw all of social life as reflecting a kind of frame inviting frame analysis and, in a sense, this book is a series of snapshots of social life as marked by the pandemic frame (Goffman 1974).

The chapters that follow range from micro-studies of solo toy-hospital play and Zoom playdates of techno-mischief during quarantine to large-scale studies of families in their communities. The authors are researchers and practitioners in Australia, Canada, England, Finland, Ireland, Japan, Scotland, Serbia, Sudan, South Korea, the United States and Wales. Cultures studied include families from different social classes and different speech communities. The editors sent out invitations to major international organizations involved in play research and advocacy: the International Play Association, the Association for the Study of Play, and journals including the *International Journal of Play*, along with scholarly organizations in psychology, folklore and anthropology. We thank the *International Journal of Play* for allowing permission to include versions of chapters here from their double special issue on 'Play: Resilience and Vulnerability in Difficult Circumstances' (2021-22), the Royal Anthropological Institute and Folklore Society in the United Kingdom for encouraging our editors' participation in its conference 'Creativity during COVID Lockdown: Life and Renewal During the Pandemic' (2021), and the Play Observatory team for its symposium 'Pandemic Play Experiences: Practices Activities/Objects/Texts' (2022). These conferences served as a scholarly introduction to several of the authors in this book.

We recognize that many parts of the world are struggling with basics and the pandemic continues as new variants of the virus emerge. Initially intending to collect a more global portrait of pandemic play, we are therefore still honored to be including the work of so many colleagues from so many different countries. At the same time, we acknowledge that there are many other play stories to be told from around the world and from under-represented peoples, and we hope that they will emerge in due course. That the primary contributions here come from English-speaking countries says more about the networking of scholarship than the true availability of research in the countries that we are missing. Meanwhile, for those seeking more global information about the anthropology of play, we recommend Helen Schwartzman's *Transformations: The Anthropology of Play* (1978), Melvin Konner's *The Evolution of Childhood* (2010), and David Lancy's *The Anthropology of Childhood: Cherubs, Chattel, Changelings* (2022). Schwartzman speaks of western biases in the description of normative play and Konner reminds us that, for many cultures, 'teaching, observational learning, and play are combined, and in effect, become one process' (2010: 517). Konner suggests that studies of play must be situated in larger studies of cultural practice, as we have attempted to do in this volume. Lancy's book includes a society index from Angola to Yacqui and notes that in communities where food sourcing is the primary activity and labor-demanding, play decreases. We do know that play, like sleep, can disappear in moments of high stress. We hope that this book sparks further study across the globe, documenting diverse pandemic frame cycles.

Play in a Covid Frame is one of the first books to focus exclusively on play during the pandemic. This will likely not be the only pandemic in our lifetime, however, and the questions it raises are relevant beyond the specifics of Covid-19. How can play help us stay vibrant? How can play help us adapt to new challenges? What distinctive cultural variations have emerged in this time and what creative activities do many groups have in common? How are young people, adults, and communities utilizing objects like toys, along with public, private and online spaces, as tools to deal with the isolation of this moment? When we treat children and young people as creative agents who are able to talk to us theatrically through the things they make and the ways they move, there is much to learn about them individually and collectively. We cannot assume that we know what they are experiencing, or what they need, until we observe them in careful detail like folklorists and ethnographers do.

What Is a Folkloristic Approach to Pandemic Play?

Folklorists study artistic communication—the genres of games, toys, songs, tales, jokes, material culture, festivals and other forms of performance. Folklorists value the oral in times dominated by print and its authority, along with informal means of learning and realization. Folkloristic approaches have been comparative, diachronic and synchronic. They may espouse an ethnographic approach but have an awareness of analogues and connections in space and time. Folklore studies may then take an historical approach, looking at threads of continuity and change, and focusing on 're-creation', the crafting of meaning in this process. They may also take a geographical approach, examining the flow and distribution of specific creative forms and genres, and they may take a cross-cultural or comparative approach. Often, folklorists study pieces of culture that are overlooked, art outside the museum, music outside the concert hall. Steve Zeitlin, author of *The Poetry of Everyday Life*, writes, 'Folklorists work to document, interpret, present, and advocate for forms of cultural expression that society may view as marginalized or insignificant, but which are often at the core of a community's identity and culture' (2021:19). If the folklorists of childhood and of play across the life course offer any wisdom, it is in the genres of play, games, humour, and toys that the strangeness of the adult world emerges.

In the 1950s, for example, Iona and Peter Opie documented children in Wolstanton, England, playing a tag game called Germ, one in Cranford called Fever, and in Wales they played the Plague (1969: 119). In 1968, Jeanne Pitre Soileau recorded this one in New Orleans, USA, also recorded similarly by the Opies in the United Kingdom:

> Call the doctor quick, quick, quick.
> Doctor, Doctor, will I die?
> Close your eyes and count to five,
> 1-2-3-4-5.
> (Soileau 2016: 58; cf. Opie and Opie 1959: 34)

In the 1980s, Vivian Gussin Paley famously audio-taped the play in her Chicago preschool; a four-year-old told another that the bad guys they were fighting were 'wet to death'. His friend countered, 'But if I touch anyone they could come back to life'. 'Back to life, wet to death, back to life!' (Paley 1988: 118). For Paley, children would play with death as a normal existential crisis often related to familial dramas surrounding the birth of a new sibling or power dynamics within social groups. In this book, we offer the paradox of this most unusual time—that we have witnessed the extraordinariness of Covid play as both theme and frame, and recognize that play forms have always reflected existential crises.

In the early 1990s, Beresin recorded children creating a spontaneous news programme on a playground in Philadelphia where children warned each other not to go to California 'or you'll get shot'. It was just weeks after the violence emerged in South Central Los Angeles after the brutal beating of Rodney King. The playground was filled with narratives of violence, warnings about travel to other cities and warnings about violence on the boulevard, spurred on by the presence of the author's video camera, an impromptu report of the 'newses' of the day (Beresin 2010). After September 11, 2001, in another Philadelphia playground, one nine-year-old sang to her softly:

> World Trade Center is falling down, falling down, falling down,
> World Trade Center is falling down, Oh-on top of us.
> (Beresin 2002)

Play allows children to repeat things they have seen and heard, retell it and remould it until it makes some kind of sense as a coping mechanism.

And yet some things we encounter make no sense at all, and sometimes it is not the job of play to try and make sense. In order to tackle such a large field, this volume includes perspectives from a range of disciplines beyond folklore and anthropology: psychology, sociology, art history, education, communication, cultural studies, early childhood studies, as well as the perspectives of health advocates, project managers, educators, playworkers, artists, and park, game and toy designers.

Individual children or families are not the unit of study here; it is the play of human beings caught up in the pandemic and affected by its associated regimes, restrictions and consequences. Drawing from folklore, the activity and the talk around the activity is the focus, deeply rooted in its various settings or contexts, whether it be the home, the schoolyard, the street or the park. Unlike anthropology, the place itself is not the primary frame but the cultural context is considered essential as a window into understanding. The activities belong to a place and time, and also reflect our global collective struggle. What folklorists do is to document, preserve and study these play genres as a reflection of the past and the present. Some connect it to archival material, some to oral history and some compare the material cross culturally. This volume does some of all the above within the larger window of child and family study. After such a time of anxiety and fear, of disruption to our normal social networks, of no sleep, of constant reminders about risk, death and loss, play, and the documentation of it in this volume, offers a set of counter-narratives: that we have been cut off and frightened and yet we are very much alive and connected. So, we play chase. And we compose satires. And we run from safety to danger to safety again. We play in forts and under tables. We make things and destroy them. We label things and relabel them, and label them again.

Psychologist and folklorist Brian Sutton-Smith spoke of the 'triviality barrier of play', that somehow the deep and poetic process of human playful expression has to fight for its legitimacy alongside other more respected containers of paradox like art or religion (1997). It is a well-accepted cliché that play is 'fun' and yet play may sometimes evoke surrealism and sad emotions (Axline 1947; Erikson 1975; Freud 1995 [1907]; Klein 1932). Games are as much about failure as they are about success, as meditation can be said to be a form of controlled suffering. Both are a type of practice for the unknown and both can make room for complex feelings (Juul 2013; Beck 2021). In the complexity of emotions at play, we make emotional space for experimentation, adjustment, renewal and healing. It is hoped that this work demonstrates that in the lightness of play lies a corresponding space for heaviness, and that schools and child care programmes, if they are serious about helping students readjust post-pandemic, will all safeguard time for play and recess.

Children fearful or not sleeping well? *Make time for play.*
Children overwhelmed by academic catch up? *Make time for play.*
Children antisocial? *Make time for play.*
Need a way to address social-emotional learning on a regular basis? *Make time for play.*

One hundred years of developmental psychology from such divergent authors as Sigmund Freud, Jean Piaget and Lev Vygotsky point to the absolute necessity of play for children and of the creative forces connected to play itself (Freud 1995 [1907]; Elkind 2008; Piaget 1962; Vygotsky 1978).

We still do not know what play is exactly, but we know that when it is missing it is a sign of ill health. Brian Sutton-Smith's aphorism 'the opposite of play is not work—it's depression' applies to toddlers and high schoolers, to college students and senior citizens. As D. W. Winnicott wrote, play has much to do with reality, offering a transition from our attachments to our interdependence. Toys and games serve to challenge our thinking, to allow us to puzzle and sort through the illogic of the present. Freud's student Erik Erikson would nod and say that after play we are refreshed as if after a good night's sleep (Erikson 1950; Winnicott 1971). This is true, even in a time of tremendous insomnia.

Covid has been an extremely limiting constraint for some, limiting social time, touch, sound, movement and the visual communication of the human face (Steiner and Veel 2021). Games themselves are artificial constraints and so potentially prepare us for such moments of serious constraint. In games, we limit running around to certain patterns or we use fewer words, like the mini crossword puzzle. Play scholar Johann Huizinga wrote that play is itself associated with its own magic circle, its own artificial limits and boundaries (1938). Katie Salen and Eric Zimmerman called play 'free movement in a more rigid structure' (2004;

304). Games and play can be then considered as the ultimate preparation for challenging times and this is true for humans as well as for animals (Fagen 1981; Burghardt 2005). It is also true that for some, the pandemic gave them more time but less geographical freedom, leading to more family time and less peer time, or more time with siblings and less with friends. It is clear that no one scholarly discipline holds all the tools for understanding the complexity of play and the complexity of this time frame. So, this book will turn and turn again to the lenses of sociology, anthropology, folklore, history and psychology as we attempt to shed light on pandemic play.

Adults play; often it appears through the arts and through crafts. We have seen bakeries serve coronavirus-shaped breads, round balls with the characteristic protruding sticks on all sides, like the icon of the virus (Kirshenblatt-Gimblett 2021). Some have turned to creative ways of decorating and personalizing masks, for example, in some cases donating hand-sewn masks to hospitals and schools. Some museums have hosted art made during Covid, notably New York's Arts Westchester's exhibit, 'Together ApART: Reflections during Covid', featuring diverse art forms. Highlights included Jennifer Larrabee's quilt made from remnants left over from mask making and Rebecca Thomas' inventive flamenco dance recorded at home with a mustachioed broom and bucket faux partner. Thomas danced and played with the motif of cleaning and scrubbing to keep her family safe. These play forms exaggerate the basics—what it means to eat, to cover ourselves, to wash, to move during the pandemic.

Play is the seed of all creativity. The Irish poet and theologian Pádraig Ó Tuama writes:

> The creative is not just a decoration. It's not a luxury. The creative is an element. And 'the creative' doesn't have to mean I'm going to go and write an orchestral suite. It might be I'm going to make a scarf with my terrible knitting, for instance, or a pie, or write a letter. It isn't something to turn to when you've time. It's something that makes time and something that, in a time of constraint, actually allows time to expand. (Ó Tuama, 2022)

Sometimes play creates and sometimes it destroys, making room for new ideas and new creations.

The goals of *Play in a Covid Frame* are threefold: to witness what anthropologist Victor Turner called 'the human seriousness of play', to document a diversity of human inventiveness during the novel coronavirus and to attempt to crystalize a useful definition of play itself through descriptive portraiture (Turner 1982). If we note what play is and does informally, it may help families, schools and other programmes that work with children safeguard time for play in the future and not confuse it with other similar-looking activities, like organized adult-led recess, art class or gym. Even in solitary play there are cultural frames and the hidden rhetoric of toy or game designers. We cannot help but play in community even when we are by ourselves. As videogame scholar Chris Bateman writes, 'No one plays alone' (2017). Like art, play is fundamentally a form of dialogue (Bakhtin 1981; Bateson 1972), so studying social play in a time of fluctuation in isolation can prove particularly useful as we search for strategies to live together on this planet.

Following the metaphor of the frame, the book is divided into three sections: landscapes, portraits and shifting frames. Landscape chapters focus on larger projects, with a particular emphasis on the built environment or playground. Portraits contain smaller-scale case studies, sometimes as small as a single toy or as large as play in a specific town. The third section raises new questions by studying hybrid play in different forms. Specifically, our landscape section begins with Julia Bishop's examination of Covid-themed chase games as they emerged in the pandemic, largely as evidenced through the eyes of adults on Twitter. Živka Krnjaja and Nevena Mitranić look at 'play as the common space' in the Serbian lockdown. Holly Sienkiewicz, Jenn Beideman, Beatriz LeBron, Shanielia Lewis, Emma Morrison, Lydia Rivera and Dina Faticone describe a 'resident-driven play-based agenda' in Rochester, New York, addressing Covid interventions there. Maria O'Dwyer, Carmel Hannan, and Patricia Neville focus on social class and play access during Covid in the Republic of Ireland. Pete King points to how adventure playgrounds in the United Kingdom responded to both Covid and the first lockdown there, while Mitsunari Terada, Mariia Ermilova and Hitoshi Shimamura document facility management of Covid restrictions in a youth centre complex in Japan. This section contains wider lenses.

The portrait section includes Katriina Heljakka's study of plush toys as 'objects of resilience' during Covid in Finland through the intergenerational display of teddy bears. Anna Beresin chronicles the pandemic as frame, theme and provocation as families searched for communal play spaces in three different communities in the US city of Philadelphia, Pennsylvania. There is a sense of ambiguity here, as many families denied the appearance of the virus in their children's play but acknowledged that their children were constantly playing 'going to the doctor'. Caron Carter offers parents' perspectives on their children's friendships during the pandemic in England, highlighting a sense of loss and their renewed understanding of children's social worlds. William Renel and Jessica Thom recount 'disabled-led play' and advocacy during Covid in England with their programme *Touretteshero*. Nicolas Le Bigre toys with Covid play innovations and vulnerability in Scotland, offering a nuanced look at improvised cultural offerings, from 'Clapping for Carers' to chalked botanical signage. Suzanne M. Egan, Jennifer Pope, Chloé Beatty and Clara Hoyne bring us findings from the Play and Learning Early Years (PLEY) Covid-19 Study in Ireland. Like these authors, Pool Ip Dong addresses the play of young children but this time in South Korea. Many of the portraits focus on toys and crafts during Covid, balancing both the specificities and the universals of pandemic play. The section finishes with John Potter and Michelle Cannon's photo essay excerpted from the Play Observatory which documented a range of children's play experiences during Covid-19.

The shifting frames section opens with Martha Radice's study of 'Yardi-Gras' in New Orleans. (No, Yardi-Gras is not a typo.) Judy McKinty, Ruth Hazleton and Danni von der Borch describe children finding 'new ways to play' during the pandemic in Australia. Beresin returns with a microanalysis of techno-mischief during a Zoom playdate. Yinka Olusoga and Catherine Bannister problematize the complexity of children's masking during the pandemic, sharing personal accounts of mask decoration and identity play. We finish with Heather Shirey's 'Art in the Streets: Playful Politics in the Work of the Velvet Bandit and SudaLove', representing Covid-related graffiti art in the work of two artists, one from the San Francisco Bay area in the USA and one from Sudan.

Young people's art appears in specific chapters but also forms a montage at the end of the portraits and shifting frames sections, highlighting young people's direct participation in curating their own documentation. Following the model of Robert Coles' works *Children of Crisis* (1967), *The Moral Life of Children* (1986a), *The Political Life of Children* (1986b) and *The Spiritual Life of Children* (1986c), *Play in a Covid Frame* honours not just the words of children, youth, adults and communities but their designs, their bodily intelligence. In conclusion, Beresin and Bishop flip the title and examine 'Covid in a Play Frame', making connections between play theory, folklore and public health, as we examine the pandemic not just as one episode but as an ongoing global challenge. Concrete suggestions for those who work and play directly with children, youth and adults are offered as a postscript, created collectively on Zoom with the contributing authors, a virtual conference designed to meet new challenges and meet each other.

It is hoped that this book will demonstrate youthful sophistication at play along with familial innovation during the pandemic, and remind us to safeguard time and public space for exaggerated playful activity and art. We who write, study or work in play, or who aim to keep our lives playful, must shift our understanding of play's importance in community life, as play remains a most trivialized topic of study in all fields and a most sidelined activity in most countries' public schooling. Play moves into open spaces, coming out of restricted ones. In this spirit, *Play in a Covid Frame* has been made open access by design, as free as possible.

Works Cited

Abramson, Ashley. 2022. 'Children's Mental Health Is in Crisis', *Monitor on Psychology Trends Report*, 53: 69, https://www.apa.org/monitor/2022/01/special-childrens-mental-health

Alabdulkarim, Sarah Omar, et al. 2022. 'Preschool Children's Drawings: A Reflection on Children's Needs within the Learning Environment Post COVID-19 Pandemic School Closure', *Journal of Research in Childhood Education*, 36: 203-18, https://doi.org/10.1080/02568543.2021.1921887

Axline, Virginia. 1947. *Play Therapy: The Inner Dynamics of Childhood* (Boston: Houghton Mifflin)

Bakhtin, Mikhail. 1981. *The Dialogic Imagination* (Austin: Texas University Press)

Bateman, Chris. 2017. 'No-one Plays Alone', *DiGRA: Transactions of the Digital Games Research Association*, 3.2: 5-36, https://doi.org/10.26503/todigra.v3i2.67

Bateson, Gregory. 1972. *Steps to an Ecology of Mind* (New York: Ballentine)

Beresin, Anna. 2002. 'Children's Expressive Culture in Light of September 11, 2001', *Anthropology and Education Quarterly*, 33: 331-37

——. 2011. *Recess Battles: Playing, Fighting, and Storytelling* (Jackson, MS: University of Mississippi Press)

——. 2020. Playful Introduction, *International Journal of Play*, 9: 275-76, https://doi.org/10.1080/21594937.2020.1805967

Burghardt, Gordon. 2005. *The Genesis of Animal Play: Testing the Limits* (Cambridge, MA: MIT Press)

Beck, Charlotte Joko. 2021. *Ordinary Wonder: Zen Life and Practice* (Boulder, CO: Shambhala Press)

Coles, Robert. 1967. *Children of Crisis* (New York: Little, Brown & Co.)

——. 1986a. *The Moral Life of Children* (Boston: Atlantic Monthly Press)

——. 1986b. *The Spiritual Life of Children* (Boston: Atlantic Monthly Press)

——. 1986c. *The Political Life of Children* (Boston: Atlantic Monthly Press)

Delacruz, Jenny. 2020. *Momma, Can I Sleep With You Tonight? Helping Children Cope with the Impact of Covid-19* (Philadelphia, PA: Cobbs Creek)

Elkind, David. 2008. 'The Power of Play: Learning What Comes Naturally', *American Journal of Play*, 1: 1-6

Erikson, Erik. 1950. *Childhood and Society* (New York: Norton)

——. 1975. *Studies of Play* (New York: Arno)

Fagen, Robert. 1981. *Animal Play Behavior* (New York: Oxford University Press)

Freud, Sigmund. 1995 [1907]. 'Creative Writers and Day-Dreaming,' in *On Freud's 'Creative Writers and Day-dreaming'*, ed. by Ethel Spector Person, Peter Fonagy and Sérvulo Augusto Figueira (New Haven: Yale University Press), pp. 143-49

Goffman, Erving. 1974. *Frame Analysis* (Cambridge, MA: Harvard University Press)

Hillis, Susan D., et al. 2021. 'Global Minimum Estimates of Children Affected by Covid-19-Associated Orphanhood and Deaths of Caregivers: A Modeling Study', *The Lancet*, 398: 391–402, https://doi.org/10.1016/S0140-6736(21)01253-8

Huizinga, Johan. 1938. *Homo Ludens: A Study of the Play-Element in Culture* (New York: Random House)

Juul, Jesper. 2013. *The Art of Failure: An Essay on the Pain of Playing Video Games.* (Cambridge, MA: MIT Press)

Kara, Helen, and Su-Ming Khoo (eds). 2020. *Researching in the Age of Covid-19, Volume 2: Care and Resilience* (Bristol: Bristol University Press), https://doi.org/10.46692/9781447360414

Kidman, Rachel, and others. 2021. 'Estimates and Projections of Covid-19 and Parental Death in the US', *JAMA Pediatrics*, 175: 745-56, https://doi.org/10.1001/jamapediatrics.2021.0161

Kirshenblatt-Gimblett, Barbara. 2021. 'Anticipatory Heritage', *Heritage, Folklore, and the Public Sphere*, American Folklore Society Folklore Talks, https://youtu.be/_paUiQ4lmOc

Klein, Melanie. 1932/1975 *The Psycho-analysis of Children*, trans. by A. Strachey (London: Hogarth)

Konner, Melvin. 2010. *The Evolution of Childhood: Relationships, Emotions, Mind.* (Cambridge, MA: Belknap Press of Harvard University)

Lancy, David. 2022. *The Anthropology of Childhood: Cherubs, Chattel, Changelings*, 3rd edn (Cambridge: Cambridge University Press)

Ó Tuama, Pádraig. 2022. *Poetry Unbound, Bonus: An Invitation from Pádraig and Krista. On Being with Krista Tippett*, 28 March, https://onbeing.org/programs/bonus-an-invitation-from-padraig-and-krista/

Opie, Iona, and Peter Opie. 1959. *The Lore and Language of Schoolchildren* (Oxford: Clarendon Press)

——. 1969. *Children's Games in Street and Playground* (Oxford: Oxford University Press)

Paley, Vivian Gussen. 1988. *Bad Guys Don't Have Birthdays: Fantasy Play at Four* (Chicago: University of Chicago Press)

Salen, Katie and Eric Zimmerman. 2004. *Rules of Play: Game Design Fundamentals* (Cambridge, MA: MIT Press)

Sama, Bhupinder Kaur, et al. 2021. 'Implications of Covid-19 Induced Nationwide Lockdown on Children's Behaviour in Punjab, India', *Child Care Health Development*, 47: 128-35, https://doi.org/10.1111/cch.12816

Schwartzman, Helen. 1978. *Transformations: The Anthropology of Children's Play* (New York: Plenum)

Soileau, Jeanne Pitre. 2016. *Yo' Mama, Mary Mack, and Boudreaux and Thibodeaux: Louisiana Children's Folklore and Play* (Jackson, MS: University of Mississippi Press)

Steiner, Henriette and Kristin Veel. 2021. *Touch in the Time of Corona: Reflections on Love, Care, and Vulnerability in the Pandemic* (Berlin: De Gruyter)

Sutton-Smith, Brian. 1997. *The Ambiguity of Play* (Cambridge, MA: Harvard University Press)

Turner, Victor. 1982. *From Ritual to Theatre: The Human Seriousness of Play* (New York: Performing Arts Journal Press)

Vygotsky, Lev. 1978. *Mind in Society: The Development of Higher Psychological Processes*, ed. by M. Cole (Cambridge, MA: Harvard University Press)

Weedy, Simon. 2020. 'Concern Over the Record Number of Child Mental Health Referrals in England and Wales', *Child in the City Online Newsletter,* 9, https:// www.childinthecity.org/2021/09/30/concern-over-record-number-of-child-mental-health-referrals-in-england-and-wales/

Winnicott, D. W. 1971. *Playing and Reality* (London: Tavistock)

Zeitlin, Steve. 2016. *The Poetry of Everyday Life: Storytelling and the Art of Awareness* (Ithaca, NY: Cornell University Press)

——. 2021. 'Folklore's Four Sisters: Scholarship, Fieldwork, Activism, and Artistry'. *Voices: Journal of New York Folklore*, 47: 19-21, https://citylore.org/folklores-four-sisters/

LANDSCAPES

'April 1, 2021'

1. 'Tag, You've Got Coronavirus!' Chase Games in a Covid Frame

Julia Bishop

Touch chase is one of the oldest and most widespread forms of play in the childhood repertoire. It is elegantly simple in conception—the chaser role changes from one player to another when the latter is caught— yet amenable to adaptation in a myriad of ways. Its requirements are likewise simple—a defined space to move around in and more than one player, plus an agreement to chase or be chased according to rules agreed by the players to govern a particular game. These affordances have led to huge variety as well as the remarkable recurrence of certain forms and elements.[1]

Touch chase is often high on the list in surveys of games popular among children in the school playground during breaktimes (e.g. Blatchford, Creeser and Mooney 1990). Yet, there is generally little detail as to which children it is popular with and how frequently, in what forms and for what reasons chasing is played. Likewise, for such a universal kind of play, there are few in-depth or international studies. Part of many children's everyday experience in middle childhood (around six to twelve years), touch chase often goes unnoticed by adults, although

---

[1] An international survey and bibliography of touch chase is lacking but one of the earliest references in the English language occurs in *Francis Willughby's Book of Games*, compiled in the 1660s (Cram, Forgeng and Johnston 2003), and variants have been documented continuously from the nineteenth century on (see, for example, Gomme 1984 [1894, 1898]; Newell 1963 [1903]; Sutton-Smith 1972 [1959]; Opie and Opie 1969; Knapp and Knapp 1976; Virtanen 1978; Schwartzman 1978; Bronner 1988; Roud 2010). For animal chase games involving role reversal, see Burghardt 2005.

   https://doi.org/10.11647/OBP.0326.01

they might recognize having played it themselves as children, and may intervene if it leads to injury, conflict or aggression (Blatchford 1994).

At the time of the global spread of the novel coronavirus SARS-CoV-2 in early 2020, however, adults quickly became aware that children were incorporating elements into their play that related to what was happening in the wider world. Among the reports that started to crop up, especially on social media, were some which spoke of chase games with names like Coronavirus Tag, Corona Tip, Infection and Covid Tiggy. In these, the chaser was typically cast as the coronavirus, or as having Covid-19, and they had to chase the others and transmit it to them:

> 'You got the Covid' (Place unknown, 20 March 2021, Twitter)
> 'CORONA CORONA!' (Place unknown, 22 September 2021, Twitter)
> 'Run he's infected!' (Place unknown, 5 November 2020, Twitter)
> 'Tag you've got coronavirus!' (Canada, 23 March 2020, Twitter)

Children were also adapting their chase games to circumvent or accommodate social distancing measures:

> The students aren't allowed to touch hands, so they've invented 'corona rules' for all their normal games. We're about to play 'corona rules mushroom tag' and it involves a lot of elbows. (Australia, 19 March 2020, Twitter).

Adult responses varied. Some expressed sadness and pessimism at the emergence of coronavirus chasing games, some reacted with amusement, and others saw them as potentially dangerous, victimizing or inappropriate, on the one hand, or educational, therapeutic or creative on the other. Incongruity and bemusement were common. 'Just heard that the kids at the local primary school were playing "Coronavirus Tag" this morning before bell. Not sure whether to laugh or cry', tweeted a parent in the UK in March 2020. 'It's bizarre hearing 8 year olds asking their friends if they can play Corona', posted a member of staff at a Swedish school nine months later.

This chapter examines accounts of coronavirus-related chase games gathered from scholarly research, news reports and social media posts for insights into how the games were played, by whom and in what countries and settings, how they came about and why, and how they relate to earlier chasing games. The focus is on any touch chase games which have been inflected by the Covid-19 pandemic in the way they were played, be this in terms of rules, roles, language and terminology, embodied practices, imagined scenarios, use of space and/or proxemics. Beneath the similar-sounding names are varied and dynamic games. As I have described elsewhere, there is thus not one coronavirus tag game but many (Bishop 2023). They emerged rapidly and in many places at once, continued to be reported for at least two years (although with dwindling frequency), and generally seem to have been the result of children's own initiatives. Touch chase games relating to current affairs are not a new phenomenon (Eberle 2016), and neither are those relating to illness and affliction (e.g. Opie and Opie 1969: 75–78), but in the case of Covid-19, they are probably the most widely spread and extensively reported instances. They have the potential to shed light on children's practices and experiences of chasing play, and highlight the importance of taking it seriously and considering its nuances.

Tracing Chasing in a Pandemic: Social Research and Social Media as Sources

Due to the conditions of the pandemic and the widespread and rapid emergence of the games, I have had to rely on others' accounts, predominantly those of other adults, rather than direct observation of and research with children themselves. These comprise i) research projects documenting aspects of everyday life during the pandemic using online surveys and video call interviews, ii) journalists' reports and iii) individuals' posts on social media. Projects focusing specifically on children's lives and play experiences include the 'Play and Learning in the Early Years (PLEY) Covid-19 Survey in Ireland' (discussed by Egan and others in Chapter 12), the 'Pandemic Play Project in Australia' (see McKinty and Hazleton 2022, and also Chapter 16 in the present volume) and the 'Play Observatory' in the UK (Cowan et al. 2021, and Potter and Cannon in Chapter 14).[2] The news reports derive from the

---

2   I am grateful to Suzanne Egan and Judy McKinty, Ruth Hazleton and Danni von der Borch for making their data available to me and clarifying details. Sincere

UK, Denmark and the USA (BBC 2020, Christian 2020, Smith 2020, Cray 2020, Hunter and Jaber 2020, Griffiths 2020). One drew on accounts garnered through an appeal made via the news outlet's Facebook page for parents (Bologna 2020a, 2020b).

By far the most numerous reports of Coronavirus Tag appeared on Twitter, however. With over two million daily active users worldwide (Dean 2022), the platform is increasingly being used as a source of data in scholarly research (Ahmed 2021). In particular, it can provide real-time and 'naturally occurring' information on attitudes, responses and networks (Sloan and Quan-Haase 2017). Social media, including Twitter, were of particular importance during the pandemic as a source of information and means of conversation, especially during periods of social distancing and lockdown (Chen et al. 2020). It is not surprising that it has proved an important source for this study. Previously folklorists have focused on folklore as transmitted and created on social media and in digital communication (Blank 2012, De Seta 2020, Peck and Blank 2020). In this case, social media, and specifically Twitter, has been drawn on as a major source of information about children's folklore taking place in face-to-face settings.

To locate 'tweets' (messages of up to 280 characters posted on Twitter) relating to Coronavirus Tag, I used the platform's own advanced search function, employing such terms as 'coronavirus', 'covid', 'corona', 'pandemic', and 'infection' in various combinations with 'tig', 'tiggy', 'tag', 'chase', 'playground' and 'game'. Twitter users can connect their content and make it more findable by tagging a keyword or topic with a hashtag (#) to link it to other tweets incorporating the same hashtag. I therefore searched on #coronavirustag, #coronatag, #covidtag, #covidgames, #pandemicplay and #pandemictag. A wide range of terms and some educated guesswork was required since the name of the game, and the way it is described and hashtagged, is variable. Further searches became necessary as new names and possible hashtags (such as #kidsarefunny corona) were discovered. Searches containing the

thanks to my colleagues on the Play Observatory project (2020–2022)—John Potter, Kate Cowan and Michelle Potter at the Institute of Education, University College London (UCL), Yinka Olusoga and Catherine Bannister at the School of Education, University of Sheffield, and Valerio Signorelli at the Bartlett Centre for Advanced Spatial Analysis at UCL—for their support of my ongoing research into Coronavirus Tag.

term 'tag' returned many irrelevant results given the use of this term in a different sense within the platform itself.

Only tweets stating that a person had directly observed play, or were reporting first-hand testimony about it, were used. This resulted in 247 examples. Tweets are thus the source of approximately 75% of the 331 examples of coronavirus tag games assembled in total for this research. There are undoubtedly more to be uncovered and it should be noted that the resulting data is currently confined to English-language examples only.

There is currently considerable debate concerning the ethics of using Twitter data in academic research (Ahmed, Bath and Demartini 2017, Ahmed 2021). It is important to note that Twitter's terms of service and privacy policy clearly state that tweets are in the public domain and users are able to restrict who has access to them if they wish. Users can also opt to be known by a pseudonym rather than their real name when they tweet. There are still ethical issues to consider, however, such as the lack of informed consent from users and the possibility that they could be identified (insofar as they have made themselves identifiable on the platform) from the words of their tweet, and whether this would cause them harm or put them at risk. There is also the difficulty of being able to sufficiently contextualize Twitter content and to obtain demographic profiles of those providing it (e.g. Fiesler and Proferes 2018; Sloan 2017). While it is theoretically possible to contact individuals via the platform to gain consent, this has proved difficult in practice. Not all have enabled direct messaging and, as described in a British Educational Research Association case study (Pennacchia 2019), the process proved complex and time-consuming, and had a patchy response.

The following approach to the use of Twitter data in this study has received ethical approval from the University of Sheffield, UK. Tweets have been harvested to provide details of children's touch chase play in its many manifestations. The central focus is on the attributes of the game and those playing it (their age and gender), and when (date and time of day) and where (geographical location and specific setting) this was happening. The identity of the person tweeting is only of interest inasmuch as it sheds light on the context in which they have observed or heard about the game—as a teacher or parent, for example—and the context in which they may pass comment on it.

The tweets themselves are not consistent in mentioning the date and place of the game they describe so the date it was tweeted and the geographical location of the person tweeting have been taken as the next best clues. The date of the tweet is always clear but establishing a person's location has generally meant consulting their personal profile to see whether they have included their location. For Twitter users to do so is optional, however, so it has not been possible to establish the location of the game in all cases. It is also possible that the location of the person tweeting is not the same as that where the game was being played.

Due to my focus on tweets as a source of information about children's games rather than the person posting, and the minimal use of personal data, the risk of harm to those tweeting is judged to be low. I have therefore not attempted to seek consent from the individuals whose tweets I draw on. Instead, all tweets reproduced here are presented anonymously excluding the author's Twitter handle and the tweet url. Geographical location, also potentially identifying, has been limited to country. Any tweets that reveal personal information about the children playing the game, such as their names, have been redacted, and any photographs and films of children included have not been used.

Nevertheless, quotations from tweets appearing below are mostly presented verbatim and as such could be traced on Twitter. Verbatim quotations are at the heart of much qualitative research, however, and in this case they contain details that would be difficult to paraphrase and it is important not to distort. The quoted examples have been selected with care and the status of all the tweets used in the study as in-the-moment conversational reports is fully acknowledged.

Data Overview

To date the number of examples of coronavirus tag games gathered from all sources combined is 331. The vast majority (roughly 97%) of these examples comprise adult observations of children and adult-reported children's testimony.[3] Many are necessarily brief and inevitably

---

3   Twitter's terms of service allow users aged 13 years and over but the content of
     coronavirus tag tweets makes it clear they were being posted by adults.

partial, omitting details that might seem mundane to an adult and instead tending to focus on the more striking aspects of the play. As a result, the accounts are uneven and there is no easy way to check the reliability of the information they contain. There is also minimal or no contextualization in terms of the players' identities and the norms of play in that particular setting nor in wider socio-cultural terms. Even so, they are of significant value when taken together as an indicator of children's experiences and provide unique insights into aspects of their everyday lives that would otherwise have gone undocumented. The corpus does contain a small amount of testimony gathered directly from children who have played coronavirus chase games, including first-hand audio-recorded accounts gathered as part of the Pandemic Play and the Play Observatory projects, and a number of these are drawn on below.

The overall corpus covers the period February 2020 to April 2022. The examples emanate from at least eighteen different countries, as far as it has been possible to ascertain their geographical provenance in the case of the Twitter data, as discussed above. Their geographical distribution is shown in (Figure 1.1).

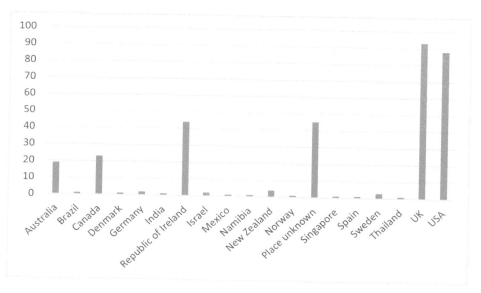

Figure 1.1 Instances of coronavirus tag games per country (Feb. 2020–Apr. 2022)
Created by Julia Bishop, CC BY-NC 4.0

Approximately 39% of the reports mention the age of the children involved and this ranges from three to eighteen years, sometimes as part of mixed-age groups, such as older and younger siblings, and sometimes including parents. The majority of ages mentioned (120 out of 149 instances) are in the range six to eleven years. There is likewise reference to gender in some of the accounts but this is generally in terms of the child from whom the information comes rather than an indicator of the composition of the group who were playing the game.

In terms of chronology the earliest reference to Coronavirus Tag so far discovered was reported in a tweet from Australia (4 February 2020):

> Dropped the son at school. Boys playing tag. One yells: I'M CORONA VIRUS AND I'LL CATCH Y'ALL! Sad times.

Further reports quickly followed on social media. Taken together with later accounts that date the playing of the game to this period, they evidence a huge surge in observations of coronavirus tag games in March 2020, comprising 131 instances or 39% of the total number of examples found over the 27-month period (Figure 1.2).

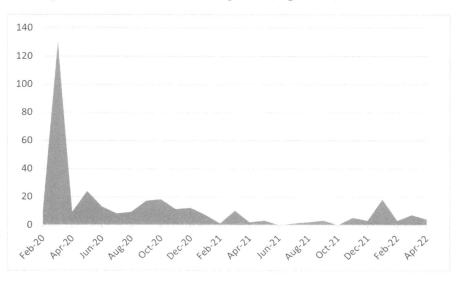

Figure 1.2 Instances of coronavirus tag games by date played
Created by Julia Bishop, CC BY-NC 4.0

In many countries represented by these tweets, this was immediately before schools were closed and just over half of the instances dated to

March mention or imply school as the setting for these games, many explicitly referring to breaktime. The number may well be higher as a number of descriptions do not mention any setting. It seems reasonable to take the number of observations as indicative of a sudden craze for coronavirus chase games among children at this time. The number of instances then drops steeply but there are small increases in June and September 2020, March 2021 and January 2022 which may in turn be indicative of actual increases in the frequency of the game following children's return(s) to school after further closures.

School is not the only setting of the games, however. Neighbourhood streets, parks and in the countryside are also mentioned, and gardens or backyards are implied in versions played on a trampoline. There is also an instance at an airport terminal, another at a swimming pool and an account by a ten-year-old of an attempt to adapt the game for playing remotely using mobile phones (Play Observatory PLCS3-20210702-at1 2023).

At school, the games were played among peers in the playground but during lockdowns, this changed to family members, often with siblings or cousins, sometimes parents, and occasionally other children in the neighbourhood.

From Coronavirus Tags to 'Corona Rules' Tags

1) Coronavirus Tags

Just as touch chase games in general are many and varied, so too are their coronavirus-related incarnations. The idea that the chaser personifies the virus or is infected with it is common to the vast majority. Within these, several types of game can be discerned depending on the way in which the role of the chaser is carried out and what happens to players who are caught, insofar as the accounts contain this information. These also suggest the immediate antecedents on which the players have drawn.

Successive chaser games of Coronavirus Tag, for example, resemble Plain Tag or Ordinary Tag in that the player who is caught immediately takes over the role of the chaser and the original chaser becomes one of the players trying to elude their touch, but cast in terms of contagion ('Whomever was "it" had the virus and only got rid of it by tagging someone else'). Examples come from the USA, Canada, the UK and Israel, in some cases with further refinements, such as in the means of tagging another player (e.g. 'you run after each other, and when you get a meter away, you clap—and then that person is it', tweeted from Israel on 16 May 2020). Alternative ways of tagging are common and are discussed further below.

In cumulative chaser games, on the other hand, the person caught joins forces with the chaser so that the number of those chasing proliferates, as described by Griffin for the Pandemic Play Project:

Recording 1.3 Corona Tip and Corona Bullrush, Griffin, aged nine, Australia, 18 June 2020

To listen to this piece online scan the QR code or follow this link: https://soundcloud.com/user-661596830/griffin-9-corona-tip-and-corona-bullrush

Recorded by Mithra Cox, 2020, CC BY-NC-ND 4.0[4]

Griffin	At school I've invented a game with my friends called Corona Tip. And this game's rules is basically the same as Tip except it's basically if you get tipped you're in corona. And it's build ups. And that means it's basically a game-.
Interviewer	What does builds ups mean?
Griffin	Build ups mean like when it gets longer and longer. Like, if you tip someone, they're in with you.
Interviewer	I see. So you get to have more than one person in?
Griffin	No. So you start off with only one person. But once they tip a couple of people they're also in with that person. And we've also invented one called Corona Bullrush which is Bullrush except it's also build ups.

---

4   Special thanks to Griffin and and Mithra for permission to include this audio clip in this chapter, and to Judy McKinty of the Pandemic Play Project for facilitating this.

| Interviewer | And what-, when you're in, you're in corona? Is that how it works? |
| Griffin | Yeah, if you get tipped, you're basically in corona. |

These games are variations of games sometimes known in Australia respectively as Build up Tips and Bullrush (for pre-pandemic examples, see the *Childhood, Tradition and Change* project website, 2011). Again, there are accounts of similar coronavirus chase games from Ireland, the UK, the USA and Canada. In the Canadian example, the proliferating chasers must also hold hands which 'was against the school protocol but it was fun' (9 October 2020, Twitter).

A further form of coronavirus tag games involves the elimination of those caught, either temporarily or for the rest of the game. A tweet from Germany recounts that 'one child plays the #SuperSpreader and has to tag the others. The winner is the one who hasn't been tagged' (24 September 2020). Elsewhere, it is said that the players so caught may be impounded or 'die' unless they can tag someone else within a certain timescale (such as 'if you were tagged, you had 20 seconds to tag someone else or you were "dead"', reported in a tweet from the USA on 10 March 2020), giving games similarities to those with cumulative chasers. In another example, from the UK, the players 'have to be locked in "the zone"—that's the climbing frame at the school playground— for the rest of lunchtime with no human rights' (BBC 2020). There are shades here of the jail in Cops and Robbers where players may remain for the rest of the game or be able to be released by players who are still free (Roud 2010: 32). The reference to human rights may echo concerns raised in relation to restrictions introduced during the pandemic (e.g. Amnesty International 2020).

Ways in which tagged players can be untagged or 'released', thereby delaying or overturning the transfer of the chaser role, represent one of the most creative parts of coronavirus tag games. Sometimes the onus is on the player who has been caught (e.g. 'if you're tagged you have 5 seconds to get to the vaccine house (hut) otherwise you have it too', reported a UK tweet on 28 November 2020) but more commonly it is up to another player. Not surprisingly, medical care or the receiving of a 'vaccine' is a common scenario in coronavirus tag games and is accomplished by a whole range of gestural, verbal, spatial and material means:

> 1 player is the virus. Virus tags people with elbow. Once tagged must get vaccine within 10 seconds or joins virus tag team. 2 other players are doctors who give vaccine (untag person with elbow). If doctor tags original virus player, the game is over. Doctor then becomes the virus or take turns (Place unknown, 10 September 2020, Twitter)

> Kids in Brazil have started playing a new variation on tag called COVID. One kid is coronavirus and has to tag the others to infect them, while another is an ambulance and has to drag tagged players to a marked space, the "hospital", to get them back in the game (Brazil, 15 March 2022, Twitter)

Some children in Australia ruled that 'if you shout "vaccinated" it's the equivalent of having a forcefield but only lasts 6 seconds' (4 September 2021, Twitter). Sometimes a prop is involved, such as a pen or balloon pump, by which the players pretend to administer the injection.

Many adults saw connections between the coronavirus games they witnessed and the well-known game of Stuck in the Mud or Freeze Tag:

> One person is COVID. If they tag you, you have to freeze in place. Another person is the vaccine who runs around unfreezing people by tapping them twice, 'because you need two shots!' (USA, 13 January 2022, Twitter)

> It's basically 'stuck in the mud' but when you tag someone you have to shout 'isolate' and you free someone by tapping them while shouting 'vaccinate' (UK, 18 January 2022, Twitter)

A UK example contributed to the Play Observatory described 'lots of playing stuck in the mud as the coronavirus in school during bubble playtime. Pretend hand wash sets you free' (Play Observatory PL186A1/S004/d1 2023). This appears to be an adaptation of Toilet Tig in which the free player pushes down on the outstretched arm of the player who has been caught, simulating flushing (cf. Roud 2010: 21). In the coronavirus tag version, the same or similar gesture presumably suggested the action of the pump on a soap dispenser bottle.

Other ways of releasing tagged players appear directly inspired by current affairs:

> P3s [6- to 7-year-olds] have apparently worked out the rules for coronavirus tig. One is it, all folks tagged also become it. If you get tagged by someone without 'the coronavirus touch' and manage to sing Happy Birthday twice, you're free. Tagged by the 'touch' mid song? Start again.

Tweeted from the UK on 4 March 2020, this was just three days after public health announcements urging people to wash their hands for at least twenty seconds, accompanied by ministers' colourful advice to gauge the time by singing the song 'Happy Birthday' twice through (Bloom 2020). This in turn prompted a wave of popular humour, including internet memes and alternative song suggestions as well as this ingenious tag game.

Another UK example that contained an echo of current affairs ruled that if players were 'tagged with "Tory" they're not allowed to eat until someone tags them with "Rashford"'. This refers to the campaign by Manchester United footballer Marcus Rashford for the government to provide meal vouchers for children in poorer families over the summer break of 2020 (BBC Newsround 2020).

Temporary immunity from being caught also featured in coronavirus tag games. Surprisingly, pretending to wear a mask, for instance by putting a hand or sleeve to one's face, was infrequently reported, maybe because this would have been too easy a way of evading being tagged. Instead, there were more traditional methods, such as sitting with crossed legs (Australia), and getting 'off-ground' (given a pandemic twist in a UK tweet on 5 March 2020 stating, 'The benches are doctors. You can't be virused there'). Nevertheless, public health measures in the US presumably inspired one game in which 'you can stop someone tagging you by yelling "Clorox" [a brand of bleach]' (3 April 2020, USA, Twitter).

2) 'Corona Rules' Tags

As the name suggests, the idea of a significant touch is central to games of touch chase for 'a touch with the tip of the finger is enough to transform a player's part in the game', not only from chased to chaser but also from tagged player to freed one (Opie and Opie 1969: 62, 64). Yet, a number of tweets from the UK, USA and Australia mention that children are not allowed to touch hands at school or in some cases touch each other at all. This does not seem to have been official advice as such for schools which, at the outset in the UK at least, stressed hand and respiratory hygiene, disinfection, ventilation and managing potential cases (Department for Education 2020). It does seem to have been a practical way of trying to reduce close physical contact between children in educational settings, including at playtime. Such rules had significant implications for children's everyday play practices and friendships in general (see Carter, Chapter 9 in this volume, and Larivière-Bastien et al. 2022). In the case of chase games, the restrictions threatened their very basis and the possibility of playing them at all and there are a few reports of them being shut down or completely banned.

Likewise, physical distancing measures led to changes to breaktime routines and play space. This resulted in fewer outside breaks for some, and staggered playtimes for others. Several UK child contributors to the Play Observatory spoke of their experience of this at primary school on their return to school in September 2020. Ten-year-old Louis described how the staggered playtimes meant that he was separated from his friends (from whom he had already been isolated during the first UK lockdown) because they were in another class (Play Observatory PLCS1-20210603-at1 2023). Others described how the physical division of school playgrounds also led to separation from peers (Play Observatory PLCS10-20211208-at1 2023). Space in which to run around was consequently more limited and this in turn meant that tag games were not viable because 'the space didn't let you play it' (Play Observatory PLCS8-20211125-at1 2023).

Children responded to these physical and temporal constraints in schools with a number of gestural and spatial variations in the way they played tag games in general, whether or not they were playing games involving a coronavirus chaser. Many were children's own initiatives (e.g. Griffiths 2020). A common example was the introduction of the rule that coming within a certain distance of others, usually one or two metres, was the equivalent of tagging them, the transfer sometimes being marked by a shout or clap. Others avoided touching by using their elbow to tag people or throwing a ball or equivalent object at them, echoing previously well documented games such as Ball Tig and

Dodgeball which operate on the same principle (Opies 1969: 73–74, Roud 2020: 35–36). Similar games were among those that took place at home during lockdowns with siblings. In cases where children had access to a trampoline, for example, they developed games such as Dodge the Virus which used a sensory ball that resembled images of the coronavirus (Beresin 2020: 275). Shadow tag, another older game (Douglas 1916, Opie and Opie 1969: 86) in which the chaser has to stand on another's shadow in order to tag them, also made a comeback, sometimes led by teachers (e.g. Play Observatory PLCS7-20211029-at1 2023), but only playable on a sunny day.

Commended by adults, who sometimes supplied foam 'noodles' (normally used in swimming pool games) as another means of playing 'no-touch tag', these games and modifications were not always considered particularly effective by children in practice. Covid Tig is 'rubbish', commented one eight-year-old boy, because 'no-one can agree what 2 metres is' (20 October 2020, UK, Twitter) and a thirteen-year-old explained that 'Shadow tig is really easy to cheat at. All you say is, "You weren't standing on my shadow. You were standing on your own shadow. Doesn't count. You have to be fully standing on my shadow" (Play Observatory PLCS3-20210702-at1 2023). Compliance with social distancing measures could thus cause ambiguity in a game and lead to frustration or disagreement.

At the other extreme, there are a number of reports in which children are described as breathing, sneezing, spitting or coughing on players to avoid tagging them by touch:

> Long chat with year six [ten- to eleven-year-olds] about behaviour, hygiene etc. Fifteen mins later coronavirus IT was going on. Run after someone and cough on them and they are IT. (UK, pre-23 March 2020, Twitter)

These accounts suggest that some children deliberately adopted a more challenging or oppositional response to the imposition of social distancing rules, and have parallels in examples where children are reported as breaking the 'no touch' rules:

> Took 8 yo to the playground thinking some outside play would be ok. The other kids made up a new kind of tag called Corona Virus Tag. You not only have to touch the other kid but hold them

for 10 seconds "to let the germs spread." (20 March 2020, Canada, Twitter)

We should exercise caution, however. Reports may be exaggerated or children's actions misunderstood. There are also descriptions, for example, in which coughing is said to be intended as a sign of having been tagged:

> If you are caught you have to cough as you now have COVID! (UK, 18 March 2021, Twitter)

or of being the tagger:

> The one who's it keeps coughing and the rest of them running around yelling oh no coronavirus!!! (Canada, 15 March 2020, Twitter).

The practice of coughing may still be regarded as risky under the circumstances but the intention may be realism (enhancing the chaser role) or pragmatism (identifying those tagged) and not necessarily malice or dissent.

Functions of Coronavirus Tag Games

A number of social media posts and journalist reports of Coronavirus Tag offer the interpretation that these games enable children to 'process' or 'make sense of' events in their lives or specifically that they are a means of playing out anxieties about the pandemic (e.g. Christian 2020). In this approach, coronavirus tag games are interpreted in terms of the pandemic. The following section attempts to turn things around and explore ways in which creating and playing the various coronavirus tags may have functioned for children as a way of keeping the pandemic in view but trying to centre children's own experiences and perceptions of play. Functions identified include amusement, maintenance of social interaction and friendship with peers in the face of public health restrictions, intensified emotional expression and escape, risk-taking, the expression of dissent, a means of discrimination against individuals and groups, and stimulus to innovation, humour and re-creation. They are not intended as an exhaustive list and, with little direct testimony from children or contextual information, they can only suggest possible multiple and varying functions from the players' points of view.

Pre-pandemic research by Howard et al. found that children 'show a great deal of emotional attachment to play, feeling happy, sometimes elated, while playing[,] and a host of negative emotions when not able to play' and when left out of play (2017: 387). Children's emotional responses to coronavirus tag games, where reported, are likewise predominantly described as fun, enjoyable and a favourite activity, associated with laughter, pleasure, and shouting, screaming and yelling. There are few direct reports of negative responses, the main one being disapproval of games breaking social distancing rules. In this sense, coronavirus tag games were no different from any other games in children's repertoires, in that they were often valued as an opportunity to express their identities and emotions freely, and to escape from everyday reality (Howard et al. 2017).

As described above, there is some evidence that children began to adapt the rules of their chase games as soon as social distancing measures were introduced at school so that they could continue playing a favoured game despite the constraints. The need for 'corona rules' helps to account for the huge surge in reports of coronavirus tag games—with a new name to distinguish them from the established ones—in March 2020 as these measures were first being brought in. Thus, a function of re-creating and playing these games for children was to allow them to continue engaging in something akin to one of their established practices of social interaction with their peers. Given that play of all kinds has an important role in supporting the development and maintenance of children's friendships (Blatchford 1998), this may have become even more important when children returned to school *en masse* following periods of separation from their peers, accounting for persistent reports of coronavirus tag games beyond the initial surge. For similar reasons, they were also potentially important for those children who for various reasons continued to attend school during lockdowns and found themselves mixing with new classmates and mixed-age groups.

The need to accommodate distancing measures posed the potentially enjoyable challenge of finding substitutes for touch and spatial proximity. Not all children wanted to engage with these possibilities, however, some finding the alternatives limited, and some opting to play other games instead at this time, such as ones which needed less space and did not involve tagging people (e.g. Play Observatory PLCS10-20211208-at1 2023).

Other children apparently set out to challenge and resist constraints by deliberately invoking taboo actions and subverting or breaking the restrictions. In these cases, the games provided a means of dissent as well as an expression of bravado.

What comes through particularly strongly in the data, however, is not just the need to adapt touch chase games to accommodate and resist restrictions on physical contact and proximity. Rather, it is the way in which, for children, the pandemic opened up possibilities for reimagining their existing repertoire of games by furnishing a common set of cultural resources. Identifying the chaser with the coronavirus or Covid led to all kinds of innovations which, even while other resources (such as playground equipment) were limited, acted as a catalyst for creativity and experimentation. These functioned to alleviate everyday routine and possible boredom, bringing about a sense of novelty to, and ownership over, the outcome. If correct, this represents another possible reason for the huge surge in games evident in the March 2020 reports and, with unfolding of events as the pandemic progressed, suggests that the pandemic was a continuing source of inspiration for some time after.

The personification of the coronavirus and inclusion of scenarios suggested by current affairs also introduces a socio-dramatic element to touch chase, allowing for play-acting the parts of being scared and being scary, as in Monster Tag games more generally. The fact that coronavirus was a real life threat, however, potentially intensified the thrill of the game and heightened the 'phantasmagoric' dimension of this play (Sutton-Smith 1997). This created a context in which shouting, yelling and screaming were permitted. Thus the games allowed the exploration not only of fear but also of power, an opportunity to let go of inhibitions which, as Howard et al. found, children value in their play (2017: 384), and to be 'larger (louder?) than life', an exaggerated version of themselves (see Beresin, Chapter 17 for an extended discussion of exaggeration in online play).

Another function of children's incorporation of verbal, gestural, material, behavioural, spatial and proxemic elements associated with the pandemic into their touch chase games was the creation of incongruities through which they could exercise their wit and ingenuity. This can be seen as a form of 'quoting', in the widest sense and in multimodal terms. In this process, as Finnegan identifies, the 'far and near' are held in productive tension with each other:

> The distancing [involved in quoting another] in turn draws the quoted voice and text near, seizing and judging it: standing back not just to externalise but to claim the right to hold an attitude to it, whether of approval, caution, admiration, disavowal, analysis, interpretation, irony, reference...
>
> [...] Quoting in its infinity of manifestations is at once 'there and away' and 'here and now'. It is both to distinguish the words and voices [and embodied communication] of others and to make them our own, both distancing and claiming. (2011: 263)

Thus, in coronavirus chase games, children made opportunities for experimentation, redefinition, inversion, humour, mockery and resistance which not only 'made sense' of the pandemic—and the adult world's response it—but *non*sense.

Pre-pandemic research into children's play has also highlighted the ambiguity of play and its potential to exclude and stigmatize certain players. McDonnell's study of play narratives, for example, quotes a child as saying, 'I had loads of friends but they're not my friends because they're running from me... He said "AAAAH run from him!"' (2019: 260). It is easy to see how coronavirus tag games have similar potential to stigmatize, isolate and disempower by casting the chaser as contagious and manoeuvring them into an unwitting or unwanted chaser role. The data contains a handful of examples in which this was, or may have been, the case and these are all based on racialized conceptions of the pandemic and its provenance:

> Students were playing a game called coronavirus tag which was targeted towards Asian students. (USA, 16 February 2020, Twitter)

Racialized verbal and physical attacks involving people of all ages were certainly documented during the pandemic (see, for example, Human Rights Watch 2020). The brevity and decontextualization of reports of these instances that took place within touch chase games makes them difficult to examine critically and the paucity of evidence likewise makes it hard to gauge how widespread such practices were. It is nonetheless essential to acknowledge this potential in chasing play, which can easily be overlooked or dismissed as 'only a game' by adults and so go unchallenged (McDonnell 2019: 259–60).

'Topical' Tags and 'Contaminating Games' in Historical Perspective

Topical Tags

Children's reframing of elements drawn from global flows of information or 'mediascapes' (Appadurai 1990) in their play has a long history (for an overview, see Marsh 2014). Mediascapes provide 'large and complex repertoires of images, narratives and "ethnoscapes" to viewers throughout the world, in which the world of commodities and the world of "news" and politics is profoundly mixed' (Appadurai 1990: 299). Characters and associated plot elements drawn from popular culture and news may thus be introduced into touch chase games. These may be generic, as in Cops and Robbers with their associated 'jail', and Witches and Fairies with their cauldron or stewpot, or specific to the latest television series, films and storybooks (Roud 2010: 18–19; for a storybook example, see British Library 2011).

An example of this is the emergence of zombie-related tag games. These show the influence of the modern zombie figure and the zombie apocalypse trope found in books, comics, films, cartoons and videogames (Conrich 2015). They seem to have become popular, at least in the UK, in the 2010s (e.g. Willett 2015; Bishop 2023). In popular culture, the zombie figure is often associated with the concept of a deadly virus, those infected then becoming zombies themselves whose proliferation threatens, in terms of the trope, to overrun the world. The humans pitted against them must avoid infection in order to survive. These scenarios have obvious parallels with both cumulative and elimination tags, and indeed tag games with names relating to zombies and infection are often reported as taking these forms (see, for example, Holben 2020). Zombie and infection names, together with Build Ups names (noted above in Australia and also found in my own fieldwork at a Yorkshire primary school in 2010 and 2018) and Family Tig (Roud 2010: 20), appear to have superseded earlier names for proliferating chaser games, such as Help Chase and All Man He (Opie and Opie 1969: 89). Even in the mid-twentieth century, however, children in Fulham in West London reported playing Gorilla, in which 'immediately one is court [caught] he becomes a goriller with the original one', again suggesting the influence of films and comics of that time (quoted in Opie and Opie 1969: 89).

Thus, children may re-create any form of tag game to make it topical by imbuing the chaser and chased roles, and sometimes other roles besides, with characterizations inspired by contemporary mediascapes. In addition, they may update existing topical tags in similar fashion. This is exactly what seems to have happened during the pandemic. The personified coronavirus or Covid-infected chaser turned games such as Stuck in the Mud into topical tags, with knock-on refinements as described above. Likewise, games called Covid Zombies and Zombie Tag Coronavirus emerged, some cumulative or eliminatory in form— 'once tagged you become an infected walking zombie', reported a tweet from Ireland in October 2020, 'game continues to last child standing who restarts the game'. Infection Tag, meanwhile, rapidly took on a new resonance, alarming to adults, even without a modification of its name:

"Parenting in the Age of Coronavirus"
A one-act play by me and my kid
Kid: "At recess, we played this fun game called Infection"
Me: "THAT SOUNDS VERY DANGEROUS YOU SHOULD NOT PLAY THAT"
Kid: "Mama, calm down, it's basically tag"
Me: *dies of anxiety anyway*
FIN (26 Feb 2020, USA, Twitter).

Next we briefly consider 'contaminating games' before considering the relationship between topical tags and contaminating games.

Contaminating Games

Coronavirus tag also belongs to a class of games in which the chaser's touch has a 'noxious effect' (Opie and Opie 1969: 75). Childlore researchers Iona and Peter Opie dubbed these 'contaminating games', commenting:

Chasing games could well be termed 'contaminating games' were it not that the children themselves do not, on the whole, think of the chaser's touch as being strange or contagious. Their pleasure in chasing games seems to lie simply in the exercise and excitement of chasing and being chased; and the contagious element, which possibly had significance in the past, is today uppermost in their minds only in some unpleasant aberrations, which are here relegated to a subsection. (1969: 62)

In the Opies' experience, such forms were the exception rather than the rule among children in mid-twentieth-century Britain. They comprise games in which the chaser has a disease, affliction or undesirable personal characteristic which is transmitted to another player by their touch. These include games involving the fictitious Lurgy and Aggie Touch, disease-related games such as Germ, the Plague and Fever, and undesirable person forms, such as Lodgers and the [Person's name] Touch (1969: 75–78). The Opies stress that during the game, and even after it, 'the suspension of disbelief in the game's pretence can be absolute: the feeling is unfeigned that the chaser's touch is unhealthy' (1969: 77).

Touch chase games of this kind have been documented in many countries of the world. The Opies cite examples from New Zealand, Spain and Italy, as well as a nineteenth-century example from Madagascar in which the chaser was known as *bôka*, 'a leper' (1969: 77). The most extensively studied and enduring contaminating game is Cooties, a form particularly widespread in America where it dates from at least the 1930s and '40s (Knapp and Knapp 1973; cf. Bronner 2011: 213–17). Cooties are a fictitious undesirable affliction, transmitted through touch or physical proximity, often from a member of the opposite sex. The main way of ridding oneself of them is to pass them on to someone else. This can be done surreptitiously or can be more overt, giving rise to Cooties Tag (Samuelson 1980).

In the second half of the twentieth century and into the twenty-first, there has been a whole catalogue of disease-related chase games, memories (but few details) of which were prompted by social media posts about Coronavirus Tag. These not only included AIDS Tag (cf. Goldstein 2004: 1–3) but also Ebola, MERS, Swine Flu Edition [Tag], TB and Polio.

There have also been newer incarnations of imaginary afflictions, such as the Cheese Touch—made famous (and topical) in Jeff Kinney's book *Diary of a Wimpy Kid* (2007), and spinoff film (2010)—and Virus (Roud 2010: 32), in which the touch of a particular person is rendered undesirable. Both of these games appear to have been used as starting points by children for the development of coronavirus tag games. A tweet from Australia, for example, described a game of Coronavirus Tiggy played at school which 'consisted of getting touched with "virus cheese." If you get "virus cheese" by being tagged, you become "infected" and you have to chase others in the game' (18 March 2020). Similarly, ten-year-old Louis, interviewed for the Play Observatory project, explained how the game of Virus played with his friends became Coronavirus Infection, a topical tag and contaminating game relating to the pandemic:

> L   Well in my class people used to call it, like somebody's
>   virus, like the [Harvey] virus, the [Leo] virus, or
>   something like that. And then because we just, like
>   coronavirus was all over the news, like 'Oh, it's spread
>   across China', and 'there's a new variant in India'. It's like–.
>
> Int   So it was like a game that you played before with a
>   different name, and then it kind of changed it?
>
> L   Yeah, yeah. (Play Observatory PLCS1-20210603-at1 2023)

It is not difficult to see how games of noxious touch can be used to stigmatize and isolate individuals deemed undesirable or unpopular. Yet, in the case of Louis and his friends, the game appears to be experienced in a good-natured way. This also seems to be true of the majority of examples gathered for this research, although this is by no means certain, for we lack the voices of those who played them and the specifics of how they were played.

What makes the difference between contaminating games experienced as good-natured and those intended and/or experienced as discriminating and excluding? It is not possible to do justice to this question here. Contaminating games are complex and, every time they are played, the outcome is subject to a range of factors: the nature of the players' relationships with each other, the nature of the disease, characteristic or affliction around which they are framed (which, like Cooties, may be shifting and ambiguous), and social structures and discourses around otherness and inequality by which they are informed.

The tone of contaminating games and the way they are experienced by players is also affected by the form that they take. The games of noxious touch, as described by children to the Opies, are successive chaser games. The possibility of singling out an individual is greater in these as only one person is the source of contamination at a time and the game is basically one person against all. If there is a release element too, then the solidarity of those tagged with those remaining free is reinforced and the chaser is more isolated in terms of the game. For a strong chaser whose social status within the group is reasonably assured and equal, this may be a welcome challenge but for a weaker player and/or one whose status is unequal, ambiguous and not assured, the power dynamics inherent in the game may be experienced very differently. In cumulative chaser games, on the other hand, those tagged swap sides so it is the chaser who receives assistance and who becomes less isolated, provided they can catch another in the first place. In the elimination form, one person is again pitted against all the other players but their kudos grows as they catch others and they can progress to the status of 'winner' when all other players are 'out'.

It is only possible to distinguish the form of the game definitively in thirty-three of the coronavirus tag game examples gathered for this study but, of those, it is notable that twenty-seven are cumulative or eliminating. Given the power dynamics inherent in the different forms of tag games, it would be interesting to know if this is indicative of a more general increase in the popularity of cumulative and eliminating games of tag from the time of the Opies' research in the third quarter of the twentieth century to now.

Conclusion

Coronavirus Tag has been shown to be a wide range of games in practice, ingeniously imbued with an array of details gleaned from, and inspired by, mediascapes as well as necessitated by local conditions. Many of these emerged at speed in many different places more or less simultaneously in the early days of the pandemic in the Global North and particularly at times when children were at school together. It has been possible to see parallels and antecedents which fostered the games' creation, their widespread occurrence and their variety. Just as American folklorist Herbert Halpert argued in relation to traditional song—that 'the presence or absence of parodies or local songs is a test of the vitality of a folk song tradition. If singers do not make up new songs, or manipulate the old materials, we have one indication that the singing tradition in that area has become fossilised' (1951: 40)—we can see the creation of coronavirus tag games as indicative of the contemporary vitality of touch chase play more generally among children.

As we have seen, the games take a number of different basic forms—successive, cumulative and eliminatory—and may embed mechanisms of release and immunity. I have argued that the form of the game adopted by the players is an important determinant of its potential and actual power dynamics which in turn impacts on players' experiences of the various roles and rules. I have also sketched a range of potential functions for coronavirus tag games for further investigation, research in which the participation of players themselves is crucial. The suggested functions attempt to foreground their experiences and are intended to acknowledge the possibility of multiple functions, rather than a priori and universalizing ones which may prioritize adults' sensibilities over those of the players. A historical and comparative perspective has shed light on the ambiguities of the game, its continuities with the past in terms of topical and contaminating elements, but also the differences of its specifics and its meanings in the contemporary context.

It is fully acknowledged that this study has relied almost entirely on adult testimony and that the majority of accounts are highly abbreviated. It nonetheless shows the interest and importance of sampling children's play repertoires on a regular basis, preferably on the basis of observation and children's own testimony, to understand everyday practices in play and peer interaction, their sensitivity to current affairs and wider discourses, including as shaped by contemporary mediascapes, and to detect changes over time and in space.

In this case, a comparative focus has helped to highlight that what children did in making their games of coronavirus tag is in fact just one example of what they do on a day-to-day basis when there is no pandemic. Children are in perpetual counterpoint with each other and the adult world and express this in their play, including their chase games. Coronavirus Tag drew adults' attention to these processes and led to their documentation but also gave the impression that this was something special to the pandemic. World affairs and the mediascape never stop furnishing many other possibilities for topical play, such as the widely acclaimed South Korean series *Squid Game* on Netflix (Sharma 2021) and possibly the Russian invasion of Ukraine in February 2022. There are important insights to be gained from looking at the detail of play—to try and do justice to its variety, its responsiveness to catalysts both global and local, and the experiences of the people who are its architects. This in turn will add nuance to our understandings of children's social lives and expressive culture, and the synergies between the two.

Works Cited

Ahmed, Wasim. 2021. 'Using Twitter as a Data Source: An Overview of Social Media Research Tools', https://blogs.lse.ac.uk/impactofsocialsciences/2021/05/18/using-twitter-as-a-data-source-an-overview-of-social-media-research-tools-2021/

Ahmed, Wasim, Peter A. Bath, and Gianluca Demartini. 2017. 'Using Twitter as a Data Source: An Overview of Ethical, Legal, and Methodological Challenges', in *The Ethics of Online Research: Volume 2*, ed. by Kandy Woodfield (Bingley, UK: Emerald), pp. 79–107, https://doi.org/10.1108/S2398-601820180000002004

Amnesty International. 2020. 'Explainer: Seven Ways the Coronavirus Affects Human Rights', https://www.amnesty.org/en/latest/news/2020/02/explainer-seven-ways-the-coronavirus-affects-human-rights/

Appadurai, Arjun. 1990. 'Disjuncture and Difference in the Global Cultural Economy', *Theory, Culture & Society*, 7: 295–310, https://doi.org/10.1177/026327690007002017

BBC News. 2020. 'Coronavirus Outbreak: How Are Children Responding?' *Global News Podcast*, 2 March, https://www.bbc.co.uk/sounds/play/p0856tth

BBC Newsround. 2020. 'Marcus Rashford Forces Government U-turn after Food Voucher Campaign', 16 June, https://www.bbc.co.uk/newsround/53061952

Beresin, Anna. 2020. 'Playful Introduction to 9.3', *International Journal of Play*, 9: 275–76, https://doi.org/10.1080/21594937.2020.1805967

Bishop, Julia. 2023. 'Recreation and Re-creation in Children's Pandemic Chasing Games', in *Creativity during Covid Lockdowns*, ed. by Patricia Lysaght, David Shankland and James H. Grayson (Canon Pyon, UK: Sean Kingston)

Blatchford, Peter. 1994. 'Research on Children's School Playground Behaviour in the United Kingdom: A Review', in *Breaktime and the School*, ed. by Peter Blatchford and Sonia Sharp (London: Routledge), pp. 15–35

——. 1998. *Social Life in School: Pupils' Experience of Breaktime and Recess from 7 to 16 Years* (London: Falmer Press)

Blatchford, Peter, Rosemary Creeser, and Ann Mooney. 1990. 'Playground Games and Playtime: The Children's View', *Educational Research*, 32: 163–74, https://doi.org/10.1080/0013188900320301

Blank, Trevor J. (ed.). 2012. *Folk Culture in the Digital Age: The Emergent Dynamics of Human Interaction* (Logan: Utah State University Press)

Bloom, Dan. 2020. 'Coronavirus: UK government Tells Children to Sing Happy Birthday while Washing Hands', *Mirror*, 1 March, https://www.mirror.co.uk/news/politics/coronavirus-uk-government-tells-children-21608374

Bologna, Caroline. 2020a. '35 Tweets about Parenting in the Age of Coronavirus', *HuffPost*, 10 March, https://www.huffingtonpost.co.uk/entry/coronavirus-parenting-tweets_l_5e66af39c5b605572809d9bf

——. 2020b. 'Coronavirus Tag? The Pandemic Has Become Part of Kids' Playtime', *HuffPost*, 12 March, https://www.huffingtonpost.co.uk/entry/coronavirus-tag-kids-playtime_l_5e680a01c5b6670e7300297e

British Library. 2011. 'Jack Frost and Sally Sunshine' [video], https://www.bl.uk/collection-items/jack-frost-and-sally-sunshine

Bronner, Simon J. 1988. *American Children's Folklore* (Little Rock, AR: August House)

——. 2011. *Explaining Traditions: Folk Behavior in Modern Culture* (Lexington: University Press of Kentucky)

Burghardt, G.M. 2005. *The Genesis of Animal Play: Testing the Limits* (Cambridge, MA: MIT Press)

Burn, Andrew. 2014. 'Children's Playground Games in the New Media Age', in *Children's Games in the New Media Age: Childlore, Media and the Playground*, ed. by Andrew Burn and Chris Richards (Farnham: Ashgate), pp. 1–30

Chen, Emily, Kristina Lerman, and Emilio Ferrara. 2020. 'Tracking Social Media Discourse About the COVID-19 Pandemic: Development of a Public Coronavirus Twitter Data Set JMIR Public Health Surveillance', 6, https://doi.org/10.2196/19273

Childhood, Tradition and Change [Australia]. 2011, https://ctac.esrc.unimelb.edu.au/index.html

Christian, Bonnie. 2020. 'Children Playing "Coronavirus" Game in UK Playgrounds, Mother Says', *Evening Standard*, 2 March, https://www.standard.co.uk/news/uk/coronavirus-game-in-uk-playgrounds-a4376506.html#comments-area

Conrich, Ian. 2015. 'An Infected Population: Zombie Culture and the Modern Monstrous', in *The Zombie Renaissance in Popular Culture*, ed. by Laura Hubner, Marcus Leaning, and Paul Manning (London: Palgrave Macmillan), pp. 16–25, https://doi.org/10.1057/9781137276506_2

Cowan, Kate, et al. 2021. 'Children's Digital Play during the COVID-19 Pandemic: Insights from the Play Observatory', *Journal of e-Learning and Knowledge Society*, 17: 8–17, https://doi.org/10.20368/1971-8829/1135590

Cram, David, Jeffrey L. Forgeng, and Dorothy Johnston. 2003. *Francis Willughby's Book of Games: A Seventeenth-Century Treatise on Sports, Games and Pastimes* (London: Routledge)

Cray, Kate. 2020. 'How the Coronavirus Is Influencing Children's Play', *Atlantic*, 1 April, https://www.theatlantic.com/family/archive/2020/04/coronavirus-tag-and-other-games-kids-play-during-a-pandemic/609253/

De Seta, Gabriele. 2020. 'Digital Folklore' in *Second International Handbook of Internet Research*, ed. by Jeremy Hunsinger, Matthew M. Allen and Lisbeth Klastrup (Dordrecht: Springer), pp. 167–83, https://doi.org/10.1007/978-94-024-1555-1_36

Dean, Brian. 2022. 'How Many People Use Twitter in 2022? [New Twitter Stats]', https://backlinko.com/twitter-users

Department for Education. 2020. *Actions for Schools during the Coronavirus Outbreak*   https://www.gov.uk/government/publications/actions-for-schools-during-the-coronavirus-outbreak

Douglas, Norman. 1916. *London Street Games* (London: St Catherine Press)

Eberle, Scott G. 2016. 'Trump Tag: Playing Politics on the Playground', *Psychology Today*, 31 May, https://www.psychologytoday.com/gb/blog/play-in-mind/201605/trump-tag

Fiesler, Casey, and Nicholas Proferes. 2018. '"Participant" Perceptions of Twitter Research Ethics', *Social Media + Society*, 4: 1–14, https://doi.org/10.1177/2056305118763366

Finnegan, Ruth. 2011. *Why Do We Quote? The Culture and History of Quotation* (Cambridge: Open Book Publishers), https://doi.org/10.11647/OBP.0012

Goldstein, Diane E. 2004. *Once Upon a Virus: AIDS Legends and Vernacular Risk Perception* (Logan: Utah State University Press)

Gomme, Alice B. 1984 [1894, 1898]. *The Traditional Games of England, Scotland, and Ireland* (London: Thames & Hudson)

Griffiths, Sian. 2020. 'Children Let Off Steam with Covid Games'. *Times*, 6 December, https://www.thetimes.co.uk/article/children-let-off-steam-with-covid-games-nkwnlccg9

Holben, Henry. 2020. 'A Letter to COVID', Milligan University Digital Repository COVID-19 Collection, http://hdl.handle.net/11558/5097

Howard, Justine, et al. 2017. 'Play in Middle Childhood: Everyday Play Behaviour and Associated Emotions', *Children & Society*, 31: 378–89, https://doi.org/10.1111/chso.12208

Human Rights Watch. 2020. *Covid-19 Fueling Anti-Asian Racism and Xenophobia Worldwide*, 12 May, https://www.hrw.org/news/2020/05/12/covid-19-fueling-anti-asian-racism-and-xenophobia-worldwide

Hunter, Molly, and Ziad Jaber. 2020. 'Touch a Shadow, "You're it!": New Routines as Denmark Returns to School after Coronavirus Lockdown', *NBC News*, 26 April, https://www.nbcnews.com/news/world/touch-shadow-you-re-it-new-routines-denmark-returns-school-n1192611

Knapp, Mary, and Herbert Knapp. 1973. 'Tradition and Change in American Playground Language', *Journal of American Folklore* 86: 131–41

——. 1976. *One Potato, Two Potato: The Folklore of American Children* (New York: Norton)

Larivière-Bastien, Danaë, et al. 2022. 'Children's Perspectives on Friendships and Socialization during the COVID-19 Pandemic: A Qualitative Approach', *Child: Care, Health and Development*, 48, 1017–030, https://doi.org/10.1111/cch.12998

Marsh, Jackie. 2014. 'Media, Popular Culture and Play', in *The SAGE Handbook of Play and Learning in Early Childhood*, ed. by Liz Brooker, Mindy Blaise and Susan Edwards (London: SAGE), pp. 403–14, https://dx.doi.org/10.4135/9781473907850.n34

McDonnell, Susan. 2019. 'Nonsense and Possibility: Ambiguity, Rupture and Reproduction in Children's Play/ful Narratives', *Children's Geographies*, 17: 251–65, https://doi.org/10.1080/14733285.2018.1492701

McKinty, Judy, and Ruth Hazleton. 2022. 'The Pandemic Play Project: Documenting Kids' Culture during COVID-19', *International Journal of Play*, 11: 12–33, https://doi.org/10.1080/21594937.2022.2042940

Newell, William Wells 1963 [1903]. *Games and Songs of American Children*, 2nd edn (New York: Dover)

Opie, Iona, and Opie, Peter. 1969. *Children's Games in Street and Playground* (Oxford: Clarendon Press)

Peck, Andrew, and Trevor J. Blank. 2020. *Folklore and Social Media* (Logan: Utah State University Press)

Pennacchia, Jodie (ed.). 2019. *BERA Research Ethics Case Studies, 1: Twitter, Data Collection and Informed Consent* (London: British Educational Research Association), https://www.bera.ac.uk/publication/twitter-data-collection-informed-consent

Play Observatory PL186A1/S004/d1. 2023. https://doi.org/10.15131/shef.data.21198142

Play Observatory PLCS1-20210603-at1. 2023. Louis (10 years) amd Jonathan (parent), interviewed by John Potter and Kate Cowan, 3 June 2021, https://doi.org/10.15131/shef.data.22012898

Play Observatory, PLCS3-20210702-at1. 2023. X1 (13 years) and X2 (10 years), interviewed by John Potter and Kate Cowan, 2 July 2021, https://doi.org/10.15131/shef.data.22012898

Play Observatory PLCS7-20211029-at1. 2023. Beatrice (pseudonym) (7 years) and Olivia (parent), interviewed by John Potter and Kate Cowan, 29 October 2021, https://doi.org/10.15131/shef.data.22012898

Play Observatory PLCS8-20211125-at1. 2023. Eli (7 years) and Rachel (parent), interviewed by John Potter and Julia Bishop, 25 November 2021, https://doi.org/10.15131/shef.data.22012898

Play Observatory PLCS10-20211208-at1. 2023. Harry (12 years), interviewed by John Potter and Michelle Cannon, 8 December 2021, https://doi.org/10.15131/shef.data.22012898

Roud, Steve. 2010. *The Lore of the Playground: One Hundred Years of Children's Games, Rhymes and Traditions* (London: Random House)

Samuelson, Sue. 1980. 'The Cooties Complex', *Western Folklore*, 39: 198–210, https://doi.org/10.2307/1499801

Sandseter, Ellen Beate Hansen, and Rasmus Kleppe. 2019. 'Outdoor Risky Play', in *Encyclopedia on Early Childhood Development*, ed. by Richard E. Tremblay, Michel Boivin, Ray DeV. Peters, https://www.child-encyclopedia.com/outdoor-play/according-experts/outdoor-risky-play

Schwartzman, Helen B. 1978. *Transformations: The Anthropology of Children's Play* (New York: Plenum Press)

Sharma, Ruchira. 2021. 'Squid Game: Why You Should Not Panic about Reports Children Are Copying the Games from the Netflix Series', *iNews*, 13 October, https://inews.co.uk/news/squid-game-games-netflix-series-challenges-reports-children-copying-warning-explained-1246173

Sloan, Luke. 2017. 'Social Science "Lite"? Deriving Demographic Proxies', in *The SAGE Handbook of Social Media Research Methods*, ed. by Luke Sloan and Anabel Quan-Haase (London: SAGE), pp. 90–104

Sloan, Luke, and Anabel Quan-Haase (eds). 2017. *The SAGE Handbook of Social Media Research Methods* (London: SAGE)

Smith, Mary. 2020. Letter, *Guardian*, 4 March, https://www.theguardian.com/world/2020/mar/04/childrens-games-are-going-viral

Sutton-Smith, Brian. 1972 [1959] 'The Games of New Zealand Children', in *The Folkgames of Children*, American Folklore Society Bibliographical and Special Series, 24 (Austin: University of Texas Press), pp. 5–257

——. 1997. *The Ambiguity of Play* (Cambridge, MA: Harvard University Press)

Virtanen, L. 1978. *Children's Lore*. Studia Fennica, 22 (Helsinki: Suomalaisen Kirjallisuuden Suera [Finnish Literature Society])

Willett, Rebekah. 2015. 'Everyday Game Design on a School Playground: Children as Bricoleurs', *International Journal of Play*, 4: 32–44, https://doi.org/10.1080/21594937.2015.1017305

2. Gathered in Play:
Play as the Common Space during the Covid-19 Lockdown in Serbia

Živka Krnjaja and Nevena Mitranić

Introduction

The devastating effects of Covid-19 led to health, economic and social crisis, threatening all aspects of life and the basic norms of the functioning of human society (Krnjaja 2021). It is unpredictable for how long the crisis might continue and whether life will ever return to 'life as we know it'. A particularly troubling question is how current conditions might impact future generations. Although children were not so heavily influenced by the first waves of the virus, mental health specialists warned that they were all—or soon would be—psychologically suffering from the consequences of the pandemic (Villarreal 2020). Experts of various profiles warn of increased depression, anxiety, aggression and dependence on digital technologies, even among the youngest (Fegert et al. 2020; Montag and Elhai 2020). The most endangered group might be children of preschool age, whose learning and development are conditioned by opportunities to achieve quality relationships with peers and adults, to participate and contribute in their close environments, to create purpose in joint activities with others and to playfully research, develop and express their ideas (Pavlović Breneselović 2010)—all of which was denied to them in the conditions of a pandemic.

Families, especially the guardians of small children, experienced great social pressure. A review of the available texts created for families

 https://doi.org/10.11647/OBP.0326.02

during the Covid-19 crisis indicates that the responsibilities they took on focused on issues of physical health and hygiene, mental health of the child and the entire family, compensation for the lack of social relations and occasions, and educational progress through joint participation in educational activities (Purešević 2021). Knowing that a lot of families have more than one child and that most of the guardians still had their own jobs to attend to, at least remotely, it is clear that the task of 'keeping it together' in a time of crisis was not easy—and still is not so.

During 2020, families and children in Serbia were faced with the same challenges mentioned above. On 16 March 2020, a state of emergency and physical isolation was declared in Serbia. Nationwide lockdown followed with the closure of all non-essential businesses and all educational institutions. However, it was imperative to maintain education in any manner possible, so it was transferred in Serbia (as elsewhere) to a digital environment. This sudden shift to distance learning proved to be a challenge, revealing a lack of digital competencies more amongst adults than amongst children, and a lack of devices in many homes, but mostly revealing confusion as to where the sudden changes were leading us, and which educational values we should strive to cherish (Miškeljin 2021).

In view of the need to establish remote support for children, families, and practitioners in education, the Ministry of Education, Science and Technological Development (MOESTD), working together with the Department of Preschool Pedagogy (Faculty of Philosophy, University of Belgrade), determined the priorities of the preschool education system in the publication *Preschool Upbringing and Education during the Covid-19 Epidemic* (Ministry of Education, Science and Technological Development 2020). As in many other countries (see, for example, Pramling Samuelsson, Wagner and Ødegard 2020), maintaining communication and supporting children and families was considered a top priority during the closure.

According to the National Preschool Curriculum Framework *Years of Ascent* (Ministry of Education, Science and Technological Development 2018), the family is considered the primary educator of a child and the first context in which a child's learning and development take place. During lockdown, the preschool education system was responsible for empowering families by offering information, advice, and ideas for joint participation of children and adults in different activities, promoting a sense of belonging, togetherness, and the development of creativity as main priorities (Ministry of Education, Science and Technological Development 2020). Preschool teachers were encouraged to communicate with children and families through different available means and media (such as Viber, YouTube, and Facebook), offering them new resources, useful information, and a platform for mutual communication and exchange. Suggestions for resources and information, as well as proposals that might be made or given, resolutely stress the importance of common play between children and adults.

As a priority for its actions, the MOESTD declared the mobilization and activation of all theresources available in the system of preschool education to competently respond to the challenges society was facing (Ministry of Education, Science and Technological Development 2020). Through joint action of different partners in the preschool educational system (educational policymakers, researchers, practitioners), the MOESTD established the website *Let's Connect, Let's Empowerin the Covid-19 Crisis* as a public digital repository of relevant information and inspiring materials for guardians and practitioners. One of the sections on the website is specifically intended for suggestions for common play created by the Department of Preschool Pedagogy and various practitioners who work in preschool institutions (preschool teachers, pedagogues, and psychologists).

With the desire to nurture a sense of togetherness in the ethical and pedagogical relation of joint research and mutual care, the teachers from the Department of Preschool Pedagogy and the students taking the undergraduate course 'Child's Play and Creativity' developed a resource entitled *The Treasury for Common Play between Children and Adults*. The *Treasury* is an illustrated publication with suggestions about different playful situations and activities that children and parents could undertake while isolating at home. The *Treasury* was also meant to serve preschool teachers in communicating suggestions to families and creating new treasuries together with them. In the digital version, the *Treasury* was posted on the *Let's Connect, Let's Empower in the Covid-19 Crisis* website as well as on the official websites of various professional associations and organizations for parents.

In this paper, we will present an understanding of play which serves as a basis for this common action of teachers and students and *The Treasury for Common Play between Children and Adults*. Further, we will present a study of families' experiences of participation in different situations and activities encouraged by the *Treasury* during isolation.

How We Gathered in Play

Research Context

When the lockdown in Serbia was announced, the Faculty of Philosophy, University of Belgrade switched to online classes. Working through digital collaborative and conferencing platforms, we as teachers tried to create space for students to understand their professional role in the conditions of the Covid-19 crisis and to strengthen their competencies to support children and families. It was important for us to model possible ways to connect the higher education community with policymakers and practitioners as a key aspect of the professional engagement of a pedagogue and to provide students with an opportunity to gain experience and learn through active involvement in supporting the preschool education community during the crisis. As a result, we suggested that students jointly prepare a collection of playful situations and activities in which children and adults could engage together during home isolation.

We consider the task of advocating for play and building support for children and adults to play together in times of crisis highly beneficial. Play is recognized as an essential right of every child (United Nations 1989) and promoted as important even in periods of crisis. Through previous research into child's play in different emergency contexts, play's strong potential for the development of rehabilitation and resilience has been well established (Feldman 2019). Play has been seen as a powerful medium through which children manage their emotions, examine difficult situations, experiment with possible reactions and outcomes, and gain a feeling of control (International Play Association 2020; Feldman 2019). But advocating for play in times of crisis is often subordinated to a therapeutic-rehabilitation framework, which uses play as a 'diversion' for rehabilitative and educational activities to orientate children towards certain objectives (Boyd Webb 2015).

In a post-developmental paradigm shift, which we promote through our faculty courses with students, the transformative and creative potential of play has been positioned as central to its importance. Play drives the capacity for flexibility to act in changed conditions, to look for alternatives and, following them, to act autonomously and competently. Dealing with the experiences and the environment through the acts of play opens up possibilities for the child to twist the boundaries of everyday events, to reinterpret their own and others' deeds, and to create different spacetimes that have the potential to alter previously established meanings (Marjanović-Shane and White 2014).

Krnjaja (2012) outlines that developing the idea of play as the capacity for flexibility in action leads towards understanding and supporting play not as an activity, but as an approach or 'attitude towards life' (Marjanović 1987; Edmiston 2005) or 'existential action of a human being' (Fink 2000)—the very attitude and existential action allowing human beings to work with the tensions affirmatively and constructively, exploring their powers and predicaments and those of the world. It is an attitude based on enthusiasm that moves us to the next experience (Manning 2012), the sensed potential of the beginning (Manning 2009) in which everything is possible, and an attitude based on the exploration of moods, emotions, and different emotional responses through a range of strategies including courage, bravery, resilience, and sociability (Krnjaja 2012a; Fleer 2009; Lester and Russell 2008; Marjanović 1987). It is also an attitude that allows us to use familiar knowledge in new, imagined contexts and manners and connects and reconstructs previous experiences and knowledge (Krnjaja 2012a; Fleer 2009), enabling us to rethink the meaning of the world and to move beyond existing ways of being and understanding, not only in the situations of play, but also throughout our entire experience of life (Lester and Russell 2010).

As such, the liberatory work of play is central to the democratic project (Khattar and Callaghan 2016; Mitranić 2016), not only as a support in the realization of the rights of the child, but also as a pathway to establishing a just and caring community even in difficult times. Accordingly, the most important argument for our initiative to create a collection of playful situations and activities for children and adults was the relational nature of play—play being the embodied process of becoming together, a space between us: 'above the ground, between goals and between players, around the ball on all sides' (Massumi 2002). The very activity of playing counters disconnection and social isolation, fostering a sense of belonging, inclusion, and acceptance (International Play Association 2020) and provides players, most notably children, with an opportunity to acquire social capital and enjoy social well-being (Pavlović Breneselović 2010; Lester and Russell 2008). Common play between children and adults additionally carries the strong potential for developing creative ways to think and act together and connecting the community as a whole (Krnjaja 2012b), which we consider to be a priority in times of crisis. This might be a strong opportunity for collaborative work between teachers, students, practitioners, and families, as well as between children and adults in the further development of early childhood practice.

The opportunity for children and adults to jointly create the collection of playful situations and activities in times of crisis provided students with an experiential task, based on active and bold involvement, research and negotiation, critical and ethical thinking, joint endeavour, and mutual trust (Mitranić and Purešević 2021). We instructed students on how to search for and develop different ideas based on the theories of play which we had discussed in the course.

The main principles we established for creating suggestions were: a) to respect play for its own sake (as opposed to subordinating play to a dialectic purpose), b) to encourage togetherness and mutual care through play (as opposed to competition), and c) to respect different family conditions when proposing the space and materials for play. Students worked in small groups and posted their suggestions on Padlet, a collaborative online platform. Groups discussed and adjusted suggestions among themselves. We as teachers also commented, posted our suggestions and ideas, and drew attention to the previously established principles.

After two weeks of collaborative work, we combined a collection of forty proposals and created an illustrated publication called *The Treasury for Common Play between Children and Adults* (Figures 2.1 and 2.2). This publication was sent to the MOESTD and relevant professional associations of preschool education. The *Treasury* was posted on the MOESTD website *Let's Connect, Let's Empower in the Covid-19 Crisis* as well as on the official websites of professional associations, but it soon went viral and was shared via social media, blogs and websites for parents (Figure 2.3).

Figure 2.1 *The Treasury for Common Play between Children and Adults* (main page), April 2020. Available on the MOESTD website https://mpn.gov.rs/vesti/riznica-igara-za-decu-i-odrasle/ Created by 4th-year students and teachers in the Department of Preschool Pedagogy, University of Belgrade, CC BY-NC 4.0

Figure 2.2 *The Treasury for Common Play between Children and Adults* (introduction), April 2020. Available on the MOESTD website https://mpn.gov.rs/vesti/riznica-igara-za-decu-i-odrasle/ Created by 4th-year students and teachers in the Department of Preschool Pedagogy, University of Belgrade, CC BY-NC 4.0

Figure 2.3 Screenshot of *The Treasury for Common Play between Children and Adults* on the MOESTD website https://mpn.gov.rs/vesti/riznica-igara-za-decu-i-odrasle/
Image by the authors, CC BY-NC 4.0

Preschool teachers were encouraged to use the *Treasury* as a resource in their remote work with children and families. The teachers chose several of the suggestions every week. They sent them to families to choose one or more proposals to try out, encouraging them to play and make further suggestions as to what is usually played and enjoyed in their family. Along with the proposals, the teachers asked the parents to send feedback about the play experience with the children, and to share it with other children and families through the established media of communication in kindergarten groups (mostly Viber groups). During the week, each family chose some of the play suggestions offered and exchanged observations and suggestions on how the play unfolded. Based on the feedback and comments of parents and children about their experiences of play, the preschool teachers made compilations of the experiences using the digital tool *StoryJumper*. They supplemented the *Treasury* with new suggestions for common play between children and adults.

Research Method

In the research we present in this paper, we focused on the experiences of families and children for whom the support through play was intended. Our goal was to explore the families' experiences of playing in home isolation, encouraged by *The Treasury for Common Play between Children and Adults.* In investigating family experiences, we used interpretative phenomenological analysis (Wilig 2013). We worked with the preschool teachers of three kindergarten groups of children aged between two and six years (a total of sixty-seven families were included) at one kindergarten in Belgrade. Together, we collected notes about the experiences of play that parents sent to teachers of kindergarten groups during their first two weeks of using the *Treasury*. All parents were informed about our research and gave consent for their notes and photographs to be used without hiding faces or identities. There were no descriptions that contained negative comments, nor was there a family that did not send a documented experience of play, at least through a photograph or a video. The number of documented contributions sent by families mostly depended on the nature of the parents' work. In this research, we have focused on short textual notes. The analysis did not include photographs and videos sent by parents that did not contain a textual record (twenty-nine attachments) and fourteen notes from parents from all three groups (five in the first group, four in the second group, and five in the third group) in which the term 'task' was used in addition to the term 'play' (so, for example, 'see how successful we were in performing this task'). As a result, we analyzed twenty-four short textual notes, or eight notes from each group. The length of the text of the notes selected for analysis ranged from thirty-one to one hundred and ten words.

After several readings of the collected notes, multiple topics emerged in the analysis. These are further integrated into four main themes considered as reflective of the essence of the experience of play for parents and children in home isolation: 1) feelings related to play, 2) resources and environments, 3) shared experiences, and 4) parent initiatives.

Research Findings

1) Feelings Related to Play

The theme of expressing feelings related to play emphasizes the satisfaction and fulfilment in play as opposed to the dominant feelings of helplessness, fear, and confusion that we have all faced during the Covid-19 lockdown. Parents described play as a way to experience delight and self-satisfaction both for them and their children.

I've noticed that we are all excitedly waiting for a new proposal. (N1)

In their notes, the parents presented play as an amusement that filled the whole family with pleasure:

It is creative and interesting to us, we were all happy, playing still goes on! (N7)

This activity, 'Strange Balloons', brought us great pleasure! (N23)

Parents associated play with a feeling of satisfaction and fulfillment, and as a way to spend quality family time.

We hid things around the house and mapped places on the plan of the apartment: 'Pirate Alexander (One-eyed Aca) is getting ready to go in search of buried treasure with his map!' The whole family played, and we had such a great and imaginative time! (N8)

This is how we told our story, and many things came out of it! We started to tell the story 'While travelling, I love to...' and we added objects, toys, drew a little, and it turned out to be very fun and imaginative. Mila was thrilled, her brother is sure to join her, and time has flown by for us in the family. (N13)

Parents described pleasure and fulfillment as their main feelings while playing:

The proposals are very interesting. It often happens that we adults play and children watch—play is constant, only the audience changes! (N2)

The parents also presented a feeling of satisfaction and fulfillment in play as a way to distance themselves from reality:

Such fun at home and such gloom all around us. (N12)

Thanks for the great ideas; play helps us forget a little about these difficult days. (N22)

2) Resources and Environments

We generated the theme of opportunities for playful research from several topics that emerged in the analysis of the notes: an exploration of different materials and objects in the house that families used for play, discovery of the potential of different spaces in the house through play, experimentation with different variations of the suggested proposals, and examination of one's identities and roles as well as power in play.

Parents mentioned the materials and the household items they had used in play which had not been used as a means for play in their house before:

> 'The Magic Line'—We really liked this activity. Dunja makes her path using various decorative ribbons found in the house and even toilet paper. (N2)

> 'Sneak Under the Rainbow'—Check out this art of ours! We are playing with sunlight and colours, and this is a glass of water shining and making a rainbow! (N16)

The different spaces in the house that parents mentioned in their notes show that families discovered the potential for play in different places as places, which they had not used in that manner before.

> 'Spider Web'—I don't know how it works for you, but we made a web out of kitchen towels. The whole corridor is networked. (N15)

> 'Hopscotch'—Here, my friends, see how the entire apartment can be turned into a big hopscotch! (N24)

Almost every day, parents sent new notes about the variations they introduced into the proposals with their children, which opened up new opportunities for experimentation for them:

> 'The Miraculous Glasses'—We played by pouring water from glass to glass with straws, and then we tried with a perforated ladle. Peter says: 'I pour a little water and then it leaks into this, then into that, then into this, each goes into a different glass! Wow, great!' (N9)

'Strange Balloons'—We had two balloons. We filled one with flour and one with rice. Then we squeezed them, bent them, made various shapes. The very material with which we filled the balloons took us further into play. We played a game of finding out what was at the bottom of the box filled with flour. Then my child enjoyed dipping his fingers into the flour and making various patterns on it. (N23)

The parents presented their experiences of play as an opportunity to test their physical skills and vitality.

Marko is delighted with the game 'Ball in the Labyrinth'. He easily led the ball through the maze while my husband and I had difficulties. (O6)

'Spider Web'—Playing for the third day in a row, we are more active than ever! (N15) (Figure 2.4)

Figure 2.4 Family photograph of father and child playing Spider Web, May 2020.

According to the parents' notes, play allowed them to explore different cultural identities and roles with their children:

'Hidden Treasure'—Today, we were thinking about how the pirates dressed and why they needed all those things. Here is how we dressed like pirates, setting off in a treasure hunt! (N4)

'Game of Shadows'—Yes, this is a real theatre. It's not difficult; we made various characters, heroes, animals, and some basic shapes which we can turn into a ship or whatever we want. We cut everything out of cardboard trays. And look, the entire stories of shadows! The whole family is having fun! (N20) (Figure 2.5)

Figure 2.5 Family photograph of father and child playing Game of Shadows, April 2020.

3) Shared Experiences

In the parents' notes, we noticed their need to share the experience of play. Considering the number of notes, photographs, and videos that parents sent to preschool teachers, we tend to conclude that this need goes beyond the domain of 'obligation'. A multitude of collected notes indicates that play functioned as an inspiring and safe space in which to share family experiences and connect different actors of the kindergarten group as a community during the lockdown. Also, as mentioned above in the discussion of the first main theme, parents recognized play as a way for a family to connect, to share, and to spend quality time together:

This is our treehouse; only Miki can climb there—that's because he practised, but we made it all together. The ideas are great! (N21)

The shadows are phenomenal—you try to draw a large drawing using a shadow. We line up the animals and draw shadows on the paper on the wall. Then we move the animals away to see how much they have grown! We can't stop playing. (N20)

Parents shared the experience of playing as their children taught them— for instance, games they played in kindergarten and liked to repeat:

'Birds in Nests'—We played Miša's favourite game from kindergarten in our yard today. Miša taught us how to play, and we played it together several times. (N11)

According to the parents' notes, the proposals suggested by the preschool teachers contributed to the siblings playing together more than ever before:

Every day, Marko looks forward to your ideas. His brother is keen on joining him and playing with him. (N10)

'My Hidden Space'—Using our curtains, we've separated one part of the room and made our 'universe' in it. The 'universe' is very interesting. Now David and Luka are playing together so nicely, which was not common before. (N14)

According to the parents' notes, the exchange of experiences and proposals with the preschool teacher helped the children to maintain a sense of belonging and connection with the teacher and other children from the kindergarten group:

My child kisses the photos of his friends while we're watching the photos and recordings shared on the Viber group. (N 17)

Mine too. (N1; N23)

Our child became interested in your suggestions only when she saw the photos of her friends playing. (N6)

Not only did the parents send their notes about play to the preschool teacher, but they almost always exchanged them with other parents via the Viber group. When the teachers suggested 'Fantastic Story' and 'Story from the Family Album', twenty families joined them. Parents filmed the children and themselves as they told stories together, and then the educators made a joint collection of stories and passed them on to each family:

> Now, friends, this is our story. [...] (video while the child tells the story) (N19)

> Let's see how Stefan's magic sword defeated the monster! (video) (N11)

Sharing the experiences of play, especially situations based on storytelling, encouraged parents to remember their favourite stories from childhood and not only tell them to their children, but also to record themselves while telling a story and to share the video with the other children and parents:

> Friends, my favourite story is 'Ugly Duckling'. I don't know why it was called ugly because it was not ugly at all; it was just different. One day [...] (N11) (Figure 2.6)

Figure 2.6 Family photographs of the whole family engaged in storytelling, May 2020

Playing and sharing experiences with the other children and families encouraged children and parents to engage in other activities outside of play and to make toys together:

> We played the 'Magic World of Sculpture'. We played with the dough and then we decided to knead and make doughnuts. We used various moulds and made figures. At the end, we ate everything. Here are the photos... We can't wait for new suggestions! (N14)

> We made an hourglass out of cornflour and two plastic water bottles. Lule never puts the hourglass down and measures our time in everything we do. (N4)

4) Parent Initiatives

In the parents' notes, expressions of the initiative to continue playing could be referred to as the initiative to use new materials and objects for play and to find websites with new proposals for playful situations and activities:

> The ideas have never been better! But try it like this, we enjoyed it—spread a net across the middle of the yard or an old table, you can use rackets and balls, but you can also drag below it, throw above it, be as imaginative as we were. (N5)

> We suggest that you take two or three glasses and tie them with straws. [...] (photo). Try it; it's a lot of fun... and it requires concentration. (N8)

A large number of suggestions which the parents devised with their children and proposed to other children and families can be seen in the parents' notes.

> Friends, we came up with the game 'Swing'—it takes two pairs, both of which hold hands. Then the first couple squat and say the name of an animal. Then the other two, the other couple, squat and say something about that animal. The first couple gets up.

When they come up with a new idea, they say it and squat again. (N3)

We made a game with four cards with the symbols of pirates (an anchor, a skull, a ship, and pirates). Parents' explanation: 'The game is for three players: two players stand next to the symbol and the third player gives them a sign on which symbol they should stand next to and how many times. The game is played faster and faster. We'll save this game and bring it to the kindergarten when we return so that we can play it all together'. (N10)

Discussion

The research findings concerning parents' and children's experiences of play during lockdown can be seen in light of the capacity for flexibility as a key element of play and the backbone of resilience. The openness of play always containing the possibility to 'go beyond' can be recognized in the experiences noted by the parents—an initiative reflected in the new propositions and modifications of proposed suggestions. We can conclude that play functioned as a safe context for families both individually and mutually, eliminating fear of error and evaluation (Marjanović 1987; Lester and Russell 2008). Common play enabled the exchange and creation of novel, original relations (Henricks 2014), and engagement with multiple possibilities of ideas, materials, and spaces for play. In this context, teachers' strategy of suggesting more proposals from which families could choose and encouraging parents to supplement this list with their own suggestions proved to be beneficial for the quality and further development of playful experiences. We noted how common play between children and adults helped families to clarify, reflect on and even transform different feelings they experienced, both within situations of play and outside them. A comparison between the feelings in play and the perception of reality due to the Covid-19 pandemic indicates that, to parents, play was a source of pleasant feelings and relaxation from everyday tension. Almost all parents' notes contain words of gratitude addressed to the preschool teachers and the suggestions for play they have sent, confirming that the experience of play represented 'a stock of good things' (Vellacott 2007) amidst harsh everyday conditions.

Thus we come to the question of play's creative potential, expressed as a transformative mode of human functioning (Sicart 2014; Krnjaja 2012a; Marjanović 1987), allowing the player to engage as a whole being in understanding and responding to their environment (Krnjaja 2012a). The imagination and transformation that parents write about in their notes are present in the search for new activities and new possibilities for play. Experiences of play enabled families to explore different perspectives and relationships, different roles and imagined contexts, to transform their living space and harmonize their actions, creating a safe space for mutual exchange. Further, the shared experience of playing and exploring possibilities for play, not just between children and adults, but also between families and different professionals in early childhood education, created 'time and space' of its own amidst social crisis and isolation. Thus, common play created new and affirmative possibilities to be and become together in this world.

It is here that the relational nature of play is shown—through mutual connection and togetherness, shared power, and exchange. The relational nature of play is confirmed in the parents' notes on multiple levels: in the family circle, through joint play of children with siblings and parents, and outside of the family circle, through the exchange of proposals and experiences of play with the preschool teacher and other families from the kindergarten group. The expressed need to exchange experiences, to learn from each other in play and to learn about possibilities for play reflects families' desire to stay connected, overcoming isolation and physical distance. Beyond the support for common play, the opportunity for different actors to get involved, to initiate, and to share, supported the sense of belonging and the further development of social capital and social well-being for children and adults as well (International Play Association 2020; Pavlović Breneselović 2010; Lester and Russell 2008). Common play as an experience, as well as a framework for action, enabled families and different professionals to decontextualize the established power relations—between children and adults, parents and teachers, practitioners and experts—and to develop new ones based on sympathy, care, and a joint struggle to thrive together, despite current conditions.

In this manner, we consider it necessary to point out the limitations of our research focused exclusively on families' experiences of play in home isolation. Families and children are active participants in the broader community of preschool education. Their experiences of play are shaped by the support provided during home isolation and by broader interactions with the professional and social communities. Nevertheless, the openness of our research to the experiences of families and children, and their acceptance as active participants of that research, gives us a basis to view the research findings in the context of the values we seek to cultivate in play as well as in preschool education as a whole.

Recommendations for Practice

Based on the significance of play, which we discovered in researching the quality of families' experiences of play during the lockdown, as well as our experience as university teachers teaching the course 'Child's Play and Creativity' during the Covid-19 pandemic, we can offer two recommendations for education:

1. **Connecting participants at different levels of the education system** through the interaction of the academic community, educational policymakers, practitioners, families and children contributes to an awareness of the importance of play in education, and rejects its common treatment in kindergarten and school right through to academic studies as something 'trivial' and separate from learning (Reid and Wood 2016).

2. **Education established on creative potential** has the power to function as a deeply responsible social practice, which makes play necessary in further rethinking education in the context of the multiple crises we are facing. The future of education lies in practices that strengthen all of its actors to face the unexpected and to work constructively with challenges. Through joint creation and further practical usage and expansion of *The Treasury for Common Play between Children and Adults*, we are convinced that a learning process based on creative potential encourages cooperation, research, initiative, mutual harmonization, and reflection, thus strengthening the sense of professional contribution.

Works Cited

Boyd Webb, Nancy (ed.) 2015. *Play Therapy with Children and Adolescents in Crisis* (New York: Guilford)

Edmiston, Brian. 2008. *Forming Ethical Identities in Early Childhood Play* (Abingdon: Routledge), https://doi.org/10.4324/9780203934739

Eichberg, Henning. 2018. 'Play against Alienation?' in *The Philosophy of Play as Life: Towards a Global Ethos of Management*, ed. by Wendy Russell, Emily Ryal and Malcom MacLean (London: Routledge), pp. 211–26, https://doi.org/10.4324/9781315454139-16

Fegert, Jorg. M., et al. 2020. 'Challenges and Burden of the Coronavirus 2019 (Covid-19) Pandemic for Child and Adolescent Mental Health: A Narrative Review to Highlight Clinical and Research Needs in the Acute Phase and the Long Return to Normality', *Child and Adolescent Psychiatry and Mental Health*, 14, (2020), https://doi.org/10.1186/s13034-020-00329-3

Feldman, Daniel. 2019. 'Children's Play in the Shadow of War', *American Journal of Play*, 11 (3): 288–307

Fink, Eugen. 2000. *Igra kao simbol svijeta* [Play as Symbol of the World] (Zagreb: Demetra)

Fleer, Marilyn. (2009). 'A Cultural-Historical Perspective on Play: Play as a Leading Activity Across Cultural Communities', in *Play and Learning in Early Childhood Settings: International Perspectives*, ed. by Marilyn Fleer and Ingrid Pramling Samuelsson (Berlin: Springer), pp. 1–18, https://doi.org/10.1007/978-1-4020-8498-0_1

Henricks, Thomas. 2014. 'Play as Self-Realization: Toward a General Theory of Play', *American Journal of Play*, 6: 190–213

International Play Association. 2020. *Play in Crisis: Support for Parents and Carers* (International Play Association), http://ipaworld.org/wp-content/uploads/2020/04/IPA-Play-in-Crisis-Booklet-for-parents-and-carers-2020.pdf

Khattar, Randa and Callaghan, Karyn. 2016. 'Playing with Play: A Playful Reconnaissance', in *Play: A Theory of Learning and Change*, ed. by Tara Brabazon (Berlin: Springer), pp. 27–33, https://doi.org/10.1007/978-3-319-25549-1_3

Krnjaja, Živka. 2012a. 'Igra na ranim uzrastima [Play in Early Years]', in *Standardi za razvoj i učenje dece ranih uzrasta u Srbiji*, ed. by Aleksandar Baucal (Beograd: Institut za psihologiju), pp. 113–32

——. 2012b. '*Igra kao susret: koautorski prostor u zajedničkoj igri dece i odraslih* [Play as an Encounter: Coauthorial Space in Common Play between Children and Adults]', *Etnoantropološki problemi*, 7: 251–67

——. 2021. 'Predškolsko vaspitanje i obrazovanje u vreme „korona krize": fizička izolacija i „efekat tunela"[Preschool Education in Times of Corona-Crises: Physical Isolation and "Tunnel Effect"]', in *Obrazovanje u vreme kovid krize: Gde smo i kuda dalje*, ed. by Vera Spasenović (Beograd: Filozofski fakultet), pp. 67–82

Lester, Stuart, and Russell, Wendy. 2008. *Play for a Change. Play, Policy and Practice: A Review of Contemporary Perspectives* (London: Play England)

——. 2010. *Children's Right to Play: An Examination of the Importance of Play in the Lives of Children Worldwide*, Working Paper, 57 (The Hague, Netherlands: Bernard van Leer Foundation)

Manning, Erin. 2009. *Relationscapes: Movement, Art, Philosophy* (Cambridge: MIT Press), https://doi.org/10.7551/mitpress/9780262134903.001.0001

——. 2012. *Always More Than One* (Durham: Duke University Press), https://doi.org/10.1515/9780822395829

Marjanović-Shane, Ana, and Jane E. White. 2014. 'When the Footlights Are Off: A Bakhtinian Interrogation of Play as Postupok', *International Journal of Play*, 3: 119–35, https://doi.org/10.1080/21594937.2014.931686

Marjanović, Aleksandra. 1979. 'Stvaralaštvo, igra i vaspitanje predškolskog deteta [Creativity, Play and Upbringing of Preschool Child]', *Predškolsko dete*, 1–2: 3–33

——. 1987. 'Dečja igra i stvaralaštvo [Child's Play and Creativity]',*Predškolsko dete*, 1–4: 85–101

Massumi, Brian. 2002. *Parables for the Virtual: Movement, Affect, Sensation* (Durham: Duke University Press)

Ministry of Education, Science and Technological Development. 2018. 'Pravilnik o Osnovama programa predškolskog vaspitanja i obrazovanja Godine uzleta [National Curriculum Framework for Early Childhood Education: Years of Ascent]', http://www.mpn.gov.rs/wpcontent/uploads/2018/09/OSNOVE-PROGRAMA-.pdf

——. 2020. 'Predškolsko vaspitanje i obrazovanje u vreme epidemije Covid-19 [Preschool Education and Upbringing in the Times of Covid-19 Epidemic]', http://www.mpn.gov.rs/wpcontent/uploads/2020/03/pred%C5%A1kolsko-vest_pdf.pdf

Mitranić, Nevena, and Dragana Purešević. 2021. 'Kompetentnost pedagoga u doba krize [The Competence of Pedagogues in Times of Crisis]', in *Vaspitanje i obrazovanje u digitalnom okruženju*, ed. by Ivana Jeremić, Nataša Nikolić, and Nikola Koruga (Beograd: Institut za pedagogiju i andragogiju), pp. 239–46

Mitranić, Nevena. 2016. 'Smernice za društvenu podršku dečjoj igri [Guidelines for Social Support to Child's Play]', *Nastava i vaspitanje*, 65: 411–25

Miškeljin, Lidija. 2021. 'Pristupi obrazovne politike predškolskom vaspitanju i obrazovanju u doba krize [Approaches of Educational Policies to Early Childhood Education in Times of Crises]', in *Obrazovanje u vreme kovid krize: Gde smo i kuda dalje*, ed. by Vera Spasenović (Begrad: Filozofski fakultet), pp. 101–18

Montag, Christian, and Jon D. Elhai. 2020. 'Discussing Digital Technology Overuse in Children and Adolescents during the Covid-19 Pandemic and Beyond: On the Importance of Considering Affective Neuroscience Theory', *Addictive Behaviors Reports*, 12, https://doi.org/10.1016/j.abrep.2020.100313

Pavlović Breneselović, Dragana. 2010. 'Dobrobit deteta u programu naspram programa za dobrobit [The Wellbeing of Child in the Curriculum vs Programing for Wellbeing]', *Nastava i vaspitanje*, 59: 251–64

Pramling Samuelsson, Ingrid, Judith T. Wagner, and Elin Erikson Ødegaard. 2020. 'The Coronavirus Pandemic and Lessons Learned in Preschools in Norway, Sweden and the United States: OMEP Policy Forum', *International Journal of Early Childhood*, 52: 129–44, https://doi.org/10.1007/s13158-020-00267-3

Purešević, Dragana. 2021. 'Vrtić na daljinu u vreme Covid-19 krize: Perspektiva roditelja [Distance-Kindergarten in Times of Covid-19 Crisis: Parents' Perspectives]', in *Obrazovanje u vreme kovid krize: Gde smo i kuda dalje*, ed. by Vera Spasenović (Beograd: Filozofski fakultet), pp. 133–50

Reid, Jo-Anne, and Denise May Wood. 2016. 'Practice Play in Learning to Teach: Performing a Teaching Body', in *Play: A Theory of Learning and Change*, ed. by Tara Brabazon (Berlin: Springer), pp. 147–65

Sicart, Miguel. 2014. *Play Matters* (Chicago: MIT Press), https://doi.org/10.7551/mitpress/10042.001.0001

United Nations. 1989. *Convention on the Rights of the Child*, https://www.unicef.org.uk/wp-content/uploads/2010/05/UNCRC_united_nations_convention_on_the_rights_of_the_child.pdf

Villarreal, Alexandra. 2020. '"The Most Stressful Time Ever": How Coronavirus Affects Children's Mental Health', *The Guardian*, 17 April, https://www.theguardian.com/society/2020/apr/17/us-children-mental-health-coronavirus

Vellacott, Julie. 2007. 'Resilience: A Psychoanalytical Exploration', *British Journal of Psychotherapy*, 23: 163–70, https://doi.org/10.1111/j.1752-0118.2007.00015.x

Wilig, Carla. 2013. *Introducing Qualitative Research in Psychology* (New York: McGraw-Hill Education)

3. Up, Down, Stop, Go, and Everything In Between: Promoting a Resident-Driven Play-Based Agenda during a Global Pandemic in Rochester, New York

Holly Sienkiewicz, Jenn Beideman, Beatriz LeBron, Shanielia Lewis, Emma Morrison, Lydia Rivera, and Dina Faticone

Effects of the Covid-19 Pandemic on Children

Throughout the nation, healthcare providers, advocates, parents and caregivers are raising red flags about Covid-19's impact on children's mental health and well-being. Rates of psychological distress, including anxiety and depression, have increased in children and youth since the pandemic began. Symptoms of depression and anxiety among youth have doubled to twenty-five percent and twenty percent respectively (Racine et al. 2021). Emergency department visits for suspected suicide attempts were fifty-one percent higher for adolescent girls in early 2021 compared with the same time period in 2019 (Yard et al. 2021). Additionally, pandemic-related cancellations of in-person activities made it more difficult to identify mental health concerns and indications of child abuse (Stewart 2020). Children and youth of colour experienced

https://doi.org/10.11647/OBP.0326.03

additional race-based stressors throughout the course of the pandemic. The murder of George Floyd and many other Black Americans by law enforcement officers, Covid-related hate crimes committed against Asian Americans, increased gun violence and widening political polarity further affect one's mental health.

The benefits of play have the potential to mitigate the impact of pandemic-related trauma. Play relieves stress and reduces anxiety by providing time for relaxation, increasing connectedness with family and friends, and allowing children to make sense of changes by 'playing out' their traumas (International Play Equipment Manufacturers Association 2020). Clinicians and child serving agencies agree that opportunities for play will be vital to children's mental health as they recover from pandemic-related trauma and anxiety (American Academy of Pediatrics 2021; Clay 2020; Global Recess Alliance 2020; Hadani and Vey 2020; Harvard Center for the Developing Child 2020; International Play Association 2020).

Play benefits children in all developmental areas. It aids both physical and cognitive development by strengthening muscles, bones, vital organs and brain functions in children (Clements 2004). Play supports maintaining healthy weight and facilitates the development of key brain functions, including focus and cognitive control (Clements 2004). Playful learning is directly correlated with teachers' reports of less fidgeting, improved behaviour and listening, and greater focus (Slater et al. 2012). An hour of active play improves academic outcomes (Sattelmair and Ratey 2009) and opportunities for integrated play throughout the day cause a student's brain to function more efficiently, leading to improved concentration (Chaddock et al. 2010). Socially, play is crucial to developing language skills, empathy, imagination, self-regulation and life skills, such as cooperation and problem solving (Miller and Almon 2009). Opportunities for play support children's emotional health by reducing feelings of anxiety and providing a means of working through complex feelings and emotions (US Department of Health and Human Services 2008). Additionally, play supports children in building healthy relationships with their peers and adults (Murphey et al. 2014). Strong relationships with adults are critical protective factors as children navigate trauma and events throughout their lives. Children who have strong and healthy relationships with adults are more likely to stay on track developmentally (Ginsburg et al. 2007) and better able to navigate toxic stress caused by poverty, racism and adverse childhood experiences (Shonkoff, Boyce and McEwen 2009). Play is a quality of life indicator and the foundation to whole child health. It makes for happier and healthier children. Opportunities for both structured and unstructured play are vital for children's education, health, well-being and success.

Despite its many advantages, not all children benefit equally from play. Black and Latino children have historically been discriminated against in the ways in which they move and play within educational systems and during out-of-school time. Students of colour are watched more intently than White students and are forced to navigate 'white gaze' in their everyday settings (schools, neighbourhoods, after-school programming, etc.), often leading to feelings of being watched, judged and not welcomed (Esposito 2011). White gaze also persists in the form of surveillance by school authorities, police and educators, leading to students of colour being adultified and their actions criminalized, as their view of play is seen as violent compared to White students whose play may be viewed as innocent, fun and therefore protected (Wright 2021).

Setting

Rochester is a mid-sized city in Western New York, USA, that continues to bear the effects of concentrated poverty and residential segregation. Redlining exists to this day and racial covenants developed in the 1930s and '40s still appear in many deeds to homes, restricting properties from being sold to, or occupied by, people of colour. With approximately 210,000 residents, 39.4% identify as Black alone, 6.2% identify as two or more races, and 19.4% identify as Latino (53%) (US Census Bureau 2021); one third of city residents live in poverty (31.3%) (Rochester-Monroe Anti-Poverty Initiative 2020). More than 40% of Black and Latino residents are poor, 20% of residents lack a high school diploma, and 47.7% of children live in poverty. The city's extreme poverty rate is over 15% and Rochester is the third poorest city in the nation when compared to the largest seventy-five metropolitan areas (Rochester-Monroe Anti-Poverty Initiative 2020). An astounding 72.2% of White residents own their homes, whereas the same is true for just 31.5% of Black residents. Throughout the nine county Finger Lakes region, 68%

of Black adults and 53% of Latinos live in poverty, compared to only 12% of White adults (Common Ground Health 2020). Inequities persist amongst all economic, education and health outcomes.

Rochester is home to 3500 acres of park and green space. Despite seemingly adequate park space, many kids do not have access to safe and accessible places to play or be physically active. Just one quarter of the city's residents thought their neighbourhood was great for children to play outdoors compared to sixty-four percent of residents in neighbouring suburbs (Common Ground Health, My Health Story 2018). Past Healthi Kids surveys found that only seventeen percent of youth reported playing at parks and playgrounds, with eighty-two percent of all play occurring in vacant lots, parking lots or streets. Two thirds of residents (65%) did not feel safe letting their child walk to a park in their own neighbourhood (Healthi Kids 2022). These numbers are alarming but not surprising, resulting from decades of structural policies, institutions and environments that perpetuated systemic racism locally.

Vast inequities in educational and health outcomes exist as well. In 2021, graduation rates of the Rochester City School District (RCSD) increased to sixty-eight percent, up eighteen percent since 2013 (Murphy and Stern 2021), and despite ninety percent of the RCSD student population being children and youth of colour, eighty-two percent of teachers in the district are White, creating one of the largest gaps between diversity of a student body and the diversity of teaching staff within the state of New York (Education Trust New York 2017). The health disparities prevalent at the community level persist with youth of colour. African American and Latino children and families in the City of Rochester experience worse health outcomes than the White/non-Latino population in Monroe County, including higher rates of obesity and increased likelihood of premature mortality (Common Ground Health 2021). Black children and youth in Monroe County are nearly two times as likely to report three or more Adverse Childhood Experiences than White students (29% versus 16%) (Common Ground Health 2021). Furthermore, the pandemic exacerbated existing disparities with Black and Latino residents in Monroe County dying from Covid-19 at a rate three times higher than Whites and were five times more likely to be hospitalized (Common Ground Health 2020).

Healthi Kids Coalition

The Healthi Kids Coalition formed in 2008 as a grassroots initiative of Common Ground Health advocating for safe and accessible play spaces in schools and neighbourhoods in Rochester. With over eighty members, Healthi Kids partners to transform policies, systems and environments to support physical, social, emotional and cognitive development of all kids from birth to eight years old. We embrace the diversity of all family structures in our community and believe in the power of youth and resident voices to co-create solutions. Our resident-led advocacy agenda prioritizes healthy learning environments, foundations for health in early childhood, equitable communities and the power of play. The coalition recognizes the need to eradicate inequities caused by racism, adverse childhood experiences, poverty, ableism and community violence, and to support the youngest members of our community. We work to advance policies to ensure that all kids regardless of ZIP code, economic status, sexual orientation, gender, race, religion, or ability have the support they need for the healthiest start in life.

Healthi Kids recognizes the importance of play to children's overall health and well-being. Advancing safe and accessible opportunities for play in schools and neighbourhoods are key focal points of our work. Our work to advance play in schools began in 2009 when we partnered with students and their families to assess the frequency with which recess was being offered in schools. This led to the creation of a recess report card demonstrating inequities in play between students in the Rochester City School District and students in suburban districts throughout the rest of the county. In 2014, Healthi Kids partnered with the RCSD Parent Advisory Council to find a district-wide solution to ensure that no child was denied recess. Together we advocated that every child, regardless of ability, would have daily active recess and that recess could not be taken away as a form of punishment. This work led to the creation of a twenty-minute mandatory daily active recess policy within the RCSD. We supported schools with the implementation of these policies by providing technical assistance, resources and materials, in addition to partnering with national experts to provide ongoing professional development opportunities for administrators, staff, and teachers across the district.

Our work to advance play in neighbourhoods began between 2010 and 2013 when we partnered with community members in five neighbourhoods throughout the city to conduct playability assessments to answer questions about where kids were playing and what we could do to improve existing play spaces. Results revealed that access to play in parks and at playgrounds is limited, causing kids to play in non-traditional spaces like streets, sidewalks, empty lots and parking lots. Results further indicated that neighbourhood and traffic safety, unsafe access to parks, and unkempt playgrounds are key barriers that deter parents from letting their children play outdoors altogether.

Armed with data, residents advocated for a number of policies, systems and environmental changes to address neighbourhood safety, policies and programmes to slow down traffic, improve walkability and bikeability, and promote playability. Examples of action taken include amending the city-wide speed bump policy, advocating for a complete streets policy, pushing to lower the residential speed limit and creating a way for residents to communicate crime prevention needs in their neighbourhood. This initial work documented inequities in access to play amongst children in Rochester and evolved to form the PlayROCs Advocacy Committee as part of the Healthi Kids Coalition.

PlayROCs Advocacy Committee

The PlayROCs Advocacy Committee grew out of the Healthi Kids Coalition in 2015. Residents affiliated with this committee led a grassroots campaign convening neighbourhood associations, block clubs, churches, community organizations and nonprofits to build and advance a play-based agenda. The team of thirty-two resident leaders and organizational partners created an agenda that advances a community vision for play, advocates for change, recognizes community bright spots and coordinates community resources. For the past seven years, the committee has advocated for play and playful learning to be prominently featured in Rochester 2034, the city's comprehensive plan. We piloted innovative built environment strategies, such as story walks, a downtown Play Walk and other tactical urbanism installations, in addition to working with the City's Department of Recreation and Human Services to transform their approaches to encourage neighbourhood play by piloting play streets and creating a playful sidewalk policy. The campaign amplifies community voices and catalyzes city residents to bring play back into the daily lives of Rochester's children.

The Healthi Kids Coalition and PlayROCs Advocacy Committee are community-engaged entities in which residents, parents, caregivers and youth are embedded throughout planning and implementation processes. In December 2019, the PlayROCs Advocacy Committee identified potential policy levers to continue to advance their play-based agenda. To truly make a difference in the lives of city children, residents were aware of the need to expand their work to the Rochester City School District. The committee was planning this expanded portfolio of work when the Covid-19 pandemic began in March 2020. The abrupt closing of schools and community centres in conjunction with social isolation and the lack of play opportunities underscored the importance of this work.

Early in the pandemic, members of the committee raised the alarm about the impact Covid-19 was having on their children. Increased social isolation, the effects of online learning and the chronic toxic stress experienced by families were affecting our children physically and mentally. This caused the committee to develop an advocacy agenda addressing the need for unstructured play throughout Covid-19. Goals of the agenda included safeguarding play in learning environments, ensuring children across Rochester had access to play and advocating for changes in the built environment to support play in everyday spaces. This chapter documents the programmatic response of the coalition and advocacy committee during the pandemic and was not designed as a research study.

Advocating for Supportive Play Environments during Covid-19

Since its inception, the PlayROCs Advocacy Committee has worked to transform Rochester's public settings into more playful spaces. The committee wanted to ensure that environmental changes continued to occur throughout the pandemic. During this time, we piloted innovative place-making approaches, like story walks and playful sidewalks. Teams created playful sidewalks in several neighbourhoods and expanded the downtown Play Walk to include an element called 'the Ripple', a tactical urbanism installation featuring constantly changing colours, rotating panels and pixelated illustrations. Local teens were integral to designing these spaces and installations. One teen recalled that 'the Ripple was developed by city teens for the benefit of our community. It is exciting to see our vision of what we wanted to see at the Play Walk become a reality'. We also continued to advocate for built environment changes that promoted play in several city capital improvement projects and worked alongside the city's Department of Recreation and Human Services to advance their 'Ten Minute Walk to Park' plan.

Coordinating Resources to Advance Play at Home

Families expressed that they were overloaded with information when researching play activities for children during Covid, but rarely did they have the necessary materials to implement the lessons or ideas seen online. Healthi Kids and PlayROCs Advocacy Committee members actively worked to ensure that children had access to unstructured play materials early in the pandemic. Together we assembled and distributed play kits, partnered with the city to support Covid-friendly programming and infrastructure that prioritizes unstructured, resident-driven play (e.g. toy libraries, bringing recreational programming and staff to non-traditional spaces, and play streets), and coordinated community resources to share with families during the pandemic. To date (as of May 2022), Healthi Kids, in partnership with the City of Rochester Department of Recreation and Human Services, has distributed 6500 play kits to kids at thirty-two different locations throughout the city. The kits focused on unstructured play materials for children aged two to ten years old and included frisbees, sidewalk chalk, crayons, football, beach ball, jump ropes, colouring books and flyers on the importance of play, all in a drawstring bag. For the first wave of distribution, kits were distributed at every R-Center and at School 8 through the school meal programme. Since then, Healthi Kids staff have heard from members of the PlayROCs advocacy committee and other neighbourhood associations that we need to expand this distribution network to ensure that all kids have access to the kits. One member of the committee summarized her thoughts:

Prior to Covid, members of the PlayROCs Advocacy Committee rallied their neighbours to plan activities with kids in the neighbourhood and at our local R-Center. Because of Covid contagion and restrictions, we were limited with what we could do. With the play kits, we are trying to provide positive things for our kids to focus on while they are dealing with all the uncertainty of Covid. Through play kits, I have been able to keep my great-grandkids active and entertained while they're at home, as I still worry about letting them play at playgrounds and touching equipment after other kids, for my own health and theirs.

We will continue to engage our grassroots network of sixty neighbourhood associations, block clubs, churches and residents across the City of Rochester to distribute kits. Each group can sign up to receive a certain number of play kits to distribute directly to children in their neighbourhood.

A Community Vision for Playful Learning

To prioritize play during Covid and build a community vision for playful learning in the RCSD, we worked with partner agencies to host listening sessions and conducted a short survey to get feedback from parents and students. Listening sessions occurred between May and September 2021 and included ninety-six caregivers, students and organizational leaders. Additionally, 115 survey responses were collected between April and August 2021. This multi-pronged approach allowed the team to hear from students and families about the perceived importance of playful learning, a landscape analysis of what was and was not happening in their schools, and what they would want to see happen in their schools and across the district to advance playful learning opportunities.

The PlayROCs Advocacy Committee worked together with RCSD family and student leaders and organizational partners to build an authentic vision reflecting family and student voices. From these discussions, Rochester City School District students and families developed the following vision statement for playful learning:

Play is central to the education and well-being of our children. To support our kids, we must maximize the potential of play in a culturally responsive and sustaining way within our education system. All children (pre-kindergarten through grade twelve) in the Rochester City School District must have equitable access to playful learning and unstructured play opportunities throughout the day (in school, out of school, and during the summer).

To carry out this vision, families and students urged leadership to prioritize six elements including focusing on mental health, implementing playful learning within a culturally responsive framework, focusing on inclusion, providing more opportunities for play outside of the classroom, embedding playful learning in the curriculum and ensuring consistent enforcement of policies.

1. Focus on mental health and emotional well-being: Parents and families were all too aware of and worried about the impact Covid-19 has had on their children. One parent shared, 'Play is meaningful. It can bring out the happiness in you and keep you young, help to release mental anguish and physical pain, keep you spiritually connected. This is what our students need right now'. Participants shared how playful learning should be prioritized to support children's mental health and well-being following pandemic-related trauma.

2. Implement playful learning within a culturally responsive framework: Participants wanted to ensure that a playful learning framework was implemented that was student-centred and affirmed racial, linguistic and cultural identities. One adult participant shared, 'I wish we had a culturally responsive school district that did everything from pedagogy to curriculum to the way we look at play and social interaction'. A student leader also confirmed the need for the vision to be implemented within a culturally responsive lens, stating the need for 'hiring and retaining teachers who look like our students, who are Black and Latinx and speak other languages. We want anti-racist trainings and responsive curriculum. Play is part of all of that... play and outside spaces and learning environments are really important'. Hiring and retaining Black and Latino teachers is a vital step in ensuring that 'learning encounters [are] more relevant to and effective for [ethnically diverse students]' (Gay 2010: 31). Furthermore,

teachers need the time and space to reflect on their perceptions of and interactions with students of colour. Playful learning should be advanced within a paradigm that celebrates the way Black and Latino children play and centres their voices in the learning process instead of requiring students to assimilate to Eurocentric culture (Wright 2021).

3. Focus on inclusion: Participants shared that they would like to see playful learning opportunities inclusive of all students, including those with disabilities. One participant shared how students with disabilities were excluded from playful learning opportunities. 'Students with disabilities are not seeing modifications being made. If the child couldn't play the game, [they] had to research the game and write a report about the game. That is not supporting playful learning for that child'. Adaptations and accommodations need to be available for students with disabilities to ensure all children have access to playful learning.

4. Provide more opportunities outside of the classroom: Participants also want more opportunities for playful learning outside of the physical classroom, such as playing outside, outdoor lessons, field trips and other experiential learning opportunities. One student leader shared, 'Covid-19 took away a lot of our play opportunities. I wish we had more hands-on play and field trips. Things that get us away from our laptops and desks'. Families and students added that it is a challenge to know what opportunities are available outside of the school setting.

5. Embed playful learning into curriculums and daily practice: Family and student leaders stated that embedding playful learning into curriculum and daily instructional practice is critical to ensure that all kids have equitable access to play. Examples of this include field trips, Math-in-Movement curriculum, learning centres and incorporating music in the classroom. One participant shared, 'when kids are engaged because it's relevant and of interest to them, then they'll learn!' Another shared that currently, 'play is an afterthought, not woven into the day'. Many stressed their concerns that

some playful learning opportunities are dependent on school resources and teachers' perceptions of play.

6. Ensure consistent enforcement of policies: Some playful learning opportunities do exist and if policies were enforced, it would go a long way to supporting a vision for playful learning. One parent shared frustration with the daily recess policy implementation, stating that 'the policy does not allow to take away play time as a punishment, but some schools do! How are we enforcing this?' Building a framework of accountability around existing district policies is a first step to ensuring playful learning happens within the district. Without this framework, administrators and teachers have limited incentive to implement playful learning.

While creating this vision for playful learning, families and students developed guiding principles for its implementation in the RCSD and our community. Families felt strongly that playful learning opportunities should be offered for students in pre-kindergarten through to grade twelve to ensure that every child has access to play throughout their educational experience. Playful learning includes both structured and unstructured activities and, most importantly, a playful learning framework must be culturally responsive, sustaining and inclusive. Teachers and staff should receive appropriate anti-racism training and be cognizant of potential biases that they bring to the classroom, including perceiving children of colour to be older than they actually are and thus more culpable for their actions. Any approach to learning should not vilify, adultify, or persecute Black and Latino children for the way they learn, grow and play.

Implementing the Vision for Playful Learning

The PlayROCs Advocacy Committee looked at play activities within three broad categories, including

- unstructured play opportunities (e.g. recess and brain breaks)
- play embedded in curriculum and instructional practices (e.g. physical education, art, music, field trips, experiential learning activities) and

- play opportunities during out-of-school time (e.g. school clubs, after-school programmes, sports teams).

Students, parents and caregivers prioritized unstructured playful learning, specifically access to recess, as the most essential element of their vision. A student leader stated, 'Kids need to have recess. A lot of kids, if you don't turn in your homework, you don't get recess. But that's not fair. When you take away recess, you're taking away our education'.

By embedding playful learning in curriculum and instructional practices, RCSD's pre-kindergarten programme is an exemplary model and has consistently ranked as one of the best in the nation for the past two decades. Play is the primary learning mechanism in this programme. Teachers set up the classroom each day with diverse, open-ended materials for children to explore and learn through creativity, trial and error, and fun, based on the nationally recognized HighScope pre-k curriculum. Daily routines include a 'plan-do-review' sequence, inspiring children to choose what they will, carry out their ideas and reflect upon the activities with adults and other children. These higher-level thinking skills are linked to the development of executive functions necessary for success in school and life. Parents and students want to see this model of embedding play into the curriculum implemented (with adaptations as necessary based on age) for all grade levels and to include more opportunities for experiential learning, field trips, art, music and physical education programmes.

Structured play generally entails an adult 'providing direction and a specific task in order for children to learn a new skill', such as Capture the Flag or board games (Playground Centre 2021). This form of play is particularly important in the classroom, as it allows children to practise achieving an established goal in a fun and effective way. It also teaches valuable life skills, such as active listening, cooperation and sportsmanship (Chatzipanteli and Adamakis 2022). Educators must understand the importance of play in achieving learning outcomes and 'design age-appropriate experiences that both stimulate and gratify children's natural curiosity and desire to understand their world' (New York State Department of Education 2021a), with the goal for 'early childhood education settings, including schools [...] to build capacity by strengthening cognitive and social development through intentional play experiences' (New York State Department of Education 2021b). An

RCSD parent leader expressed that 'right now, play and learning are seen as separate from one another. Play is not appreciated for the value it brings as part of our kids' educational experience'.

Students and parents also expressed the desire for more playful learning opportunities in out-of-school programmes and settings. Out-of-school time (OST) programmes are additional venues for playful learning to occur and many students receive the benefits of music, art, field trips, experiential learning and unstructured play within these settings. OST programmes provide a foundation for playful learning by integrating the things families and students have identified as important into their learning experiences. Nationally, kids of all ages spend an average of eighteen-and-a-half hours a week in OST programmes, amounting to nearly thirty-six percent of additional instructional time outside of the school day (Redd et al. 2012). OST programmes can help promote social-emotional skills, support overall health and well-being, explore new opportunities and address the opportunity gap for students in traditionally under-resourced neighbourhoods, providing care for students while their families work (Healthi Kids 2017; Vandell, Reisner and Pierce 2007).

A child's access to play in Rochester largely depends on their school and/or teacher. Families, community partners and students pointed to the inequitable distribution of existing resources. Families shared that while some schools have 'all of the resources', others have none. They want to see these resources available to all district students. Some teachers report feeling tethered to their school's curriculum, which prioritizes teaching to a test rather than providing opportunities for play. At the same time, many parents believe teachers either do not want to or do not know how to utilize play to teach or engage with children. Inconsistent implementation of policies and allocation of resources across district buildings have families increasingly concerned with RCSD's intent to promote playful learning. The Healthi Kids Coalition continues to support the implementation of this vision by coordinating resources, advocating for district policy amendments and providing professional development opportunities to district staff, students and families.

Effects of Covid-19 on Children and Youth in Rochester

The negative effects of the pandemic will be felt for decades to come, especially by parents, children and youth living in poverty. During the 2020–21 academic year, all suburban schools within Monroe County implemented hybrid learning models utilizing both in-person and virtual options with some suburban schools returning to full-time in-person learning by the end of that year. RCSD remained remote for the entire school year without a hybrid option. Children were physically out of schools for over a year, with the expectations that even our youngest children would learn online. This situation created impossible scenarios for working parents and contributed to a decline in academic outcomes across the district, fewer opportunities for play and further social isolation for our city's youth.

Locally, parents and caregivers worry about reduced opportunities for their children to play. The vast majority of parents (87%) agree that play is more important now than ever before because it encourages self-confidence, less screen time and more physical activity; however, only two in five families report that their children are playing more now than before the pandemic (International Play Equipment Manufacturers Association 2020). Parents with limited options feel that they are failing their children. One parent shared, 'I've failed in reference to where my kids were and where they are now. I'm an advocate for play, but due to Covid, my family's gone backwards instead of forwards'. Parents and caregivers shared that they tried to encourage play by finding opportunities outside of school, but play activities were limited during this time. A parent leader within the RCSD stated, '[Playful learning is] even more important now than before...[there's a] huge gap in social interactions that our children have. This needs to be a core element to everything we do—parents, teachers, leaders'. Another caregiver offered, '[My kids are] still trying to understand how things have changed and what's going on. It's still difficult to explain to them everything that's happened. [Covid-19] has changed them' (Table Talk Primary Caregiver Participant). Another parent advocate summarized the effects on children who have been able to access play compared with those who have not:

We have seen more clearly than ever how the wellness of children is affected by play or the lack of it. As a parent, I noticed and experienced that during the pandemic, when consistent opportunities for play, connection, and exploration were provided in schools and other spaces, children seemed to be more able to maintain and cultivate a sense of wellness. They seemed better able to navigate the challenges and uncertainty. The converse was also true. Children and families who did not have access to resources and environments that maintained a culture of play, exploration, and connection seemed to be more vulnerable to stress and crisis.

When we prioritize building healthy relationships through play, play-based learning, recess and out-of-school time, we have the potential to mitigate the trauma and impact of the pandemic on our children. All children within the Rochester City School District deserve this opportunity.

Ensuring Equitable Opportunities for Play

Not all children have access to safe spaces to play. Data from the Healthi Kids Coalition's playability plan demonstrates that over sixty percent of parents in the City of Rochester say the lack of safe places to play in their neighbourhood is a problem, eighty-two percent of kids throughout the city do not play in traditional parks or playgrounds (Healthi Kids 2016) and sixty-five percent of residents state that they would not feel safe letting their child walk to a park in their neighbourhood (Healthi Kids 2022). Results from a large regional survey reveal that only one quarter of city residents believe their neighbourhood is great for children to play outdoors, a figure three times lower than responses from their suburban counterparts (Common Ground Health 2018). Barriers to play in Rochester neighbourhoods have been identified by residents through multiple studies. Top barriers to neighbourhood play include neighbourhood safety, traffic safety and the condition of playgrounds (Healthi Kids 2016).

Families and students in the RCSD have stressed that if play is not happening in neighbourhoods, then we must ensure that playful opportunities are happening throughout the school day. A PlayROCs

Advocacy Committee Member stated that 'It's important we focus on play in schools because [not all kids have the] opportunity to play in their neighbourhood'. To advance our community's playful learning vision, we must examine play and playful learning through a lens accounting for anti-racism, diversity, equity and inclusion.

The Work Continues

Common Ground Health catalyzed residents across the city to re-conceptualize traditional notions of play, while continuing to advocate for safe and accessible play for all. Covid-19 elevated the importance of this work, as play became an opportunity to facilitate healing and promote resilience in children during a time of chronic uncertainty. Residents are actively planning the next phase of work focused on additional investments in play infrastructure at home and at school on behalf of the school district, city and county. However, advocating with local government takes time and residents are unwilling to sit back and wait for bureaucratic red tape to clear. Efforts are underway to create an 'unstructured play' endowment fund with a local foundation to support residents, neighbourhood associations, block clubs, parent-teacher organizations and the faith community to fund innovative initiatives that promote unstructured play in neighbourhoods and in schools. This will help to provide a mechanism to fund resident-led solutions to address current barriers to play. This fund will also enable supporters in the community to have a dedicated space to donate funds towards these initiatives. The funding could be used to pilot and implement several strategies in neighbourhoods including but not limited to: story walks, playful sidewalks, interactive elements in public spaces, play streets, play kits, recess kits, weather-appropriate clothing for outdoor play, pop-up programming in neighbourhoods, youth workers in parks, play materials in neighbourhoods (e.g. ball bins, toy libraries) and additional innovative ideas that support play in neighbourhoods and at school. This fund would be managed by the foundation and governed by members of the PlayROCs Advocacy Committee. Should this fund be eligible to residents in the broader Finger Lakes region, we will identify residents from other geographic locations to review their applications as well. This fund will allow children in the Greater Rochester and Finger Lakes region to have enhanced access to play by supporting interventions in their neighbourhood.

Play is critical to the physical, social-emotional and cognitive development of children and a child's preferred way of learning. When we live in kid-friendly environments that support play, the likelihood of chronic disease, obesity, behavioural health issues and crime-related injury decrease. When we provide kids with time and space for unstructured play, we provide them with the opportunity to grow, learn and improve their overall academic performance. A parent advocate reflected on their work with Healthi Kids and the PlayROCs Advocacy Committee:

> Our work together has taught me about the link between play and healthy being, especially for children. During Covid, I was able to use the knowledge and tools I gained to ensure the wellness of myself and my child. Even though life was challenging at times, I knew to include play to help us stay connected, joyous and motivated. We have an amazing opportunity to positively impact children and families via play, something we often overlook when it comes to our wellbeing. As we experienced the pandemic, we had to be more innovative and expand our ideas of what play is, how we experience play together and how we could stay connected, even while being physically apart.

Play is critical for children throughout periods of trauma. It provides opportunities for children to heal and build essential relationships with caregivers, and allows for the release of ongoing stressors. The most critical thing our community can do for our children to mitigate the toxic and chronic stress of a pandemic is to let them play.

Works Cited

American Academy of Pediatrics. 2021. 'COVID-19 Interim Guidance: Return to Sports and Physical Activity', https://www.aap.org/en/pages/2019-novel-coronavirus-Covid-19-infections/clinical-guidance/Covid-19-interim-guidance-return-to-sports/

Chaddock, Laura, et al. 2010. 'Basal Ganglia Volume Is Associated with Aerobic Fitness in Preadolescent Children', *Developmental Neuroscience*, 32: 249–56, https://doi.org/10.1159/000316648

Chatzipanteli, Athanasia, and Manolis Adamakis. 2022. 'Social Interaction through Structured Play Activities in Early Childhood', in *Handbook of Research on Using Motor Games in Teaching and Learning Strategy*, ed. by Pedro Gil-Madrona (La Mancha: IGI Global), pp. 80–99, https://doi. org/10.4018/978-1-7998-9621-0.ch005

Clay, Rebecca A. 2020. 'The Serious Business of Play', https://www.apa.org/ topics/Covid-19/children-unstructured-play

Clements, Rhonda. 2004. 'An Investigation of the Status of Outdoor Play', *Contemporary Issues in Early Childhood*, 5: 68–80, https://doi.org/10.2304/ ciec.2004.5.1.10

Common Ground Health. 2018. 'My Health Story: Perceptions of Outdoor Play Environments (Monroe County), https://www.commongroundhealth.org/ insights/library/perceptions-of-outdoor-play-environments

——. 2021. *The Color of Health: The Devastating Toll of Racism on Black Lives* (Rochester, NY: Common Ground Health), https://media.cmsmax.com/ ravk3pgz5ktlujs1r08ci/37712-common-ground-health-book-reader-spreads-fix.pdf

Education Trust. 2017. *See Our Truth: The State of Teacher and School Leader Diversity in New York, and Why It matters for Students, Educators and our Future* (New York: Education Trust), https://s3.documentcloud.org/documents/4110263/See-Our-Truth-DIGITAL-v-2-Reduced.pdf

Esposito, Jennifer. 2011. 'Negotiating the Gaze and Learning the Hidden Curriculum: A Critical Race Analysis of the Embodiment of Female Students of Color at a Predominantly White Institution', *Journal for Critical Education Policy Studies*, 9: 143–64, http://www.jceps.com/wp-content/uploads/ PDFs/09-2-09.pdf

Gay, Geneva. 2010. *Culturally Responsive Teaching: Theory, Research, and Practice* (New York: Teachers College Press), https://www.cwu.edu/ teaching-learning/sites/cts.cwu.edu.teaching-learning/files/documents/ CulturallyResponsiveTeaching_TheoryResearchandPractice,%20 Geneva%20Gay.PDF

Ginsburg, Kenneth R., et al. 2007. 'The Importance of Play in Promoting Healthy Child Development and Maintaining Strong Parent-Child Bonds', *Pediatrics*, 119: 112–91, https://doi.org/10.1542/peds.2006-2697

Global Recess Alliance. 2020. 'Statement on Recess', https://globalrecessalliance. org/statement-on-recess/

Hadani, Helen Shwe, and Jennifer S. Vey. 2020. 'Playful Learning in Everyday Places during the COVID-19 Crisis—and Beyond' (Brookings Institute), https://www.brookings.edu/blog/education-plus-development/2020/04/07/playful-learning-in-everyday-spaces-during-the-Covid-19-crisis-and-beyond/

Harvard Center on the Developing Child. 2020. 'Stress, Resilience, and the Role of Science: Responding to the Coronavirus Pandemic', https://developingchild. harvard.edu/stress-resilience-and-the-role-of-science-responding-to-the-coronavirus-pandemic/

Healthi Kids. 2016. *Data Brief: State of Play in Rochester, NY*, https://media. cmsmax.com/9p433trpk8pdaaywwkfzb/healthi-kids-state-of-play-in-rochester-ny-data-brief-2016.pdf

——. 2017. *Expand Out of School Time Opportunities in Rochester*, https://media. cmsmax.com/9p433trpk8pdaaywwkfzb/benefits-of-after-school-grasa-advocacy-committee-2017.pdf

——. 2022. *PlayROCs the Rochester City School District: A Community Vision for Playful Learning*, https://media.cmsmax.com/9p433trpk8pdaaywwkfzb/ cgh-41-cgh-playrocs-report-r7.pdf

International Play Association. 2020. *Play in Crisis: Support for Parents and Carers* (International Play Association), http://ipaworld.org/wp-content/ uploads/2020/04/IPA-Play-in-Crisis-Booklet-for-parents-and-carers-2020. pdf

International Play Equipment Manufacturers Association. 2020. 'Survey on the Importance of Play and the Mental Impacts of Social Injustice in the U.S. (Voice of Play)', https://voiceofplay.org/2020-survey/

Miller, Edward, and Joan Almon. 2009. *Crisis in the Kindergarten: Why Children Need to Play in School* (College Park, MD: Alliance for Childhood), https:// eric.ed.gov/?id=ED504839

Murphey, David, et al. 2014. *Are the Children Well? A Model and Recommendations for Promoting the Mental Wellness of the Nation's Young People* (Robert Wood Johnson Foundation and Child Trends), https://www.childtrends.org/ wp-content/uploads/2014/07/2014-33AreChildrenWellRWJF.pdf

Murphy, Justin and Gary Stern. 2021. 'RCSD Graduation Rate Rises to 68%, Highest in Years, Brockport and Greece Also Make Gains', *Rochester Democrat and Chronicle*, 14 January, https://www. democratandchronicle.com/story/news/education/2021/01/14/ rcsd-graduation-rate-2020-68-regents-local/4157954001/

New York State Department of Education. 2021a. *Introduction to the New York State Next Generation Early Learning Standards*, http://www.nysed.gov/ common/nysed/files/introduction-to-the-nys-early-learning-standards.pdf

——. 2021b. *Play: Understanding the Value of Play*, http://www.nysed.gov/ common/nysed/files/programs/early-learning/value-of-play-birth-through-3rd-grade.pdf

Stewart, Nikita. 2020. 'Child Abuse Cases Drop 51 Percent: The Authorities are Very Worried', *New York Times*, 9 June

Playground Centre. 2021 'Unstructured vs Structured Play and Examples', https://www.playgroundcentre.com/unstructured-vs-structured-play

Racine, Nicole, et al. 2021. 'Global Prevalence of Depressive and Anxiety Symptoms in Children and Adolescents during COVID-19: A Meta-Analysis', *JAMA Pediatrics*, 175: 1142–50, https://doi.org/10.1001/jamapediatrics.2021.2482

Redd, Zakia, et al. 2012. *Expanding Time for Learning both Inside and Outside the Classroom: A Review of the Evidence Base* (Child Trends and the Wallace Foundation), https://www.wallacefoundation.org/knowledge-center/Documents/Expanding-Time%20for-Learning-Both-Inside-and-Outside-the-Classroom.pdf

Rochester-Monroe Anti-Poverty Initiative. 2020. 'U.S. Census Data Show Rochester Poverty Rate, Child Poverty Rate Decreases', https://www.actrochester.org/tinymce/source/US%20Census%20Update%202020.pdf

Sattelmair, Jacob, and John J. Ratey. 2009. 'Physically Active Play and Cognition: An Academic Matter?', *Journal of Play*, 1: 365–74, https://files.eric.ed.gov/fulltext/EJ1068997.pdf

Shonkoff, Jack P., W. Thomas Boyce, and Bruce S. McEwen. 2009. 'Neuroscience, Molecular Biology, and the Childhood Roots of Health Disparities: Building a New Framework for Health Promotion and Disease Prevention', *JAMA*, 301: 2252–259, https://doi.org/10.1001/jama.2009.754

Slater, Sandy, et al. 2012. 'The Impact of State Laws and District Policies on Physical Education and Recess Practices in a Nationally Representative Sample of US Public Elementary Schools', *Archives of Pediatrics and Adolescent Medicine*, 166: 311–16, https://doi.org/10.1001/archpediatrics.2011.1133

US Census Bureau. 2021. 'QuickFacts: Rochester City, New York', https://www.census.gov/quickfacts/fact/table/rochestercitynewyork/PST045221#qf-headnote-a

US Department of Health and Human Services. 2008. 'Physical Activity Guidelines for Americans', http://www.health.gov/paguidelines

Vandell, Deborah, Elizabeth Reisner, and Kim Pierce. 2007. *Outcomes Linked to High-Quality Afterschool Programs: Longitudinal Findings from the Study of Promising Afterschool Programs*, https://www.purdue.edu/hhs/hdfs/fii/wp-content/uploads/2015/07/s_iafis04c04.pdf

Wright, Brian. 2021. 'What's Play Got to Do with It? Reimagining and Recapturing the Freedom and Spirit of Free Play in Cultural Spaces', Keynote address for PlayROCs the Rochester City School District Presentation, https://www.youtube.com/watch?v=enUmF-2tdTQ&t=2225s

Yard, Ellen, et al. 2021. 'Emergency Department Visits for Suspected Suicide Attempts among Persons Aged 12–25 Years before and during the COVID-19 Pandemic - United States, January 2019-May 2021', *Morbidity and Mortality Weekly Report*, 70: 888–94, http://dx.doi.org/10.15585/mmwr.mm7024e1

4. 'Let Them Play': Exploring Class, the Play Divide and the Impact of Covid-19 in the Republic of Ireland

Maria O'Dwyer, Carmel Hannan, and Patricia Neville

Play and Ireland: An Overview

Bruner's work in the 1970s oriented play as the basis for the 'flexibility of thought' which underpins the immense problem-solving abilities and creativity of humans (1972). In more simple terms, the long period of biological immaturity in humans provides us with ample opportunities to practise and develop our play skills. These play skills then support mental, physical, socio-emotional, cognitive and social development. Play is inarguably a multi-faceted phenomenon. While it is a feature of all societies, its prevalence and forms vary across them, as the very nature of childhood itself and the value of play are culturally and environmentally shaped. Indeed, play itself has been described as 'pedagogic culture' (Arnott and Duncan 2019), created by the interplay between the contextual cues, such as space, interpersonal collaborations and materials, that frame young children's creative play.

Running parallel to these macro-developments in the conceptualisation of play and its function, there is a concern internationally that children's free play has decreased, especially for middle-class, female, young and

https://doi.org/10.11647/OBP.0326.04

ethnic minority children (Holloway and Pimlott-Wilson 2014). Play has become individualized and 'pedagogised', that is, play has been configured as a means 'to limit the risks of certain biographies and to offer children and adolescents the best possible start in life' (Frahsa and Thiel 2020: 2). This has given rise to a decline in free play and outdoor play which are packaged as more risky (Carver, Timperio and Crawford 2008, Timperio et al. 2004; Powell, Ambardekar and Sheehan 2005; Veitch et al. 2006; Farley et al. 2007). Play has also been medicalized, e.g. as an antidote to a childhood obesity pandemic (Demetriou et al. 2019; Tremblay et al. 2015; Australian Government Department of Health 2014).

The ludic landscape of Ireland has also been shaped by related societal trends. Opportunities for and access to play have changed significantly in Ireland over the last two decades, with a notable reduction in opportunities for free, unstructured play. A primary driver of the development of the Irish early childhood education and care (ECEC) sector, through the highs of the Celtic Tiger (economic boom) to the lows of the pursuant recession, has been labour activation. While ECEC provision is delivered through a variety of play-based curricula, the nature of care means that much of it is adult-led and children are grouped according to age, resulting in less exposure to mixed-age peer play. This period has also been characterized by an increasing desire by public bodies to avoid litigation by risk-assessing playgrounds and public parks (i.e. the preference for soft rubber 'flooring' over natural woodchips, etc.). The rising role of technology and its integration into toy making and marketing offer what Gosso and Almeida Carvalho describe as 'an increasing variety of sedentary and often individualised and highly-structured toys and games which allow little space for children's creativity in the exploration and collective construction of play objects and materials' (2013: 6). This has led to what could be described as a 'sanitization' of play, whereby our desire to nurture and support children in safe environments has resulted in more structured and less risky play. There exist, therefore, competing national discourses of safety and protection versus play and autonomy in the structuring of children's everyday lives in Ireland (Kernan and Devine 2010).

This trend of play becoming more structured is evident in Ireland as elsewhere and it has been related to the hurried child syndrome (Elkind 1981; Frost 2011). Smyth (2016) studied young children in Ireland and their involvement in creative play (such as painting, drawing and playing make-believe games) as well as the more traditional cultural pursuits of reading and attending educational or cultural events with their parents. Even at the early age of five, gender and social background differences are apparent in children's exposure to these activities. Children from highly educated or middle-class families, for example, watch much less television than their peers regardless of child gender (Smyth 2016).

American, US and UK literature acknowledges that 'class gaps in structured activity participation' exist (Bennett, Lutz, and Jayaram 2012: 133), revealing the existence of different 'parental logics' by middle- and lower-class parents, with middle-class parents seeing extra-curricular activities, including play, as vehicles for creating and securing social status (e.g. Chin and Phillips 2004; Bennett 2012; Laureau 2003; Vincent and Ball 2007; Aurini, Missaghian and Milian 2020). Despite this, there has been scant engagement with this theory and associated research in Irish childhood studies. Little has been written about how child play is mediated by social class in Ireland. This book chapter takes the opportunity to reflect upon this under-researched topic to present an appraisal of how class insinuates and configures Irish children's play. The disruptive impact that Covid-19 has had on children's opportunity for structured play, as revealed in the *Growing Up in Ireland* study, will form the basis of this chapter, acting as a timely case study into the play divide in Ireland. The research discussed here represents the preliminary findings of our study and are part of an ongoing piece of work into the play divide in Ireland.

The Play Divide in Ireland

There is a growing body of research that children's play or, more specifically, what parents allow their children to do as playful activity, is heavily inscribed with class aspirations and significations. For instance, it has been found that middle-class parents tend to enrol their young children in extracurricular creative and sporting activities more readily than working-class parents. The reason for this is not merely a question of financial means; middle-class parents look upon such activities as a way of 'distinguishing' their child for the middle class (e.g. Vincent and Ball 2007). As active promoters of their children's social capital, middle-class parents have identified play and structured activities as a means of securing social mobility and status for their children. This act of 'concerted cultivation' (Lareau 2000, 2003) distinguished the 'parenting logic' of middle-class parents from the 'natural' parenting approach of working-class parents, i.e., letting the children find their own way in the world (Lareau 2000, 2003; Chin and Phillips 2004: 186).

Before moving on, it is important to discuss what we mean by social class, in particular the nature of this categorization in the Irish context. Many commentators have debated the political exceptionalism of Ireland being one of the few countries in Western Europe that did not experience an industrial revolution. The ensuing absence of an industrial class living in densely populated, urban cities and the continued prevalence of agricultural production contributed to the development of a political culture based on the local community rather than class-based struggle (e.g. O'Carroll 1987). Confirmation that notions of 'class' were articulated differently in Irish society from the 1930s to 1990s can be found in the oral history records from that time. There, the word 'class' was rarely used by its participants. That was not to say that their oral histories were devoid of an awareness of social difference and status. Rather, what followed was a nuanced understanding of class mediated by place in which rural participants discussed social status in terms of land ownership (big/small farmers) and urban participants discussed social difference in terms of employment type (Cronin 2007: 34-35). Other signifiers of class were diet/food, e.g. Sunday dinners (Cronin 2007: 37). Even though Irish society has undergone a process of 'accelerated modernization' since the mid-1990s—successive cycles of economic boom (Celtic Tiger economy 1994-2007) and bust (recession 2008-) and changing demographic trends based on inward and outward migration—the growing divide between rural and urban areas, lower fertility rates and the rise of working mothers and the associated issue of affordable childcare (e.g. Power et al. 2012; Cullen and Murphy 2020; Coulter and Arqueros-Fernandez 2020), and rurality and place still rank as important signifiers of class.

It is worth highlighting that a 'play divide' has emerged consistently in Ireland for the last twenty to thirty years. While numerous studies (Stirrup, Evans, and Davies 2016) consider the reproduction of social class and cultural hierarchies in early childhood care and education settings, little research has focused on play as an expression of class demarcation or divide. In Ireland, this is perhaps most perceptible in outdoor play practices and norms. In 2010, *How Are Our Kids*, a large-scale study, explored the needs and experiences of children and families in Limerick city, with a particular emphasis on Regeneration Communities, that is, the most deprived areas of the city. The description of the lives of children and families paints a picture of a poorer quality of life, poor experiences of childhood and worse outcomes across a wide range of indicators of child well-being between children living in the most deprived neighbourhoods of Limerick city. While crime, anti-social behaviour and community safety were issues in the Regeneration Communities, parents reported concerns for the impact of this on older children and teenagers. Younger children, however, appear to have benefitted from greater freedom in these neighbourhoods. Strong community networks, intergenerational living (availability and proximity of extended family) and the more traditional 'it takes a village' approach to child-rearing influenced this freedom. The findings indicate that in communities experiencing much higher than average levels of socio-economic disadvantage and relative deprivation, children engaged more in outdoor play. It could be argued that there is a traditional element to these outdoor play opportunities, whereby children are afforded responsibility at an earlier age, older siblings look after younger ones and micro mobility (i.e. the use of scooters, skateboards, quad bikes and, in some cases, horses) is more normalized. This is, essentially, the kind of unstructured outdoor play that would have typified Ireland in the 1980s, where children played outside independently, daily and for significant periods of time. This stands in contrast to the play experiences of young children in middle-class areas where scheduled 'play dates', extra-curricular activities and paid childcare are more common. Lee et al. (2021) contend that individual, parental, and proximal physical (home) and social environments appear to play a role in children's outdoor play and time, along with ecological factors such as seasonality, rurality, etc. The study in Limerick city would indicate that is very much the case.

The Impact of a Global Pandemic on Play

The World Health Organization officially declared that the world was in the grasp of a coronavirus (Covid-19) pandemic on 11 March 2020. In the following two years in European and longer elsewhere, all social, health and economic systems have been trying to respond to unprecedented demands and challenges. Anthropologists call such an event a 'liminal moment in which a given order that is considered normal or desired is dissolved, breaks down, and is affected by a decomposition or unbalance that needs to be restored' (Visacovky 2017: 7). As 'the tranny of the urgent' (Davis and Bennett 2016) crisis management mode took over, world leaders and global systems tried to make sense of and adjust to an unprecedented threat to global health and well-being. This period of profound disruption took many forms. These include, but are not limited to, a deceleration of everyday life, the shrinkage of social spaces, the collapsing of work and domestic spaces, the closure of schools and businesses, and the accelerated digitalization of society (Fuchs 2020, Devine et al. 2020, OECD 2020). While many were struggling to stand still amidst the whirlwind of change, Covid-19 also provided the sober reminder of how stratified society is with pre-existing social and health inequalities gaining added poignancy and severity (e.g. Public Health England 2020; Raharja, Tamara and Kolt 2020; Sze et al. 2020). The psycho-social and educational impact of children living in a pandemic also came under scrutiny. How, and in what way, would children's social, emotional and educational development be affected by living through a pandemic? Early Irish evidence suggested the widening of educational gaps (e.g. Darmody 2021; Doyle 2020; Mohan et al. 2020).

For researchers in the Republic of Ireland this question took on added poignancy because the nation enacted one of the harshest lockdown responses compared with other countries (Hale et al. 2021). All Irish schools were closed for 141 school days, from 13 March to 30 June 2020 which marked the end of the academic year. This was the longest school closure period in the history of the state as well as in comparison with other comparative OECD countries (Richardson et al. 2020). In all, approximately one million children and young people (Central Statistics Office 2020) (or 1 in 5 of the Irish population) were directly affected by this pandemic response. Unsurprisingly, there has been a raft of studies exploring the educational impact of Covid-19 on Irish school-aged children (e.g. Chzhen et al. 2022; Flynn et al. 2021). These Irish studies confirm trends being witnessed across other developed countries (Rao and Fisher 2021), namely, that the sudden shift to remote/distance learning confirmed long-standing educational inequalities, regarding access to digital technologies (Armitage and Nellums 2020; Chzhen et al. 2022: 2) and families' capacity/ability to support their child's learning (Doyle 2020; Chzhen et al. 2022: 2). While digital supports were available to both primary and secondary level schools to help offset these digital disparities, such as in the form of loaning schemes for laptops to disadvantaged families, available research reveals the absence of a standardized approach to how schools administered and allocated these emergency digital resources (Brown 2021; Burke and Dempsey 2020; Cullinan et al. 2021). Such educational disruption was also recognized as impacting on children's well-being and learning resulting in feelings of social isolation and loneliness (Flynn et al. 2021).

While the play divide received little attention, there has been a growth in the study of the digital divide. Some authors contend that digital technology is displacing other, more wholesome activities, such as the intellectually or physically beneficial pastimes of reading or playing outdoors in certain social groups. Proponents of this school of thought associate increased time with digital technology with the increased sedentarism of twenty-first century childhood. For others, the content that young people find online, such as violence-infused gaming or online predators masquerading as children, is the cause for concern (Gentile et al. 2017). Regardless of whether you support the displacement theory or content theory regarding digital media and children, the fact that we are living in a digitalized, networked society is inescapable. Children, parents, policy makers and legislative structures all broker affirmative and transformative ways of working with digital technology.

The Republic of Ireland, like other developed countries, has taken a keen interest in developing evidence-based, research-informed policies to safeguard its young citizens against the excesses of digital technology (e.g. O'Neill and Dinh 2013; Government of Ireland 2018; Children's Research Network 2020). Research confirms that the pattern of digital usage among young children in Ireland is largely similar to their European counterparts (O'Neill, Grehan and Olaffson 2011; O'Neill and Dinh 2015, Smahel et al. 2020). In 2010, Irish children spent one hour in average online (O'Neill and Dinh 2015), this rose to 2.1 hours a day during the week and 3.4 hours a day at weekends by 2020 (National Advisory Council for Online Safety 2021: 22). The smartphone is the most popular social media device. In 2014, thirty-five percent of children used a smartphone (O'Neill and Dinh 2015), this rose to seventy percent in 2020 (National Advisory Council for Online Safety 2021: 9, 10). Children as young as eight are using a smartphone, with the majority between the ages of 11 and 12 (Cybersafe Kids 2020, 2021, 2022). Irish young children are regular and at times heavy users of digital technology, as indicated by the increase in screen time over the past decade (e.g. Bohnert and Garcia 2020), with online entertainment and social networking as the two main reasons why young children used the internet (O'Neil and Dinh 2015).

The top five online activities of Irish children are as follows: watching video clips (58%), listening to music online (55%), communicating with family and friends (53%), playing online games (40%), using social networking (38%) (National Advisory Council for Online Safety 2021:24). Using the internet for school purposes was lower down their priorities (34%) (National Advisory Council for Online Safety 2021: 24). When disaggregated according to age and gender a distinct pattern emerges. Generally, social internet usage increases with age, for both genders. However, certain activities reveal a marked gendered effect. Thirteen- to seventeen-year-old girls are more likely to use the internet for schoolwork (51% compared to 35%), social networking (62% compared with 51%) and communicating with family and friends (70% compared with 66%), compared to boys. Boys more likely to use the internet to watch video clips (73% compared to 61%) and game than girls (56% compared to 34%) (National Advisory Council for Online Safety 2021: 24). This trend represents a pattern is also found among the nine- to twelve-year age groups.

At first glance, this body of work promotes a conventional and easily comparable view of Irish children's engagement with digital technology vis-à-vis other EU countries. However, when we explore Irish play data more closely we find an alternative and more interesting situation. Despite the paucity of research into children's play in Ireland (Rowicki and McGovern 2018), some studies have touched on a more complex pattern involving class, gender and geographical factors.

A 2007 school survey and focus group study involving 292 children aged between the ages of four and twelve years from ten primary schools across Ireland found that outdoor active play, like football, was the most popular form of social play (Downey, Hayes and O'Neill 2007). Interestingly seventy percent of this category were male and from a rural background (Downey, Hayes and O'Neill 2007: 15). This was followed by chasing and then digital technology/games (Downey, Hayes, and O'Neill 2007: 15). Again, it was more likely for males from a rural background (Downey, Hayes and O'Neill 2007: 15). Digital technology came first in the options for solo play (Downey, Hayes, and O'Neill 2007: 15). Again this play preference was more commonly expressed by boys than girls, and those from a rural background (Downey, Hayes and O'Neill 2007: 15). Fifty percent of children surveyed played computer games, whereas twenty-five percent cited readings as a favoured pastime (Downey, Hayes, and O'Neill 2007: 15)

Rowicki and McGovern's analysis (2018) of time use in *Growing Up in Ireland* employing diary data from 2007-2008 when the children were aged nine, and from wave 2 of the study when they were aged thirteen, offers a more contemporary glimpse into Irish childhood. Girls at age nine spent fifty minutes playing sports each day, regardless of socio-economic group. This fell for all by age thirteen but especially for those from lower socio-economic groups (twelve minutes versus twenty-nine minutes). All girls spend more time on media from nine to thirteen years of age. At age thirteen, children from lower SES spent more time (108 minutes) with digital technology compared with higher socio-economic status (86 minutes). The situation was reversed with unstructured play with girls from working-class backgrounds recording an increase in unstructured play time from age nine to thirteen (fifteen minutes per day) compared with a decrease of two and ten minutes for girls from higher socio-economic groups. Overall, girls and boys from lower socio-economic groups spend less time in sport activities and more time using digital technology at age thirteen.

Helster conceptualizes these socio-digital inequalities as 'systematic differences between individuals from different backgrounds in the opportunities and abilities to translate digital engagement into benefits and avoid the harm' (2021: 34). Recent research in Ireland has compared two cohorts of children growing up in the 'digital age' using data from the *Growing Up in Ireland* study. In 2017-2018, nine-year-old children spent more time on digital devices and social media, while in 2007-2008, nine-year-old children spent more time watching TV and adopted less diversified forms of media engagement (Bohnert and Gracia 2021). The study found that the effects of digital use on socio-emotional well-being were quite similar by gender and socio-economic group in both cohorts.

The digital divide in classroom technology use has received much attention given the school-level inequalities witnessed during Covid-19. Yet little work has focused on social class and the daily lives of children during the pandemic. The next section will outline differences in the lives of children as reported by the children themselves during Covid-19.

Data

The *Growing Up in Ireland* (GUI) study started in 2006 and follows the progress of two groups of children: around eight thousand nine-year-olds (Cohort '98) and ten thousand nine-month-olds (Cohort '08). The members of Cohort '98 are now aged about twenty-four years and those of Cohort '08 are around thirteen years old. The following results refer to the experiences of the '08 cohort, who filled in a special Covid-19 survey in December 2020 when they were aged twelve. The survey's timing coincided with the relaxation of what were the most severe (Level 5) restrictions after the second wave of Covid-19 in the autumn. The survey was brief, taking about ten minutes to complete online, and focused on a relatively small number of key experiences and outcomes. As with all online surveys, the response rate was lower than face-to-face interviews, so that 3901 surveys were completed by parents and 3301 by twelve-year-olds.

Changes in Free Time

As many facilities were closed, families spent more time at home together. Many parents of twelve-year-olds reported enjoying time with their family (sixty-three percent said this was 'always true') and doing more activities together (forty-eight percent 'always true'). But they also had less time to themselves (thirty-one percent 'always true'). The twelve-year-olds were asked to compare their lifestyles at the time of the survey (December 2020) to the period just before the pandemic struck (March 2020). Figure 4.1 shows the percentages who described doing particular activities 'more' or 'less' often than before. According to the children, there are substantial changes in the amount of time they spent on different types of activities as a result of the pandemic and associated restrictions.

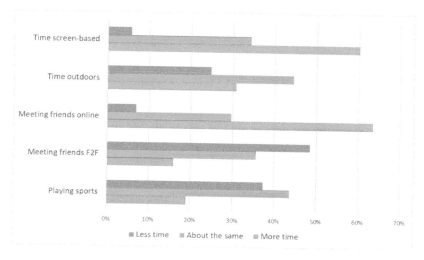

Figure 4.1 Child reports on differences in time spent on classes of activities in December 2020 compared with March 2020, before the pandemic (data source: Infant '08 Cohort, wave 5 and Covid survey, *Growing Up in Ireland* study)

In December 2020, therefore, most twelve-year-olds reported increases in time spent with family, on informal screen activities and talking to friends online or by phone and less time with friends face-to-face and playing sports (see Figure 4.1). There are, however, some important differences in these activities by child gender and family social class. In terms of gender, girls were significantly more likely to report spending more time meeting up with friends online or over the phone (sixty-nine percent compared to fifty-nine percent of boys at $p<0.00$). The nature of female relationships has often been characterized as more about sharing and intimate confiding than the more instrumental approach taken in male friendships (see, for example, O'Connor 1992).

In terms of social class differences, there was an under-representation of families from lone parent, poor and working-class backgrounds in this online Covid-19 survey (see Kelly et al. 2021). This means that the results do not represent the population in terms of these characteristics.

Despite this, some class divides are evident in terms of the time children reported spending outdoors and online. Children from families where occupational/employment information was missing or unavailable (due to parents not being employed) were more likely to report spending less time outdoors in December 2020 compared to March of that year. In addition, children from unskilled manual backgrounds were most likely to report spending less time online (note the small n=20). In addition, as further evidence of Lareau's conceptions of concerted cultivation, there were significant class differences in taking part in organized cultural activities, like music and drama classes (chi2=24.6919 P=0.038). Caution is however advised in interpreting these figures, given the small numbers in certain class categories.

A more fruitful way to highlight the impact of the pandemic on children's free time is to look at differences between rural and urban Ireland. Children and childhood is rural Ireland has been a topic of study for some time (Tovey 1992; Curtin and Varley 1994; Devine 2008; Gray 2014). Much of the work drew on the role of children in the stem-family system in the first half of the twentieth century and then later, their role in farming families. Little attention has focused on the differences in experience of childhood in rural versus urban contexts in current times. This is especially important in the context of the pandemic where the availability of high-speed broadband and public transport was limited in many rural areas.

In the *Growing Up in Ireland* study, there was a clear divide in how the pandemic impacted children based on their location. In December 2020, children in urban areas were significantly more likely to report that they were spending less time outdoors compared to children growing up in rural areas of Ireland (see Figure 4.2). Compared to children living in urban areas, children growing up in rural areas were more likely to report spending the same or more time outdoors in December 2020 compared to March of that year. We do not have information in the study on what the children were doing outdoors, but we do have information of the time spent online. There was no rural/urban divide in the time children reported to spend online. There were, however, significant differences in who the children reported spending time with. Children in rural areas were more likely to report spending more time with family compared to children in urban areas (chi2 = 24.2303 P= 0.000), whereas children in urban areas were more likely to report seeing their friends face-to-face.

This may simply be related to the closer proximity to friends in urban areas. This analysis does raise more questions than answers and allows us the first glimpse into how the lives of children have changed during the pandemic, as reported by the children themselves.

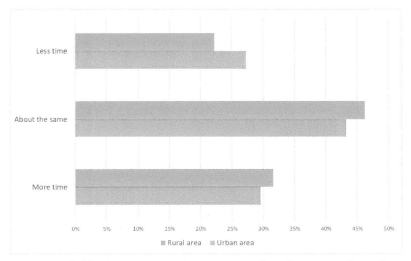

Figure 4.2 Children's comparison of time spent outdoors by region in December 2020 compared with March 2020, before the pandemic (data source: Infant '08 Cohort, wave 5 and Covid survey, *Growing Up in Ireland* study)

Discussion and Conclusion

The onset of a global pandemic and its associated socio-cultural disruptions has re-established the importance of researching child development and well-being as it is configured in Irish society. We acknowledge the growing interest in accessing the psycho-social and educational impact of an extensive school closure policy on Irish school-aged children and the role digital technologies played during this liminal time. As a point of departure, we have adopted a class-based approach to play, and how its form and function has evolved alongside rapid social change and challenges (Cullen and Murphy 2020; Coulter and Acqueros-Fernandez 2020). Against this critical framework, play in Ireland displays distinct class, gender and geographical significance. Little attention has been given over to contemplating the 'play divide' in Ireland more generally and how this socially determined pattern of play was impacted by the social and educational restrictions put in place in response to Covid-19. Rather, the focus has been on the digital divide within and outside the classroom, be that a virtual class or not. Our analysis of GUI data found that the 'play divide' continued during the first lockdown of spring 2020, however, class and geographical location gave rise to more nuance in the configuration of this 'play divide'. While children spent more time with their families, this 'indoor time' took on different significance for children from urban and rural backgrounds. Digital technology was used to remain connected with friends, while children from rural backgrounds tended to spend more time with family than those from urban backgrounds. Researchers are still trying to explain why this may be the case. One possible reason could include the uneven distribution of broadband connectivity across the Republic, where there is better connectivity in Dublin and in more urbanized location compared with rural locations (Central Statistics Office 2021). Urban children have more access to and opportunity for online activities compared to rural children. The lack of affordable and accessible early childcare arrangements in Ireland could also contribute to why families in rural locations have fewer opportunities to be apart (OECD 2021). Children living in manual occupations households also spent less time online, suggesting that the high financial cost associated with being online in Ireland is prohibitive and dissaudes regular use (Pope 2017). These findings confirm that configurations of play are heavily inscribed by class and that the rural-urban divide in Ireland continues to act as a significant social marker of difference in terms of the Irish domestic sphere.

Research into childhood and children in Ireland only emerged in the late 1990s and since then has grown into an area of burgeoning scholarship (e.g. Buckley and Riordan 2017; Hay 2020). This chapter has outlined the knowledge and research gaps in this field of enquiry of the 'play divide' in Ireland and explored whether the Covid-19 restriction had an impact on the constitution of this 'play divide'. While the work is preliminary, it points to the importance of place, space and class in terms of the 'play divide' and calls for further work into its consequences as a mediator in the linkage between social class and child outcomes.

Works Cited

Armitage, Richard, and Laura B. Nellums. 2020. 'Considering Inequalities in the School Closure Response to COVID-19', *The Lancet Global Health*, 8: e644, https://doi.org/10.1016/S2214-109X(20)30116-9

Arnott, Lorna, and Pauline Duncan. 2019. 'Exploring the Pedagogic Culture of Creative Play in Early Childhood Education', *Journal of Early Childhood Research*, 17: 309-28, https://doi.org/10.26503/todigra.v3i2.67

Aurini, Janice, Rod Missaghian, and Roger Pizzaro Milian. 2020. 'Educational Status Hierarchies, After-School Activities and Parenting Logics: Lessons from Canada', *Sociology of Education*, 93: 173-89, https://doi.org/10.1177/0038040720908

Australian Government Department of Health. 2014. *Move and Play Every Day: National Physical Activity Recommendations for Children 0–5 Years* (Canberra: Department of Health)

Bennett, Pamela. R, Amy C. Lutz, and Lakshmi Jayaram. 2012. 'Beyond the Schoolyard: The Role of Parenting Logics, Financial Resources and Social Institutions in the Social Class Gap in Structured Activity Participation', *Sociology of Education*, 85: 131-57, https://doi.org/10.1177/0038040711431

Bohnert, Melissa, and Pablo Garcia. 2021. 'Emerging Digital Generations? Impacts of Child Digital Use on Mental and Socioemotional Well-Being across Two Cohorts in Ireland, 2007–2018', *Child Indicators Research*, 14: 629–59, https://doi.org/10.1007/s12187-020-09767-z

Brown, Sharon. 2021. 'Readiness, Barriers and Strategies for Dealing with Unexpected Organisational Change: A Case Study of Irish Secondary Schools During the Covid-19 Pandemic', unpublished Master's thesis in Business Administration, Dublin Business School, https://esource.dbs.ie/handle/10788/4314

Bruner, Jerome S. 1972. 'Nature and Uses of Immaturity', *American Psychologist*, 27: 687-708

Buckley, Sarah-Anne, and Susannah Riordan. 2017. 'Childhood Since 1740', in *The Cambridge Social History of Modern Ireland*, ed. by Eugenio Biagini and Mary E. Daly (Cambridge: Cambridge University Press), p. 328

Burke, Jolanta, and Marcella Dempsey. 2020. *Covid-19 Practice in Primary Schools in Ireland Report* (Maynooth, Ireland: Maynooth University Department of Education), https://www.into.ie/app/uploads/2020/04/Covid-19-Practice-in-Primary-Schools-Report-1.pdf

Carver, Alison, Anna Timperio, and David Crawford. 2008. 'Playing It Safe: The Influence of Neighbourhood Safety on Children's Physical Activity: A Review', *Health & Place*, 14: 217-27, https://doi.org/10.1016/j.healthplace.2007.06.004

Central Statistics Office. 2020. *Department of Education Statistics* (Dublin: Central Statistics Office), https://www.cso.ie/en/databases/departmentofeducation/

——. 2021. 'Internet Coverage and Usage in Ireland 2021', https://www.cso.ie/en/releasesandpublications/ep/p-isshict/internetcoverageandusageinireland2021/householdinternetconnectivity/

Children's Research Network. 2020. 'Growing Up in the Digital Environment', *Children's Research Digest*, 6, https://www.childrensresearchnetwork.org/knowledge/resources/digest-growing-up-in-the-digital-environment

Chin, Tiffani, and Meredith Phillips. 2004. 'Social Reproduction and Child-rearing Practices: Social Class, Children's Agency and the Summer Activity Gap', *Sociology of Education*, 77: 185-210, https://doi.org/10.1177/003804070407700

Chzhen, Yekatarina, et al. 2022. 'Learning in a Pandemic: Primary School children's Emotional Engagement with Remote Schooling during the spring 2020 Covid-19 Lockdown in Ireland', *Child Indicators Research*, 15: 1517–538, https://doi.org/10.1007/s12187-022-09922-8

Coulter, Colin, and Francisco Arqueros-Fernandaz. 2020. 'The Distortions of the Irish "Recovery"', *Critical Social Policy*, 40: 89-107, https://doi.org/10.1177/02610183198389

Cronin, Maura. 2007. 'Class and Status in Twentieth Century Ireland: The Evidence of Oral History', *Soathar*, 32: 33-43

Cullen, Pauline, and Mary Murphy. 2020. 'Responses to the COVID-19 Crisis in Ireland: From Feminized to Feminist', *Gender, Work & Organization*, 28: 348-65, https://doi.org/10.1111/gwao.12596

Cullinan, John, et al. 2021. 'The Disconnected: COVID-19 and Disparities in Access in Quality Broadband for Higher Education Students', *International Journal of Educational Technology in Higher Education*, 18: 26, https://ulir.ul.ie/handle/10344/10160

Cybersafe Kids. 2020. Annual Report 2019. https://www.cybersafekids.ie/wp-content/uploads/2021/02/csi_annual_report_2019.pdf

Cybersafe Kids. 2021. Academic Year in Review 2020. https://www.cybersafekids.ie/wp-content/uploads/2021/09/CSK_Annual_Report_2020_web.pdf

Cybersafe Kids. 2022. Academic Year in Review 2021-22. https://www.cybersafekids.ie/wp-content/uploads/2022/09/CSK_YearInReview_2021-2022_FINAL.pdf

Davis, Sara, and Belinda Barrett. 2016. 'A Gendered Human Rights Analysis of Ebola and Zika: Locating Gender in Global Health Emergencies', *International Affairs*, 92: 1049-060, https://doi.org/10.1111/1468-2346.12704

Demetriou, Yolanda, et al. 2019. 'Germany's 2018 Report Card on Physical Activity for Children and Youth', *German Journal of Exercise and Sport Research*, 49: 113–26, https://doi.org/10.1007/s12662-019-00578-1

Devine, D., et al. 2020. *Children's School Lives: An Introduction*, Children's School Lives Report, 1 (Dublin: University College Dublin), https://cslstudy. wpenginepowered.com/wp-content/uploads/2020/12/CSL-Annual-Report-1-Final.pdf

Doyle, Orla. 2020. *COVID-19: Exacerbating Educational Inequalities?* (Dublin: Public Policy)

Farley, Thomas A., et al. 2007. 'Safe Play Spaces to Promote Physical Activity in Inner-City Children: Results from a Pilot Study of an Environmental Intervention', *American Journal of Public Health*, 97: 1625-631, https://doi. org/10.2105/AJPH.2006.092692

Flynn, Niamh, et al. 2021. '"Schooling at Home" in Ireland during COVID-19: Parents' and Students' Perspectives on Overall Impact, Continuity of Interest, and Impact on Learning', *Irish Educational Studies*, 40: 217-26, https://doi.org /10.1080/03323315.2021.1916558

Frahsa, Annika, and Ansgar Thiel. 2020. 'Can Functionalised Play Make Children Happy? A Critical Sociology Perspective', *Frontiers in Public Health*, 8: 571054, https://doi.org/10.3389/fpubh.2020.571054

Frost, Joe L. 2010. *A History of Children's Play and Play Environments: Towards a Contemporary Child-Saving Movement* (London: Routledge)

Fuchs, Christian. 2020. 'Everyday Life and Everyday Communication in Coronavirus Capitalism', *triple Cs: Communication, Capitalism & Critique*, 18: 375-99, https://doi.org/10.31269/triplec.v18i1.1167

Gentile, D. A., et al. 2017. 'Bedroom Media: One Risk Factor for Development', *Developmental Psychology, 53*: 2340–355, https://doi.org/10.1037/dev0000399

Gosso, Yumi, and Anna Maria Almeida Carvalho. 2013. 'Play and Cultural Context', in *Encyclopedia on Early Childhood Development*, ed. by Richard E. Tremblay, Michel Boivin, and Ray DeV. Peters, https://www.child-encyclopedia.com/play/according-experts/play-and-cultural-context

Government of Ireland. 2018. *Action Plan For Online Safety 2018-2019*, https:// assets.gov.ie/27511/0b1dcff060c64be2867350deea28549a.pdf

Hale, Thomas, et al. 2021. 'A Global Panel Database of Pandemic Policies (Oxford COVID-19 Government Response Tracker)', *Nature Human Behaviour*, 5: 529–38, https://doi.org/10.1038/s41562-021-01079-8

Hay, Marnie. 2020. 'Centuries of Irish Childhoods', *Irish Economic and Social History*, 47: 3-9, https://doi.org/10.1177/0332489320950077

Helsper, Ellen. 2021. *The Digital Disconnect: The Social Causes and Consequences of Digital Inequalities* (London: SAGE)

Holloway, Sarah L, and Helena Pimlott-Wilson. 2014. 'Enriching Children, Institutionalizing Childhood? Geographies of Play, Extracurricular Activities, and Parenting in England', *Annals of the Association of American Geographers*, 104: 613–27, https://doi.org/10.1080/00045608.2013.846167

Horgan, Denis, et al. 2020. 'Digitalisation and COVID-19: The Perfect Storm', *Biomedicine Hub*, 5: 1-23, https://doi.org/10.1159/000511232

Humphreys, Eileen, Des McCafferty, and Ann Higgins. 2011. *How Are Our Kids? Experiences and Needs of Children and Families in Limerick City with a Particular Emphasis on Limerick's Regeneration Areas* (Limerick: Limerick City Children's Services Committee)

Kelly, Lisa, et al. 2022. *Growing Up in Ireland: A Summary Guide of the COVID-19 Web Survey for Cohorts '08 and '98* (Dublin: n.p.), https://www.growingup.ie/pubs/20210909-Summary-Guide-Covid-Survey.pdf

Kernan, Margaret, and Dympna Devine. 2010. 'Being Confined Within? Constructions of the Good Childhood and Outdoor Play in Early Childhood Education and Care Settings in Ireland', *Children and Society*, 24: 371–85, https://doi.org/10.1111/j.1099-0860.2009.00249.x

Knight, Sara. 2009. *Forest Schools & Outdoor Learning in the Early Years* (London: Sage)

Lareau, Annette. 2000. 'Social Class and the Daily Lives of Children: A Study from the United States', *Childhood*, 7: 155–71, https://doi.org/10.1177/0907568200007002002

——. 2003. *Unequal Childhoods: Class, Race, and Family Life* (Berkeley: University of California Press)

Lee, Eun-Young, et al. 2021. 'Systematic Review of the Correlates of Outdoor Play and Time among Children aged 3-12 Years', *International Journal of Behavioral Nutrition and Physical Activity*, 18: 41, https://doi.org/10.1186/s12966-021-01097-9

McBride, Deborah L. 2012. 'Children and Outdoor Play', *Journal of Pediatric Nursing*, 27: 421-22, https://doi.org/10.1016/j.pedn.2012.04.001

Mohan, Gretta, et al. 2020. *Learning for All? Second-Level Education in Ireland During Covid-19*, ESRI Survey and Statistical Report Series, 92, https://www.esri.ie/pubs/SUSTAT92.pdf

National Advisory Council for Online Safety. 2021. Report of a National Survey of Children, their Parents, and Adults regarding Online Safety 2021, https://www.gov.ie/en/publication/1f19b-report-of-a-national-survey-of-children-their-parents-and-adults-regarding-online-safety/?referrer=http://www.gov.ie/onlinesafetyreport/

O'Connor, Pat. 1992. *Friendships Between Women: A Critical Review* (New York: Guilford Press)

OECD. 2021. *Country Note: Ireland*, https://www.oecd.org/education/school/StartingStrongVI-CountryNote-Ireland.pdf

McCoy, Selina, Amanda Quail, and Emer Symth. 2012. *Growing Up in Ireland: Influences on 9 Year Olds' Learning: Home, Schooling, and Community*, Child

Cohort Research Report, 3 (Dublin: Government Publications), https://www.growingup.ie/pubs/BKMNEXT204.pdf

O'Carroll, John Patrick. 1987. 'Strokes, Cute Hoors and Sneaking Regarders: The Influence of Local Culture on Irish Political Style', *Irish Political Studies*, 2: 77-92

O'Neill, Brian, Simon Grehan, and Kjartan Olaffson. 2011. *Risks and Safety for Children on the Internet: The Ireland Report* (London: LSE EU Kids Online), https://www2.lse.ac.uk/media-and-communications/assets/documents/research/eu-kids-online/participant-countries/ireland/IrishReport.pdf

O'Neill, Brian and Thuy Dinh. 2013. *Children and the Internet in Ireland: Research and Policy Perspectives*, Digital Childhoods Working Paper Series, 4 (Dublin: Technological University Dublin), https://arrow.tudublin.ie/aaschmedcon/32/

———. 2015. *Net Children Go Mobile: Full Findings from Ireland* (Dublin: Technological University Dublin), https://arrow.tudublin.ie/cserrep/55/

Pope, Conor. 2017. 'Ireland One of the Priciest Developed Countries for Broadband', *Irish Times*, 17 November, https://www.irishtimes.com/news/ireland/irish-news/ireland-one-of-priciest-developed-countries-for-broadband-1.3298978

Powell, Elizabeth C., Erin J. Ambardekar, and Karen M. Sheehan. 2005. 'Poor Neighborhoods: Safe Playgrounds', *Journal of Urban Health*, 82: 403–10, https://doi.org/10.1093/jurban/jti099

Power, Martin. J., et al. 2012. *An Introduction to Irish Society: Transitions and Change* (Essex: Pearson)

Public Health England. 2020. *Disparities in the Risk and Outcomes of COVID-19*, https://assets.publishing.service.gov.uk/government/uploads/system/uploads/attachment_data/file/908434/Disparities_in_the_risk_and_outcomes_of_COVID_August_2020_update.pdf

Raharja, Anthony, Alice Tamara, and Li Teng Kok. 2021. 'Association between Ethnicity and Severe COVID-19 Disease: A Systematic Review and Meta-Analysis', *Journal of Racial and Ethnic Health Disparities*, 8: 1563-572, https://doi.org/10.1007/s40615-020-00921-5

Rao, Nirmala, and Phillip A Fisher. 2021. 'The Impact of COVID-19 Pandemic on Child and Adolescent Development around the World', *Child Development*, 92: e738-e748, https://doi.org/10.1111/cdev.13653

Richardson, Dominic, et al. 2020. *Supporting Families and Children beyond COVID-19: Social Protection in High-Income Countries* (UNICEF Office of Research: Innocenti), http://hdl.handle.net/10993/44976

Roopnarine, Jaipaul L., and Kimberly L. Davidson. 2015. 'Parent-Child Play access Cultures: Advancing Play Research,' *American Journal of Play*, 7: 228-52

Rowicki, Slawa and Mark McGovern. 2018. 'Unequal Opportunities for Play? How Children Spend their Time in Ireland,' *Children's Research Digest*, 5: 11-19, https://childrensresearchnetwork.org/knowledge/resources/unequal-opportunities-for-play-how-children-spend-their-time-in-ireland

Sandseter, Ellen Beate Hansen. 2011. 'A Quantitative Study of ECEC Practitioners' Views and Experiences on Children's Risk-taking in Outdoor Play', unpublished paper presented at the 21st EECERA conference, Education from Birth: Research, Practices and Educational Policy

Smahel, David, Machackova, Hana, Mascheroni, Giovanna, Dedkova, Lenka, Staksrud, Elisabeth, Ólafsson, Kjartan, Livingstone, Sonia and Uwe Hasebrink. 2020. EU Kids Online 2020: Survey results from 19 countries (Issue February, pp. 156–156). https://doi. org/10.21953/lse.47fdeqj01ofo p.19.

Stirrup, Julie, John Evans, and Brian Davies. 2017. 'Learning One's Place and Position through Play: Social Class and Educational Opportunity in Early Years Education,' *International Journal of Early Years Education*, 25: 343-60, https://doi.org/10.1080/09669760.2017.1329712

Sze, Shirley, et al. 2020. 'Ethnicity and Clinical Outcomes in COVID-19: A Systematic Review and Meta-analysis', *EClinicalMedicine*, 29: 100630, https://doi.org/10.1016/j.eclinm.2020.100630

Timperio, Anna et al. 2004. 'Perceptions about the Local Neighborhood and Walking and Cycling among Children', *Preventive Medicine*, 38: 39-47, https://doi.org/10.1016/j.ypmed.2003.09.026

Tremblay, Mark, et al. 2015. 'Position Statement on Active Outdoor Play', *International Journal of Environmental Research and Public Health*, 12: 6475–505, https://doi.org/10.3390/ijerph120606475

Veitch, Jenny, et al. 2006. 'Where Do Children Usually Play? A Qualitative Study of Parents' Perceptions of Influences on Children's Active Free-Play', *Health & Place*, 12: 383-93, https://doi.org/10.1016/j.healthplace.2005.02.009

Vincent, Carol, and Stephen J. Ball. 2007. '"Making up" the Middle Class Child: Families, Activities and Class Dispositions,' *Sociology*, 41: 1061-077, https://doi.org/10.1177/0038038507082315

Viscaovky, Sergio E. 2017. 'When Time Freezes: Socio-Anthropological Research on Social Crises', *Iberoamericana-Nordic: Journal of Latin American and Caribbean Studies*, 46: 6-16, https://doi.org/10.16993/iberoamericana.103

5. How Playwork in the United Kingdom Coped with Covid-19 and the 23 March Lockdown

Pete King

Introduction

On 23 March 2020, the British Prime Minister announced a UK-wide lockdown in response to a new β-coronavirus, SARS-CoV-2 or Covid-19 (Dickson 2020). All playwork provisions closed immediately except for settings that provided childcare for parents and carers who were 'key workers' and therefore still working. This included health and social care, education and childcare, key public services, local and national government, food and other necessary goods, public safety and national security, transport and utilities, communication and financial services (Department for Education 2020).

As playworkers were not considered key workers, this resulted in the closure of adventure playgrounds and out-of-school clubs, as well as local parks and open spaces, unless the setting supported a local authority 'cluster or hub' (King 2020; Department for Education 2020). This was a single location serving a cluster of schools where the children of critical workers, later extended to include vulnerable children as well, were schooled and looked after at the end of the school day whilst their parents continued to work.

On a playwork social media online forum, one person posted the following question: 'Could playwork be considered as a key working role?' This question resonates with the development of playwork since

  https://doi.org/10.11647/OBP.0326.05

the early play clubs in the 1900s, the development of the adventure playground movement in the 1950s and, more recently, the conference paper by Gordon Sturrock and Perry Else about the playground as therapeutic space and playwork as healing (1998). The question seemed worth investigating further and formed the start of a year-long, longitudinal study, as described in this chapter.

Playwork is a profession that has roots in the United Kingdom but examples of playwork practice are also evident in other countries, such as The Netherlands (van Rooijen 2021), the USA (Patte 2018) and Hong Kong (Chan et al. 2020). Within the UK, playwork has been defined as 'a highly skilled profession that enriches and enhances children's play. It takes place where adults support children's play, but it is not driven by prescribed education or care outcomes' (SkillsActive 2010: 2).

This chapter starts with a brief historical account of the development of playwork in the UK up to the present day from two similar, yet very different origins. The chapter then focuses on four research studies into Covid-19 and playwork undertaken between March 2020 and March 2021. All of these studies were undertaken by the author and each was ethically approved by the College of Human and Health Science, Swansea University. They involved a study at the start of the March 2020 lockdown on how playwork responded to the pandemic and how playworkers had to adapt upon re-opening their gates and doors in July 2020. The study included practitioners and children at adventure playgrounds and after-school clubs across the United Kingdom. The chapter concludes by reviewing how the versatile and adaptable nature of playwork has enabled it to continue to support children and young people's play in the United Kingdom.

Historical Pathways

1) Adventure Playgrounds

Adventure playgrounds evolved from the idea of the 'junk playground' by the landscape architect Carl Theodor Sørensen (1931) and the first one opened on 15 August 1943 at Emdrupvej (sometimes referred to as Emdrup) (Cranwell 2003a), just outside Copenhagen. After visiting Emdrup in 1946, Lady Allen of Hurtwood (Allen 1968) brought the idea to the United Kingdom. The first public 'junk playground' is reported to have been set up in 1948 in Camberwell, London, by a voluntary association (Benjamin 1961). With the involvement of the National Playing Fields Association (NFPA, now called Fields in Trust) (Norman 2003), 'junk playgrounds' were re-named 'adventure playgrounds' (Cranwell 2008) in a leaflet published by the NPFA (Newstead 2017).

The child-led nature of the adventure playgrounds, which is still reflected in the Playwork Principles (Playwork Principles Scrutiny Group 2005) and according to which adults should support children's play, has been documented across the UK, for example, in London, Liverpool, Bristol and Grimsby (Benjamin 1961), Crawley (Shier 1984), Peterborough, Stevenage and Telford (Chilton 2003), Reading, Preston and Welwyn Garden City (Lambert and Pearson 1974). These adventure playgrounds were supported by a combination of voluntary committees, local authorities and the NPFA (Cranwell 2003a). Although the number of adventure playgrounds has declined since the 1970s (Chilton 2018) due to the impact of increasing health and safety regulations (Chilton 2003), for example, they are still run by voluntary committees, with funding in some cases provided by the local authority or through funding grant applications.

2) Children's Play Centres

The second pathway has been traced by Cranwell (2003b), who provides a historical account of the evolution of play settings in London between 1860 and 1940 where the 'major function of supervised out-of-school provision was to assist the state in maintaining the responsibility of working-class families to provide and protect their children in the community' (Cranwell 2003: 33). In London, the nineteenth century saw the beginnings of supervised clubs which resemble today's out-of-school provision. The supervised clubs included the Mary Ward and the Passmore Edwards Settlements, and the play centres opened by the Children's Happy Evening Association (CHEA) (Bonel and Lindon 1996; Homes 1970).

The Children's Happy Evening Association opened their first play centre in Marylebone, London in 1888 (Holmes and Massie 1970; Martin 1999), and by 1914 ran between ninety-four (Taylor 2013) and ninety-six (Holmes and Massie 1970) play centres in London and ten outside of London. In 1897, the Passmore Edwards Settlement (Holmes and Massie 1970) set up the Passmore Edwards Children's Recreation Schools which were founded by the novelist and philanthropist Mary Ward (Rappaport 2001). These developed from a Saturday morning 'playroom' at Marchmont Hall, St. Pancras in 1897, attended by 'two batches of 120' children (Trevelyan 1920: 2). Free evening and weekend play clubs were also set up to offer 'poor children respite from slum life and provide the first tentative moves towards combating juvenile delinquency' (Rappaport 2001: 731). These play clubs were funded through a combination of private financial donations and, with the passing of the Education (Administrative Provisions) Bill in 1907, through local authorities (Trevelyan 1920). In London, play centres were initially run by the CHEA, and the Passmore Edwards Children's Recreation Schools were taken over by London County Council from the 1940s up until 1990 (Cranwell 2003).

From Play Centres to the Childcare Agenda

During the 1990s and 2000s, funding was made available initially by the Conservative government in 1993 through the Out-of-School Childcare Initiative (Saunderson et al. 1995), and then by the Labour government's drive to increase quality, affordable and accessible childcare (Department for Education and Employment 1998) and out-of-school care (breakfast clubs, after-school clubs and holiday play schemes) that parents paid for their children to attend (unlike the CHEA, which was free). Although the increasing focus on childcare provision contributed to a decline in adventure playgrounds (Chilton 2003), by the 2000s there was an increase in the number of out-of-school provisions opened in primary schools (and other community venues) across the UK.

In 1993, the Conservative government provided funding for the Out-of-School Childcare Initiative (OSCI) (Education Extra 1997), also known as the Out-of-School Childcare Grant (OSCG) (Saunderson et al. 1995). OSCI/OSCG was introduced in April 1988, to provide set-up costs for out-of-school childcare (Saunderson et al. 1995) but the out-of-school clubs were reliant on fee-paying parents and carers. Within the first year of the OSCI/OSCG, two hundred different schemes had been created, providing 4400 childcare places (Saunderson et al. 1995). At the same time that the OSCI/OSCG funding finished, the UK government also changed from Conservative to Labour.

The New Labour government continued the drive to increase the workforce by providing funding to create childcare places under the National Childcare Strategy (NCS) (Department for Education and Employment 1998). The NCS was intended to support the existing voluntary sector, which was the main childcare provider, and the childcare business sector 'to ensure quality affordable childcare for children aged 0 to 14 in every neighbourhood, including both formal childcare and support for informal arrangements' (Department for Education and Employment 1998: 11) and to create '40,000 extra childcare places'. By the 2000s the number of out-of-school clubs saw a huge rise in provision (breakfast clubs, after-school clubs and holiday play schemes) (Smith and Barker 2000).

In 2020, despite limited funding opportunities due to government funding ending and the introduction of austerity measures (Voce 2015), both out-of-school provision and adventure playgrounds run by playworkers or adults who use a playwork approach remained. Although exact numbers for out-of-school provision in the UK are difficult to specify, the number of childcare settings in the UK was 13,380 (including day care, nursery and out-of-school settings) (Office for National Statistics 2015). It is also estimated that there are about 125 adventure playgrounds still operating in the UK. From the time of the 1900 play clubs to the development of the adventure playgrounds movement in the 1940s, and the recent childcare revolution, playwork fulfils an important role in some children's lives in the UK.

The Community Element of Playwork

It has been proposed that adventure playgrounds and after-school clubs might be considered as a form of community of practice (CoP) (King and Newstead 2020; King 2021a, 2021b), where CoP is defined as

[A] group of people who share a passion, a concern, or a set of problems regarding a particular topic, and who interact regularly in order to deepen their knowledge and expertise, and to learn how to do things better. A CoP is characterized by mutual learning, shared practice, inseparable membership, and joint exploration of ideas. (Mohajan 2017: 1)

The CoP of playwork can be traced back to the early days of the children's play centres and the subsequent growth of out-of-school provision (King 2021b) as well as the development of the adventure playground movement (King 2021a). For example, a CoP for adventure playgrounds has developed shared goals which are found in the twelve key elements for adventure playgrounds (Play England 2017), developed by those who work in them. However, the 2020 global event of Covid-19 created a new 'concern or a set of problems regarding a particular topic' to which the playwork community needed to respond.

The Introduction of Lockdown and the Impact on Playwork

The 23 March lockdown impacted everybody's lives, both professionally and personally. For this reason, and the unique nature of the situation, it was important to undertake research into how playwork would be affected by the pandemic at the time, rather than retrospectively. This initial study turned into an eighteen-month longitudinal study from March 2020 to September 2021, when all settings were able to re-open, and during subsequent lockdowns between October 2020 and March 2021. In total, eight research studies were undertaken of which four, from the period March-July 2020, are the focus here.

Study 1 was undertaken in March 2020 during the first UK lockdown. It involved interviewing twenty-three participants recruited from across the UK (see King 2020a for more details). Study 2 was undertaken after playwork settings re-opened in July 2020 as lockdown restrictions were eased. It involved interviews with eighteen adventure playground workers in England and Wales (King 2021a). Study 3 was also undertaken in July 2020, with fifty-four participants from across the UK completing an online survey (King 2021b). Study 4 was undertaken in March and April 2021, one year after settings re-opened in July 2020. Nine headteachers in Torfaen Borough Council, Wales, were interviewed about their perception of 'well-being playworkers' (see King 2021d for more details). The studies were UK-wide which meant that, following the initial lockdown, the restrictions (e.g. the social distancing measures in force in playwork settings) at the time of each study may have differed from one part of the UK to another.

Study 1: Can Playwork Be Considered an Essential Worker Role?

This first study explored three aspects of playwork practice from the March 2020 lockdown: the notion of playwork as a key work role, the immediate impact of Covid-19 and lockdown on playwork settings, and the question of how playwork would be undertaken post-lockdown.

When asked about their understanding of a 'key worker', playworkers in the study viewed the role as a response to the current situation, which was necessary to support the maintenance of the health and well-being of all citizens, and providing care to an individual (King 2020). In this sense, playworkers viewed themselves as key workers during the pandemic. In particular, they viewed playwork as supporting key worker parents and carers by providing childcare as part of a school 'hub'. This not only enabled parents and carers to carry out their work but also gave them peace of mind that their children were in an environment where they could enjoy themselves. This was important as not all children had access to childcare settings during lockdown:

> So, I think the number one thing is it allows the parents to do their jobs, that's the number one thing right now. But the second thing, which is what the parents keep saying to me, is how the difference it makes to them knowing that their kids are happy, they're safe, they're well cared for, their needs are being met. (Manager of an after-school club and holiday play scheme, England)

The theme of a playwork approach also emerged from the data. A playwork approach is summed up in the second playwork principle:

> Play is a process that is freely chosen, personally directed and intrinsically motivated. That is, children and young people determine and control the content and intent of their play, by following their own instincts, ideas and interests, in their own way for their own reasons (Playwork Principles Scrutiny Group 2005: 1)

Playwork focuses on the process of play, rather than any adult-directed purpose or outcome. This approach is one of the unique ways in which playworkers define their work (King 2015), where children and young people have control and autonomy in play as to how, where, with whom, and what. The implications of this approach, not only during lockdown but afterwards too, are summed up in the comment below:

> I just think as a playworker, you've got no agenda, you're there just to facilitate. And I think that, during these times, that approach would be a massive help to children, young adults [and] vulnerable individuals. And thinking about how we're going to impact on it. Going back is going to be a challenging time for all the staff, for all the children and all the parents. (Manager of a Wraparound Play Company, Wales)

A third theme that emerged was that of relationships and this reflected the important role of playwork, not just for the children and young people who attend playwork settings, but regarding relationships within the community, including for parents and carers:

> I would like now to think we're proving our worth, that we don't just play pool and table tennis, we are a vital part of the families on our estate, a vital part of their lives as well. We are key to them. So that surely makes us keyworkers? (Senior Playworker of an Adventure Playground, England)

Study 1 thus indicated that playwork was considered important not only in supporting key workers as defined by the government but was also a key worker role in itself. The second part of this study explored how playwork settings responded to the onset of lockdown and their thoughts on how playwork should continue once the lockdown eased.

At the start of the 23 March lockdown, playwork settings fell into one of three categories (King 2021c). The first category was settings that immediately closed, with all staff put on furlough, i.e. eighty percent of staff members' pre-Covid salaries were paid through the UK Government's 'coronavirus job retention scheme' (Pope and Shearer 2021). In this category, all staff ceased work and settings remained shut. For other playwork settings, one or two staff members remained employed (whilst other staff members were put on furlough) but no face-to-face playwork took place. Instead, some settings developed an 'outreach' play service where resources were left outside houses for children to collect and use. The example below is based on the 'Theory of Loose Parts' (Nicholson 1971) which states that the more resources (loose parts) children can play with, the more ideas are created in their play:

> We came up with this 'bags for play' idea where we are getting bags of loose parts out to children across the county. Particularly children who are living in disadvantaged areas or who have got social care interventions, so we're trying to get the bags out to the children who need them most. We are being true to our roots in the fact that the bag is full of stuff so it's not obvious what you may do with it. There's a bit of active stuff like skipping rope, balloons, chalk. Nice tin of water colour paints and paper. Scissors, some tape, some glue, some scrap, so it's very much true to what we do, no directions on how to use it. (Playworker for an Open Access Mobile Play Provision, England)

Some settings engaged in online interaction, running virtual play sessions, although with varying success, as indicated in the comment below:

> I'm recording videos of Mr Men videos and putting that on our website and sharing that around. We get a little bit of engagement from the parents who follow our social media, and a couple of the kids who follow our social media. But to be honest, it's a tiny fraction. I'm happy to do that and I think it provides value but the amount of value it provides in comparison to being open for play, it's obviously going to be really a tiny fraction. (Manager of an Adventure Playground, England)

Certain other settings remained open but changed their focus to support families in the communities where they were located. For example, some adventure playgrounds became, or expanded on, food bank provision:

> Quite a few families have got in touch, so the playground is kind of providing a food bank service to some of the families and other people in the community. That is still providing a service to the community although it's not adventure play. (Manager of an Adventure Playground, England)

A change in focus emerged, with playworkers supporting primary school teachers in running the 'hubs' for key worker and vulnerable children:

> Well, in regard to the service which we run seven days a week at the moment, all our provisions are closed, but we've been asked to co-ordinate and run the hubs, five hubs across the authority plus one for the special needs school. So, we are not running those play spaces or staffed play spaces, we are supporting the hubs' staffed provision for children that attend that. It's not open to all. It started first for blue light services, second it was open to any front-line services and, as from Monday, we are looking at looked-after children to be supported and have play opportunities as well. (Play Service Manager, Wales)

This example of a play service that ended up coordinating the hubs resulted in a follow-up study (Study 4), which is described in more detail later on in this chapter. Participants in the first study were also asked how they thought playwork would be able to continue post-lockdown. This led to the emergence of three themes: reduced or no playwork provision, developing new methods of delivering playwork, and the need for a more therapeutic role (King 2020).

Some feared the worst-case scenario, i.e., that playwork settings would not be able to continue, particularly those in the childcare sector who rely on parents and carers paying for their children's attendance at sessions. With most parents and carers working from home, many playwork settings in the out-of-school sector were worried about the numbers of children who would use the provision post-lockdown:

> We closed on the 23rd March as the schools shut but we were able to open during Easter which meant the staff could go off on their break. I had staff I could bring in who weren't furloughed, and we were able to open and offer cover for children. We made a loss, I would say, of £800+ that week, that fortnight. (After-school Club Manager, Wales)

Whilst funding was one issue, another was the strong possibility that the introduction of two-metre social distancing would continue in playwork settings and that playworkers would have to develop new ways of doing their job, as reflected in the comment below:

> We've fought against funding cuts and, as a profession, we're fighting back against stuff we don't like. This is something we don't like but we can't fight because we've got to keep children apart which doesn't sit well with any of us. We are just going to have to roll with it and accept this is the situation and how do we make it good. It is fairly rubbish and we've got to kind of keep it kind of happy and move on really. (Play Development Worker, Wales)

With children and young people experiencing lockdown and not being able to play in the same physical space as their friends and peers, there was a genuine feeling that the therapeutic aspects of playwork would be most required when children returned to the settings:

> So, for sure, there is going to be a high level of need and I'm expecting that our targeted support that we do, our play nurturing work, that could be very much on the up. You know people will have a real appreciation of children who are experiencing high levels of anxiety from what they've been through and the need for them to have opportunities to play in small groups or as individuals with our playworkers. (Playworker for Open Access Mobile Play Provision, England)

In July 2020 playwork settings began to re-open, although with many restrictions. It was decided that follow-up research was needed to see how playwork generally, and the different playwork settings, were able to operate. As noted above, this resulted in two further studies, one with adventure playgrounds and mobile play provision, and the other with out-of-school clubs (breakfast clubs, after-school clubs, and holiday play schemes).

Study 2: Adventure Playgrounds and Mobile Play Provision Post-Lockdown

Study 2 involved interviewing adults who work within adventure playgrounds or who offer mobile play provision in children's and young people's local parks and open spaces. Pre-Covid, these two types of provision were 'open access':

> This provision usually caters for a wide age range of children, normally aged five years and over. The purpose is to provide staffed play opportunities for children, usually in the absence of their parents. Children are not restricted in their movements, other than where related to safety matters and they are not prevented from coming and going as and when they wish. (Welsh Government 2016)

Here, children are free to come and go as they please. They do not have to stay if they choose not to. During the interviews, participants were asked how their setting ran both pre- and post-lockdown. The difference can be seen in Figures 5.1 and 5.2 below:

Access	Opening Times	Age Range	Attendance Range	Staff Range	Addition to Play
Open	Term-Time		Between 25 to 80		
	Monday to Friday 3.30pm to 7pm				
	Saturday 10am to 5pm				Provide food
	Holiday	4-17 years	Up to 200 a day (not all at the same time)	3 to 6 core staff (plus 5-10 seasonal staff)	Youth Club
	Monday to Friday 10am to 5pm				Run bespoke sessions
	Saturday 10am to 5pm				

Figure 5.1 A 'typical' adventure playground, pre-March 2020 lockdown (data from King 2021a)
CC BY-NC 4.0

Access	Opening Times	Age Range	Attendance Range
Closed and Bookable	Term-Time		
	Monday to Friday 3.30pm to 7pm		
	Saturday 10am to 5pm		
	Holiday	4-17 years	In 'Bubbles' of 15-20 and designated time slots allocated
	Monday to Friday 10am to 5pm		
	Saturday 10am to 5pm		

Figure 5.2 A 'typical' adventure playground, July 2020 (data from King 2021a)
CC BY-NC 4.0

The exact 'change in playwork practice' identified and feared in the first study became a reality, in that settings had to change from open access, with children free to arrive and leave at their will, to a closed-access, bookable provision. This resulted in fewer children using the settings. In addition, the need for a Covid-19 risk assessment increased paperwork and cleaning. This led to reduced availability of resources, particularly the 'loose part' objects which now had to be rotated and cleaned. There was also less space for children to use as they were in small groups or 'bubbles' and rotated between designated areas at different time slots. This was a big change from pre-lockdown playwork practice:

> The children didn't have the control they normally have over what they were doing, which is what play is all about, isn't it? You could argue this was activity rather than play. Because they chose to be there. I assumed they did because they turned up, the parents brought them and stuff like that and they wanted to be there. They had a good time. It was different to what they normally access in the playground. There was an element of fluidity there, if they wanted to go on a slide they would go on the slide, but it was not as free-range as it would normally be as you had to stay in these bubbles and stay separate from the other bubbles. So it was far more structured, which goes against the grain completely, you know what I mean? The activities could be adapted to some degree, but it wasn't as fluid and responsive as it normally would have been. (Manager of an Adventure Playground, England)

This reflection indicates how the 'playwork approach' of supporting the process of play was forced to 'change' in order for children to attend once again. This was quite a challenge for those using, and used to, a 'playwork approach' in their practice but it reflects the need for playworkers as a community of practice to continually adapt to solve 'shared problems' (Mohajan 2017). Thus, the main themes that emerged from the interview data were preparation for opening (increased cleaning and paperwork), reduction (in playwork ethos, children attending, resources and space), targeted service (for both new and existing users) and play behaviour (anxiety about returning and having to play with social distancing measures) (King 2021a).

Study 3: Out-of-School Settings (Breakfast Club, After-School Club and Holiday Play Scheme) Post-March 2020 Lockdown

The 'shared problems' also related to Study 3 which focused on the closed-access out-of-school clubs. Closed access in this instance designates the need for children to be booked in for sessions and to stay until collected by their parent, carer or other adults. Study 3 was an online survey. As with Study 2, participants were asked to describe a typical session pre-March 2020 lockdown and their experience at re-opening in July 2020. This is shown in Figures 5.3 and 5.4 below:

Access	Opening Times	Age Range	Number	Snack	Space	Activities
Closed and children collected or made their own way depending on their age	After-School from 3pm to 6pm	4-11 years	Average 30-40	Children self-select their snack	Supervised indoor and outdoor space children free to choose what they wanted to go	Range of resources and equipment children could choose to do

Figure 5.3 A 'typical' after-school club, pre-March 2020 lockdown (data from King 2021b)

CC BY-NC 4.0

Access	Opening Times	Age Range	Number	Snack	Space	Activities
All children collected	After-School from 3pm to 6pm	4-11 years	'Bubbles' of 15 children	Children bring snack or staff make it	Children remain in their 'Bubbles' and play either inside or outside	Resources and equipment reduced and rotated between 'Bubbles'

Figure 5.4 A 'typical' after-school club, July 2020 (data from King 2021b),
CC BY-NC 4.0

As with Study 2, Study 3 also saw a reduction in the number of children attending, the resources available and the space in which to play (King 2021b). Although there was also an increase in cleaning and paperwork, Covid-19 policies and reporting measures had to be put in place, resulting in more forms to complete. Children had to remain in 'bubbles' consisting of a group of no more than fifteen children (Public Health England 2020). A bubble would often be the same as the children's year group bubble at their school. It was necessary to ensure that enough staff were employed for the number of bubbles:

The segregation of children into bubbles is the biggest headache for me. I am lucky that we have always worked with surplus staff (minimum of 1:8 adult-to-child ratio, and usually more like 1:6). This means I now have enough staff to support each bubble (so 7 separate sets of children) and still serve snack to 72 children, but running the setting would be so much easier and more fun for the children if they could play with each other. (Manager of out-of-school provision, England)

As in Study 2, playworkers had to change their 'playwork approach' which previously involved children choosing what they wanted to play with. Four themes are related to this change in practice: maintaining service (increased policies, cleaning and financial concerns), bubbles (placement of children in year groups or age groups), play space (which had to be rearranged with designated resources and mostly outdoors), and play behaviour (more one-to-one with adults and, upon return, play behaviour was challenging) (King 2021b). As with the adventure playgrounds and mobile play provision, the closed-access, out-of-school provision led to 'shared problems' related to facilitating a play environment with fewer children, resources and space. With many out-of-school settings based in schools, the increased paperwork and greater number of staff required for bubbles made these changes specific to school-based playwork settings. Different solutions to open-access provision were needed.

The need for flexibility in playwork was anticipated by the participants in Study 1. It can be traced back to early play centres and adventure playgrounds, where issues of funding, resources and staff retention were commonplace, and remain so in different playwork settings today. It could be argued that the adaptability and versatility of playwork arises from its focus on the process of play and that this enables playworkers to respond to different situations, from adventure playgrounds to children's hospital wards. Study 4 showed how an established team of playworkers was able to respond to the sudden lockdown by coordinating and running school hubs, supported by teaching staff (King 2021d).

Study 4: 'Well-being' Playworkers

As noted above in Study 1, one playwork provider was asked to coordinate and run hubs. This was the play service of Torfaen Borough Council in South-East Wales. Torfaen Borough Council has had a play service since 2004 and, prior to Covid, provided community play provision including holiday play schemes, family sessions and respite sessions, as well as support for schools before and after the school day and during school breaktimes. During the lockdown, the play service playwork team changed their job title to 'well-being playworkers' to reflect their new focus of supporting children and young people. During the first lockdown in March 2020, the same well-being playworkers were allocated to one of the six hubs in Torfaen, working with the teaching staff who were scheduled to work that day. This proved to be very successful and led to Study 4, which involved interviewing the headteachers linked to each of the six hubs about their views of the well-being playworkers.

The headteachers from the six primary schools to which the six hubs were attached were asked for their views on the well-being playworkers during the first lockdown and after it was eased in July 2020. Three clear themes emerged: strong relationships (with the children, staff and school, and the wider community), the fact that these playworkers were a part of the school team (running the lockdown hubs, offering bespoke provision and providing academic support), and provided quality service (with their adaptable play practice, trained staff and resources provided). Some of the headteachers had had experience of the play service before lockdown but for others these hubs were the first experience. There was a clear similarity between the themes and subthemes that emerged from the headteachers in this study (i.e., the importance of relationships and adaptable play practice) and those that emerged from Study 1 involving playwork professionals.

The Torfaen play service, as with many other play organizations across the UK, was already familiar with the hub concept since this is often applied for holiday play schemes and open-access adventure playgrounds. What was evident and acknowledged by the headteachers and school staff working in the hubs was that well-being playworkers undertook a playwork approach with children in formal education. The well-being playworkers, and importantly the same playworkers attending the same hubs each day, provided some day-to-day consistency for the children with a familiar face. The more informal approach of the well-being playworkers, for instance the fact that they were addressed by their first names), provided what Burghardt (2005) termed a 'relaxed field' that enabled children to play, with the well-being playworkers supporting the process of play:

> It's the way they just interact with the children, and they chat to the children, and I suppose the activities that they do, like the sporting activities, the creative activities, the fact they are a constant. (Headteacher 2, Wales)

This is not to say that teaching staff played an unimportant or passive role but the well-being playworkers were more experienced and skilled in their ability to adapt quickly in developing the hub (King 2020), which the play service had been running in the community since 2004 via holiday play schemes in Torfaen.

The designation of playwork as a key worker role in terms of 'relationships' and 'adaptability' in Study 1 was perceived by playwork professionals, whilst in Study 4 it was acknowledged by headteachers. The two different perspectives indicate the importance of play, and playworkers, in supporting children, families and schools during the first lockdown and beyond.

Conclusion

As argued throughout this chapter, playwork has always had to be adaptable and versatile and this was evident in many ways during the lockdown period. For example, as a result of austerity and welfare reform, there has been an increase in the number of food banks (Lambie-Mumford and Green 2015) which resulted in some adventure playgrounds either forming or increasing food-bank provision. This is not new in playwork praxis considering that the formation and development of the nineteenth-century play clubs and 1950s adventure playgrounds took place in low socio-economic communities:

> Most playwork is done in areas of chronic emotional, cultural and often financial deprivation. If this were not so, the needs for [adventure] playgrounds of this kind and criticisms of the

environments in which they are placed would only be minimal. (Hughes 1975: 2)

The more recent out-of-school clubs did not become food banks but they supported children and young people in different ways by providing services and running at a loss. Although not sustainable, this demonstrated playwork's flexibility during the lockdown period and beyond.

The four research studies included in this chapter contribute to the social history of playwork during the pandemic. The four studies considered the lived experience of the participants as they were experiencing lockdown and the effects of Covid-19 on a professional level. Changes had to be put in place and this relied on the sharing of ideas and problems that did occur during the pandemic for both adventure playground and mobile play provision (King 2021a) and the out-of-school club sector (King 2021b).

Whilst schools and other childcare-related settings were provided with government guidance upon re-opening, this was not the case for many playwork settings. Instead, guidance to adapt settings often came through other sources, such as London Play, who developed guidance for adventure playgrounds.

From a playwork praxis perspective, the current Covid-19 pandemic has shown how playwork adapted and demonstrated versatility to support children, young people and their families within their communities. Whether this involved providing food, delivering play resources or virtual play sessions, playwork continued, if not directly face-to-face. Where face-to-face delivery was still undertaken, this occurred in very controlled conditions and during the lockdown within the local authority hubs. The very nature of playwork praxis, such as not knowing which children may attend at a given time (as in pre-Covid open access) or having different children booked into after-school clubs and holiday play schemes, enabled a 'playwork approach' to supporting the provision of play for hub teaching staff and, in the case study outlined here, coordinating the hubs. The idea of 'uncertainty' in playwork can be traced back to the nineteenth-century play clubs and the adventure playground movement. This suggests that playwork will continue to adapt to survive in the face of future uncertainty.

Works Cited

Allen of Hurtwood, Lady Marjorie. 1968. *Planning for Play* (London: Thames and Hudson)

Benjamin, Joe. 1961. *In Search of Adventure: A Study of the Junk Playground* (London: National Council of Social Service)

Bonel, Paul, and Jennie Lindon. 1996. *Good Practice in Playwork* (Cheltenham: Stanley Thornley)

Burghardt, Gordon M. 2005. *The Genesis of Animal Play: Testing the Limit* (Cambridge, MA: MIT Press)

Chan, Pauline, et al. 2020. 'Playwork Play Works', in *Playwork Practice at the Margins*, ed. by Jennifer Cartmel and Rick Worch (London: Routledge), pp. 39-56

Chilton, Tony. 2003. *Adventure Playgrounds in the Twenty-First Century*, in *Playwork: Theory and Practice*, ed. by Fraser Brown (Maidenhead: Open University Press), pp. 114-27

——. 2018. 'Adventure Playgrounds: A Brief History', in *Aspects of Playwork*, Play and Culture Studies, 14, ed. by Fraser Brown and Bob Hughes (London: Hamilton Books), pp. 157-78

Cranwell, Keith. 2003a. 'Towards a History of Adventure Playgrounds 1931–2000', in *An Architecture of Play: A Survey of London's Adventure Playgrounds*, ed. by Nils Norman (London: Four Corners Books), pp. 17-26, https://www.play-scapes.com/wp-content/uploads/2015/03/Architecture-Of-Play1.pdf

——. 2003b. 'Towards Playwork: An Historical Introduction to Children's Out-of-school Play Organisations in London (1860-1940)', in *Playwork: Theory and Practice*, ed. by Fraser Brown (Maidenhead: Open University Press), pp. 32-47

Department for Education. 2020. *Guidance: Critical Workers and Vulnerable Children Who Can Access Schools or Educational Settings*, 19 March, https://www.gov.uk/government/publications/coronavirus-covid-19-maintaining-educational-provision

Department for Education and Employment. 1998. *Meeting the Childcare Challenge: Green Paper* (London: HMSO)

Dickson, Annabelle. 2020. 'Boris Johnson Announces Coronavirus Lockdown in UK', *Politico*, 23 March, https://www.politico.eu/article/boris-johnson-announces-coronavirus-lockdown-in-uk/

Education Extra. 1997. *Out of School Childcare Initiative: Succeeding Out of School* (London: Department for Education and Employment)

Holmes, Anthea, and Peter Massie. 1970. *Children's Play: A Study of Needs and Opportunities* (London: Michael Joseph)

Hughes, Bob. 1975. *Notes for Adventure Playworkers* (London: CYAG Publications)

King, Pete. 2015. 'The Possible Futures for Playwork Project: A Thematic Analysis', *Journal of Playwork Practice*, 2: 143–56, https://doi.org/10.1332/205 316215X14762005141752

——. 2020. 'Can Playwork Have a Key Working Role?' *International Journal of Playwork Practice*, 1, https://doi.org/10.25035/ijpp.01.01.07

——. 2021a. 'How Have Adventure Playgrounds in the United Kingdom Adapted Post-March Lockdown in 2020?' *International Journal of Playwork Practice, 2*, https://doi.org/10.25035/ijpp.02.01.05

——. 2021b. 'How Have After-school Clubs Adapted in the United Kingdom Post-March Lockdown?' *Journal of Childhood, Education and Society*, 2: 106-16, https://doi.org/10.37291/2717638X.202122100

——. 2021c. 'The Impact of Covid-19 on Playwork Practice', *Child Care in Practice*, https://doi.org/10.1080/13575279.2020.1860904

——. 2021d. 'Well-being Playworkers in Primary School: A Headteacher's Perspective', *Education 3-13*, https://doi.org/10.1080/03004279.2021.1971276

King, Pete, and Shelly Newstead. 2020. 'Demographic Data and Barriers to Professionalisation in Playwork', *Journal of Vocational Education and Training*, 73: 591-604, https://doi.org/10.1080/13636820.2020.1744694

Lambie-Mumford, Hannah, and Mark A. Green. 2015 'Austerity, Welfare Reform and the Rising Use of Food Banks by Children in England and Wales', *Area*, 49: 273-79, https://doi.org/10.1111/area.12233

Lambert, Jack, and Jenny Pearson. 1974. *Adventure Playgrounds* (Harmondsworth: Penguin)

Mohajan, Haradhan K. 2017. 'Roles of Communities of Practice for the Development of the Society', *Journal of Economic Development, Environment and People*, 6.3: 27-46

Newstead, Shelly, and Pete King. 2021. 'What Is the Purpose of Playwork?' *Child Care in Practice*, https://doi.org/10.1080/13575279.2021.1958752

Norman, Nils. 2003. Introduction to *An Architecture of Play: A Survey of London's Adventure Playgrounds*, ed. by Nils Norman (London: Four Corners Books), pp. 7-16, https://www.play-scapes.com/wp-content/uploads/2015/03/Architecture-Of-Play1.pdf

Office for National Statistics. 2021. *Childcare Providers in Regions of the United Kingdom*, https://www.ons.gov.uk/file?uri=/businessindustryandtrade/business/activitysizeandlocation/adhocs/005704childcareprovidersinregionsoftheunitedkingdom/ah009.xls

Patte, Michael. 2018. 'Playwork in America: Past, Current and Future Trends', in *Aspects of Playwork: Play and Culture Studies, Volume 14*, ed. by Fraser Brown and Bob Hughes (New York: Hamilton Books), pp. 63-78

Play England. 2017. *Adventure Playgrounds: The Essential Elements* [*Updated Briefing*], https://www.playengland.org.uk/s/Adventure-Playgrounds-gph4.pdf

Playwork Principles Scrutiny Group. 2005. *The Playwork Principles*, https://playwales.org.uk/login/uploaded/documents/Playwork%20Principles/playwork%20principles.pdf

Pope, Thomas, and Eleanor Shearer. 2021. *The Coronavirus Job Retention Scheme: How Successful Has the Furlough Scheme Been and What Should Happen Next?* (Institute for Government), https://www.instituteforgovernment.org.uk/sites/default/files/publications/coronavirus-job-retention-scheme-success.pdf

Public Health England. 2020. 'Guidance: How to Stop the Spread of Coronavirus (COVID-19), https://www.gov.uk/government/publications/coronavirus-covid-19-meeting-with-others-safely-social-distancing/coronavirus-covid-19-meeting-with-others-safely-social-distancing

Rappaport, Helen. 2001. *Encyclopedia of Women Social Reformers*, I (Santa Barbara, CA: ABC-CLIO)

van Rooijen, Martin. 2021. 'Developing a Playwork Perspective from Dutch Research Experience', in *Further Perspectives on Researching Play from a Playwork Perspective: Process, Playfulness, Rights-Based and Critical Reflection*, ed. by Pete King and Shelly Newstead (London: Routledge), pp. 58-78

Saunderson, Ian, et al. 1995. *The Out-of-School Childcare Grant Initiative: An Interim Evaluation* (Leeds: Leeds Metropolitan University)

Shier, Harry. 1984. *Adventure Playgrounds: An Introduction* (London: National Playing Fields Association)

SkillsActive. 2010. *SkillsActive UK Play and Playwork Education and Skills Strategy 2011–2016* (London: SkillsActive)

Smith, Fiona, and John Barker. 2000. 'Contested Spaces: Children's Experiences of Out-of-School Care in England and Wales', *Area 33*: 169-76, https://doi.org/10.1177/0907568200007003005

Sturrock, Gordon, and Perry Else. 2007 [1998]. 'The Playground as Therapeutic Space: Playwork as Healing (known as "The Colorado Paper")', in *Therapeutic Playwork Reader One*, ed. by Perry Else and Gordon Sturrock (Southampton: Common Threads), pp. 73-104

Trevelyan, Janet P. 1920. *Evening Play Centres for Children* (London: Methuen)

Voce, Adrian. 2015. *Policy for Play: Responding to Children's Forgotten Right* (Bristol: Policy Press)

Waters, Philip. 2018. 'Playing at Research: Playfulness as a Form of Knowing and Being in Research with Children', in *Researching Play from a Playwork Perspective*, ed. by Pete King and Shelly Newstead (London: Routledge), pp. 73-89

Welsh Government. 2016. *National Minimum Standards for Regulated Childcare for Children up to the Age of 12 Years*, https://careinspectorate.wales/sites/default/files/2018-01/160411regchildcareen.pdf

6. Playworkers' Experiences, Children's Rights and Covid-19: A Case Study of Kodomo Yume Park, Japan[1]

Mitsunari Terada, Mariia Ermilova, and Hitoshi Shimamura

Children in Japan during Covid-19

The Japanese fiscal year ends in March and begins in April. During this time people are busy moving, submitting tax reports, renewing contracts and documents, and graduating and starting school. When Covid-19 struck, all of Japan's schools closed. Many graduation ceremonies were cancelled or moved online, and the new year began in confusion. Club activities and private lessons were also cancelled. From April 2020, the first state of emergency was announced (see Figure 6.1). Shopping centres and amusement parks were all closed. The number of infected people was low so, in July 2020, the government launched the 'Go to Travel' campaign to promote domestic tourism. However, this led to the subsequent spread of Covid-19.

---

1   We would like to thank the Yume Park manager Daisuke Tomokane, the Director of NPO Tamariba Nishino Hiroyuki, and the playworkers who made it possible to organize interviews and investigate activities in Yume Park during Covid-19. This work was supported by the Japanese Society for the Promotion of Science KAKENHI Grant Number 22K14912.

During the Covid-19 pandemic, Japan was characterized by unique phenomena: despite the low number of official restrictions and 'hard' measures, the population exhibited high compliance with the recommendations to stay home, avoiding the 'three C's'—closed spaces, crowded places and close-contact settings. This high-level compliance was due to peer pressure in Japanese society, which means that stigma is attached to those who break rules and behave egotistically in ways that compromise the community's safety. Violators of rules, condemned by the community, attract strong verbal and nonverbal feedback— looks, questions, threats, attitudes and even physical actions (attacks on property, etc.). During the pandemic, the phenomenon of the 'self-restraint police' (*jishuku keisatsu*) emerged, whereby community members would spy on one another to ensure that everyone was adhering to the safety regulations and would punish those who did not comply with them (Katafuchi, Kenichi and Managi 2021: 71). The phenomenon resulted in several suicides by those infected with Covid-19 because the infected individuals could not face the resulting social condemnation. Therefore, adherence to the restrictions ensured the containment of Covid-19 in Japan, but it also had very negative consequences. This specific cultural phenomenon of peer pressure also affected children's welfare.

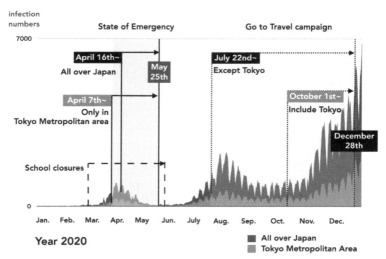

Figure 6.1 Timeline of Covid-19 in Japan, 2020 (based on data from Ministry of Health, Labour and Welfare, Japan)
Created by Mitsunari Terada, CC BY-NC-ND 4.0

Play comes naturally to growing children. They cannot fully control their body movements, voice, or energy. Children and caregivers during the pandemic were constantly under pressure from two sides: first, their neighbours and family members who, working at home, complained about noise from children (many apartments are poorly soundproofed) and second, the wider community complained about 'children going out' and playing freely despite the recommendation to stay home, thereby exacerbating the spread of Covid-19. Children and their caregivers did not have a place in which to simply be: the children's need to play and move was ignored by adults who found themselves in high-pressure situations. This is reflected in the number of domestic violence reports, which increased during the pandemic, as well as the increased suicide rate among women (the main caregivers) and schoolchildren. The female suicide rate reached unprecedented levels, surpassing the male suicide rate for the first time in many years (Ministry of Health, Labour and Welfare et al. 2021: 9). This has also been linked to job losses, as women hold the majority of temporary insecure positions and service jobs.

Japan's National Centre for Child Health and Development conducted a survey on how children perceived the changes associated with Covid-19. Japan's Ministry of Health, Labour and Welfare reported that suicides among students, including those in elementary and junior high schools, reached 1039 in 2020, the highest since the government began compiling data on suicides in 1978 (Ministry of Health, Labour and Welfare et al. 2021: 9).

The 'National Online Survey of Children's Well-being during the COVID-19 Pandemic in Japan' offers a snapshot of children's and caregivers' situations (National Centre for Child Health and Development 2021): 'Can't meet friends' (76%) was listed as the top concern among schoolchildren during the 'stay at home' mandate in the first wave of Covid-19, followed by 'Can't go to school' (63%), 'Can't play outside' (54%) and 'Worried about study' (52%). At least thirty-nine percent of children reported that they '[hadn't] kept in contact with friends', and screen time increased by seventy-two percent compared to the previous year.

Regarding stigma relating to Covid-19 infection, sixty-three percent of children agreed that 'I want to keep it a secret if my family were to catch Covid-19'. Several pages of the report are devoted to gathering children's direct voices. Children spoke about the unfair attitudes of adults regarding their needs: 'Why are adults allowed to gather in large groups? A stranger got angry with us when we were playing' (a seven-year-old boy). A twelve-year-old girl said 'Do not treat us like germs/ virus', likely referring to adults' attitudes towards children in public spaces. Another girl wrote in her response, 'To my teacher: You give us too much homework. Also, seven periods a day are too much' (National Centre for Child Health and Development 2021). Many children wrote that they wanted their opinions to be heard. Parents and teachers seemed too busy and children lacked one-on-one time. For example, a seventh-grade boy (between twelve and thirteen years old) wrote, 'I want my teachers to listen to me in a room where I feel safe to talk to them and not be heard by other students', and 'It's not easy to ask for advice. I need someone to help me do that' (a fourth-grade girl, between nine and ten years old). The guardians' responses revealed that twenty-nine percent of caregivers have moderate to severe depressive symptoms (National Centre for Child Health and Development 2021). During Covid-19, while children obviously had plenty of time to play, they did not always have a suitable space in which to do so. They felt lonely and perceived the adults' nervousness as well as worrying about 'falling behind in their study at school' (Terada and Shimamura 2020).

The information presented above demonstrates that many children in Japan need a safe place in which to play and the opportunity to communicate with someone who will listen. When the pandemic separated them from their friends, they urged their parents to work harder and to care about the opinions of others. Providing a place for children to visit, and in which to play and communicate with others was an objective that kept Yume Park open when Covid-19 struck. In this chapter, we will discuss the decision to keep Yume Park open for children, safeguarding their right to play despite government restrictions and regional preventive measures, and how this was made possible through the efforts of the playworkers who accommodated visitors to the park.

Our aims are as follows:

- to investigate how children's play and participation changed during the Covid-19 restrictions in the outdoor space of Yume Park

- to examine how playworkers adjusted the park's usual policies in response to the emergency.

Data Acquired

The authors interviewed managers and playworkers in their twenties and thirties, while writing memos, during a three-day visit to Yume Park. Playworkers were interviewed in groups of three or four people. A group interview format was chosen in order to stimulate conversation and help playworkers to remember the events of 2020. A timeline of events was reconstructed in an interview with Daisuke Tomokane, current manager of the Yume Park facility. To prepare questions for interviews, we were advised by Yume Park leaders to look through the documentary created by one of Yume Park's fans as the pandemic unfolded. A professional filmmaker, working on a voluntary basis, captured segments of playworkers' meetings and interviewed a few of the parents visiting the park, and posted them on his company's YouTube channel, Group Gendai.

The data therefore consists of the following: interviews conducted by the authors in early 2022; official statistics on visitor numbers collected by playworkers between March and August 2020, and augmented by a documentary on Yume Park (Group Gendai 2021); newspaper articles, and research articles. The park values its visitors' privacy highly, and so we were not granted access to diary entries containing personal data. The study was conducted with the ethical approval of the leader of NPO Tamariba, which manages Kodomo Yume Park facilities and Kawasaki City office. All playworkers were interviewed with their informed consent.

Kodomo Yume Park, Kawasaki City

Historical Background

Kodomo Yume Park (henceforth Yume Park), translated from Japanese as 'Children's Dream Park', is a youth centre complex that ensures children's freedoms, allowing children from different backgrounds to play together in a safe environment. It was established in Kawasaki City in 2003 in accordance with Japan's first local ordinance on children's rights, an interpretation of the United Nations Convention on the Rights of the Child (CRC) following the Japanese government's ratification of the latter (Kinoshita 2007: 270).

The facility, founded and owned by Kawasaki City, is managed by the NPO [Non-Profit Organization], Tamariba. It aims to provide a space in which children may play freely, a place in which to be—*ibasho* (Tanaka 2021: 7)—and an alternative education system in which each child receives individual attention, in contrast to standard schools in which children differing from the norm may be 'left behind'.

Hiroyuki Nishino, the director of Yume Park, was one of the first educators to voice concerns about children's rights in Japan. Based on Articles 28 and 31 of the UN CRC, he pursued the idea of creating a third space in which children could play freely and receive education. He favours an approach wherein the initiative comes from the child, or at least wherein adults do not attempt to impose 'programmed' activities on to children, but rather to support children in their natural drive to play. The alienation and isolation reported by Japanese children in a UNICEF survey (Nagata 2016: 243) raised concerns among educational professionals. Nishino's approach is characterized by chaos and diversity: 'It is important to mix the people, abled and not abled, all different—we are all learning from each other'.

Kawasaki has a reputation for teen violence, with several cases attaining prominence in the media during the last decade. The city owes its diverse population to its industrial past and its foreign labour force. Disparities are extreme here: on the edge of Tokyo, the mingling of middle-class families' offspring and children from socially vulnerable families (e.g. children of single parents, sometimes foreigners) create an environment that is particularly conducive to bullying (*ijime*) and exclusion. The problem is likely rooted in the Japanese education system, wherein children's time is strictly regulated by adults: students spend all day at school with lessons in the morning and club activities (*bukatsu*) in the evening. Schoolchildren thus experience only two places: home and school. Occasionally, some children's home environments are unsafe or poor (for example, their parents or single parent may work all day, have substance abuse problems or mental health issues, etc.). School would ideally offer such children a safe space, but on the contrary they are often bullied or ignored at school for being 'weird'. Where might these children find a third space exempt from strict school rules and domestic issues?

To further compound the problem, the culture of groupism occasionally reaches the point of absurdity in Japanese public schools, as seen in certain high-profile court cases involving teachers who forced children to dye their natural brown hair black to promote conformity.

Yume Park was created in response to these issues and to accommodate any child in need, or those who do not wish to attend public school for whatever reason. Yume Park's open space approach for children has been referred to as 'free school' by various publications. It does indeed provide children with graduate certification without attendance at formal educational facilities. However, Nishino prefers to call it 'En'—a 'free space' rather than 'free school'—to appeal to children who prefer to think that they are not attending a place called 'school'.

'In "Free Space En", we are creating living space, going shopping, cooking, cleaning. Then, as we spend time together, we learn more about each other and nurture close relationships', says director Nishino.

'"It is nice that you were born, it is nice to see you here, I am glad to know you" is the message we need to transfer to children every day so that they flourish like flowers', he concludes, asserting that Yume Park's mission is the recognition of each person as valuable and worthy, simply by virtue of their existence in this world.

Facilities and Organisation

Yume Park's facilities are described below (see Figure 6.2).

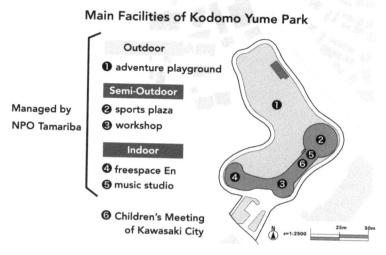

Figure 6.2 Main facilities of Yume Park mentioned in this chapter
Created by Mitsunari Terada, CC BY-NC-ND 4.0

Outdoor

1. Adventure playground. The outdoor space in Yume Park includes a small garden, lots for growing vegetables and parking spaces, etc. as well as one of the biggest adventure playgrounds within the urban sprawl of Tokyo's megalopolis. The adventure playground is equipped with hand-made slides, swings and towers, water pools and mountains of clay-like soil (see Figure 6.3). Various tools and materials, such as hammers, nails, saws, wheelbarrows and lumber, are provided. Playworkers are available to help the children should they need it.

Figure 6.3 Scenery of adventure playground in Yume Park before Covid-19
Photo by Hitoshi Shimamura, CC BY-NC-ND 4.0

2. The sports area is a semi-covered concrete hall (with baskets, gates, a flat floor for ball games, etc.)

Indoor

3. Free Space *En* is managed by NPO Tamariba, an alternative education facility and free school which children attend instead of regular school, a so-called *ibasho* (Tanaka 2021: 7).

4. Music studio

5. Kawasaki City children's meeting room

There is also a garden and farmland on the outside and multiple rooms available for rent and use.

From here on, we will use the umbrella term 'Yume Park' to refer to the entire facility.

Management and Children's Participation Rules in Yume Park

A banner at Yume Park bears the message 'No prohibitions'. Children are encouraged to do whatever they like provided that they do not harm themselves or others. No strict rules are universally applied in Yume Park, but rather rules are created within relationships and situations, and negotiated by participants within those situations. The interviews with the playworkers highlighted that people always question the reasoning behind newly established rules and form a habit of critical thinking, rather than blindly accepting the opinions of others. For example, if one group is playing ball games while younger children also wish to use the space, the older children understand that they must accommodate smaller children.

The Playworker's Role Includes Facilitating Children's Participation

Playworkers perform the facilitating role in the adventure playground. They are involved in the day-to-day management as well as event planning and preparation. They welcome visitors and make them feel at home in addition to stimulating the children's play. As Nishino mentioned, children do not always express themselves verbally, therefore non-verbal communication can be considered participation too. Therefore, children's play in Yume Park is any act of participation.

At least once a day, playworkers attend reflection and planning meetings, where they discuss the children's condition, equipment maintenance and risk management. These meetings are sometimes held indoors in the 'staff only' rooms, but more frequently outside, so that the children do not miss the opportunity to participate in them (see Figure 6.4). The interviews suggest that this 'flexible' system is taken as a given, with no formal guidelines recommending that they 'include the children's voices, which would make it necessary to hold the meetings outdoors'. These participatory meetings were described as occurring naturally, when appropriate, or even spontaneously. The general culture of Yume Park (as a facility committed to the Convention on the Rights of the Child) involves close communication to understand children's needs, and assistance in needs fulfilment by all employees.

The playworkers' routine at Yume Park also includes daily journal entries about the day's occurrences. This system was designed to keep all playworkers working various shifts informed and to facilitate continuity in communication with the children. For example, if Playworker A worked on Monday and learned something important about a child's personal life, feelings and challenges, they could record it in the journal so that Playworker B, working on Tuesday, would be informed about the context. This system ensures continuous support for the children who visit Yume Park on a regular basis. This 'diary' allows the playworkers to record the joys and burdens of the day on paper, thus clearing their minds, as well as allowing them to communicate indirectly with one another.

Figure 6.4 Daily reflections of playworkers outside; children join naturally
Photo courtesy of Kawasaki Kodomo Yume Park, CC BY-NC-ND 4.0

Although the Yume Park facility is a designated children's space, it is managed mainly by adults. However, children are considered among the facility's stakeholders, and are invited to express their opinions on various issues and to manage spaces. It thus appears that children's participation can be facilitated when adults can provide adequate risk management and a safe environment. One of the main roles carried out by the playworkers is risk management: they eliminate hazards and provide a safe space for children's free play. Children can manage risks by themselves; however, hazards (unexpected physical dangers above a certain threat level) must be removed.

However, when adults do not know how to ensure safety, it becomes difficult to create a space suitable for children's play. The director, Nishino, said that Covid-19 offered an opportunity to renew relationships between adults and children because neither group had pandemic experience, and both 'stood at the zero level'. Some might disagree, arguing that adults lost the psychological confidence required to manage the situation, including their primary role of ensuring safety. However, Nishino likely sought to interpret the negative situation in a positive light in a bid to keep spirits high during difficult times and to try to frame the crisis as an opportunity for people to become closer to one another.

In the next section, to contextualize Yume Park's achievement in protecting the child's right to play, we will first offer an overview of Japan's Covid-19 timeline and the local government's response, before characterizing children's play and the general circumstances of Japanese society during the pandemic.

Reflections on Yume Park's Actions to Ensure Freedom of Play

Our contribution focuses on the beginning of the pandemic (March to August 2020), when there was general confusion around how to perform usual activities within a Covid framework. The absence of a clear understanding of how to behave is of the greatest interest in our analysis. Therefore, we have not described autumn 2020, when Yume Park implemented its annual festival or the period post-2021, when the situation stabilized.

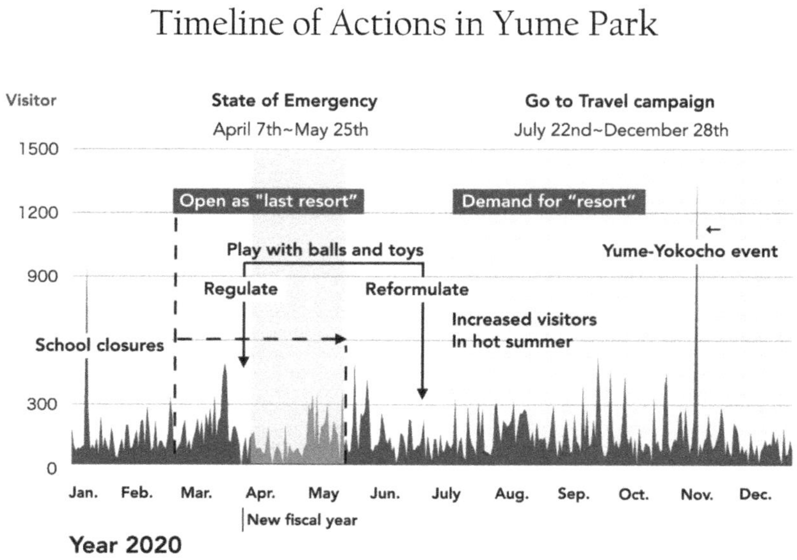

Timeline of Actions in Yume Park

Figure 6.5 Timeline of Yume Park, 2020 (based on data from Kawasaki City)
Created by Mitsunari Terada, CC BY-NC-ND 4.0

At the beginning of March 2020 in Japan, the government imposed restrictions on activities in public facilities in a bid to curb the spread of Covid-19. The closure of public schools was among the first responses. Because Yume Park is a public facility, it too was under consideration for closure. Through the concerted effort of Yume Park representatives and city officers, the facility was kept open as a 'last resort' (see discussion topic A below), with several changes to its rules and functions as preventive measures (see discussion topics B, C and D below). This decision was based on an understanding of Yume Park's importance as a place for Kawasaki's most vulnerable children and families. Yume Park's director also used various media—television, newspapers, social networks—to emphasize the importance of supporting children with such facilities during the pandemic. Under the first emergency call, the number of users declined compared to the usual figures, but some children continued to visit, as it was their 'space'.

From the end of Golden Week—a series of holidays clustered and observed at the end of April and beginning of May in Japan—the number of visitors to Yume Park increased (see Figure 6.5). Once the school year started, the number of visitors stabilized. However, with the hot summer that followed and pandemic-related regulations—including the advice to stay home—people turned to Yume Park as an accessible recreational space. Playworkers perceived this tendency as a misuse of Yume Park, believing that it was being treated as a holiday 'resort'. The playworkers were risking their lives supporting children's play in the context of the stressful restrictions (see Section C below). Yume Park had to impose measures to prevent overcrowding and adjust its ethos accordingly (see Section D below).

Discussion of Topics Emerging from Interviews

The discussion that follows is based on four themes (A–D) that emerged from interviews with Yume Park's playworkers and leaders.

A. Should Children's Facilities Be Open for Play Rights in Uncertain Times?

As we mentioned in the introduction, many public facilities for children were closed, especially in the beginning of the pandemic in 2020. This is an understandable measure to avoid spread of infection. Within these circumstances, the attempt to ensure safety for all by imposing stay-at-home policies posed the risk that some children would become unsafe.

Therefore, Yume Park's solution was to remain open to support children's rights. This decision is also supported by the International Play Association, which underlines the importance of play in crisis as a coping mechanism (International Play Association 2020).

In March 2020, as Japan was formulating its emergency measures, Yume Park was preparing to keep its doors open. It was clear to Nishino that those children whose need for care and support was greatest might lose a place where they could go and talk. He argued that Yume Park should be kept open as 'the last resort' (*saigo no toride*—literally, 'the last fortress') in an interview with NHK, Japan's public media channel, that was later quoted in newspapers (NHK 2021). Nishino understood that children and parents were facing a particularly difficult situation, and many caregivers told playworkers that Yume Park was the only place in which they felt safe. In the Group Gendai documentary, one mother told the camera, 'The children wanted to play outside. They were quite aggressive, having to stay home, punching the walls. It was difficult'.

Another female visitor told the camera, 'The apartment owner told us off because we are so noisy as a family. It was difficult, so we decided to come to Yume Park from time to time. So if there were no place like this, that would be just unbearable'. Considering society's failure to acknowledge children's needs to play, to make noise and to simply be, whether in their apartments or outdoors, Yume Park offered a crucial source of support during the pandemic. Interviewees often mentioned 'other people's eyes', which, in Japanese, means the attention and pressure from other community members.

Director Nishino pointed out in his interview,

> Children usually cannot ask for help by words, so they give us signals by their body language—strange movements or irritation. So when the environment turns against children, as in the case of Covid restrictions, we had to keep the place open, in order for children to have a place to be. Because, as I said, children can't ask for help or advice by words, usually, you know, so if they just have a place to be, where someone listens and pays attention to them, that's the way to help them.

With this argument, he described his determination at the beginning of the pandemic in 2020 as follows:

> At the end of February, when I heard that the government planned to close public schools, I went to the city office and spoke to the officers: 'We need Yume Park open now more than ever before'. They understood. Because it was established in accordance with the Child's Right to Play Article, they accepted my request.

Some playworkers were hesitant at the beginning of 2020, as the growing panic and uncertainty caused much confusion. Announcements (Japanese cities have speakers installed throughout them for such announcements in case of disasters) sounded daily, with the message urging citizens to 'PLEASE STAY HOME'. However, learning directly from children and parents, the playworkers gradually acknowledged the need to keep Yume Park's gates open:

> During Covid times, children reported increased abuse from parents, and parenthood difficulties were reported by parents. We created a time and space for people to come and talk about these

issues in their family—parents in trouble, children in trouble. There was a news report about a son who attacked a family with a knife, so it was very scary to hear.

Some playworkers shared Nishino's determination from the outset.

The discussion about the necessity to keep Yume Park open relates closely to the following two themes: making new rules and the burden of working during the reality of a pandemic.

B. Controversy of Encouraging Interactive Play within Social Distance Requirements

During the pandemic, playworkers shouldered a heavy burden. First, they risked infection while working 'in the field' with visitors, and second, they were responsible for comforting the children. At the time, no one considered that the burden for playworkers might be too great. One of the playworkers reflected:

> When the coronavirus struck, we all suddenly became more distant, because we had to keep our distance, as the officials recommended. We did not have experience of pandemic situations, so we relied on recommendations like wearing masks, not talking, keeping our distance. So, we found ourselves quite isolated—less personal communication took place between staff, and a kind of alienation developed.

Three of the playworkers interviewed had worked at the park for four years, while the others had worked there for ten and six years. Regardless of their age, they were experienced playworkers.

The most difficult aspect for playworkers was losing their role of encouraging children's play:

> I felt that I had lost my very essence, to support children's play and encourage them—I could not do that. When I tried to speak to one visitor, she rolled her eyes at me—"What nonsense to speak in a pandemic!"—her face said to me. I was losing confidence in my role and the sense of meaning in being there.

It is clear that the playworkers experienced an identity crisis amid the anti-Covid measures, as their normal actions—facilitating communication between people and the environment—could cause transmission, spreading the virus among visitors. They were losing their role. Additionally, as the new school year began in April, it was difficult to establish relationships with the new children, with fewer opportunities for talk and interaction in the context of 'social distancing' (see Figure 6.6).

A playworker shared her thoughts about the stress of working during 2020:

> I live with my elderly parents and take the train to work every day. So, every time I put my family's lives at risk, not only in the park, meeting visitors, but also on the way home. It was hard, constantly being afraid of getting infected and passing it on to someone else.

Another playworker who had been working in Yume Park for ten years said:

> At the time, I was so scared so I was thinking it would be good to get the coronavirus quickly—I hoped to get immunity and relief from being afraid.

Another male playworker also said that he feared becoming infected because he travelled to work on an overcrowded train.

A female playworker shared her concerns about childhoods in the pandemic:

> Who will take the responsibility for these children growing up without touch? We were thinking together with the children, what is it to live? We thought about it, being just a heartbeat, but without relationships with people, is that a life?

During the interviews with playworkers, we discovered that they did not discuss their own feelings much during the most hectic times. Although they continued to record daily occurrences in the journals, they never discussed their own doubts, fears, and despondencies, likely due to the diary's public nature and its informative function. The playworkers themselves only realized retrospectively that they were psychologically exhausted.

Figure 6.6 Children play on water slide in 2016 and in 2020 with social distancing
Photo courtesy of Kawasaki Kodomo Yume Park, CC BY-NC-ND 4.0

C. The Need for New Rules at Odds with the Usual Policy of Yume Park

Supporting children's play rights, Yume Park succeeded in staying open with zero infection in the facility. As before the pandemic, children had a place to play. However, it was crucial that facility managers reacted quickly to ensure safety and to limit some play activities without negotiating new rules with children as they would usually do. Reasons for this were: time limitations, pressure from society (all other facilities were closed), uncertainty regarding the dynamics of the virus spread, and an urge to comply with governmental policies like the 'state of emergency'.

During spring vacation and school closures, many schoolchildren from around the neighbourhood came to play ball games, as they used to do in public school at *bukatsu*—(club activities in Japanese schools, from *bu*, 'club' and *katsu*, 'activity'). In many public parks, especially in the Tokyo metropolitan area, there is a high rate of ball game prohibition (Terada and Kinoshita 2020: 52). However, playworkers soon realized that the risk of spreading the virus was high with up to fifty children running close together and fighting for the ball. The playworkers' struggle to impose prohibitions is evident in the following passage:

The junior high schoolers were coming to play basketball in big groups, and when I approached them to ask them not to play and explained that many people were touching the same ball and moving closely together, they asked me, 'why then is it ok to use the carpenter's tools in the adventure playground?' I did not know how to resolve this issue, and I felt it was dangerous because the number of people infected was growing by the hour at this time and I was worried that we would have to close it [Yume Park] if a virus cluster occurred. And I strongly felt it was a place for people who have no other place to be, mostly, you know, for them we keep it open, and these claims from schoolchildren who wanted to play basketball were a little irritating to hear. I had to make judgements relying on my estimation and analysis. For example, today this child needs this the most, so it is OK to allow him/her to do this and that. We had to make many decisions every day, taking responsibility. We were constantly puzzled and troubled by the necessity to decide what was good and what was bad in each situation.

Of course, it would have been easier if everything had been definitively decided all at once. However, this is not how Yume Park works. As noted above, the rules in Yume Park are flexible, situated and bound up in relationships. Typically, they are changed and acknowledged based on negotiation and reasoning. However, during a pandemic, changes to rules must be implemented swiftly: from 4 April, visitors were no longer permitted to use balls and toys, whether rented or their own. Exceptionally in Yume Park's history, rules were changing from day to day and these changes were implemented from the top down.

For playworkers, one of the key questions was 'Can we accept that adults should determine the rules of children's facilities to minimize the risk of Covid-19?' One playworker spoke of early April, before the announcement of Japan's national state of emergency on 7 April:

It seemed that there was no choice but to accept the 'no balls, no toys' policy, because a state of emergency would be announced soon. Should we have asked the children's opinions, even though there was no possibility of changing the rules at that time?

At the time, playworkers still did not know how to enforce appropriate safety measures against the virus, so the strictest safety was necessary. Nonetheless, as play professionals, they thought constantly about how best to support children's rights to play and participate.

Amid the regulations, children began creating new forms of play in spite of the limitations. For example, they made paper balls instead of using the prohibited basketballs or footballs. Soon, paper balls were also regulated, so children started balancing on the pipe to keep their distance from each other and touching the ball with a stick, etc.

During the first months of Covid-19, from March to May, rules were swiftly decided without the children's participation. However, in June several factors led to their re-formulation. First, children were persistent in their desire to play and were constantly questioning the rules, seeking to compromise play and safety measures, and so a series of discussions between children and playworkers took place (see Figure 6.7). Second, Yume Park's culture prioritizes children's voices in deciding new rules. Owing to this culture of children's participation in rulemaking, Yume Park reinstated the mechanism for constantly updating the rules regarding balls and toys, depending on the situation.

Figure 6.7 Children and playworkers reformulating the rules together in the adventure playground

Photo courtesy of Kawasaki Kodomo Yume Park, CC BY-NC-ND 4.0

D. Dealing with Conflict: When 'Last Resort' Turns into 'Just a Resort'

From the end of July, with the arrival of the hot weather, playworkers observed a growing demand for outdoor play and increased visitor numbers. As a consequence of the prevalent shaming culture, many people travelled from other prefectures, trying to escape their neighbourhoods' watchful eyes so that they could enjoy outdoor play secretly. Others turned to Yume Park because other recreational facilities were closed, and travelling by train or plane was considered a step too far. More and more people came to have 'picnics', as Yume Park was officially open and welcoming visitors as a self-proclaimed 'last resort', whereas local Tokyo parks still advised that people refrain from visiting.

It seemed to the playworkers that Yume Park was being overused. First, huge visitor numbers prevented the formation of close relationships. Second, people's lack of familiarity with the culture of the playground led to misunderstanding and stress on both sides: people behaved like customers in a shopping centre, asking for and ordering tools or playground features, for example. Yume Park was turning into a 'resort' in which a kaleidoscopic array of consumers needed to be served quickly and to their full satisfaction. Furthermore, the pandemic was not yet over and preventive measures, such as social distancing and mask wearing, were still in place.

This loss of human interaction in the adventure playground had been unpleasant but necessary. As a result, the playworkers created communication boards and duplicated the playground equipment. Signs were erected to explain the playground's functions and rules, thereby avoiding direct communication so as to help prevent the spread of Covid. These signs reminded visitors not to eat, drink or picnic on the facility and to stay for no more than three hours at once. The duplication of playground equipment reduced the load on single structures and minimized the density of queues for each structure.

The various users had different situations: some had nowhere safe to be; others had no place to picnic and were bored at home. Everybody wanted to go outdoors and enjoy the opportunity to play freely. Demands for outdoor play should be satisfied accordingly but, in the case of Yume Park, the playworkers felt that the 'last resort' status was being 'misused'. Playworkers, faced with the risk of Covid-19 infection, with up to seven hundred visitors per day, felt conflicted.

Conclusion

In this chapter we have shared Yume Park's effort to remain open to ensure the fulfilment of children's rights, focusing on the beginning of the pandemic in 2020 (approximately March to August). Currently, in 2022, Yume Park still has zero recorded cases of Covid-19 and successfully implemented annual events like Yume Yokocho Festival (where children create their own shops and sell products) in 2020 and 2021.

Current Yume Park director Tomokane said, 'We don't want to show the attitude that we cannot do things because of Covid; we want to show how we can do things, even in the pandemic. It is because children are living right now'. Play is about actively engaging with the world and creativity is about finding a way to do something. If adults find reasons to be passive because of Covid, children may as well lose hope.

School closures during lockdowns increased demand for outdoor play facilities and compelled Yume Park managers and playworkers to impose limitations and rules without the usual negotiation process during the first months of restrictions. They were then adjusted in response to the evolving situation, which enabled a re-negotiation with the children, in accordance with the facility's human-centred culture. This was made possible thanks to the selfless efforts of the playworkers who, often neglecting their own psychological needs, continued to go to work and make decisions on the ground, within the framework of a roughly designated safety zone. Rules were developed with the children's input based on foundational information about the virus, and measures, such as minimum social distancing between people or the need to sterilise one's hands with alcohol, were incorporated into the park's day-to-day running.

Covid-19 was a new challenge that forced adults to consider how they could support the child's right to play in a new environment, for which the potential to apply previous experience was limited. The interviews with Yume Park's managers and playworkers revealed that the park's staff have a strong sense of its identity, support children's rights, and are willing to endure hardship in pursuit of this mission. This was made possible through daily meetings, reflections, and discussions, in a practice and culture that had been applied and nurtured for almost two decades. The Covid emergency confirmed that a strategy that may previously be seen as highly idealistic was in fact useful when a pandemic required people to reflect and adapt regularly.

Works Cited

Group Gendai. 2021. *Documentary Series about Yume Park during Pandemic*, https://youtu.be/j9gRT9A_s-0

Katafuchi, Yuya, Kenichi Kurita, and Managi Shunsuke. 2021. 'COVID-19 with Stigma: Theory and Evidence from Mobility Data', *Economics of Disasters and Climate Change*, 5: 71–95, https://doi.org/10.1007/s41885-020-00077-w

Kinoshita, Isami. 2007. 'Children's Participation in Japan: An Overview of Municipal Strategies and Citizen Movements', *Children, Youth and Environments*, 17: 269-86

Ministry of Health, Labour and Welfare of Japan and others. 2021. *Suicide Situation in 2020*, https://www.mhlw.go.jp/content/R2kakutei-01.pdf

Nagata, Yoshiyuki. 2016. 'Fostering Alternative Education in Society: The Caring Communities of "Children's Dream Park" and "Free Space En" in Japan', in *The Palgrave International Handbook of Alternative Education*, ed. Helen E. Lees and Nel Noddings (London: Palgrave Macmillan), pp. 241-56

National Centre for Child Health and Development. 2021. *National Online Survey of Children's Well-being During the COVID-19 Pandemic in Japan*, https://www.ncchd.go.jp/center/activity/covid19_kodomo/report/digestreport_en.html

NHK [Japan Broadcasting Corporation]. 2021. *Children's Dream Park: About Children Who Do Not Attend School*, https://www.nhk.or.jp/shutoken/yokohama/article/000/66/

International Play Association, 2020. *Play in Crisis*, https://ipaworld.org/resources/for-parents-and-carers-play-in-crisis/

Tanaka, Haruhiko. 2021. 'Development of the *Ibasho* Concept in Japanese Education and Youth Work: *Ibasho* as a Place of Refuge and Empowerment for Excluded People', *Educational Studies in Japan*, 15: 3-15, https://doi.org/10.7571/esjkyoiku.15.3

Terada, Mitsunari, and Isami Kinoshita. 2020. 'Research on Local Governmental Restrictions for Ball Play in Block Parks', *Landscape Research Japan Online*, 13: 52–58, https://doi.org/10.5632/jilaonline.13.52

Terada, Mitsunari, and Hitoshi Shimamura. 2020. 'Finally Got Free Time? Could Public Spaces Reverse Children's Play-Deficit in Post-Pandemic Japan?' Unpublished conference paper presented at the 'IPA-World Play and Public Place Seminar, 4: State of Play in Cities'

PORTRAITS

'Cough'
Drawing on schoolyard fence, Philadelphia, 1 July 2021
Photo by Anna Beresin, CC BY-NC 4.0

7. Objects of Resilience: Plush Perspectives on Pandemic Toy Play[1]

Katriina Heljakka

Introduction

'Objects embody unique information about the nature of man in society', writes Susan Pearce (1994: 125). Relations with material things have powerful consequences for human experience, as objects serve to express dynamic processes within people, and between people and the total environment (Csikszentmihalyi and Rochberg-Halton 1981). All three-dimensional objects are active instruments of communication, and in particular of non-verbal communication (Volonté 2010).

During a certain age in the child's development, 'artefacts become its principal means of articulating feelings and desires' (Miller 1987: 99). Following Piaget's idea of thinking with and through objects is a feature of childhood that adults abandon (Eberle 2009). Nevertheless, from infancy onwards, we are not only touching objects but are also being touched by objects.

This chapter takes an interest in the role of soft toys and meaning making in relation to them in play during the Covid-19 health crisis. Toys are the material artefacts of play. However, toys, Rossie explains, are frequently described as objects and not as instruments of play. For

---

1   This research was conducted in affiliation with the University of Turku's Pori Laboratory of Play, Finland.

this reason, the play activity is not analyzed with the same care as the toy itself (Rossie 2005). The chapter at hand takes an interest in how plush toys have been used in play during the ongoing pandemic and attempts to analyze the play patterns and player motivations with the same care given to the toys under scrutiny.

To 'play with' an object is to experience the satisfaction of trying to control it (Henricks 2006). Sometimes playing with toys extends beyond the physical manipulation and control of objects into the meanings created and communicated about human matters. Earlier work suggests how concepts such as play value and toy play experiences can be analyzed. First, toys as designed objects may accrue meanings and play value in terms of their aesthetics, ergonomics of use, age appropriateness, durability, safety, educational affordances and entertainment value (Heljakka 2013). Second, experiences in relation to toys, and toy play in particular, may be structured by using a framework with physical, functional, fictive and affective dimensions (Paavilainen and Heljakka 2018). Contemporary toys as three-dimensional, material playthings may in other words be considered as *physical* entities that can be manipulated in terms of object play. Usually, the toys are *functional* in terms of both their playability—they are intended to be used in play of some kind and afford, for example, possibilities to pose and display them in different ways. Toys of the contemporary kind often also include a *fictional* aspect—they may due to their personality as character toys have a backstory of some kind. In the simplest sense, they may have a name and a personality described in a few sentences. On the other hand, they can be tied to transmedia franchises or story worlds. Toys are also objects and vehicles which communicate emotions (Shillito 2011). Therefore, the toy play experience usually includes an *affective* component, which means that the player forms an emotional bond with the plaything. The study presented in this chapter demonstrates how all of the aforementioned dimensions of toy experiences are relevant, when considering their use in the context of play during the pandemic.

In Western societies, toys are mass-produced objects often tied to transmedia phenomena and popular storytelling. The chapter focuses on a universally recognized character toy with connections to news media and has long-standing roots in the history of toy making and play with plush toys—the teddy bear. The teddy bear is the world's first mass-marketed toy (Leclerc 2008) and one of the most recognized and popular character toys universally. In 1998, the teddy bear was elected to the Strong National Museum of Play's National Toy Hall of Fame (Strong Museum n.d.). The year 2002 was celebrated in North America, Europe and Asia as the hundredth birthday of the origin of the teddy bear (Varga 2009). At the time of writing this chapter, the teddy bear is celebrating its 120th birthday as one of the oldest transmedial toy phenomena.

The teddy bear and its 'huggability' results from a long evolution from the first, more 'realistic' bears marketed by toy makers Mitchom and Steiff in the early 1900s to 'the teddy bears we came to know and love look more like cubs, rounded, wide-eyed, big-eared, stubby-limbed, and most important, needy' (Eberle 2009: 74; for extensive research on the teddy bear's origins and evolution, see Varga 2009). As discussed in this chapter, teddy bears and other 'cutified' plush suggest a need to be cuddled and nurtured but, as proposed in the chapter, also have the capacity to 'give back' by providing their human counterparts crucial playful support and a communicative means in times of crisis.

The Sensory, Sentimental and Survivalist Potentiality of Plush

The aim of this chapter is to deepen the understanding of object play during the beginning and continuation of the Covid-19 pandemic. By focusing on play patterns with soft toys or plush, as these toy characters are sometimes referred to in the North-American context, the author strives to form an understanding of the relevance of these toys for 'pandemic toy play' (Heljakka 2020).

Toys are most often associated with childhood and considered as suitable gifts for a child: 'These small objects, pretty or ugly, clean or dirty, are a comfort to a child, often a best and closest friend' (de Sarigny 1971: 6). As Fleming notes, 'toys are infinitely adaptable and can take on meanings other than those they originally came with' (1996: 67). Indeed, children have a way of doing things with toys over and beyond the apparent character of the toy (Sutton-Smith 1986). Toys can and do have dual function, one in the minds of adults and another in the culture of children (Chudacoff 2007).

What makes toys particularly valuable artefacts for the child is the fact that they may become transitional objects in the child's relationship with its mother, relationships with the world of things and other people (Sutton-Smith 1986). Donald Winnicott (1896-1971) is one of the most influential theorists on object play. Winnicott's conception of transitional objects highlights the psychological significance of the child's early 'not-me' objects: for example, the attachment the child forms to a soft toy (Crozier 1994).

The transitional space between mother and child both connects and separates them. It is the 'either-or' or the 'neither-nor'. Soft toys may help the child to move away from the mother by operating as substitutes for maternal presence. They are loved fiercely, and, in the strongest instances, never leave the child (Ivy 2010). What Winnicott notes about this relation between the human self and the material object is that it 'establishes here an underdetermined space, a blur between fantasy and reality' (Marks-Tarlow 2010: 43).

Doll designer Käthe Kruse maintained that the way to a child's heart was not through the eyes in the form of a perfectly miniaturized doll, but through its hands in the shape of a soft toy (Reinelt 1988). According to 'Dr Toy', Stevanne Auerbach, the ideal toy relationship is 'that the child not only enjoys it from the beginning, but they want to go back to the toy, that they get attached to it, a teddy bear' (Heljakka 2013: 175).

Long-term relationships with toys are formed with those characters that communicate vulnerability and call out for nurturing and care: '[soft toy animals,] in so far as they are humanized, in the sense of being endowed by a child and parents with human qualities, including the ability to 'look back', to communicate and to receive communications, they share the function of companion and friend, protector and protected' (Newson and Newson 1979: 90). Moreover, stuffed toy animals are stimulating, visual and material playthings. The connection between the player and the plush can be soothing. In play with soft toys the sensory stimuli extend to emotional attachment between the player and the toy. In this way, plush toys function as a source of communication (Auerbach 2004).

Earlier literature on teddy bears acknowledges them as 'ambassadors of love', which have evolved from being a mother substitute to an adult fetish, an item of adult idolatry resulting from commercial nostalgic production of the teddies in the post-1950s (Varga 2009: 72; 76). These soft toys especially may, in their players' hands and minds, turn into personalities, inanimate friends and quiet confidants who have their place on our shelves, sofas and even—in our hearts.

Ruckenstein (2011) proposes that toys could be thought of in terms of their potentiality. The goal of this chapter is to investigate how this potentiality materializes in plush characters which often represent commercial playthings. Cook describes how commercial objects are believed to retain 'some kind of taint that renders inauthentic most any practice associated with it. [...] It is artificial because it was borne of, and exists in the realm of commercial goods and commodity production' (2009: 90). Nevertheless, Belk has noted how even contemporary mass-produced objects may be thought to have 'magical' properties, from the capacity to protect their owners from harm to the capacity to cure, empower and bring good luck (Belk 1991; cf. Crozier 1994). The potentiality of toys manifests on one level in their supposed 'liveliness', achieved through animism and the human tendency to anthropomorphize.

Animism, the belief that objects, animals and plants have spiritual lives of their own, connects with the idea of bringing toys to life. In this tradition of thinking, objects are given agency so that the manipulable object is believed to encompass supernatural qualities. Again, anthropomorphizing refers to the tendency of attributing a human form or personality to things that are not human. Humans are predisposed to anthropomorphize, to project human emotions and beliefs on to anything (Norman 2004). In terms of relationships with toys, this tendency to 'animate the inanimate' is also visible in adult toy play (Heljakka 2013).

Anthropomorphization is extended to all sorts of objects: 'the toys that emerge from the toy cupboard are all granted mobility, feelings, and desires' (Kuznets 1994: 144). Karl Groos writes in the *Play of Man*, 'the child playing with the doll raises the lifeless thing temporarily to a place of a symbol of life. He lends the doll his own soul whenever he answers a question for it: he lends to it his feelings, conceptions and aspirations' (Groos and Baldwin 2010 [1901]: 203).

Plush toys tend to attract players of many ages. Toy types such as traditional, animal-themed soft toys, and toy characters that lean on the fantastic in their aesthetics, seem to cater best to the request for gender-neutrality (Heljakka 2013). The popularity of teddy bears is not limited by gender. Cross explains the allure of the teddy bear for wider audiences of players, including young males: 'Unlike the doll, long linked with girls' gender role-playing, the bear has had wild and primitive "boyish" associations, thus making it appropriate for male companionship' (2004: 53). According to the survey conducted by the hotel chain Travelodge in Britain and Spain, a large number of 'bear-toting travelers are men'. The hotel had, over twelve months, 'reunited more than 75 000 bears with their owners' (Mayerowitz 2010). The study conducted in Britain in 2010 revealed that twenty-five percent of the men who answered the survey said that they take their teddy bear away with them on business trips because it reminds them of home (Mayerowitz 2010).

Throughout the times when toys have been produced industrially, adults have used them as bribes, instruments for bonding and affection (Chudacoff 2007). Adult imagination in connection to character toys of the contemporary kind results often in relational interactions with the teddy bear toy (Varga 2009).

The teddy bear is considered an emotional plaything that brings comfort to its owner, no matter the age or gender of the player. Doll researcher Jaqueline Fulmer has discovered that there are many Americans who creatively express their identity through the medium of dolls (including soft toys like teddy bears) and that they constitute a thriving and diverse subculture with the potential of connecting people during a crisis (2009).

'Why should children be the only ones to enjoy stuffed animals?', Dr. Toy Stevanne Auerbach rightly asks (2004: 112). During the Covid-19 pandemic, teddy bears and other plush animals have illustrated the ability to bind people—children, adults and seniors—together during crisis. By introducing the #teddychallenge, the first goal of this chapter is to accentuate teddy bears' potentiality as playthings with intergenerational appeal. The second is to illustrate how plush toys, in particular, continue to thrive as objects that channel a survivalist attitude—a theme of interest to past and present investigations of teddy bears.

'Name a social, health or environmental disaster and the teddy follows', Donna Varga aptly claims (2009: 81). Indeed, plush animals have been employed in both moments of collective mourning as well as deliberate trauma management, as for instance with *trauma teddies*, used in association with mass disasters in Australia during the devastating bushfires of 2019-2022. The idea of trauma teddies is that emergency personnel carry them around to give to children and adults who have experienced trauma.

To conquer despair, teddy bears have also been used to commemorate national tragedies, such as the car crash death of the United Kingdom's Princess Diana (Varga 2009: 79, 81; Fulmer 2009: 92). In fact, Varga notes how the teddy is reified as a therapeutic artefact that is able to provide *bearapy* (2009: 72; 79). Cook positions the teddy bear as 'a readily recognizable symbol of loss and object of comfort' (2009: 89) which, according to Sturken, 'make[s] us feel better about the way things are' by its presence alone (2007: 7). In this way, teddies fill their function to serve humans in practical and existential ways—as comforters to hug and as bearers of hope to hold on to.

From allowing sensory and sentimental gratification, plush creatures move on to promote survival in the name of toy activism. Earlier work on serious uses of toys presents the possibility of using character toys in 'toy activism'. Toy activism, as formulated by Heljakka, refers to harnessing character toys, such as dolls, action figures and animal characters, including various soft toys, to make visible or to promote a political, ethical or emphatic goal (2020, 2021).

Toy activism is not a new phenomenon. In the 1980s, giving teddy bears to AIDS sufferers was a means of extending contact in an indirect way to the forbidden bodies of the ill and the dying. Originally these were personal gifts but, by the end of the decade, they had become an essential part of the growth of AIDS activism (Harris 1994: 55-56; cf. Varga 2009: 79). The findings of the study presented in this chapter aim to highlight the important continuous and active role of toys in fighting the negative effects of a global health crisis through toy play and, in particular, the seemingly endless presence of the teddy bear in times of crisis.

Method

Play has been studied via diverse methods, such as observation in a natural environment, observation in a structured environment, interviews and questionnaires, and examinations of toy inventories, pictures and photographic records, or other evidence of children's play (Smith 2010). In this study, object play is addressed and analyzed in the light of the empirical data collected from different sources, namely media articles, personal interviews conducted online and 'live' toy photography posted on Twitter, Facebook, and Instagram, following the idea of triangulation (see, for example, Stake 1995).

In order to study the phenomenon of the Teddy Challenge, the author conducted a research trilogy with phases performed in March-April 2020, June-July 2020, and the spring of 2021. First, the study sought to map out the phenomenon by analyzing articles collected online from news media in Finland, the USA and the UK. Second, online interviews with seven toy players from Finland, the UK and Singapore were carried out in order to find out about toy play patterns in general during the lockdown period of spring-summer 2020. Third, and finally, the study analyzed pandemic toy play during the second wave of the Covid-19 virus in Finland through a thematic analysis of a new set of online toy photographs relating to the replaying of the #teddychallenge and shared by regional Finnish news media in March-April 2021.

Data collection	Phase of study	Analysis
100 toy photographs, photo-play (or toy photography) posted on Twitter, Facebook or Instagram during March–April 2020 with the hashtag #nallejahti [#teddychallenge] 13 media articles, including newspaper articles and other media materials such as blog writings (4 international and 9 Finnish) March–April 2020	*First phase of study, March–April 2020*	The researcher conducted a visual content analysis on the materials by investigating: where (indoors/outdoors) and how the teddy/teddies were displayed (posed and positioned), how many teddies were in the photograph, and if there were recognizable elements of storytelling in the photographs, such as combinations of props, clothing etc. (visual elements) or written messages (verbal elements). The researcher conducted a thematic analysis on the materials by investigating how the media articles defined the teddy challenge. This part of the research was reported in a publication (Heljakka 2020).

7 qualitative interviews with examples of photo-play (or toy photography) were conducted online with adult toy players (all female, aged 30–75 years) from Finland, UK, and Singapore	*Second phase of study, July 2020*	The researcher asked the following questions: 1. *Did you participate in the teddy challenge in spring–summer 2020?* 2. *Tell me about your toy play activities during March–June 2020?* 3. *Please send examples of photo-play created during the Covid-19 pandemic.* The interviewees were requested to send in examples of their own photo-play created during the Covid-19 pandemic. The answers and instances of photo-play were scrutinized with the help of content analysis. The themes were then linked to the topics of resistance, resourcefulness, and resilience as identified in the first phase of the study. This part of the research was reported in a publication (Heljakka 2021).
260 toy photographs, photo-play (or toy photography) published in newspaper SK in March-April 2021 related to its localized teddy challenge with an interest in mobilizing the toys Three media articles covering the localized challenge	*Third phase of study, March–April 2021/2022*	The researcher conducted a visual content analysis on the materials by investigating: where (indoors/outdoors) and how the teddy/teddies were displayed (posed and positioned), how many teddies were in the photograph, and if there were recognizable elements of storytelling in the photographs, such as combinations of props, clothing etc. (visual elements) or written messages, such as captions written for the photo-play (verbal elements). The researcher conducted a thematic analysis on the materials by investigating how the media articles defined and depicted the results of the localized teddy challenge. The findings of this sub-study are reported in the chapter at hand.

Figure 7.1 Data collection and analysis: Methods used for the three-part study

Liberated through Toys: Three Stages of Pandemic Toy Play Investigated

Unusual and uncertain times seem to influence toy design to produce novel playthings. Toys focusing on development of prosocial tendencies, such as empathy, emerged in the 2000s, but the beginning of the Covid-19 pandemic caused an upsurge in the toy market's offering of character toys depicting figurines and dolls as action heroes serving as guardians of our well-being. For example, in response to the ongoing health crisis, Mattel launched a series called Fisher-Price *Thank You Heroes*, including collections of plastic play figures consisting of series of nurses, doctors, delivery drivers and emergency medical technicians, as well as a series of 'community champions', 'who work hard every day to help us stay healthy, safe and stocked with everything we need'. Furthermore, in 2021 the company launched a Barbie toy portrait of the real doctor Sarah Gilbert, a developer of the Covid-19 vaccine (Reuters 2021).

Instead of new toys that draw their design inspiration from the human heroes of the ongoing pandemic, the study explained in this chapter focuses on a universally recognized and loved plaything—the teddy bear. Teddy bear plush can be found in many homes and can consequently be considered a sustainable toy which represents long-term play value for players of many ages. According to an article published in the *Telegraph*, more than half of Britons still have a teddy bear from childhood and the average teddy bear is twenty-seven years old (Telegraph 2010). Besides their role as domestic artefacts with decorative and affective value, teddy bears have featured in professional portraiture of children. Plush toys have been deliberately used as props in portrait photographs—the practice of photographing a child with his or her favourite teddy bear, for example, was common by 1907 (Walsh 2005).

In the contemporary world, plush characters come alive in 'photo-play' (toy photography), a popular play pattern associated mainly with character toys, such as dolls, action figures and soft toys, dependent on camera technologies, social sharing and most of all the creativity and imagination of the players. The largest part of contemporary photo-play illustrates character toys displayed in arrangements of various sorts.

The making of toy displays requires versatile physical properties and mechanical affordances of the toys, such as articulated limbs which are either overstuffed for sturdiness or have an overtly soft stuffing to achieve a slouchy and huggable appearance. The design of teddy bears has made them poseable from the beginning. The poseability of teddy bears differentiated them from the early commercial dolls that were mostly made of wood, composition or porcelain—the teddy bear was a more 'huggable' toy from the beginning (Walsh 2005).

The photo-play explained in the following section has made use of the teddy bear's affordances in terms of aesthetics and poseability. In other words, they allow creative and experiential toy photography due to their articulation and looks which, combined with current camera technologies, breathe life into the toys and invite anthropomorphization of the playthings. Photo-play is central for analyses of #teddychallenge, which took place in three consecutive phases of study, elaborated on in the next sections of the chapter.

Figure 7.2 Photo-played display of three plush toys taking part in the #teddychallenge, 2020

Photo by Katriina Heljakka, CC BY-NC 4.0

Ludounity: The #teddychallenge as Playing for the Common Good

Long before the Covid-19 pandemic, Donna Varga wrote about 'the attempt to replace the dearth of social contact with a material object' (Varga 2009: 81). Approximately ten years after Varga's foundational research on teddy bear cultures was published, teddies and other plush toys appeared in window screens as a firsthand, communal reaction to the uncertainties presented by the new health crises in association with the outbreak of the Covid-19 virus. The simultaneous occurrence of teddy bear displays in many countries, and even different continents, accentuated the human need for participatory play, the essentiality of photo-play and the social sharing of the activity. The play pattern was also accompanied by a gamified goal—a challenge based on the spotting of teddies offline in windows of houses and online through the screens of mobile devices and social media that attracted players of different ages. Inviting children and adults to create, narrativize and hunt for toy displays, the #teddychallenge became a popular phenomenon widely covered by the media across the globe.

While players could take part in the challenge online by looking at the toy displays photographed and shared by others on social media, offline participation in the #teddychallenge began with setting up a display of toys in a window. In Daniel Miller's view, a visual display is always complemented by the possibility of a story (Miller 2008) and the visually displayed stories of teddy bears are a documented part of early commercial toy history. An example of this is the fact that 'after the 1912 Titanic sinking, Steiff produced black mourning bears; these were part of a window display at Harrods and for sale' (Cockrill 2001; cf. Varga 2009: 76).

The first phase of the study examined the phenomenon of the teddy challenge, analyzing its motivations, messages and manifestations. As a physically and spatially emerging form of play, it was perceived as a gesture of solitary play. Moreover, there was a strong social statement lurking behind the window screens, a form of toy activism that sent out a message about the mental and creative agility and empowerment of players living in quarantine. The motivation for the teddy challenge, then, was to join forces in the name of social play. The message of the

#teddychallenge was a pledge for togetherness. Finally, the manifestations were as creative as the players in terms of their skills in handicrafts, storytelling, displaying wit or willingness to place toys centre-stage with the purpose of functioning as stand-ins and spokespersons. The first phase of research revealed *playing for the common good* as a strategy for surviving a socially challenging moment in time. In the beginning of the pandemic, the world was at (toy) play for 'ludounity' (Heljakka 2020).

Intergenerationality: The #teddychallenge as an Intergenerational Play Practice

According to Bengtson, multigenerational relationships will be more important in the twenty-first century for three reasons: a) demographic changes of an ageing population, b) the importance of grandparents fulfilling family functions, and c) the strength of intergenerational solidarity over time (Bengtson 2001; cf. Cohen and Waite-Stupiansky 2012). The second phase of research on the #teddychallenge included interview material and photo-play from participants in three countries and demonstrated how resistance, resourcefulness and playful resilience appeared in toy play during the Covid-19 pandemic as an intergenerational practice with solitary and social qualities (Heljakka 2021). Pandemic toy play, employing teddy bears and other toy friends during the spring and summer of 2020, illustrated how playthings were displayed, narrated, photo-played and shared on social media to counteract experiences of loneliness and isolation by communicating positive playful messages of emotional survival. Players of different ages joined in the teddy challenge as displayers, spectators or social media activists, demonstrating how toy activism for a common cause may lead to many forms of play, including intergenerational play that enhances well-being. As a public form of toy play, the #teddychallenge sent out its message to grandparents and grandchildren, as well as to anyone else interested in being invited to participate in this form of hybrid play, and translated messages of support and solidarity in the form of physical toy displays, sometimes accompanied by written messages.

Optimism and Future-orientedness: The #teddychallenge as a Regional and Mobile Play Experience

The final phase of the study sought to investigate play during spring 2021 on a national and local level. To understand how pandemic toy play happened at a later phase of the health crisis, the author investigated regional play, encouraged through a photo-play challenge created by the local media, the daily newspaper *SK*, published in Western Finland.

This phase of the study represented another perspective on pandemic toy play—a replayed play pattern made familiar by the firsthand #teddychallenge—and combined it with the idea of regional toy tourism, or rather, toyrism (Heljakka & Räikkönen 2021), i.e. making one's 'toy friends' mobile and capturing their adventures on camera. The news media invited locals to take their toys out for photo-play in nearby areas through an invitation to play presented online. In a matter of days, some one hundred photo-plays were generated and, after a few days more, the news media had collected 260 instances of photo-play from their readers.

The analysis of these photos showed how teddies and other plush were taken on outings in regional locations and attractions. Afterwards, some of the instances of photo-play were published in the local newspaper's online and printed versions (Kauppi 2021).

In the photos, the plush were shown out and about, engrossed in leisurely, even sporty activities, like sunbathing, skiing, on sledges, climbing, hiking, having picnics, barbecuing, baking, gardening flowers, and visiting local sights and playgrounds. These playful images, taken in March 2021, by and large depicted activities that many human beings seemed to have done regionally before the pandemic one year earlier, in March 2020. At this point, the toys were depicted spending time outdoors close to home and seeking the calming yet energizing effect of visiting natural landscapes and local attractions during outdoor excursions, or resorting to homely and comforting activities within the domestic space, spending time with the family.

In this way, the third phase of research highlighted toy play as an activity that reflected playful resilience—optimism and orientation towards a brighter future through imaginative, creative and narrative object play mainly conducted outdoors in the public sphere and sending out a strong signal of the presence of play in challenging times. Together with the detected themes of ludounity, intergenerationality, optimism and future-orientedness, the results of the three-part study on pandemic toy play contribute to an understanding of the development of plush characters into 'objects of resilience'—an evolutionary concept visualized in Figure 7.3, and discussed in the final part of this chapter.

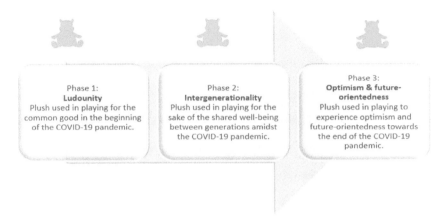

Figure 7.3 Development of plush characters into 'objects of resilience'—an evolutionary concept
Created by Katriina Heljakka, CC BY-NC 4.0

Discussion: Main Facets of the #teddychallenge

Play is neurologically a reactive itch of the amygdala, one that responds to archetypical shock, anger, fear, disgust or sadness. But play also includes a frontal-lobe counter, reaching for triumphant control and happiness and pride. (Sutton-Smith 2017: 61)

Cultures work out their feelings at play (Eberle and the Strong National Museum of Play 2009). As the quote from Sutton-Smith tells us, play is about more than combatting negativity—it is also largely about enjoyment; happiness and pride: 'Play makes life more worth living than is the case without it. And this leads logically to the notion that optimism and flexibility are essential correlates of play' (Sutton-Smith 2017: 224).

Imagination, inclusion and communality were the main features of the play pattern showcased by everyday players as well as enterprises and authorities represented in the media articles of the first phase of research. With the detected aspects of resistance, resourcefulness and resilience, the interviewees who participated in the second phase of research demonstrated the multifaceted nature of toy play during the pandemic. In the third phase, the analysis of the photo-play showed how toy players maintained a positive and hopeful spirit by showing their plush toys taking an active part in outdoor activities transported to participate in local toyrism.

According to the three-part study presented in this chapter, it becomes evident that toys have the power to comfort and inspire large numbers of people (Fulmer 2009). Moreover, they are fantastic creatures that are used to channel and display the products of the collective human imagination, optimistic mindset and a survivalist attitude through play in public space.

The three-part study explained in this chapter highlights mature toy players not only as solitary object players but also as social and intergenerational object players highly involved and engaged in proactive play. The #teddychallenge shows how the teddy bear, as a representative of childhood innocence, has evolved to encompass 'social, emotional, and material capacities of transformative love', and to become 'a humanitarian ambassador' (Varga 2009: 72-73).

Brian Sutton-Smith refers to Goffman when writing: 'whatever play is, it always runs parallel to our lives, serving as a respite from ordinary events and a lesson on how life can actually be better than it is' (Sutton-Smith 2017: 67). As toy play during the Covid-19 pandemic has proven, 'we don't play in order to distract ourselves from the world, but in order to partake in it' (Bogost 2016: 233). Play is resourceful in many ways; in playing we orientate ourselves towards opportunities, seek solutions and allow ourselves to think positively about our options. Furthermore, play is social interaction as much as it is private action (Henricks 2015: 101). As shown in the chapter at hand, play is about action as much as it is about reaction and response to what the world throws in our way.

The purpose of this chapter was to explain a study with an interest to examine, describe, and increase the understanding of toy play during the Covid-19 pandemic. The three-part study showed first how the

#teddychallenge evolved from a play pattern of toys being displayed and shown in windows by themselves, and second, how the teddies and other toys were liberated to move out and about with their human counterparts as the restrictions on social distancing and physical mobility slowly dissolved thanks to the introduction of vaccines around the world. Third, the study revealed how toys were taken out on excursions and depicted enjoying life in a replaying of the #teddychallenge, as encouraged by regional news media.

In the consecutive phases of the research, the author noted how communality of play emerged in the #teddychallenge, and how it illustrated a case of playing for the common good through a sense of togetherness of generations and belonging in communities. Cohen and Waite-Stupiansky claim that 'there is little doubt that play is the unifying factor in allowing participants the opportunity to communicate and share the joys and wonders that play provides' (2012: 69). In contemporary times, plush toys have proven their power as intergenerational playthings. In this way, play has moved from being object-centred to relationship-centred (Henricks 2015, quoting the work of Daniil Elkonin)—and more specifically about relationships between generations of adults and children strengthened through toy play.

The #teddychallenge also highlighted how toy play among the mature participants of the challenge is not about nostalgia for the past but, even more so, about interactions with toys as a response to the human condition here and now. Moreover, photo-play with plush included both toys old and new, illustrating that the toy relations of today may include all kinds of plush toys—historical and contemporary.

In association with the evolution of the teddy bear, Donna Varga has written about 'a belief in the object's transformational possibilities' (2009: 79). In light of the findings of the study investigating the #teddychallenge, it is possible to think about the play pattern as a form of toy activism which addresses the capacity of plush to function as *objects of resilience.*

Resilience is 'a process to harness resources in order to sustain well-being' and the idea of progress—moving forward—is an important component of resilience (Southwick et al. 2014). In times of crisis, adults mentally resort to reinspecting objects of resilience, such as plush creatures like teddy bears—as 'emissaries of hope' (Varga 2009: 84).

As shown in this chapter, during the Covid-19 pandemic, plush toys have worked as objects of resilience—artefacts that mobilize the human in physical, cognitive and emotional ways, strengthening our trust in survival and channelling our trust in a return to normalcy.

Conclusions: Bearers of Optimism and Hope

Toys, and soft plush creatures in particular, are both symbols of loss and sorrow but, precisely because of that, they are also bearers of optimism and hope. At the time of finalizing this study, the war between Russia and Ukraine broke out, bringing to the forefront other kinds of toy activists. The idea of toys as artefacts of hope materialized recently in the toy activist protests against Russia's attack on Ukraine, where dolls were taken to show compassion for the victims of war.

The protective aura of plush as a gift given to soothe children (and others) during crisis (Cook 2009) became even clearer during the writing of this chapter through the droves of people fleeing the war. Finnish broadcaster YLE showcased a photography project by Abdulhamid Hosmas (YLE 2022) who portrayed Ukrainian children holding on to their character toys after they had crossed the border. A few days later, a Facebook post (In Ukraine 2022) showcased an image of a bridge on which plush toys were hung, informing passers-by that the 'Romanian border police and citizens have turned the pedestrian bridge linking Ukraine and Romania at Sighetu Marmației into a toy bridge'. On the bridge, the toys were displayed for grabbing by children passing through on their way out of the country. Consequently, instead of leisurely toyrism as a form of toy mobility, this human tragedy has resulted in migration of donated toys, and as such represents humans' recent wish to harness play for the common good (Heljakka 2020).

During the Covid-19 pandemic the monetary value of playthings became irrelevant and economic exchange value was replaced by emotional exchange value (Cook 2009). Toys' capacity to move people emerges here in both physical and affective terms—the first instances of the #teddychallenge were built on the idea of the teddy bear hunt encouraging people to move about in their neighbourhood to spot teddies in gardens and windows so as—more importantly—to raise spirits despite physical and social distancing. The #teddychallenge, as a byproduct of the pandemic, reveals human beings' neediness towards toys. Plush characters function as protective, personal and intimate trustees and comforters but also, and more poignantly, as 'a portal of human contact' (Fulmer 2009: 93).

Faith in the teddy bear's presence to make everything better (Varga 2009: 81) seems again a timely wish of players all over the world. Amidst the ongoing war in Ukraine and the still lingering health crisis caused by the Covid-19 virus, toys communicate a playfulness otherwise absent in the everyday lives of those suffering from mental and physical stress. For this reason, toys can be viewed as personal and shared objects of resilience for players of many ages. As relational artefacts, they are about longevity and sustainable relationships (Heljakka 2022). Play celebrates being present and living in the moment while being supported by familiar and comforting toys.

In adult toy cultures, the object relations and interactions are still partly confined to the intimacies of domestic space. In children's toy relationships, however, plush creatures are forever present, brought into the public space, grasped tightly in the arms of the child, channelling comfort and reassurance. But times change, and so do human relations with toys. And more importantly, societal ideas of teddy bears and other character toys are acknowledged to encompass powers of their own. The time has come to realize the importance of anthropomorphized entities functioning as mirrors, extensions and avatars (Heljakka 2023). Moreover, they have increasingly gained the capacity of independence and ability to function as toy activists. All the same, toys are not insignificant, but highly important artefacts channelling messages of hope and survival. Teddy bears, and plush creatures in general, have during the Covid-19 pandemic proved their capacity as emblems of collective hope and toy activists communicating faith in brighter times to come.

Time will tell how the materiality of these playthings will evolve but what is known now is that tangibility as an affordance is hard to replace. More importantly, what we seek from objects of resilience, besides sensory gratification, is familiarity and friendliness, poseability and huggability, a chance to care for, grow attached to, and build affectionate relationships with them—all while seeking the possibility of seeing the human behind the thingness.

This chapter has highlighted how the appetite for object play during challenging times is a sign of mental strength and playful resilience—a willingness to sustain well-being, human psychological endurance and survival. The three-part investigation and synthesis of pandemic toy play illustrates how, in times of crisis, toys may transform from intimate, transitional objects to communal objects of resilience. As proposed in the chapter, the #teddychallenge represents a form of toy activism in which toy characters act as messengers of socially significant statements. Playing and toying for the common good by combining character toys with online sharing, imaginative acts of physical object displays, socially shared photo-play and hybrid play culture, all thrive and channel a strong message of ludounity: by playing together, we will survive. Bearers of hope in shared play—the plush toys conceptualized in this chapter as objects of resilience—are an important tool for achieving ludounity.

Works Cited

Auerbach, Stevanne. 2004. *Smart Play, Smart Toys: How to Raise a Child with a High Play Quotient* (USA: Educational Insights)

Bengtson, Vern L. 2001. 'Beyond the Nuclear Family: The Increasing Importance of Multigenerational Bonds', *Journal of Marriage and the Family*, 63: 1–16, https://doi.org/10.1111/j.1741-3737.2001.00001.x

Boehm, Helen. 1986. *The Right Toys: A Guide to Selecting the Best Toys for Children* (Toronto: Bantam)

Bogost, Ian. 2016. *Play Anything: The Pleasure of Limits, the Uses of Boredom, and the Secret of Games* (London: Basic Books)

Chudacoff, Howard P. 2007. *Children at Play. An American History* (New York: New York University Press)

Cockrill, Pauline. 2001. *The Teddy Bear Encyclopedia* (New York: Dorling Kindersley)

Cohen, Lynn E., and Sandra Waite-Stupiansky. 2012. 'Play for All Ages: An Exploration of Intergenerational Play', in *Play: A Polyphony of Research, Theories and Issues*, ed. by Lynn E. Cohen and Sandra Waite-Stupiansky, Play and Culture Studies, 12 (Lanham, MD: University Press of America), pp. 61–80

Cook, Daniel T. 2009. 'Responses', *Cultural Analysis*, 8: 89–91

Cross, Gary. 2008. *Men to Boys. The Making of Modern Immaturity* (New York: Columbia University Press)

Crozier, Ray. 1994. *Manufactured Pleasures: Psychological Responses to Design* (Manchester: Manchester University Press)

Csikszentmihalyi, Mihaily, and Eugene Rochberg-Halton. 1981. *The Meaning of Things. Domestic Symbols and the Self* (Cambridge: Cambridge University Press)

de Sarigny, Rudi. 1971. *Good Design in Soft Toys* (London: Mills and Boon)

Eberle, Scott G., and the Strong National Museum of Play. 2009. *Classic Toys of the National Toy Hall of Fame: A Celebration of the Greatest Toys of All Time!* (Philadelphia: Running Press)

In Ukraine. 2022. [Toy Bridge Facebook post], 17 March, https://www.facebook.com/1448090885498011/posts/2749767311997022/

Fleming, Dan. 1996. *Powerplay: Children, Toys and Popular Culture* (Manchester: Manchester University Press)

Fulmer, Jacqueline. 2009. 'Teddy Bear Culture[s]', *Cultural Analysis*, 8: 92–96

Groos, Karl, and Elizabeth Baldwin. 2010 [1901]. *The Play of Man* (Memphis, TN: General Books)

Harris, Daniel. 1994. 'Making Kitsch from AIDS: A Disease with a Gift Shop of Its Own', *Harper's Magazine*, July: 55–56

Heljakka, Katriina. 2013. *Principles of Adult Play(fulness) in Contemporary Toy Cultures. From Wow to Flow to Glow* (Helsinki: Aalto Arts Books)

——. 2020. 'Pandemic Toy Play against Social Distancing: Teddy Bears, Window-Screens and Playing for the Common Good in Times of Self-Isolation', *Wider Screen*, 11 May, https://widerscreen.fi/numerot/ajankohtaista/pandemic-toy-play-against-social-distancing-teddy-bears-window-screens-and-playing-for-the-common-good-in-times-of-self-isolation/

——. 2021. 'Liberated through Teddy Bears: Resistance, Resourcefulness, and Resilience in Toy Play during the COVID-19 Pandemic,' *International Journal of Play*, 10: 387–404, https://doi.org/10.1080/21594937.2021.2005402

——. 2022. 'On Longevity and Lost Toys: Sustainable Approaches to Toy Design and Contemporary Play', in *Toys and Sustainability* by Subramanian Senthilkannan Muthu (Singapore: Springer Singapore), pp. 19–37

——. 2023. 'Masked Belles and Beasts: Uncovering Toys as Extensions, Avatars and Activists in Human Identity Play', in *Masks and Human Connections: Disruptive Meanings and Cultural Challenges*, ed. by Luísa Magalhães and Cândido Oliveira Martins (Cham: Springer International), pp. 29-45

Heljakka, Katriina, and Juulia Räikkönen. 2021. 'Puzzling out "Toyrism": Conceptualizing Value Co-Creation in Toy Tourism', *Tourism Management Perspectives*, 38: 100791, https://doi.org/10.1016/j.tmp.2021.100791

Henricks, Thomas S. 2006. *Play Reconsidered. Sociological Perspectives on Human Expression* (Urbana: University of Illinois Press)

——. 2015. 'Sociological Perspectives on Play', in *The Handbook of the Study of Play*, ed. by James E. Johnson et al. (Lanham, MD: Rowman & Littlefield and the Strong Museum of Play), II, pp. 101–20

Ivy, Marilyn. 2010. 'The Art of Cute Little Things: Nara Yoshimoto's Parapolitics,' in *Fanthropologies*, Mechademia, 5, ed. by Frenchy Lunning (Minneapolis: University of Minnesota Press), pp. 3–29

Kauppi, Sari. 2021. 'Nallegalleria', *Satakunnan Kansa*, https://www.satakunnankansa.fi/satakunta/art-2000007863021.html

Kuznets, Lois. 1994. *When Toys Come Alive, Narratives of Animation, Metamorphosis and Development* (New Haven: Yale University Press)

Laatikainen, Satu. 2011. 'Lelu on leikin asia [A Toy Is an Issue of Play]', *Yhteishyvä*, 12: 72–74

Leclerc, Rémi. 2008. 'Character Toys: Toying with Identity, Playing with Emotion', unpublished presentation at the Design and Emotion Conference, Hong Kong Polytechnic University, 6-9 October

Marks-Tarlow, Terry. 2010. 'The Fractal Self at Play', *American Journal of Play*, 3: 31–62

Mayerowitz, Scott. 2010. 'Bedtime Story: 1-in-4 Grown Men Travel with a Stuffed Animal', *ABC News*, http://abcnews.go.com/Travel/grown-men-travel-stuffed-animals-teddybears-dogs/story?id=11463664

Miller, Daniel. 1987. *Material Culture and Mass Consumption* (Padstow: Basic Blackwell)

Newson, John, and Elizabeth Newson. 1979. *Toys and Playthings* (New York: Pantheon Books)

Ngai, Sianne. 2005. 'The Cuteness of the AvantGarde', *Critical Inquiry*, 31: 811–47

Norman, Donald. 2004. *Emotional Design: Why We Love (or Hate) Everyday Things* (New York: Basic Books)

Paavilainen, Janne, and Katriina Heljakka. 2018. 'Analysis Workshop II: Hybrid Money Games and Toys', in *Hybrid Social Play Final Report*, ed. by Janne Paavilainen and others, Trim Research Reports, 26, pp. 16–18, http://urn.fi/URN:ISBN:978-952-03-0751-6

Pearce, Susan M. 1994. 'Thinking about Things', in *Interpreting Objects and Collections*, ed. by Susan M. Pearce (London: Routledge), pp. 125–32

Reinelt, Sabine. 1988. *Käthe Kruse: Leben und Werk* (Weingarten: Kunstverlag Weingarten)

Reuters. 2021. 'Barbie Debuts Doll in Likeness of British COVID-19 Vaccine Developer', 4 August, https://www.reuters.com/world/uk/barbie-debuts-doll-likeness-british-Covid-19-vaccine-developer-2021-08-03/

Rossie, Jean-Pierre. 2005. Toys, Play, Culture and Society: Anthropological Approach with Reference to North Africa and the Sahara (Stockholm: SITREC)

Ruckenstein, Minna. 2011. 'Toying with the World. Children, Virtual Pets and the Value of Mobility', *Childhood*, 17: 1–14, https://doi.org/10.1177/090756820935281

Shillito, Adam. 2011. 'Toy Design', unpublished presentation at the 'From Rags to Apps' conference, Shenkar College Tel Aviv, author notes

Smith, Peter K. 2010. *Children and Play* (Chichester: Wiley-Blackwell), https://doi.org/10.1002/9781444311006

Southwick, Steven M., et al. 2014. 'Resilience Definitions, Theory, and Challenges: Interdisciplinary Perspectives', *European Journal of Psychotraumatology*, 5: https://doi.org/10.3402/ejpt.v5.25338

Stake, Robert E. 1995. *Qualitative Research: Studying How Things Work.* (New York: Guilford Press)

Strong Museum. n.d. 'The National Toy Hall of Fame: Teddy Bear', https://www.museumofplay.org/toys/teddy-bear/

Sturken, Marita. 2007. *Tourists of History: Memory, Kitsch, and Consumerism from Oklahoma City to Ground Zero* (Durham, NC: Duke University Press)

Sutton-Smith, Brian. 1986. *Toys as Culture* (New York: Gardner Press)

——. 2017. *Play for Life: Play Theory and Play as Emotional Survival*, comp. and ed. by Charles Lamar Phillips and others (Rochester, NY: The Strong)

Telegraph, The. 2010. 'Third of Adults "still take teddy bear to bed"', 16 August, https://www.telegraph.co.uk/news/newstopics/howaboutthat/7947502/Third-of-adults-still-take-teddy-bear-to-bed.html

Varga, Donna. 2009. 'Gifting the Bear and a Nostalgic Desire for Childhood Innocence', *Cultural Analysis*, 8: 71–96

Volonté, Paolo G. 2010. 'Communicative Objects,' in *Design Semiotics in Use: Semiotics in the Study of Meaning Formation, Signification and Communication*, ed. by S. Vihma, School of Art and Design Publication series, A 100 (Helsinki: Aalto University), pp. 112–128

Walsh, Tim. 2005. *Timeless Toys: Classic Toys and the Playmakers Who Created Them* (Kansas City: Andrews McMeel)

YLE. 2022. 'My Teddy is My Refuge', https://yle.fi/uutiset/3-12344876

8. 'This Is the Ambulance, This Truck': Covid as Frame, Theme and Provocation in Philadelphia, USA

Anna Beresin

When the school playgrounds reopened after quarantine, you could find most parents, grandparents and babysitters picking up their children after school, or observing their children's lingering play, gathering at the edges, moving slowly from periphery to centre. Like their movements, this essay begins with a wide-angle lens, describing play and conversations about play with parents and guardians in three public school communities in Philadelphia, Pennsylvania, during the winter and spring of 2020-2021. In Philadelphia, America's poorest large city, one school community studied here is mostly minority and middle-class in a racially integrated neighbourhood with access to parks and trees, one a mostly white, upper middle-class school community in the centre of the city, and one an almost exclusively minority, working-class school in an under-resourced, minority community. The first two have elaborate new playgrounds augmented by extensive parent-sourced fundraising. The third has no playground outside at all but a privately funded rooftop playground is in the cards as the neighbourhood struggles with gentrification. It is not unusual in this city for playground access to be so unequal, and this can be considered a social justice issue reflecting racist housing development (Beresin in press; Feldman 2019).

  https://doi.org/10.11647/OBP.0326.08

With ethical approval provided by the University of the Sciences, fifty adults participated in this study as well as their available children if both parties approved. In this chapter, we will see intersectional power dynamics and intertextual expressivity while the families described access to toys, games and common play spaces during the different phases of the pandemic. Although the challenges faced by each community were different, the themes of play were universal. This essay highlights the pandemic's influence on healthy children's social lives within their playground communities, and the pandemic's emergence as a frame and theme, and then narrows in on children's micro-world-building.

At the middle-class school, I was regularly greeted by two mothers who sat as sentries on the steps leading to the school's playground. Children spiralled toward and away from the mothers, checking in about snack permissions, one small girl always carrying a large stuffed animal of indeterminate species. The mom noted that the girl carries her 'stuffy' with her now, wherever she goes. The mothers served as this yard's gatekeepers, perched on the edge of the schoolyard play world while other adults leaned on the playground fence containing the newly augmented series of rope climbers, swirling slides, and variously levelled steps on a padded area. There were basketball hoops complete with nets, smaller-sized plastic ball funnels, and a wide nearby area with a painted oval for running and biking on concrete.

Twenty minutes away at the upper middle-class schoolyard, the greeters were a team of mothers and nannies sitting multiple days a week on the low wall that served as a fence for their schoolyard. Mostly women with younger children in strollers, these were the more fashionable counterparts to the first playground, guarding their charges and offering snacks while the children lingered after school to play. Their playground had also been revitalized a few years earlier with major fundraising from both the parents' association and local companies to the tune of one hundred thousand dollars. This playground sports a metal climber, several slides and, most unusual for school playgrounds, several rubberized mounds simulating small rolling hills often used as a base for Tag and for momentum-filled running or biking.

Another twenty minutes away, a third school has no playground at all. The concrete area that was designated originally for play is mostly used as a parking area for the teachers' cars. I was greeted regularly here by a grandmother picking up her granddaughter and great-niece, both of whom live with her. 'Every week a new Barbie' at the local Target provided them with a much-needed opportunity for getting outside the house during the pandemic, as outdoor play spaces were limited.

The study began as a series of videocall interviews via Zoom utilizing a snowball sample that started with my next-door neighbour's family during quarantine in the winter of 2020. Quarantines were established by each school district within each state in conjunction with local governmental decisions. As the quarantine shifted, I began weekly observational studies with ethnographic interviews in these three different school communities, each a school where I have done extensive fieldwork or had known contacts. Previous research by this author was carried out in two of the school communities, one with daily observation over several months' time, the other with weekly observation over a span of five years (Beresin 2014; Beresin 2015). The third community school is within a few blocks from my home where I have lived for twenty years. All are public kindergarten through eighth grade schools in Philadelphia with an approximate enrolment of five hundred students serving children ages five through fourteen. Parents and guardians were recruited through neighbourhood posters, parent teacher association Facebook pages, word of mouth, and on-site during conversations in the schoolyards. Children were not interviewed on the playground, as this researcher did not want to interrupt their important play time although, if approached and the parent or guardian was present, their words were recorded by hand with pen and paper. The children were invited to contribute drawings or photos of their currently favourite toys and activities, as long as there were no images of the children's faces.

All quotes that follow are verbatim, and often the adults quote their own children. Many have had a front-row seat to their children's worlds during the pandemic, given that parents were often themselves working from home, were unemployed, or were supervising their children's online schooling. At the time of the interviews, the families were healthy, although several had lost relatives to the disease. The methods here are qualitative and improvised and the material carefully transcribed, given the rush to document children's lives at the time of the novel coronavirus (Erickson 1990; Tannen 2007). As I write this, the Delta variant is receding and the Omicron variant is surging, directly affecting the young.

This author vowed to protect the families' privacy as this time was particularly vulnerable, bordering on the traumatic, according to the early Zoom interviews in this study. Ordinarily in ethnographic research, there would be more description of each person who speaks in the excerpts below. It can be said that parents' vocations ranged from the recently unemployed, some by choice, to epidemiologists, plumbers, teachers, lawyers and artists, a full range of educational backgrounds and social classes. The interviews included white European American, Latina/Latino, Asian American and African American adults. They varied in age from parents in their early twenties to late forties, all with children in one of the three kindergarten-through-eighth-grade schools in the study. The parents as a cohort voiced their appreciation and the sense that we were documenting this time together as a collage, and that it was a task worth doing.

Playgrounds

Parents and caregivers in the middle-class school playground voiced their appreciation of the newly renovated space utilized for both recess and for after-school play. This included emphatic comments relating to this particular playground, shown below in bold:

Everybody loves this playground. It's the best place to hang with other parents, **a safe watering hole.**

We come here literally every day. Never stopped. **Coming here has been a lifesaver.** We came even when it was cold, just not in the rain. My son comes here after school. Even though he hasn't been in face-to-face classes, he hasn't missed out on the socialization piece. He met every school kid at the playground.

It's much better now. We've been at this playground as much as possible since Covid started. It was closed initially, maybe in April or May it opened. We're here at least three times a week. Sometimes five. **She has a whole crew she meets here.**

The playground is so wonderful. It is such a wonderful place to safely gather with other parents after school or on the weekends. **It's just a great place for our community to be.**

Now the only place to move is the playground.

My daughter would call out to other children in the playground, 'Are you in Ms. J's class? Are you in Ms. J's class?' **Without the playground, I don't know how she'd meet her classmates in person. It really helped a lot to meet other kids, even one hour a week.** I feel for families who don't have any access to outdoor spaces. I have so much privilege. At her old school in Philly, they had a policy of having to leave the playground after fifteen minutes of play and then they close the gates. Not here! No one kicks us out. We're sometimes here until 6:30, and we can stay.

We go to the playground a lot. We meet other families here. . . The playground, we go usually once a week. It's always buzzing. I avoided it early in the pandemic. We didn't know enough about the virus, how it was transmitted, if they could get it on surfaces. So many unknowns. As months go by, we are more comfortable. We still wear masks and bring hand sanitizer. For me, it's been nice to see people once a week. I used to enjoy walking the kids to school. I missed that, seeing people, chatting. We would linger with no agenda. I really did miss that.

In the upper middle-class neighbourhood, the parents had different challenges and other advantages in terms of resources. Some children went to high-end afterschool gyms and were there on off-days when school was completely online. Some went to second homes and spent online school time in vacation-ready isolation. After school, families were supposed to leave the playground, as it was officially closed right after dismissal. Some stayed anyway. There was frustration over the idea of having to leave the playground oasis, along with a newfound appreciation for its social function for parents as well as children.

Today we were told to leave at 2:50, but we didn't! They're in six-feet-away blocks in school and only have one recess in the afternoon. At 2:50 we're supposed to leave, as of today. (Don't tell.) Tomorrow we may go to the other playground, next to the river. I can't imagine walking back home and coming here again at 4:30 when it opens again.

The school says so because more students are back in school. **Children cannot linger in the playground.** After 4:30, I can officially come back. I can't walk home and walk back. They're trying to limit Covid exposure. I don't think it's coming from the school, this directive, but from the district. At another local Philly public school nearby, they can't play on the playground until the last kid has been picked up. The principal, she shoos them off. 'Can't play here!' They stagger them after school and in the morning.

Don't tell, we're still here. It's technically not the school's playground. It's a public park. That's why there's no fence. Parents here asked for a gate but they can't do it.

We have no pod. My wife has a group of friends. That was it, united by a 'pinky promise' to be safe with each other. **We two dads ran into each other today (at the playground), a kind of 'random fathers club'.** Just tell me where to go and I go.

We are fortunate, we have neighbours with kids, all close during this whole thing. **It's a close school group here at the playground.**

They typically go to the other public playground, or stay here, on the in-person days. The younger one does her virtual days at a gym daycare. The older one does her virtual schooling at home and then goes to the same gym a few days a week, and also takes a foreign language. **All of the children they've played with are from the school. All from school.**

This is where they want to play, at this playground.

There was nothing to play with in the working-class neighbourhood schoolyard. While waiting there, children played with objects or people they brought from home and soon quickly dispersed.

Pods

Pods, self-selected small groups or bubbles for socializing, were more common in the middle-class community as families sought ways to co-parent while working, allowing their children to have much-needed social time. All three communities spoke of proximity leading to social groupings, whether they were families on the same street, in the same housing development, the same preschool, or through the importation of relatives to watch the children. For some families, it required new efforts at organizing social time:

> From what I've observed, it's about half of the kids who are in pods.

> **The Fairy Podmothers is definitely what we've become, so I spent the better part of this morning arranging with them.** 'Who wants to meet for sledding across the street?' Especially the one Pod-Mom who does still work from home—she has less of an opportunity to hang out with us in the afternoon. She has to work.

> I think it's been a really great experience for my daughter to have this pod, this safe haven experience of kids and parents who live right in our neighbourhood over a block, for her to feel secure in her community in this insecure chaotic time has helped her mentally and emotionally. I think that will carry on, even after the pandemic is under control. So, **I'm feeling hopeful that we will continue some kind of cooperative parenting approach, even after we all go back to school. It's been great that way.**

In the working-class community, sticking with the immediate family was more common:

> **It was just us. Me and him.**

> They don't socialize online. No. **They play with each other, they do.** I've been thankful they have each other.

> At home, he plays with toys. ('Toys?') LEGOs. Yes, LEGOs. Mostly games on my phone. *Roblox* and stuff. (The child chimes in, 'I

like to watch YouTube and play with my sister', as he looks at her adoringly) **Who do they play with? Each other. Only each other.**

Parents in all three communities voiced their concerns about the pandemic's impact on the children's socio-emotional lives:

> For the little one, so much of her play, her entire play, her entire memory is of the pandemic.

> My son and the girl neighbour had a conversation, **'If my mom dies, mom gets sick with Covid and dies', he said he 'would go live with them'.** He said, 'I don't remember what my friends look like without their masks'.

> The first night of the pandemic she was up for five hours, the first night we were told there would be no school. . .the stress was incredible. And you couldn't really see it, I didn't see any change in behaviour but **sleep just vanished.** It was incredible. . . She called it the Dumb Virus early on, and so we call it that. . . the pandemic doesn't show up in their play. I don't ever hear them ever imagine things that are related to it.

> Our son says if he doesn't want to do something, he'll say, **'We can't because of Covid'.** Like, 'We can't go to the amusement park because of Covid'. But also, 'I can't go for a walk because of Covid', or 'I can't go to get groceries with you because of Covid'. (*She rolls her eyes*) It's listed as a stock excuse, 'I am tired, it could be Covid'.

> **One day she was sitting and literally fell off her chair.** I don't know what exactly, she just kind of fell over. Paying attention is harder. . . She just is missing her friends more and more.

And yet,

> **Covid- it's not a negative for some children.** Some get to spend more time with their parents. Before I was working four jobs. And I still came here to pick up my daughter after school. I was beat. Now, I work from home online. I was able to sit there and teach her from home. **Covid was my break! I felt like I was part of her**

childhood. It gave me a chance to spend more time. I don't want to go back to face-to-face work. I need to be there seven hours a day to help her.

Covid as a Frame for Online Play

Covid emerged as a rationale for online play but rarely as a motif in online play. Many parents in all three communities were deeply ambivalent about screen time, a phenomenon Jay Caspian Kang calls 'the great child-rearing panic of the 21st century' (Kang 2022: 24):

> Oh God. **Any rules about screen time went out the window during Covid.**

> Online play equals YouTube. Goofy challenges. How to make slime. Spicy food challenges. She'd like to do it too, **but she knows I'm not a fan.**

> What does he play? 'Basketball!' he says excitedly. ('Outside?') **His mom lowers her voice. 'Mostly on his phone,** or on a system, a computer too'.

> If it's not outside, then they gravitate to the screens—Wii, tablet, phone, tv. **It's a battle to divert them from screens.**

> Toys? (*They all roll their eyes*) **We try to get them off the tablet, off of YouTube.** She shifts off school work and continues for an extra hour, sneakily. I ask if she's finished and she admits, 'Oh I've been finished for an hour'. Her neighbour nods. **When they're home, they revert to the screen so we try and keep them outside.**

> We regularly FaceTimed grandparents. The older one did some FaceTime with a few friends. Some out of state, some local. The younger one has one friend she FaceTimes with, and some aunts, or does Kid Messenger. Or is it Messenger Kids? They have games you can play with other people. We try to vary it. **Sadly, she could be on the computer 24/7.**

> She's hooked on it too. **She's hooked on watching, with** *Minecraft,* **when they actually have it (the toy) right there!**

Sometimes the YouTubers simulate pranks. **I hate that, so no more YouTube. But you get so tired, and you have to cook dinner and work.**

They live in the same world, but they are in different worlds. When asked, 'Don't you want to talk to your cousin and grandparents?' 'NO!' And grandparents get so mad. **Yes, grandparents get so mad on FaceTime.** But if you ask if they want to play with someone on *Minecraft*, they jump online.

It is difficult as he has ADHD. They all got distracted with YouTube and online games. I would not have introduced the computer at his age. He had to be on for school. He asks for *Minecraft*. He tried a few *Minecraft* knock-off apps. I told him **I didn't think he was ready.**

Winter was hard. They did lots of drawing tutorials on YouTube. Video chats with grandparents. (The child comes up to me cautiously and the parents explain I am studying kids play.) What do you play? **'I like to watch tv!' and runs off.** (*Parent rolls eyes*) She will often say, 'Pretend we're a family'.

They still watch way too much YouTube. Oh God. Videos of other families. They just follow rich families, that's how they make their money. Like vlogs. I don't know what it is about them, especially for her. I keep telling her, that way of living is not typical. He likes the educational stuff. She is into *Spy Ninjas*. Looks at all the reality tv. No cartoons, or shows. Just reality tv.

Online? We are pretty strict, much to my son's chagrin. We don't let them play much online. They watch PBS Kids. There are some computer games the computer teacher set up on their website. They can pick up anything from that page: *Brain Pop, ABCya, Pebble Go, Room Recess*.

His favorite thing is to play piano on a keyboard and learn from YouTube. **After school, I have him get off the screen.**

It used to be *Pokémon*. Now it's *Bakugan*.

And *LOL Dolls*. Girls are all into them.

So much time on the screen. He's hooked. Nintendo Switch. YouTube.

Some parents were adamant that online games eliminated imaginative play:

Imaginary play stopped when they were online for school. They wanted to do online games only. But it came back when we took them out of school. The older one would have been fine staying hybrid. The six-year-old, it was significant for the kindergartener when we made the change. They would say, 'When can we watch?' It was addictive. They were losing their youthful sense of wonder and creativity, so we had to set limits. And then we took them out of school completely. So much of kids' play is on the computer. It's that addictive, the nature of it.

Ah, it's unfortunate. We were a family that never had a tv. If we watched a movie, it was once a year. Now they are addicted to YouTube. My twins. It's been awful. I went to online forums, ironic huh, and spoke to the school teachers. I blocked YouTube and only did kid YouTube, and the kids figured out how to unblock it. So, I teach them to be good consumers, to make media and not just consume it. I took a class at the Penn Graduate School of Education. Piaget and Vygotsky would be rolling in their graves. Whenever they went on screens, they stopped playing and had a meltdown when the screens were stopped. But when they went back to their toys, they played instantly.

Some parents were more positive or clearly neutral about technology:

The older one does a lot of *Prodigy*, a math game. When you get things right you can get stuff at a virtual shop, fix up an avatar and dress it. The first graders, two girls and one boy—**their play was lovely.** They did superheroes often. *Pokémon* was a big theme.

The first grader takes lots of selfies and likes editing them, changing the backgrounds. YouTube Kids is like a rabbit hole. They both like it, to make crafts for dolls. The other day I had a splinter. She asked, 'Want me to get it out? Put glue on your hand, let it dry and peel off the glue. Out will come the splinter'. **How did she KNOW that? YouTube!**

Online, they play Roblox and an RPG [role-playing game]. **It's age-appropriate**, a restaurant, mall type thing, race car simulations, or *Roblox*, an off-brand *Minecraft*.

Inside, it's the sofa. That they jump on. They got Nintendo Switch. **It's a treat on weekends.** 30 minutes and we close it. She's okay with it. She's a rule follower.

He socializes online with his class. He's big into *Zelda* and *Luigi's Mansion*. Recently he's into LEGOs.

They draw and do drawing tutorials online. They can do computer, if they are doing science research. They do Xbox. ('*Xbox!*' the children echo.) *Uno*. ('*Uno!*') And Switch. Lots of *Uno*. And *Uno Attack*- you hit the button to get specific cards.

We do *Draw with Moe* for online activity. In the beginning, for a while, until depression set in. **Now it's normal.**

An older sister offers that **after her sister watches a TV show, she replays and reenacts the whole show.**

She's in Girl Scouts and that's all virtual. **They socialize online in Scouts.** She does soccer too. I do everything to try to keep her occupied. Scouts did a scavenger hunt online. Cooking online, too.

He plays in the *Minecraft* world, plays with Brazilian cousins in Canada. He waits for her to wake up.

The online world was clearly a source of tension yet also connection, even as adults also admitted that they, too, turned to television and computers for both work and recreation during the pandemic. According to the anthropologists of childhood, children's play cultures have always reflected adult work, miniature exaggerated versions of the adult world, whether it be children playing farmer in the fields of farming towns or pretending to be fishing in fishing villages (Konner 2010; Lancy 2022; Sutton-Smith 1986). It is no surprise that children turned to online building activities like *Monument Valley 11* or *Minecraft* or *Roblox* as their parents connected to Excel sheets, Word docs, and Zoom meetings. For some children and adults this online focus of school and play was stressful: 'Developmentally, they can't sit in front of a screen for seven hours'. 'My daughter said she wants "to kill the internet"'. Yet for many, online play offered a kind of transitional *mode*, a space between the world of objects and individual thoughts and the online social world of work and school.

Covid as Theme

Parents in each community have agreed that Covid as a theme has emerged in their children's play, although some were quick to deny it, as if its emergence was somehow a sign of fragility or weakness. Our conversations on Zoom and in all three school locations yielded phrases like, 'No, Covid has not come up in my children's play'. But when I offered that many children have been playing doctor or nurse, or have put masks on stuffed animals, the response has consistently been, 'Oh, they play doctor forever':

> She does a lot of, you know, **her dolls get Covid tests, her dolls get fevers, her dolls go to protests** about the teachers not being safe. Her dolls are living her life. And I'm trying to think, well the older daughter was just drawing and painting viruses. **She drew viruses, she drew antibodies. She drew vaccines. It definitely comes up.**

> A mom sighs, the **dolls and animals wear masks and are ALWAYS getting a vaccine.**

> **There's a lot of going to the doctor, going to the hospital.** That kind of stuff has definitely come up for them. I think it subsided a little bit.

> They would make like ten **masks for their dolls and stuffed animals** in virtual play.

> At the LEGO store, **the kids noticed that the LEGOs had masks**. In Switch online, you can choose to have your avatar with a mask, but she does not choose it.

When they play school, it's 'Masks on! Now we're going outside!'

When I wasn't feeling great after being vaccinated, **the kids gave me a check-up** and brought me a snack tray.

A trio of boys are running a candy, soda, and chip sale at the base of the school playground steps, hawking their wares. **One handmade sign says, 'No mask no seRvice' in large, mixed lettering.**

Half of the stories about Covid play involved exaggeration:

The young one has a doctor's kit. He's been giving us shots. **He gives us shots, me and my husband, in our eyeballs and all kinds of places.**

Covid comes up all the time. I am a nursing student in a masters' program. When I'm not nannying, I work in a Covid testing site. All told, sixty to seventy hours a week. She'll ask me questions. She's seen me in scrubs from head to toe and an N95 mask. She put one of her toys in a box and it **'couldn't play with any of the other toys because of Covid'. She puts hair scrunchies on her stuffed animals as masks. She knows what a pulse oximeter is.** She's a very curious kid. . .

I volunteer for Philadelphia Fights [Covid] and volunteer to help people get the vaccine. She asked if we give out stickers. When I said, 'No,' she said, 'What's the point of getting a vaccine if you don't get a sticker?' **So, she made stickers, printed them out.** It says, 'I got my VACSIN'. (*She shows me the image, vaccine proudly misspelled alongside a diagonal stock image of a needle and a small mask that says, 'Wear a mask'*) The child is annoyed that she's too young to get a vaccine, though. She knows what a nasal pharyngeal wall is. **It did make me sad when she put her one toy in a box, in quarantine, and said, 'You're not allowed to play with the other toys'. That toy couldn't hug the other toys.** That's been affecting her. She tells me that when they play Tag at school, they can't touch each other.

They pretended a lot of their toys had to be six feet away. Or ten feet away. Then they would ask, 'When could we be outside?'

The three-year-old likes playing with his mask like a slingshot.

Just today, we ran into a preschool friend of hers here at the playground, 'Jane'. We said, 'Hi Jane'. 'Oh no. Jane has Covid. I'm Rebecca', the other girl insisted. At first, we thought, **'Oh no, Jane has Covid,' then we realized it was an imaginary friend.** A new identity. Jane [aged 5] is now Rebecca because 'Jane has Covid'.

Sometimes exaggerated play emerged indirectly as a by-product of Covid, like these tales of escape. Here Covid frames other kinds of play:

I actually, this isn't like me, but recently **I ordered a ton of toilet paper,** 'cause there was a thing where you couldn't get it. I do not want to worry about that this year, so I had this GIANT box and I brought it in, and asked them what they wanted to do with it, and the oldest saw an airplane. They build—they do this really well. The older said, 'I see an airplane' and the four-year-old said, 'Oh yeah, let's put windows over here', and then they created this giant airplane that they were riding in for days.

The four-year-old, she's really into bags. (*She laughs*) She'll convert many things into a carrying vessel. It might be an actual bag or backpack and she'll stuff it with all kinds of stuff. I think she's going places. She might be at school. She might be going on vacation. She has the thing that she's doing. Or she'll stuff all her baby stuff into it. It's amazing what can be created into a vessel to carry something somewhere. **And then all the stuff moves to a different part of the house.** That reminds me, she asked me for a suitcase for Christmas.

When my seven-year-old went back to school recently, **the four-year-old pretended she went back to school, too.** She got dressed, took a 'first day of school picture', and packed a backpack including her 'computer'.

He's always loved his stuffed animals, but he's gotten a lot more attached to them, since all of this. And it's been like a different one every week. . . **He has this enormous elephant. He is dragging it around the house.** Every time they have show-and-tell, which is not often because it takes up so much time, and listening in to each kid do show-and-tell is the cutest thing you've ever heard, so having him haul this elephant and shoving it in front of the laptop is very funny.

One parent said her child's 'dolls were living her life'. It seems that the children are also using the toys to *play with their lives* through distorted exaggerations that may allow the fear to be managed. Vaccines are in eyeballs. Suitcases are packed and moved to different parts of the house. Masks are toyed with like slingshots and created out of hairbands. The most extreme version was the child who claimed a new imaginary identity for herself, as her real 'self' had Covid and apparently disappeared. Jean Piaget called play 'the primacy of assimilation over accommodation', meaning children will modify the information around them to fit within their own concepts, or here, to fit their own life patterns. Yet, as Brian Sutton-Smith argued in his letter to Piaget, what emerges is not a mere copying of the real world (Piaget 1962; Sutton-Smith 1971). There is an attempt at stretching reality, not just assimilating it. There also seems to be a connection between the dreamy, stretchy surrealism of play and its connection to healing, according to psychologists from Melanie Klein to Erik Erikson to Virginia Axline (Klein 1975 [1932]; Erikson 1975; Axline 1947). The child who appeared the most stressed and did not sleep for days when the pandemic erupted was the child whose play remained untouched and unstretched by the subject of Covid.

Many families spoke of stuffed animals or 'stuffies' as particularly important to the child at this time. Sometimes it was a specific toy, like the enormous stuffed elephant, and sometimes the favorite toy shifted from week to week, often within a specific line of toys. As one parent wrote about her child's stuffed animals, 'They go to school with her in the morning, hang out with her around the house and go to bed with her at night'. The object is not just a loved transitional object, it is imbued with special powers (Winnicott 1977). A theatrical object of relational connection made visible, we see them in cartoons like *Peanuts* with Linus' blanket and *Calvin and Hobbes* with Calvin's stuffed tiger. Yet, Covid has brought the discussion of comfort objects into view as mini social worlds that are controlled by the child, some of which are slept with like traditional transitional objects, some of which are collected and carried everywhere, and some of which are in beloved worlds online, serving as their own kind of electronic social bridge during isolation, all providing rituals of comfort at this time.

World-building as a Folk Practice

As parents arranged and rearranged their families' lives during the pandemic, children arranged and rearranged their toys as a folk practice in all its inequality. Their domestic world-building is not just a mirror of their real pandemic world. James Christie noted that at play 'new meanings are substituted, and actions are performed differently than when they occur in non-play settings' (Christie 1994: 205). Simple re-creation of domestic schemas in animal and human play worlds is itself often associated with extreme stress, as compared to playful schematic hybridity or inversion (Axline 1964; Burghardt 2005; Stallybrass and White 1986). In the final examples below, the children are playing out their worlds dialogically without any obvious dialogue, offering their domestic scenes as artistic offerings (Bakhtin 1981; Flanagan 2009; Pasierbska 2008; Opie, Opie and Alderson 1989; Sutton-Smith 1986, Sutton-Smith 2017), as iconic Covid puzzles.

One parent described a child's repetitive play of being ill and of being rescued, acted out through Anna and Elsa dolls from *Frozen* (Figure 8.1). This is excerpted from a longer Zoom interview.

Researcher: I'm curious which dolls or stuffed animals does she pretend to have fevers and things like that.

Parent: She has these little like kid versions of Anna and Elsa from *Frozen*. And she calls them Anya and Elsa. Like what her life is. See where they are? Always, they're always around.

Researcher: Okay.

Parent: So (it's) like her whole life. They just got a bath there on the bathroom floor. Her whole room is like these little vignettes. I actually have to clean it up. I'm glad I didn't. So, like here they are. This is the ambulance, this truck.

Researcher: The ambulance.

Parent: And that's the hospital. So, this definitely plays
                out. And there's the amusement park, right, and
                then we have our emergency vehicles that come
                to the rescue.

Figure 8.1 'Playroom' (22 February 2021), Elliott, aged five
Screenshot © Anna Beresin, 2023, and used with permission

In the example above, the movie-inspired characters play out the child's
concerns like a song on repeat but the child mixes hospital narratives
with amusement park toys as spoken by the movie characters. For
another child, world-building was reduced to architectural designs of
impossible buildings, like the art of M. C. Escher in Figure 8.2.

   For others, the pandemic was a time to turn inward and was partially
lived in a screen-filled home, shown here as Figure 8.3. This chalk
drawing of a satellite dish was found rubbed onto the schoolyard that
had no playground.

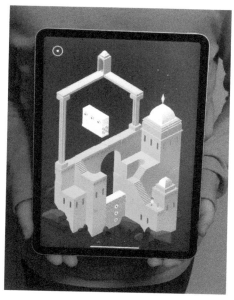

Figure 8.2 'Monument Valley, an Ustwo Puzzle Game' (23 February 2021), played by Mona, aged nine

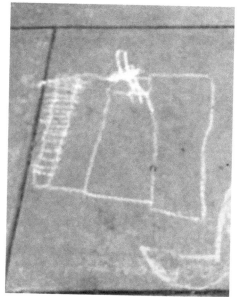

Figure 8.3 'House with Satellite Dish' (28 April 2021), chalked by a child on the schoolyard with no playground

One could say that the satellite drawing and the impossible house image do not have specific connections to the pandemic, yet the latter was chosen by a child as her favourite pandemic activity. The satellite dish was one of only three images chalked during the entire research period in the one community, alongside a faint image of a frowning girl and a lightly drawn flying superhero. Recent publications in the folklore of online play suggest that the division of the online world and the 'real' world is more permeable than previously believed (de Souza e Silva and Glover-Rijkse 2020; Willett et al. 2013). Perhaps online play—from the more passive forms of television and YouTube to the more active open worlds of computer games, video games and movie-related toy play—all can be considered a kind of world-building doll play, a spectrum ripe for research.

Brian Sutton-Smith writes, 'Children's play fantasies are not meant only to replicate the world, nor to be only its therapy; they are meant to fabricate another world that lives alongside the first one and carries on its own kind of life, a life often much more emotionally vivid than mundane reality' (1997: 158). For some children, this has been a time to go further inside the self, shown here in this drawing of a child's imagined rocket in Figure 8.4.

Figure 8.4 'Some Air', Conor (9 April 2021), aged seven

The father said it was drawn in the child's thinking place during quarantine, the glass-enclosed porch at the front of their house, as the child would go there to watch people walk by as a liminal form of social life. The rocket was up in 'some air', and when he needed 'some air' he would go to his porch. The seven-year-old took particular pride in naming his drawings himself. Note the intense marking of the box with its windows at the centre, the child simultaneously escaping the house and the pandemic world.

And some children were busy in their pods, building new frames in more than one home, transitioning from this reality to a different one.

> They've been doing a lot of building villages. Two kids will go and build like a school, and another will build a library and add on a fire station or a police station. It's almost like they're trying to find out, since we're not out in the real world, 'what does a village look like' kind of thing. There's been a lot of taking care of each other and friends taking care of each other in different ways; that's come up quite a bit. And they're really into using little figurines that they'll include when they build a LEGO house. . . They are creating their own imaginary society in a way. It's kind of interesting. All of the parents have talked about that, all have observed them in our homes. They will come to read to the others and give a prize. They are their own little society. I've never seen this kind of play play out before.

Perhaps this is play's greatest gift to our collective survival, exaggeration in communities both real and imagined, moving from this ambulance to some safe new place with air.

Works Cited

Axline, Virginia. 1947. *Play Therapy: The Inner Dynamics of Childhood* (Boston: Houghton Mifflin)

——. 1964. *Dibs in Search of Self* (New York: Ballantine)

Bakhtin, Mikhail. 1981. *The Dialogic Imagination* (Austin: Texas University Press)

Beresin, Anna. 2014. *The Art of Play: Recess and the Practice of Invention* (Philadelphia, PA: Temple University Press)

——. 2015. 'Pen Tapping: Forbidden Folklore', *Journal of Folklore and Education*, 2: 19-21, https://jfepublications.org/wp-content/uploads/2016/05/webJFE2015vol2final.pdf

——. In press. 'Unequal Resources: Space, Time, and Loose Parts and What to Do with an Uneven Playing Field', in *Play and Social Justice*, ed. by Olga Jarrett and Vera Stenhouse (Berne: Peter Lang)

Burghardt, Gordon. 2005. *The Genesis of Animal Play: Testing the Limits* (Cambridge, MA: MIT Press)

Christie, James M. 1994. 'Academic Play', in *Play and Intervention*, ed. by Joop Hellendoorn, Rimmert van der Kooij, and Brian Sutton-Smith (Albany: State University of New York Press), pp. 203-13

Erickson, Frederick. 1990. 'Qualitative Methods', in *Quantitative Methods/Qualitative Methods*, ed. by R. L. Linn and F. Erickson (New York: Macmillan), pp. 77-187

Erikson, Erik. 1975. *Studies of Play* (New York: Arno)

Feldman, Nina. 2019. 'Why Your Neighborhood School Probably Doesn't Have a Playground', *WHYY Radio* (6 February)

Flanagan, Mary. 2009. *Critical Play: Radical Game Design* (Cambridge, MA: MIT Press)

Kang, Jay Caspian. 2022. 'Ten-year-old Ryan Kaji and His Family Have Turned Videos of Him Playing with Toys into a Multimillion-dollar Empire: Why Do So Many Other Kids Want to Watch?' *New York Times*, 9 January, pp. 22-25, 47-49, https://www.nytimes.com/2022/01/05/magazine/ryan-kaji-youtube.html

Klein, Melanie. 1975 [1932]. *The Psycho-analysis of Children*, trans. by A. Strachey (London: Hogarth)

Konner, Melvin. 2010. *The Evolution of Childhood: Relationships, Emotion, Mind* (Cambridge: MA: Harvard University Press)

Lancy, David. 2022. *Anthropology of Childhood: Cherubs, Chattel, Changelings*, 3rd edn (Cambridge: Cambridge University Press)

Opie, Iona, Robert Opie, and Brian Alderson. 1989. *The Treasures of Childhood: Books, Toys, and Games from the Opie Collection* (London: Arcade)

Pasierbska, Halina. 2008. *Doll's Houses from the V&A Museum of Childhood* (London: V&A)

Piaget, Jean. 1962. *Play, Dreams, and Imitation in Childhood* (New York: Norton)

de Souza e Silva, Adriana, and Ragan Glover-Rijkse. 2020. 'Introduction: Understanding Hybrid Play', in *Hybrid Play: Crossing Boundaries in Game Design, Player Identities and Play Spaces*, ed. by Adriana de Souza e Silva and Ragan Glover-Rijkse (Routledge: London), pp. 1-12

Stallybrass, Peter, and Allon White. 1986. *The Politics and Poetics of Transgression* (Ithaca: Cornell University Press)

Sutton-Smith, Brian. 1971. 'A Reply to Piaget: A Play Theory of Copy', in *Child's Play*, ed. by R. E. Herron and B. Sutton-Smith (New York: Wiley), pp. 340-42

——. 1986. *Toys as Culture* (New York: Gardner Press)

——. 1997. *The Ambiguity of Play* (Cambridge, MA: Harvard University Press)

——. 2017. *Play for Life: Play Theory and Play as Emotional Survival* (Rochester, NY: Strong Museum of Play)

Tannen, Deborah. 2007. *Talking Voices: Repetition, Dialogue, and Imagery in Conversational Discourse* (Cambridge: Cambridge University Press)

Vygotsky, Lev. 1978. *Mind in Society: The Development of Higher Psychological Processes.* Ed. by M. Cole (Cambridge, MA: Harvard University Press)

Willett, Rebekah, Chris Richards, Jackie Marsh, Andrew Burn, and Julia Bishop. 2013. *Children, Media, and Playground Cultures: Ethnographic Studies of School Playtimes* (London: Palgrave Macmillan)

Winnicott, D. W. 1971. *Playing and Reality* (London: Tavistock)

9. Parents' Perspectives on Their Children's Play and Friendships during the Covid-19 Pandemic in England

Caron Carter

Introduction

Historically, research on children's friendships in educational contexts has been overlooked, with academic progress and attainment taking precedence. In recent years, there is growing recognition of the importance of children's friendships, particularly in relation to children's social and emotional well-being and their learning and development (Daniels et al. 2010; Hedges and Cooper 2017; Peters 2003). While the existing research is valuable, it does not address how children coped without face-to-face interactions with friends during Covid-19 lockdowns and subsequent restrictions. This topic of inquiry is crucial as schools are now tasked with supporting children with their friendships and well-being as children return post-lockdown (Education Endowment Foundation 2022; O'Toole and Simovska 2021). Relatively little is known about how children managed without their usual friendship interactions. Questions remain about how children creatively maintained play with friends and how the answers might be used to support children's friendships in the future. This chapter poses the question: What are parents' perceptions of children's play and friendships during the Covid-19 pandemic?

 https://doi.org/10.11647/OBP.0326.09

While a recent study has used online questionnaires to gather data from children (aged five to fourteen years old) about their friendships during this time (Larivière-Bastien et al. 2022: 9), to my knowledge there is no research using in-depth, semi-structured interviews with parents of young children (six- to seven-year-olds) in England.

The Affordances of Friendship

Friendship matters to children (UNICEF 2011) and affords several benefits socially, emotionally and academically (Hedges and Cooper 2017; Kragh-Muller and Isbell 2011). Quality friendships can provide children with opportunities to understand and regulate their emotions and interactions with others (Coelho et al. 2017: 813; Dunn and Cutting 1999); friendship can thus enhance children's social and emotional competences' (Engdahl 2012: 86).

A range of studies have highlighted the association between children's friendships and play. Engdahl (2012: 86) notes succinctly that 'children play with their friends, and they develop friendships while playing'. Positive play interactions with friends are therefore an important ingredient for making and maintaining children's friendships. Having friends that participate in enjoyable play has also been connected to enhanced well-being and positive school experience (Fattore, Mason and Watson 2016; Hollingsworth and Buysse 2009; Murray and Harrison 2005; Streelasky 2017). Likewise, higher levels of self-confidence and self-worth in children have been linked to the presence of stable, quality friendships (Berndt and Keefe 1995; Engle, McElwain and Lasky 2011). Research also indicates the benefits friendship can have on learning and development including improved school attainment (Ladd 1990).

However, friendship cannot be taken for granted and is not guaranteed for all children (Engdahl 2012). Not being able to make friends can have a negative impact on children. This experience can cause a child stress, damage self-esteem, affect engagement and learning, and influence their future relationships with peers (Daniels et al. 2010; Ladd 1990; Murray and Harrison, 2005). Simply having a friend or friends is not necessarily a protective factor. It is the quality of the friendships that makes the difference and can lead to higher self-worth and better school experiences (Gifford-Smith and Brownell 2003). Furthermore, friendships can be fragile and unstable, especially in younger children (Rubin et al. 2005). Therefore, children need time and space to nurture and maintain quality friendships (both in and out of school) for positive well-being and holistic development and learning (Carter 2021; Carter 2022a; Carter and Nutbrown 2016; Chan and Poulin 2007). During the Covid-19 lockdown and restrictions, this time and space for friendships was removed or radically reduced and altered.

Context: Covid-19 Pandemic

On 20 March 2020 England went into a national lockdown due to the Covid-19 pandemic. Schools were closed to most pupils with only some key workers and vulnerable children continuing to attend. During this lockdown period, households were only permitted to go out once per day for exercise or for provisions. Even when lockdown came to an end and some schools reopened in June to children in Year 1 (five- to six-year-olds) and Year 6 (ten- to eleven-year-olds), restrictions remained regarding social distancing (Department for Education 2020). For children, the lockdown and restrictions led to a lack of in-person social contact with their friends.

During lockdown and home-based learning, there was no guidance given to children and families about how to manage and maintain children's friendships. When schools fully re-opened to all children in September 2020, some official guidance for schools was issued stating that children may need pastoral care to help them reconnect socially (Department for Education 2020). Children were kept in 'bubbles' to reduce their number of contacts in school. Bubbles were groups, classes or year groups of pupils that had to be kept together; children could not play with others outside of their bubble. Consequently, many parents remained fearful or reticent about allowing their children to have social contact with friends out of school. Some children were unable to participate in their usual after-school provision/activities which were still on hiatus due to concerns about potential rises in infection rates. In summary, for many children, disruption to friendship interactions continued for several months or longer beyond the lockdown.

The adverse effects of Covid-19 social restrictions on children and families are already evident and for some the effects will be long-lasting (Goldschmidt 2020; Loades et al. 2020; Rider et al. 2021; United Nations 2020). Many families experienced stress, anxiety and depression as a result of the restrictive measures (Pascal et al. 2020). There are recent studies suggesting that the psychological impacts on children include loneliness, anxiety and struggling to cope in the absence of friends and school (Egan et al. 2021). Children have reported concerns about losing friends during the lockdown (Lundie and Law 2020). As pupils returned to school, pastoral support for children was and continues to be a high priority. Schools have also reported the need for 'long term planning for social and wellbeing interventions' (Achtaridou et al. 2022: 31), which is indicative of the legacy of the pandemic restrictions for children socially and emotionally.

The Voice of Parents

The data for this chapter are drawn from a larger pilot study on children's friendships. Fieldwork for that study took place largely before the pandemic and involved teachers, teaching assistants, lunchtime welfare supervisors and children. The initial research design did not include parents but it became apparent to me after talking to adults in school that the perspectives of parents were missing and were needed in this study. The following vignettes from participants in the larger study prompted a period of reflection for me. There were instances where school staff felt that parents did not always understand the complexity and challenge involved in handling friendship play scenarios in the school settings. In schools, staff must manage these friendship dynamics in a class of thirty or more, whereas parents have just their own child or children in mind. For example, the following commentary by a lunchtime welfare supervisor describes the challenges of working to meet the needs of both the parents and the children.

Researcher:	Do you feel that adults/teachers can support children's friendships?
Lunchtime Welfare Supervisor:	Yes. They see as well how they are in the classroom and also they have a lot of input from parents, who they want to play with, who they can play with. Some have got issues and they can't play together, they're in the same class and they can play together at break and stuff but at lunch we have to keep them separate. Some we just have to do because that's what the parents say but I know that sometimes it's discussed, why can't we teach them to play nicely, rather than keeping them apart? That's not up to us. If you've got two children that have to be kept apart and you've got one child that likes to play with both of them and that child then has to choose who they play with, which is a lot for that child.

Similarly, the following extract gives a teacher's perspective:

Researcher:	Do you feel parents are on side [with friendship issues]?
Teacher:	It tends to be, at the end of the day if there has been an issue, I'll then keep that child behind and say to the parent, this has happened in the playground today. Can you talk about it at home with them? Most parents are quite on board with it, but some parents are, kind of, 'Well they don't want to play that game'. Sometimes they're not always going to have their first choice of game. Sometimes they have to be able to negotiate or they have to be able to take the back seat sometimes. Some parents find that hard to get across to their child that actually their child is one of thirty within the class and it won't always be their child who gets to pick the game every time. Some parents and some children expect that to be the case. So some parents are less on board with that than others.

Being a parent myself, I thought it was important to explore this further. Parents often hear about happenings at school second-hand and they do not always know the full truth of a situation. Trying to support children from home with friendship scenarios, without understanding the bigger picture, is often a challenge for parents and carers. This is evident in the headteacher's comments here:

Headteacher: I can think of a friendship situation we're managing from one class, and two children are playing in separate playgrounds and have done for a number of months. That is as much to support the parents with this process as well, so they're reassured that they're not playing together, as it is for the children themselves.

Researcher: You said you know sometimes parents can have concerns and it's quite hard if you're the parent because you're not there at school?

Headteacher: It is hard, partly because when children go home, they tell the story from their perception and that isn't always the true reality. Some parents have an understanding of children and will understand that their child isn't lying, but will be telling things completely from their perspective, and therefore when they come and see us, as a school, they come from the perspective of understanding to try and find more information and to find out what the actual reality is. A few parents we have to help because they can only see it from their child's perspective and their child doesn't always have a true understanding of what has actually happened.

Following reflection on this data collection it was clear to me that the need for parent voice warranted a new strand of data. Consequently, I obtained ethical approval for some additional interviews investigating parents' perspectives on supporting children's friendships. Just when I planned to interview parents face-to-face, we went into the first Covid-19 lockdown period. This forced the interviews to go online but fortuitously the timing allowed for exploration of parents' perspectives on how this unprecedented lockdown was affecting children's friendships. Thus, the additional data collection involved parent voice exclusively—hearing parents' opinions and perceptions of their children's experiences of play and friendships during this timeframe. Therefore, I acknowledge that the data cannot be considered to be truly representative of the children's own voices and perspectives. For details on child voice, see Carter, Barley and Omar (2023).

Research Methods

As stated, the data for this chapter forms part of a larger study for which most of the fieldwork took place before Covid-19. Only the data from parents were collected during the pandemic, in June 2020 after the first lockdown. These parent interviews enabled me to investigate how children had managed play and friendship during the lockdown. The setting was an infant and preschool in the north of England providing education for children aged between three and seven years old, with approximately three hundred children on roll. To research the phenomenon of children's friendships in one setting, the methodology adopted was a single case study. The intention was not to generalize from the findings, but to allow for an in-depth investigation (Yin 2018) to discover what could be learnt from this single specific context.

Online interviews were the primary method of collecting data from the parents, with supplementary methods being fieldnotes and a reflective research diary. Individuals experience life in different ways and interpret and make meaning of life events through different lenses or perspectives (Salmons 2014). Therefore, interviews were the most appropriate method for learning about the varied perspectives of parents on their children's play and friendships during this unique period post-lockdown. The online modality had the advantage of being Covid-secure, given that we were still subject to restrictions including working from home. All of the parents interviewed stated their preference for online interviews over face-to-face meetings. Their reasons were twofold: Covid-19 safety considerations, but also the time saving and flexibility of fitting interviews around work schedules and not needing to come into schools. The parents may also have felt more comfortable in their own environment than school settings, therefore lessening any potential effects of power dynamics.

The participants were recruited through the school. Information and consent forms were emailed to parents of all three Year 2 classes (the phase focus for this research). Four female parents and one male parent agreed to participate. Greater detail on the participants is not provided here as their anonymity could be compromised. This group of five is a smaller sample of parents than anticipated prior to the pandemic. The original aim was to recruit twelve parents for this pilot. However, recruiting participants for research was more challenging during the pandemic because families and schools were under increased pressures. In these circumstances, it would have been unethical to persist in chasing potential recruits for responses in the hope of achieving a larger sample. However, it was still feasible to proceed with in-depth interviews but with a smaller number of participants. The study was approved by Sheffield Hallam University's Ethics Review Board. Informed consent was obtained in writing from all participants and they were given pseudonyms to ensure anonymity and confidentiality. All quotations by parents used in this chapter have assigned pseudonyms.

The data analysis was guided by Braun and Clarke's reflexive thematic analysis (TA) (2019). Reflexive TA is a method of 'developing, analysing and interpreting patterns across a qualitative dataset' in order to develop themes (Braun and Clarke 2022: 4). The first phase of this analytic process requires the researcher to familiarize themselves with the dataset. This required listening to the recordings, re-reading interview transcripts and fieldnotes. The second stage involved coding the data with concise labels that helped to organize the data and map it to the research question. In the third phase, initial themes were generated. Finally, the fourth stage called for revisiting, developing and reviewing the themes (Braun and Clarke 2006). The aim was to conduct a 'rich, nuanced analysis' that responded to the research question and revolved around a central concept (Braun and Clarke 2022: 97).

Findings and Analysis

The aim of this study was to investigate parents' views and perceptions of their children's play and friendships during the Covid-19 lockdown and restrictions. The main findings fall within two key themes: (1) that children adopted alternative strategies to interact with their friends creatively and playfully, and (2) parents became more grateful for their children's friendships, as did some of the children themselves.

Theme 1—Creative Strategies to Interact with Friends

The absence of face-to-face opportunities for play during the lockdown and continued restrictions led to children and families having to resort to alternative means if they wanted to maintain contact with their friends. Parents found themselves standing in place of school in their children's lives, including taking on the full-time role of teacher, but for many parents the greater challenge was providing for the holistic needs of their child. For example, Connie explained that although she felt able to support and nurture her child academically, it was more difficult to plug the gap socially.

> I think it's extremely important. I think it's one of the reasons why with the pandemic it's so important for children to be at school because I just think there's a risk—I think it's just detrimental for them not to be in school, even more so for the friendships in some ways, you know, because we're fortunate ourselves to have, you know, for me and my husband to have a good education and therefore academically in some ways we can plug those gaps when they're not at school but you can't replace the sort of friendships and the time that they spend together when they're not. Obviously, the academic educational side is really important but just thinking about the last six months, you know, we could plug some of those academic gaps by doing reading, writing, some maths with them, but there's just no replacement for the interactions with other children and what they learn in the playground and the feedback that they get from their friends, I don't think.

To meet the challenges, all parents reported strategies they had used as a family to help their children to interact with friends in creative and playful ways. Parents spoke mostly about three strategies: the use of the Zoom online meeting platform, video messages/calls and doorstep visits.

Strategy 1—Zoom

Connie recalled how her daughter had made use of Zoom during the lockdown to stay in touch with her friends, particularly her closest friend who is an only child. Connie was impressed by her daughter's creative use of Zoom:

> We did try. So we used Zoom for her to interact with some of her friends and I think she actually managed with Zoom pretty well all things considered [...] I think she was particularly good at using Zoom so they used to play games and all sorts by Zoom. They'd do little imagination games, they'd read to each other over Zoom, play Hide and Seek and I Spy and they were really quite creative in how they used Zoom.

For many children, Zoom provided a forum for play activities with friends, enabling treasure hunts, quizzes, bingo and sharing/showing LEGO and toys. These opportunities for continued imaginative play with friends, albeit through virtual contact, were vital. Time and space to nurture and maintain quality friendships were important during the lockdown and restrictions in order to support children's development, learning and well-being (Carter 2021; Carter 2022b; Carter and Nutbrown 2016). Likewise, having fun play experiences with friends promotes enhanced well-being and positive school experiences (Fattore, Mason and Watson 2016; Hollingsworth and Buysse 2009; Streelasky 2017). Maintaining friendships was also essential for the return to school; Zoom interaction could facilitate this maintenance. However, Zoom was not the best strategy for everyone. For example, Connie was aware that Zoom did not work for all of her child's friends.

> I think some of her friends really struggled with it [Zoom] and so it was harder to keep in touch with them in that way [...] but certainly that wasn't across the board [a positive Zoom experience], and I think some of her friends they did find it really difficult to use Zoom.

Another parent whose child had additional needs and found friendship more challenging, especially initiating friendships, did not feel that Zoom worked for them either.

> So he wasn't too keen on Zoom meetings with other friends because, I don't know, I think a lot of them just find them a bit dull but they did exchange, were using my phone or using their parents' phone, messages and video messages. (Andrea)

This perspective gives a sense that for many children some modes of online play with friends did not suit them. Four out of the five parents talked about how they had started with Zoom or other platforms but the novelty soon wore off. Some children, such as Andrea's son, felt uncomfortable in this arena. Parents also knew of many children who were without the technology to connect virtually with friends and this anecdotal evidence aligns with official data (Organization for Economic Co-operation and Development 2020). The upshot is that the pandemic restrictions removed or greatly reduced children's time and space for friendship interaction, removing with it the benefits provided by quality, stable friendships including higher self-confidence and self-worth (Daniels et al. 2010; Gifford-Smith and Brownell 2003; Ladd 1990; Murray and Harrison 2005). Research shows that this absence of social interaction had negative impacts on children's well-being (Lundie and Law 2020). These challenges resonate with reports by schools that they are prioritizing pastoral support for children and putting in place social, emotional and well-being initiatives (Achtaridou et al. 2022: 31).

Strategy 2—Video Messaging/Calls in the Absence of Birthday Parties

A couple of the parents said that the absence of face-to-face birthday parties during lockdown and restrictions had been significant for children. Birthday parties figure strongly in the peer culture of infant, school-age children (between four and seven years old) (Bath 2009). Andrea spoke about the absence of a birthday party having a considerable impact on her son. Instead, they had used video messages creatively to celebrate the occasion and try to fill the birthday party gap:

> Yeah. I mean it was hard because during that time from March to May I think we couldn't even meet anybody even outdoors so that was hard and he had his birthday during that time as well but what we did was some friends [...] well, they would make videos of themselves and they would send video messages to each other

so we did that and actually for his birthday I'd asked some of his close friends to record a video message for him and then collected it all together and he watched it on his birthday so he really liked that.

Nevertheless, as was the case with Zoom, video messages and calls did not work for all of the families. Melanie talked about the short-lived effectiveness of video calls for her child.

The funny thing was though, over lockdown I tried to do video calls and stuff with her friends, so she got to see them and we did that for a while but then she kind of got a bit bored of it.

Strategy 3—Doorstep Visits

Three out of the five parents spoke about doorstep visits. These were often conducted with one family standing at the bottom of the drive while members of the other family were at their doorstep or an open window. These were often friends who were located geographically nearby to one another. Sometimes gifts were also left by the front door. Lucy stated: 'We did some doorstep visits to a couple of her friends'. Doorstep visits provided opportunities for children to see each other but not for fun and enjoyable play experiences (Fattore, Mason and Watson 2016; Hollingsworth and Buysse 2009; Murray and Harrison 2005; Streelasky 2017). This finding chimes with the research of Larivière-Bastien et al. (2022: 9) which noted that 'physical closeness' between friends, an important dimension of children's friendships, was absent during Covid-19 restrictions.

To conclude this theme, it seems that all children and families in the study tried some means of virtual contact with friends. For some this worked well but for many these measures had only short-term utility. Parents felt that nothing compared to the face-to-face modality of interaction with friends, where children could experience play that was fun, enjoyable and physically close. Most parents talked about arranging outdoor play dates as soon as they were permitted to do so, as stated by Connie:

As the restrictions eased and we could see people outside and things we then did try to really make as many play dates as was allowable within the restrictions at the time.

Theme 2—The 'Newfound Joy' of Friendship

Valuing Friendship: 'You only appreciate it when it's gone'

All the parents spoke positively about the value of children's friendships and especially having experienced lockdown and social restrictions. The following quotations by parents illustrate that they found play and friendships important in different ways. Although they may have known the value of children's friendships pre-pandemic, it is interesting that all the parents elaborated on the positive affordances of play and friendship for their child during this period.

> I think she gets [...] positive reinforcement of herself. I think friendships are important for their self-confidence and self-worth. I think enjoyment, fun, you know, people who will play games and have ideas that sort of match hers and on her level [...] I think she probably gets different things from different friends I would say. (Connie)

> I definitely think there are a lot of positives to the friendships [...] I think it makes the experience of school much more enjoyable for him and he looks forward to school more now that he's got an established set of friendships there. I think overall also he feels more as a part of the class that, oh, you know, I sit with this person and I had lunch with this person and I'm going to see this person so I think there's that greater sense of belonging and also feeling more enthusiastic about going to school. Oh, I think it's really important. (Andrea)

> Yes. I think it's very hard to be able to learn and develop yourself without a peer support network and I think friendship is very much linked to your happiness and well-being isn't it and if you're not happy and feeling well and buoyant it's hard to learn, isn't it? So, yeah, I think it's very important. That being said, I'm coming at it from me being a very sociable creature and my children being very sociable creatures and I don't know whether it would be the same for a child that perhaps doesn't really want to. (Lucy)

Firstly, we have Connie valuing friendships for children's self-worth and self-confidence. This aligns with the literature on the association between these outcomes and quality, stable friendships (Daniels et al. 2010; Gifford-Smith and Brownell 2003; Murray and Harrison 2005). Connie valued the fun and enjoyment her daughter experienced when playing with others and coming up with ideas for games together. Similarly, Andrea noted that her son's experience of school had improved once he had an established group of friends. Both of these perspectives reflect research cited earlier in this chapter on the benefits of friendship and play for children's well-being and school experiences (Fattore, Mason and Watson 2016; Hollingsworth and Buysse 2009; Streelasky 2017). Finally, Lucy discussed how friendships are integral to happiness and well-being which has a knock-on effect on learning. Again, this idea is supported by research which suggests that positive friendships are associated with improved attainment (Ladd 1990).

All of the parents post-lockdown said that their children seemed to have renewed gratitude for friendships and their affordances. For instance, Connie talked about her child's response to being reunited with friends.

> Do you know what? I think they emerged out the other side of lockdown a little bit more grateful for each other which was nice [...] so I don't think she realized that she missed her friends as much as what she did when she saw them again. So it was almost like a newfound joy, I think, seeing her friends again which was nice. Has it changed? Yeah, I think because they've all sort of adapted really well and slotted straight back in, just as friends do, you know, you don't see each other for a few years or whatever, in their case probably is the equivalent of years isn't it and they've just slotted, they seem to have slotted straight back in to where they left off.

A Welcome Break from Enforced Socialization

According to some parents, lockdown was a welcome break from obligatory social interaction for their children, including those who find friendship more challenging to navigate. Andrea reported on how the break benefitted her son who has additional needs. She felt this break allowed him to have a smooth transition back into play and friendship when schools reopened.

But the good thing I've seen is that once he went back to school it's kind of happened really naturally and it almost went back instantly which was really good to see, because I was like, oh, this has been a six-month gap and what's it going to be like but it's been really good actually. I think lockdown was good for him, gave him a bit of a break and now he's gone back and he's doing much better, touch wood.

Early research does indicate that being at home during lockdown reduced stress and pressure on some children and therefore enhanced their well-being. This was particularly pertinent to children who before the pandemic had negative experiences at school such as bullying (Ziauddeen et al. 2020).

Likewise, being at home may have suited some children's personalities or inclinations. For example, Melanie talked about how her daughter simply enjoyed the break and doing things at home with her family.

I asked her was she missing her friends and was she missing school and stuff and she never was, she was very happy just being at home with her family. So she's happy with them but she does need them I think […] Yeah, she said she didn't want to go back to school, she was happy just being at home and playing and doing the stuff we did at home. I expected when she went back to school it to be more difficult. I thought it would be more of a shock and she'd be more upset but she's adapted really well to it […] She has a really nice little group of friends but, yeah, she did, she was quite self-contained and happy during lockdown.

Some families were able to spend more time together, resulting in positive interactions between children and adults (Goldschmidt 2020). Other parents also talked about the social gap being filled by a sibling(s). Some siblings were close in age or enjoyed one another's company and were able to play together imaginatively as they would with their friends.

I think having a sibling at home eased things. My two get on very, very well so by and large they'll just go off and play whatever imaginative game they're into at the time. (Lucy)

It seems that although children expressed contentment with family and siblings, these relationships could not replace their friendships, something which became evident when they returned to school. Connie's words movingly illustrate this: when her daughter was reunited with friends, it was like a 'newfound joy'.

Discussion

This chapter addresses the following research question: What are parents' perceptions of children's play and friendships during the Covid-19 pandemic? Two main insights were highlighted. First, children and families were using a range of strategies to interact virtually with friends, although none was as effective as in-person play with friends. Second, appreciation for the value of children's friendships was reignited either during lockdown or when children returned to school.

Face-to-face Play with Friends Was Irreplaceable

The findings provide new evidence about the irreplaceable nature of 'real world', face-to-face play with friends and the value of friendship and its affordances. All the parents discussed how their child had used virtual means of making contact and interacting with friends. One parent, Connie, felt that online platforms enabled her child to continue her imaginative play with peers (referred to in 'Strategy 1: Zoom' above). They continued to enjoy games like Hide and Seek and I Spy. Other parents reported that the novelty of virtual contact soon wore off because children either grew bored or realized the social limitations of the platform. Andrea and Connie recalled that some children became bored or just found it difficult to interact online.

Virtual technology was appreciated but found to be greatly inferior to the face-to-face mode of play and interaction with friends. Parents reported that children did not possess phones of their own so connecting with their friends in this way would have been new to most of them. The data indicate that use of platforms like Zoom may have supported some friendships to thrive by enabling children to show toys, play games and share tours of their homes and gardens. However, in other cases, parents reported that children seemed to find it awkward to work out what to say and how to be with friends in these new virtual spaces. These findings are consistent with emerging research by Larivière-Bastien and others (2022) which focused on children in the five-to-fourteen age range. In their study, children often found it challenging to read social cues or facial expressions through virtual interaction and some virtual conversations had awkward silences. Of course, one might speculate that lack of privacy from adults and/or siblings, compared to children's experiences in the playground for example, could contribute to the awkwardness.

Doorstep visits were another strategy used by three of the families in the present study. These visits enabled friends to see one another from afar but the interaction was deemed unsatisfactory in comparison to the usual play with friends which included fun, enjoyment and physical closeness (Fattore, Mason and Watson 2016; Hollingsworth and Buysse 2009; Larivière-Bastien et al. 2022; Murray and Harrison 2005; Streelasky 2017). These findings indicate that parents feel that their children have been socially isolated from their friends and denied the means to adequately play and interact. Essentially, this predicament stemmed from official restrictions by government and was contrary to Article 15 of the United Nations Convention on the Rights of the Child, which states that children should have the right to play with other children, form friendships and join organizations (United Nations 2013). Interaction with friends is essential for children's well-being and mental health. Indeed, in the wake of the pandemic, children now need opportunities to reconnect with friends and experience extended periods of play (Pascal et al. 2020) to counteract this social deficit. Time and space to reconnect could be allocated during the school day or in cost-free activities after school (Carter 2022b).

The Renewed Value of Friendship

A novel finding was that parents had a renewed sense of value for their children's friendships. The parents were able to articulate the specific affordances of friendship for children including self-confidence, self-worth, fun and enjoyment, a more positive experience of school and a disposition that is ready and receptive to learning. All these affordances are supported by the research literature (Fattore, Mason and Watson 2016; Hollingsworth and Buysse 2009; Larivière-Bastien et al. 2022; Murray and Harrison 2005; Streelasky 2017).

A couple of the parents felt that their children had not really missed their friendships while they were confined to their homes as they had a sibling to play with and/or felt quite contained within their family. As quoted above, Melanie recalled that her daughter was content at home and did not miss her friends. However, upon return to school the children recognized that they had missed their friends and that these special relationships were different to those with siblings and parents (Dunn 2004). Connie acknowledged that her daughter realized she had missed her friends upon being reunited with them.

There were interesting observations by some parents that their children welcomed respite from the pressure to interact socially with friends in school. Andrea, as quoted above, commented on her son benefitting from a break in social interaction with peers. Her child had additional needs and often found instigating play with friends a challenge. The pause in social activity may have been doubly beneficial for this child—it was a comfortable break in itself but the absence of friends also served eventually to reawaken his appreciation for friendships and supported his reintegration back into school.

Children's friendships may have been taken for granted by parents prior to the pandemic. When Covid-19 restrictions effectively removed opportunities for children to play and interact with friends, the unprecedented changes perhaps invited the cliché that something is not appreciated until it is gone. Lockdown put children's friendships and their positive affordances under the spotlight. A silver lining of this challenging period is that the links between children's friendships, well-being and mental health have been brought to the fore (Carter 2022b). Perhaps these illuminated links are why the parents in this study valued friendship so highly in terms of its contribution to children's happiness and development. This is in line with Carter and Nutbrown's 'pedagogy of friendship' (2016). Their approach calls for adults to value and respect children's friendships, to be knowledgeable about how young children's friendships are enacted, and to provide opportunities—time and space—for children to have agency to nurture and maintain their friendships (Carter 2022a). Where parents and educational settings value and understand the importance of friendships, they are likely to be made a genuine priority.

Implications for Future Research and Practice

There are obvious limitations to using a small sample. From a single case study involving a specific group of five parents, the findings cannot be generalized. However, the data do provide important insights into how parents perceived their children's play and friendships during the pandemic lockdown and restrictions. These valuable insights may chime with other parents' perceptions. In future research, it would be intriguing to explore parents' perspectives using a larger and heterogenous sample of in-depth qualitative interviews to add to these pilot study findings. It would be fruitful also to hear from more children directly about their experiences of play and friendship during the Covid-19 pandemic (Carter, Barley and Omar 2023). This is an important task given that children in some contexts were 'marginalised and their voices silenced' during the pandemic (Lomax and others 2021: 1). To conclude, the findings add to the existing small body of knowledge on how children and families coped in the absence of in-person interaction with friends during lockdown and restrictions. This chapter amplifies the case for parents and educational settings to provide opportunities for children's friendships to be made, re-established, nurtured and maintained during the period of Covid recovery.

Works Cited

Achtaridou, Elpida, et al. 2022. *School Recovery Strategies: Year 1 Findings* (London: Department for Education)

Bagwell, Catherine L., and Michelle E. Schmidt. 2011. *Friendships in Childhood and Adolescence* (New York: Guilford)

Bath, Caroline. 2009. Learning to Belong: Exploring Young Children's Participation at the Start of School (London: Routledge)

Berndt, Thomas. J., and Keunho Keefe. 1995. 'Friends' Influence on Adolescents' Adjustment to School', *Child Development*, 66: 1312–329, https://doi.org/10.1111/j.1467-8624.1995.tb00937.x

Braun, Virginia, and Victoria Clarke. 2006. 'Using Thematic Analysis in Psychology', *Qualitative Research in Psychology*, 3: 77–101, https://doi.org/10.1191/1478088706qp063oa

——. 2019. 'Reflecting on Reflexive Thematic Analysis', *Qualitative Research in Sport, Exercise and Health*, 11: 589–97, https://doi.org/10.1080/21596 76X.2019.1628806

——. 2022. *Thematic Analysis: A Practical Guide* (London: SAGE)

Carter, Caron. 2021. 'Navigating Young Children's Friendship Selection: Implications for Practice', *International Journal of Early Years Education*, https://doi.org/10.1080/09669760.2021.1892600

——. 2022a. 'Supporting Young Children's Friendships: The Facilitating Role of the Lunchtime Welfare Supervisor', *Pastoral Care in Education*, 1-20, https://doi.org/10.1080/02643944.2022.2054023

——. 2022b. 'What Is the Biggest Challenge Facing Pastoral Care in Education Today and How Can This Challenge Be Effectively Addressed? The Effects of the Covid-19 Pandemic on Children's Well-being', *Pastoral Care in Education*, 40: 279-86, https://doi.org/10.1080/02643944.2022.2093960

Carter, Caron, Ruth Barley, and Arwa Omar. 2023 'I wish that COVID would disappear, and we'd all be together': Maintaining Children's Friendships during the Covid-19 Pandemic', unpublished paper presented at the 'Children and Childhoods' conference, University of Suffolk, 12-13 July

Carter, Caron, and Cathy Nutbrown. 2016. 'A Pedagogy of Friendship: Young Children's Friendships and How Schools Can Support them', *International Journal of Early Years Education*, 24: 395–413, https://doi.org/10.1080/096697 60.2016.1189813

Chan, Alessandra, and François Poulin. 2007. 'Monthly Changes in the Composition of Friendship Networks in Early Adolescence', *Merrill-Palmer Quarterly*, 53: 578-602, https://www.jstor.org/stable/23096155

Coelho, Leandra, et al. 2017. 'Quality of Play, Social Acceptance and Reciprocal Friendship in Preschool Children', *European Early Childhood Education Research Journal*, 25: 812-23, https://doi.org/10.1080/1350293X.2017.1380879

Daniels, Tina, et al. 2010. 'My best friend always did and still does betray me constantly': Examining Relational and Physical Victimization within a Dyadic Friendship Context', *Canadian Journal of School Psychology*, 25: 70-83

Department for Education (DFE). 2020. *Actions for Schools during the Coronavirus Outbreak*, https://www.gov.uk/government/publications/actions-for-schools-during-the-coronavirus-outbreak

Dunn, Judy. 2004. *Children's Friendships: The Beginnings of Intimacy* (Oxford: Blackwell)

Dunn, Judy, and Alexandra L. Cutting. 1999. 'Understanding Others, and Individual Differences in Friendship Interactions in Young Children', *Social Development*, 8, 201–19

Education Endowment Foundation (EEF). 2022. *Moving Forwards, Making a Difference: A Planning Guide for Schools 2022-23*, https://

educationendowmentfoundation.org.uk/support-for-schools/ school-planning-support

Egan, Suzanne. M., et al. 2021. 'Missing Early Education and Care during the Pandemic: The Socio-Emotional Impact of the COVID-19 Crisis on Young Children', *Early Childhood Education Journal*, 49: 925-34, https://doi.org/10.1007/s10643-021-01193-2

Engle, Jennifer. M., Nancy. L. McElwain, and Nicole Lasky. 2011. 'Presence and Quality of Kindergarten Children's Friendships: Concurrent and Longitudinal Associations with Child Adjustment in the Early School Years', *Infant and Child Development*, 20: 365–86, https://doi.org/10.1002/icd.706

Engdahl, Ingrid. 2012. 'Doing Friendship during the Second Year of Life in a Swedish Preschool', *European Early Childhood Education Research Journal*, 20: 83–98, https://doi.org/10.1080/1350293X.2012.650013

Fattore, Tobia, Jan Mason, and Elizabeth Watson. 2016. *Children's Understandings of Well-being: Towards a Child Standpoint*, Children's Well-Being: Indicators and Research, 14 (Dordrecht: Springer)

Fujisawa, Keiko. K., Nobuyuki Kutsukake, and Toshikazu Hasegawa. 2008. 'Reciprocity of Prosocial Behavior in Japanese Preschool Children', *International Journal of Behavioral Development*, 32: 89–97, https://doi.org/10.1177/0165025407084055

Gifford-Smith, Mary. E., and Celia A. Brownell. 2003. 'Childhood Peer Relationships: Social Acceptance, Friendships, and Peer Networks', *Journal of School Psychology*, 41: 235–84, https://doi.org/10.1016/S0022-4405(03)00048-7

Goldschmidt, Karen. 2020. 'The COVID-19 Pandemic: Technology Use to Support the Wellbeing of Children', *Journal of Paediatric Nursing*, 53: 88–90, https://doi.org/10.1016/j.pedn.2020.04.013

Hedges, Helen, and Maria Cooper. 2017. 'Collaborative Meaning-making Using Video Footage: Teachers and Researchers Analyse Children's Working Theories about Friendship', *European Early Childhood Educational Research Journal*, 25: 398-411, https://doi.org/10.1080/1350293X.2016.1252153

Hollingsworth, Heidi. L., and Virginia Buysse. 2009. 'Establishing Friendships in Early Childhood Inclusive Settings: What Roles Do Parents and Teachers Play?', *Journal of Early Intervention*, 31: 287–307, https://doi.org/10.1177/1053815109352659

Kragh-Müller, Grethe, and Rebecca Isbell. 2010. 'Children's Perspectives on Their Everyday Lives in Child Care in Two Cultures: Denmark and the United States', *Early Childhood Education Journal*, 39: 17–27 https://doi.org/10.1007/s10643-010-0434-9

Ladd, Gary W. 1990. 'Having Friends, Keeping Friends, Making Friends, and Being Liked by Peers in the Classroom: Predictors of Children's Early School Adjustment?' *Child Development*, 61: 1081-100, https://doi.org/10.1111/j.1467-8624.1990.tb02843.x

Laursen, Brett. 2017. 'Making and Keeping Friends: The Importance of Being Similar', *Child Development Perspectives*, 11: 282–89, https://doi.org/10.1111/cdep.1224

Larivière-Bastien, Danaë, et al. 2022. Children's Perspectives on Friendships and Socialization during the COVID-19 Pandemic: A Qualitative Approach', *Child: Care, Health and Development*, 48: 1017-030, https://doi.org/10.1111/cch.12998

Loades, Maria. E., et al. 2020. 'Rapid Systematic Review: The Impact of Social Isolation and Loneliness on the Mental Health of Children and Adolescents in the Context of COVID-19', *Journal of the American Academy of Child and Adolescent Psychiatry*, 59: 1218–239, https://doi.org/10.1016/j.jaac.2020.05.009

Lomax, Helen, et al. 2022. 'Creating Online Participatory Research Spaces: Insights from Creative, Digitally Mediated Research with Children during the COVID-19 Pandemic', *Families, Relationships and Societies*, 11: 19-37, https://doi.org/10.1332/204674321X16274828934070

Lundie, David, and Jeremy Law. 2020. *Teachers' Responses and Expectations in the COVID-19 School Shutdown Period in the UK* (Glasgow: University of Glasgow)

Murray, Elizabeth, and Linda J. Harrison. 2005. 'Children's Perspectives on Their First Year of School: Introducing a New Pictorial Measure of School Stress', *European Early Childhood Education Research Journal*, 13: 111–27, https://doi.org/10.1080/13502930585209591

Organization for Economic Co-operation and Development (OECD). 2020. *Combatting Covid-19's Effect on Children*, https://www.oecd.org/coronavirus/policy-responses/combatting-covid-19-s-effect-on-children-2e1f3b2f/

O'Toole, Catriona, and Venka Simovska. 2021. 'Same Storm, Different Boats! The Impact of COVID-19 on the Wellbeing of School Communities', *Health Education*, 122: 47-61, https://doi.org/10.1108/HE-02-2021-0027

Pascal, Chris, et al. 2020. *COVID-19 and Social Mobility Impact Brief #4: Early Years. Research Brief* (The Sutton Trust), https://dera.ioe.ac.uk/35885/1/Early-Years-Impact-Brief.pdf

Peters, Sally. 2003. '"I Didn't Expect that I Would Get Tons of Friends More Each Day": Children's Experiences of Friendship during the Transition to School', *Early Years*, 23: 45-53, https://doi.org/10.1080/0957514032000045564

Rider, Elizabeth A., et al. 2021. 'Mental Health and Wellbeing of Children and Adolescents during the Covid-19 Pandemic', *BMJ*, 374: 1730, https://doi.org/10.1136/bmj.n1730

Rubin, Kenneth H., et al. 2005. 'Peer Relationships Childhood', in *Developmental Science: An Advanced Textbook*, 5th edn, ed. by Marc H. Bornstein and Michael E. Lamb (New York: Lawrence Erlbaum Associates), pp. 469-512

Salmons, Janet. 2014. *Qualitative Online Interviews: Strategies, Design, and Skills*, 2nd edn (London: SAGE)

Streelasky, Jodi. 2017. 'Tanzanian and Canadian Children's Valued School Experiences: A Cross Case Comparison', *International Journal of Early Years Education*, 25: 274–91, https://doi.org/10.1080/09669760.2017.1352491

UNICEF. 2011. *The State of the World's Children* (New York: United Nations Children's Fund)

United Nations. 1989. *Convention on the Rights of the Child*, https://www.unicef.org.uk/wp-content/uploads/2016/08/unicef-convention-rights-child-uncrc.pdf

——.2020.*Policy Brief: The Impact of Covid-19 on Children* (New York: United Nations), https://unsdg.un.org/resources/policy-brief-impact-covid-19-children

Yin, Robert K. 2018. *Case Study Research and Applications: Design and Methods*, 6th edn (Los Angeles: SAGE)

Ziauddeen, Nida, et al. 2020. 'Schools and COVID-19: Reopening Pandora's Box?', *Public Health in Practice*, 1, https://doi.org/10.1016/j.puhip.2020.100039

10. Digital Heroes of the Imagination: An Exploration of Disabled-led Play in England During the Covid-19 Pandemic

William Renel and Jessica Thom

Introduction

Since March 2020, more than 170,000 people in Britain have lost their lives to Covid-19. Of this total, approximately sixty percent have been disabled people, with learning disabled people being disproportionately affected (Bosworth et al. 2021; Public Health England 2020; Office for National Statistics 2022). Abrams and Abbott suggest that to adopt a disability studies perspective on Covid-19 is 'to ask about who we treat as essential workers in our society, who we deem worthy of valuable resources, who has value, and, ultimately, what sorts of people we deem as worthy of living in the world' (2020: 172). Between April 2020 and August 2020 seven international disability rights organizations worked together to produce the Covid-19 Disability Rights Monitor (Brennan 2020), surveying disabled people from across 134 countries. The research concluded that the pandemic has had a monumental impact on disabled people worldwide, due to inadequate measures to protect disabled people in health and social care settings, prioritization of normative bodies and minds, and a total breakdown of community services and support. The Disability Rights Monitor also highlighted the disproportionate impact of the pandemic for specific disabled people, including people of colour, those in rural areas, and children and young people.

Disability and Play

Much of the existing literature surrounding disabled children and young people and play has been developed through a medical model understanding of disability. This model frames disabled people's experiences through an individualized perspective where impairments should be fixed or treated. The medical model dehumanizes disabled bodies and minds and has engendered a problematic history of disability and play focused on assessment, diagnosis and intervention. For example, 'difficulties in sharing imaginative play' is still used in the Diagnostic and Statistical Manual of Mental Disorders (American Psychiatric Association 2013) as a criterion for diagnosing Autism Spectrum Disorder. Porter, Hernandez-Reif and Jessee (2008) note that many disabled children and young people are made to undertake 'play therapy' where a trained adult professional will use play practices to help a disabled child or young person 'to cope'. Methodologically, much of the existing literature relating to disabled children and young people's experiences of play uses comparative studies between disabled and non-disabled participants (Brodin 2005; Messier, Ferland, and Majnemer 2008), surveys of parents or siblings (Stillianesis et al. 2021; Mitchell and Lashewicz 2018; Conn and Drew 2017) and interventions that seek to 'teach' disabled children how to play like their non-disabled peers (Jahr, Eldevik and Eikeseth 2000). In recent years there are a growing number of social and critical framings of disability and childhood studies where social, cultural and political contexts are given priority over individualistic and medical perspectives. Goodley and Runswick-Cole (2010) led this call for a social turn in disability and childhood studies, contending that disabled children and young people's play has too often been characterized as a tool for diagnosis and therapy, and arguing for the emancipation of play from the domains of assessment and intervention for disabled children. The social model of childhood disability (Connors and Stalker 2007) renews existing conceptions of the sociology of childhood (Prout and James 1997) by incorporating the social (Oliver 1990) and social relational models of disability (Reeve 2012; Thomas 2003). Collectively these perspectives provide a crucial opposition to existing medical framings of disability and play. Burke and Claughton suggest that by understanding the intersecting social, cultural and political complexities of disability and play, disabled children and young people become 'active, creative agents who self-monitor, make choices and exert control over their play within unique play cultures that they construct for and between themselves' (2019: 1078).

Disability, Play and Covid-19

UNESCO described Covid-19 as a global crisis for teaching and learning with 826 million children and young people (50% of learners worldwide) without access to a household computer and 706 million (43%) without household internet (UNESCO 2020a). Disabled children and young people were amongst the most at risk from disengaging from meaningful social, learning and play opportunities during the pandemic (UNESCO 2020b; UNICEF 2020). Sabatello, Landes and McDonald (2020) argue that the true impact of Covid-19 on the experiences of disabled people remains unknown as they continue to be under-represented in impact studies due to inaccessible data collection methods. Research that has focused on disabled children and young people shows that Covid-19 created significant reductions in physical activity and play opportunities (Graber et al. 2021; Moore et al. 2021; de Lannoy 2020) alongside increases in screen time and digital media use (Manganello 2021), increases in medication (Masi 2021) and a generalized decline in mental health and wellbeing (Cacioppo et al. 2021). In the UK, research during the pandemic highlighted that the impacts of Covid-19 would not be equally distributed and were likely to widen existing inequalities (Tonkin and Whitaker 2021; Public Health Scotland 2021). In addition, pandemic-related school closures created a significant increase in the use of information and communication technologies and remote learning environments (Zarzycka et al. 2021; UNESCO 2021). Remote learning via digital platforms offers some advantages to disabled children and young people due to increased flexibility with timings, opportunities to work in different locations, access to multimodal content and different modes of interaction (Bruce et al. 2013). However, remote working can also accentuate the existing digital divide (Organisation for Economic Cooperation and Development 2001) and can only be effective when delivered alongside the appropriate infrastructure (e.g. access to wifi and electricity), accessible content (e.g. captions on videos, easy-read versions of written information), training and regular evaluation (Hashey and Stahl 2014; Chambers, Varoglu, and Kasinskaite-Buddeberg 2016). Although the foregrounding of digital play would undoubtedly work well for many children and young people, Casey and McKendrick note 'that digital play is not equally accessible to all, notably, children from low-income families, disabled children, children with additional support needs, and refugee and migrant children' (2022: 9).

Digital Heroes of the Imagination

In response to the significantly increased barriers to meaningful inclusive play opportunities for many disabled young people outlined above, Touretteshero partnered with the National Youth Theatre (NYT) to design and deliver a new, radical, disabled-led play project called 'Digital Heroes of the Imagination' (DHOTI). Touretteshero is a disabled and neurodivergent-led community interest company. Touretteshero's mission is to create an inclusive and socially just world for disabled and non-disabled people through our cultural practice (www.touretteshero. com/). NYT is a pioneering youth arts organization that empowers young people. Since 1956, NYT has engaged over 150,000 young people and reached an audience of over two billion people across the world (www.nyt.org.uk). DHOTI was the first formal partnership between Touretteshero and NYT. The project builds on previous inclusive play projects that Touretteshero has designed and delivered across the UK since 2010. At the start of the Covid-19 pandemic, Touretteshero, a disabled-led company with clinically vulnerable staff, had to make a series of difficult decisions about what work we would continue to undertake. DHOTI was one of the few creative projects that Touretteshero delivered during the pandemic. The reason we decided to prioritize this project was our feeling that meaningful inclusive play opportunities would be more significant than ever for disabled young people navigating the complexities of the pandemic. With this in mind, DHOTI builds on what Lloyd (2008) describes as equitable experiences of education—those which disrupt normative creative and learning cultures towards approaches focused on inclusion and imagination. DHOTI combines inclusive practice training for young creatives, the distribution of accessible creative resources to learning disabled young people and hybrid digital-physical play sessions for disabled young people. Between June 2020 and January 2021 two phases of DHOTI were delivered, working in partnership with special educational needs or disabilities (SEND) schools in London. The following sections of this chapter will describe the two phases of DHOTI and the core elements of the project. By detailing these elements we hope to position disabled children and young people's experiences at the centre of new discourses concerning play during the Covid-19 pandemic.

Phase 1—Pilot

The initial iteration of DHOTI was a small-scale pilot project, working with twenty-four disabled young people aged between eleven and nineteen from two classes at a SEND school in South London. The young people had a range of both physical and cognitive impairments as well as different communication preferences. Each of the students had an education, health and care (EHC) plan.[1] During the pilot phase of DHOTI the UK was in full lockdown, meaning that the project would be delivered using digital technology within people's home environments. Thirteen young people aged fourteen to twenty-five were recruited by NYT to become 'makers' and 'creative buddies' for the project. All of these young people received inclusive practice training from Touretteshero. The makers created all of the materials necessary for the project, these were collated in 'top secret' superhero kits which were delivered to the students' homes by Touretteshero—the world's first fully-fledged Tourettes superhero (Figure 10.1). The creative buddies partnered with young disabled people from the school and

---

1   An EHC plan is 'for children and young people aged up to 25 who need more support than is available through special educational needs support. EHC plans identify educational, health and social needs and set out the additional support to meet those needs' (GOV.UK n.d.).

worked through an inclusive creative process collaboratively exploring four activity areas over two three-hour workshops.

Figure 10.1 Touretteshero Delivering 'Top Secret' Superhero Kits in South London during the Covid-19 Pandemic, July 2020

Through the workshops, each of the young disabled students had opportunities to transform themselves into a new superhero, designing masks, capes and logos and creating new superhero powers and moves. The students also utilized the materials to transform their home environments into imaginative places where the superheroes could live, work and play. These included treehouses, urban cities, underwater kingdoms and intergalactic ships in outer space. The workshops culminated in short recorded videos where each of the superheroes showcased their new identities and shared their messages with the world. These included 'Mr Healthy' who helps people eat fruit and vegetables, 'Dancing Isobel' who makes people happy, and 'Super Mermaid' who rescues people that fall in the water. The majority of the messages that the superheroes created during the pilot phases reflected the context of the pandemic and the UK being in a full lockdown. Key themes included being outdoors, accessing nature, helping others and connecting with neighbours. Some of the messages that the students shared transcended the realities of the students' day-to-day lives, such as 'I have lion powers and I can walk through walls'. Other messages were self-reflective and related to the lived experiences of the students, such as 'my superpower is drawing; it helps me calm down'. Some students used spoken words and Makaton[2] to share their messages whilst others used text-to-speech devices.

Inclusive Practice Training

Touretteshero designed and delivered bespoke inclusive practice training for DHOTI. The intention was to introduce the young people from NYT who would be leading the project to disabled-led thinking and practice. The training included discussion of the different models of disability including those deemed problematic, such as the medical and charity models, and those which the project would build on, such as the social and strong social models (see Davis 1995; Oliver 1990, 2013; Crow 1996). The social model understands that people are not disabled by their impairments but by a societal failure to consider difference in how environments, systems and services are designed. The strong social model extends the social model and considers a 'more complete understanding of disability and impairment as social concepts; and a recognition of an individual's experiences of their body over time and in variable circumstances' (Crow 1996: 218). The DHOTI training included discussion of accessible and inclusive language, aiming to create a shared and consistent understanding of which words would and would not be used within the project, and the rationale for this. The training also considered differences in key terms, such as the distinction between the word impairment (the facts about someone's mind and body) and disability (the lived experience of disabling barriers). During the training sessions, each of these ideas was shared in creative ways, for example, the difference between the words impairment and disability was presented through illustrations of two colourful cereal boxes, created by Jess Thom (Figure 10.2).

---

2   Makaton is a unique visual language often used by people with learning disabilities and autistic people combining 'symbols, signs and speech to enable people to communicate' (see https://makaton.org).

Figure 10.2 Cereal boxes showing the distinction between 'impairment' and 'disability' (2020)

Discussions of language during the DHOTI training were framed by the affirmation model of disability, described as a 'non-tragic view of disability and impairment which encompasses positive social identities, both individual and collective, for disabled people grounded in the benefits of life style and life experience of being impaired and disabled' (Swain and French 2000: 569). The DHOTI training introduced central definitions of play as freely chosen, personally directed and intrinsically motivated (John and Wheyway 2004) as well as the United Nations 'right to play' (discussed later in this chapter). Following Walker's (2004) collaborative model of disability equality training, an in-depth evaluation was undertaken with the young people involved after each phase of DHOTI. During the evaluation, the young people commented:

> The training changed my perspective on disability and has enhanced how I want to make work in the future.

> I got so much from the training that I took with me into the DHOTI project. I was feeling really nervous beforehand but the training calmed me down a lot and I felt empowered to work in a more inclusive way.

DHOTI—Phase Two

During the second phase of DHOTI, the pilot project was expanded to work with 124 disabled and/or neurodivergent young people aged between eleven and nineteen from two separate SEND schools in London. During the second phases of DHOTI the UK was not in a full lockdown but schools were restricted to working in small classroom bubbles. This meant that the majority of disabled young people were back in the school buildings but were restricted to working within one classroom and one consistent group of teachers, teaching assistants and students. The young people could not connect with students from other classroom bubbles. In conversations with teachers and families of the students during phase two of DHOTI, it became apparent that the students were missing opportunities to connect with people outside of their individual classroom bubbles. Therefore, creative ways for students to connect with each other became a key focus for the second phase of the project. Twenty young people aged fourteen to twenty-five were recruited by NYT to become makers and creative buddies for the second phase of the project. All of these young people received inclusive practice training from Touretteshero. Two additional training sessions were incorporated into the second phase of the project, working with teachers and teaching assistants from the two schools. Feedback from the creative buddies during the evaluation of the second phase of the project highlighted how the training with teachers made a significant improvement in how much the teachers engaged and supported the workshops. One young person commented:

> The teachers were brilliant; they used Makaton and helped all the students take part—they were so much more involved than when we did the pilot.

The makers created 160 new top secret superhero kits which included additional tactile and sensory materials. The creative buddies used video conferencing software to join the young people in their school classrooms to work through the inclusive creative process over two three-hour workshops. These hybrid digital-physical play environments enabled meaningful creative relationships to be formed between disabled young people in London and creative buddies from across the UK.

The workshops during the second phase of DHOTI highlighted the significance of non-physical participation and interaction as a central component of inclusive play during the pandemic. The opportunities for human connection that were created during DHOTI serve, as Liddiard and others note, as a counter to normative ideas and expectations of face-to-face work as a point of superiority, affirming 'technologies as spaces ripe for human and affective connection, nurture and care, especially for marginalised people who experience barriers in the physical and social world' (2022: 7). During the workshops, the students used the materials in their superhero kits to transform their classrooms into new imaginative worlds—walls became planets, stars and solar systems. Chairs became caves and underground lakes. Doors became book covers to be opened and explored. The workshops culminated in a performance where the students showcased their new identities and shared their messages for the world within their classrooms. These performances were transmitted live between the different classrooms in the school using webcams and microphones, creating a multi-room creative exchange where each student could perform, watch and engage with their peers from across the school. The messages shared by the students ranged from humorous calls to action such as 'I am Frying Pan Man and I will make school dinners better for all' to poignant messages such as 'To all my fellow superheroes in our school, I miss our playtime and want to know if you are ok'. After the performance feedback was gathered from students in different classrooms at the school using easy-read surveys and an iPad with a text-to-speech application. The students were all positive about the experience, with the exception of two who commented that some of the messages were hard to hear during the performance. One student commented, 'it was good to see my friends in the other classes', whilst another said, 'I will be a superhero every day now, even at home with dad'.

Top Secret Superhero Kits

A central component of DHOTI was the design of multi-sensory 'Top Secret' superhero kits. Informed by the Universal Design for Learning

Framework (Rose and Meyer 2002), the materials and activities were designed to create meaningful opportunities to engage with the kit through different sensory channels, acknowledging that taking part will look and feel different for each student. Each kit included a welcome letter within a tactile visual envelope, four activity boxes—each with a distinct visual identity—easy-read instructions (Sutherland and Isherwood 2016) about how to take part, and a wealth of multi-sensory 'loose part' materials (Nicholson 1971). These materials included colourful wheelchair spoke covers, pens and sticky foam shapes (Figure 10.3). The superhero kits included materials that would be used for specific activities during the workshops but they were also designed to ensure that disabled young people had access to resources to use at home beyond the life of the project.

Figure 10.3 Top Secret Accessible Superhero Kit (2020)

Discussion

The following sections of this chapter reflect on the existing practices of inclusive play and consider how discourses of risk, resilience and the right to play are renewed by new forms of disabled-led play that emerged during the Covid-19 pandemic. Casey suggests that 'the concept of inclusive play links inseparably the right to play and the right of disabled children to participate fully in society [...] by aiming for inclusive play, we are simply aiming for the best play experiences we can offer to all children' (2010: xi).

Risk and Resistance

Risk is a central component in discourses and practices of play. Cultures of risk in relation to play activity are continuously changing and many suggest that societal shifts in Western cultures towards risk aversion have engendered an understanding of 'meaningful play' as risk-free and highly controlled (Gill 2007). Ball et al. (2019: 4) contend that a 'prominent driver of play opportunities—or lack thereof—has been the proliferate use of risk assessment'. Seale et al. (2013) argue that inclusive play and education are fundamentally an embodiment of positive risk-taking. Slee (2007) describes the primary connections between risk-taking and inclusive practices and Ainscow notes how positive risk-taking is 'essential to the creation of more inclusive forms of pedagogy' (1999: 71). Within inclusive play practice, risk-benefit assessments are often used to consider both risks and benefits towards informed judgements that consider a variety of issues relevant to localized circumstances (Ball, Gill and Spiegal 2008). Seale et al. (2013) extend this approach and present a conceptual framework of positive risk-taking in relation to disabled people's experiences of learning and play. This framework argues that 'practitioners need to balance the "what if something goes wrong" questions with "what if something goes right" questions' (2013: 240). Covid-19 presented new questions with regards to risk and disabled children and young people's play. Many SEND schools were necessarily focused on the immediate health risks that their disabled students were facing and prioritized minimizing the spread of the virus. Although this was undoubtedly a significant risk, Touretteshero was also concerned about the risks that were perhaps less obvious or given less priority in changes to SEND policy and practice. These included the social and political risks of disabled young people being isolated and disconnected from others that may be compounded by different communication preferences and the existing digital divide. Or the barriers to creative experiences for disabled children and young people through a lack of access to resources and materials.

A series of probing questions was created to frame the conversations around risk during the DHOTI project. These included:

- What are the risks to disabled young people if they can't be creative or access creative, multisensory resources?

- What are the risks to disabled young people if they can't stay creatively connected to their peers?

- What are the opportunities whilst working remotely for disabled young people to connect with other young people?

The pandemic accentuated an existing issue within discourses of risk, namely the tension between macro and micro risk practices. As Seale et al. note,

> organisations respond to what might be perceived as 'big risks' such as abuse, personal safety or educational failure at a macro level by drawing up pre-planned policies, rules and guidelines. Individuals that work with and alongside these organisations are required to negotiate their response to these risks at a micro level. (2013: 238)

During the pandemic, with schools closed and governments across the globe creating frameworks in which populations could navigate the macro level risk of the Covid-19 virus, disabled children and young people, their parents, carers, siblings and close friends were negotiating the real-world micro risks of their everyday lives. In this context, dynamic new approaches to risk, risk-assessment and risk-benefit were created. Further questions were considered during DHOTI, such as

- Is the risk of delivering a box of accessible materials directly to a disabled young person's house worth the benefit of that young person having access to the materials?

- Is the risk of using video conferencing software to work one-to-one with a disabled young person directly in their home environment (which pre-pandemic safeguarding policy would advise against) worth the benefit of the young person accessing creative activities and connections?

Within these negotiations of risk assessment and benefit new play cultures emerged, bringing together young NYT members from across the UK to build accessible resources and lead creative encounters with disabled young people in London in ways that, before the pandemic, would never have been conceived. In this context risk assessment and benefit informed new currencies of resilience in and between the young people involved. Resilience in this sense is understood as an act of resistance, following Goodley's (2005) sociocultural framework where resilience is not an individual trait or characteristic but a political response to disabling and ableist circumstances. By placing inclusion and anti-ableist thinking at the centre of the DHOTI play encounters, the risks taken at the micro level informed new instances of what Mia Mingus describes as 'access intimacy':

> That elusive, hard to describe feeling when someone else 'gets' your access needs […] Sometimes access intimacy doesn't even mean that everything is 100% accessible. Sometimes it looks like both of you trying to create access as hard as you can with no avail in an ableist world. Sometimes it is someone just sitting and holding your hand while you both stare back at an inaccessible world. (2011)

Positive Memories as Protection

DHOTI emphasized the significant role that exciting, inclusive experiences of play can have in creating lasting positive memories for disabled children and young people. Research shows that when disabled children and young people share memories of play and learning in school contexts they often focus on the barriers they experienced (Díez 2010) and moments of segregation and discrimination (Shar 2007; Connor and Ferri 2007). Reviews of public playgrounds highlight that lack of accessible play equipment and the impact on meaningful equal play opportunities for disabled children and young people (Fernelius and Christensen. 2017; Ripat and Becker 2012). This highlights how the design of a play space sends a clear message about which bodies and minds have been considered. As Hamraie (2013) suggests, designed environments are not simply static structures in which humans exist and interact, but instead environments produce lived and embodied experiences and, at times, create physical and social barriers that can reinforce structural inequalities. Through engaging with non-accessible play spaces from an early age, disabled children learn to expect less. Even when accessible equipment is present, it is often a single item within an otherwise non-accessible playground. When disabled children and young people report positive memories of play, it is often within an environment that is not only physically accessible, but also where attitudes towards disabled people are positive (Jeanes and Magee 2012). As Wenger et al. argue, 'to achieve inclusion on inclusive playgrounds, the physical, attitudinal, social, and political environments must be regarded as interrelated' (2021: 144). At Touretteshero we often talk about the idea of positive memories as protection. This notion acknowledges that disabled children and young people will encounter barriers in their lives but that having lasting positive memories of events, environments or experiences where their requirements are met can serve as protection when things are challenging. It was clear during DHOTI that Touretteshero and NYT were not in a position to remove all of the physical and attitudinal barriers that disabled children and young people were experiencing due to the Covid-19 pandemic. It was also apparent that the pandemic would create lasting negative memories for many, if not all, disabled children and young people. Therefore the need to create moments of meaningful creative connection and positive experiences for disabled children and young people was more significant than ever.

Renewing The Right to Play

The contemporary understanding of the right to play was formalized in Article 31 of the United Nations Convention on the Rights of the Child (UNCRC) which requires state parties to 'recognize the right of the child to rest and leisure, to engage in play and recreational activities appropriate to the age of the child and to participate freely in cultural life and the arts' (United Nations 1989). However, there are a number of publications that informed Article 31 of the UNCRC. The human right to rest and leisure (but not play) was established in Article 24 of the Universal Declaration of Human Rights in 1948 (United Nations 1948). Following this, the right to play was included in the Declaration of the

Rights of the Child in 1959 which notes that children 'shall have full opportunity for play and recreation, which should be directed to the same purposes as education; society and the public authorities shall endeavour to promote the enjoyment of this right' (United Nations 1959). The International Play Association's Declaration of the Child's Right to Play (1979) calls for the child's right to play as a fundamental priority for health. Despite the UNCRC being described as 'the most complete statement of children's rights ever produced [. . .] [and] the most widely-ratified international human rights treaty in history' (UNICEF n.d.), the right to play and Article 31 has also been described as forgotten, ignored, misunderstood and, therefore, the least recognized right of children and young people (Fronczek 2009; Davey and Lundy 2011).

In 2013, the United Nations published *General Comment No. 17 (2013) on the Right of the Child to Rest, Leisure, Play, Recreational Activities, Cultural Life, and the Arts (art. 31)* to reassert the significance of Article 31 as fundamental to the health, well-being and quality of a child or young person's life. Significantly, General Comment No. 17 raised specific concerns with regards to equal access and opportunities to play for disabled children. General Comment No. 17 also lists thirteen aspects of an optimum play environment through which Article 31 can be realized. These include accessible space, time, permission, materials, freedom from social exclusion and prejudice, and the recognition from adults of the value and legitimacy of a child's rights (United Nations 2013). However, it is noted that whilst Article 31 and General Comment No. 17 are widely acknowledged, they are often overlooked or under-utilized in practice (Janot and Rico 2020; Sabatello, Landes, and McDonald 2022; Tonkin and Whitaker 2021). The United Nations Convention on the Rights of Persons with Disabilities aims to assert disabled children and young people's right to play by ensuring 'that children with disabilities have equal access with other children to participation in play, recreation and leisure and sporting activities' (United Nations 2006). It is noted that much of the research regarding disabled children and young people's right to play has subsequently focused on inclusive environments and accessible play spaces (Goodley and Runswick-Cole 2010), meaning that disabled children continue to experience discrimination within these play spaces and cultures (John and Wheyway 2004).

Research suggests that in times of crisis the fundamental right to play for all children is threatened through increased barriers to play, reduced access to space and a lack of permission (Wright and Reardon 2021; Gill and Miller 2020; Heldal 2021; Chatterjee 2017). Casey and McKendrick contend that

> the Covid-19 pandemic afforded an opportunity to reappraise the status of play as a fundamental right of the child through the lens of play in crisis. However, children's right to play was curtailed as it became collateral damage when managing the threat to public health [. . .] the staged lifting of restrictions highlighted the standing of play relative to other human rights, with the desire to facilitate return to work, children's education and adult leisure being prioritised over facilitating opportunities for children's play. (2022: 13-14)

DHOTI created an opportunity to reassert the role of play as a fundamental human right and to re-energise the principles of the right to play in a practical context. Documents such as UNCRC Article 31 and General Comment No. 17 should not be considered neutral in relation to the lived and embodied realities of a crisis such as the Covid-19 pandemic. In times of crisis these documents become more important than ever as 'artifacts of knowing-making' (Hamraie 2017), helping to bridge the gap between macro considerations about population health and well-being and the everyday priorities and realities of individuals negotiating crisis.

Conclusion

This chapter has reflected on DHOTI, a radical play project led by Touretteshero and NYT during the Covid-19 pandemic in England. The chapter has considered how discourses of risk, resilience and the right to play are renewed by new forms of disabled-led play such as DHOTI. The pandemic has emphasized how disabled children and young people, their rights, and their experiences of play are so often secondary to the perspectives of their non-disabled peers. This affirms what Goodley describes as a dislocation of disabled young people from our play and educational communities where 'disabled students appear at the end of the educational conversation, as a postscript, the addendum or the complicating outliers' (2021: 122). Although Covid-19 undoubtedly created a significant threat to the fundamental right to play, DHOTI, alongside other play projects across the globe (see Casey and McKendrick 2022), highlight how a child's right to play can be actively protected, promoted, or improved during times of crisis. DHOTI suggests that we should keep taking risks and understand that risky play for disabled children and young people can lead to moments of 'access intimacy' and new understandings of resilience—not as an individual trait but as an act of anti-ableist resistance. DHOTI also highlights how positive memories can protect disabled children and young people when things become challenging. As researchers and practitioners with an interest in play, we should seek to build more inclusive cultures (in whatever context, crisis or no crisis) in which disabled people can thrive. If, as Casey and McKendrick suggest, the Covid-19 pandemic has shown 'the seeds of opportunity to sustain and strengthen our support for children's right to play' (2022: 14), then the perspectives of disabled children and young people must be brought to the centre. Disabled people hold a unique legacy of resilience and resistance to societal inequalities that predates the Covid-19 pandemic. Existing calls for the emancipation of disabled children's play (Goodley and Runswick-Cole 2010) and the Principles of Disability Justice (Berne et al. 2018) provide important building blocks in steering a critical, rights-based trajectory for play theory and practice beyond the pandemic. By thinking from an intersectional perspective, promoting leadership of the most impacted and aiming for collective access against normative expectations, new processes of play as collective liberation can emerge. And thanks to DHOTI, there are 148 new disabled superheroes who are ready to lead us into this future.

Works Cited

Abrams, Thomas, and David Abbott. 2020. 'Disability, Deadly Discourse, and Collectivity amid Coronavirus (COVID-19)', *Scandinavian Journal of Disability Research*, 22: 168–74, https://doi.org/10.16993/sjdr.732

American Psychiatric Association. 2013. *Diagnostic and Statistical Manual of Mental Disorders*, 5th edn (Arlington, VA: American Psychiatric Association)

Ainscow, Mel. 1999. *Understanding the Development of Inclusive Schools* (London: Falmer)

Ball, David, Tim Gill, and Bernard Spiegal. 2008. *Managing Risk in Play Provision: Implementation Guide* (Play England), https://dera.ioe.ac.uk/8625/1/00942-2008DOM-EN.pdf

Ball, David, et al. 2019. 'Avoiding a Dystopian Future for Children's Play', *International Journal of Play*, 8: 3-10, https://doi.org/10.1080/21594937.2019.1582844

Berne, Patricia, et al. 2018. 'Ten Principles of Disability Justice', *WSQ: Women's Studies Quarterly*, 46: 227-30, https://doi.org/10.1353/wsq.2018.0003

Bosworth, Matthew L., et al. 2021. 'Deaths Involving Covid-19 by Self-reported Disability Status during the First Two Waves of the Covid-19 Pandemic in England: A Retrospective, Population-based Cohort Study', *Lancet Public Health*, 6: e817–25, https://doi.org/10.1016/S2468-2667(21)00206-1

Brennan, Clara Siobhan. 2020. *Disability Rights during the Pandemic: A Global Report on Findings of the COVID-19 Disability Rights Monitor*, https://www.internationaldisabilityalliance.org/sites/default/files/disability_rights_during_the_pandemic_report_web_pdf_1.pdf

Brodin, Jane. 2005. 'Diversity of Aspects on Play in Children with Profound Multiple Disabilities', *Early Child Development and Care*, 175: 635–46, https://doi.org/10.1080/0300443042000266222

Bruce, David, and others. 2013. 'Multimodal Composing in Special Education: A Review of the Literature', *Journal of Special Education Technology*, 28: 25–42, https://doi.org/10.1177/0162643413028002

Burke, Jenene, and Amy Claughton. 2019. 'Playing with or Next to? The Nuanced and Complex Play of Children with Impairments', *International Journal of Inclusive Education*, 23: 1065-080, https://doi.org/10.1080/13603116.2019.1626498

Cacioppo, Marine, et al. 2021. Emerging Health Challenges for Children with Physical Disabilities and Their Parents during the Covid-19 Pandemic: The ECHO French Survey', *Annals of Physical and Rehabilitation Medicine*, 64: 101429, https://doi.org/10.1016/j.rehab.2020.08.001

Casey, Theresa. 2010. *Inclusive Play: Practical Strategies for Children from Birth to Eight* (London: SAGE)

Chambers, Dianne, Zeynep Varoglu, and Irmgarda Kasinskaite-Buddeberg. 2016. *Learning for All: Guidelines on the Inclusion of Learners with Disabilities in Open and Distance Learning*, UNESCO Programme: From Exclusion to Empowerment, https://unesdoc.unesco.org/ark:/48223/pf0000244355

Chatterjee, Sudeshna. 2017. *Access to Play for Children in Situations of Crisis: Synthesis of Research in Six Countries* (International Play Association), http://ipaworld.org/wp-content/uploads/2018/02/IPA-APC-Research-Synthesis-Report-A4.pdf

Conn, Carmel, and Sharon Drew. 2017. 'Sibling Narratives of Autistic Play Culture', *Disability & Society*, 32: 853-67, https://doi.org/10.1080/09687599.2017.1321526

Connor, D.J., and B.A. Ferri. 2007. 'The conflict within: Resistance to inclusion and other paradoxes in special education', *Disability & Society*, 22 (1): 63–77

Connors, Clare, and Kirsten Stalker. 2007. 'Childhood Experiences of Disability: Pointers to a Social Model of Childhood Disability', *Disability & Society*, 22 (1): 19–33, https://doi.org/10.1080/09687590601056162

Davey, Ciara, and Laura Lundy. 2011. 'Towards Greater Recognition of the Right to Play: An Analysis of Article 31 of the UNCRC', *Children & Society*, 25: 3–14, https://doi.org/10.1111/j.1099-0860.2009.00256.x

Davis, Lennard J. 1996. *Enforcing Normalcy: Disability, Deafness, and the Body* (London: Verso)

Díez, Anabel Moriña. 2010. 'School Memories of Young People with Disabilities: An Analysis of Barriers and Aids to Inclusion', *Disability & Society*, 25: 163-75, https://doi.org/10.1080/09687590903534346

Fernelius, Courtney L., and Keith M. Christensen. 2017. 'Systematic Review of Evidence-Based Practices for Inclusive Playground Design', *Children, Youth and Environments*, 27: 78–102, https://doi.org/10.7721/chilyoutenvi.27.3.0078

Fronczek, Valerie. 2009. 'Article 31: A Forgotten Article of the UNCRC', *Early Childhood Matters*, 113: 24–28

Gill, Tim, and Robyn Monro Miller. 2020. *Play in Lockdown: An International Study of Government and Civil Society Responses to Covid-19 and Their Impact on Children's Play and Mobility* (International Play Association), https://ipaworld.org/wp-content/uploads/2020/08/IPA-Covid-report-Final.pdf

Goodley, Dan. 2005. 'Empowerment, Self-advocacy and Resilience', *Journal of Intellectual Disabilities*, 9: 333-43, https://doi.org/10.1177/1744629505059

——. 2021. Disability and other Human Questions (Bingley: Emerald)

GOV.UK. n.d. 'Children with Special Educational Needs and Disabilities (SEND)', https://www.gov.uk/children-with-special-educational-needs/extra-SEN-help

Graber, Kelsey M., et al. 2021. 'A Rapid Review of the Impact of Quarantine and Restricted Environments on Children's Play and the Role of Play in Children's Health', *Child: Care, Health and Development*, 47: 143–53, https://doi.org/10.1111/cch.12832

Hamraie, Aimi. 2017. *Building Access: Universal Design and the Politics of Disability* (Minneapolis, MN: University of Minnesota Press)

Hamraie, Aimi. 2013. 'Designing Collective Access: A Feminist Disability Theory of Universal Design', *Disability Studies Quarterly*, 33, https://dsq-sds.org/article/view/3871/3411

Hashey Andrew I., and Skip Stahl. 2014. 'Making Online Learning Accessible for Students With Disabilities', *TEACHING Exceptional Children*, 46: 70-78, https://doi.org/10.1177/0040059914528329

Heldal, Marit. 2021. 'Perspectives on Children's Play in a Refugee Camp', *Interchange*, 52: 433–45, https://doi.org/10.1007/s10780-021-09442-4

International Play Association (IPA). 1979. 'IPA Declaration of the Child's Right to Play', http://ipaworld.org/about-us/declaration/ipa-declaration-of-the-childs-right-to-play/

Jahr, Eric, Sigmund Eldevik, and Svein Eikeseth. 2000. 'Teaching Children with Autism to Initiate and Sustain Cooperative Play', *Research in Developmental Disabilities*, 21: 151–69, https://doi.org/10.1016/S0891-4222(00)00031-7

Janot, Jaume Bantulà, and Andrés Payà Rico. 2020. 'The Right of the Child to Play in the National Reports Submitted to the Committee on the Rights of the Child', *International Journal of Play*, 9: 400–13, https://doi.org/10.1080/21594937.2020.1843803

Jeanes, Ruth, and Jonathan Magee. 2012. '"Can we play on the swings and roundabouts?": Creating Inclusive Play Spaces for Disabled Young People and Their Families', *Leisure Studies*, 31: 193-210, https://doi.org/10.1080/02614367.2011.589864

de Lannoy, Louise. 2020. 'Regional Differences in Access to the Outdoors and Outdoor Play of Canadian children and Youth during the Covid-19 Outbreak', *Canadian Journal of Public Health*, 111: 988–94, https://doi.org/10.17269/s41997-020-00412-4

Liddiard, Kirsty, et al. 2022. *Living Life to the Fullest: Disability, Youth and Voice* (Bingley: Emerald)

Lloyd, Christine. 2008. 'Removing Barriers to Achievement: A Strategy for Inclusion or Exclusion?' *International Journal of Inclusive Education*, 12: 221–36, https://doi.org/10.1080/13603110600871413

Manganello, Jennifer A. 2021. 'Media Use for Children with Disabilities in the United States during Covid-19', *Journal of Children and Media*, 15: 29–32, https://doi.org/10.1080/17482798.2020.1857281

Masi Anne, et al. 2021. 'Impact of the Covid-19 Pandemic on the Well-being of Children with Neurodevelopmental Disabilities and Their Parents', *Journal of Paediatrics and Child Health*, 57: 631-36, https://doi.org/10.1111/jpc.15285

Messier, Julie, Francine Ferland, and Annette Majnemer. 2008. 'Play Behavior of School Age Children with Intellectual Disability: Their Capacities, Interests and Attitudes', *Journal of Developmental Physical Disability*, 20: 193–207, https://doi.org/10.1007/s10882-007-9089-x

Mingus, Mia. 2011. 'Access Intimacy: The Missing Link', https://leavingevidence.wordpress.com/2011/05/05/access-intimacy-the-missing-link/

Mitchell, Jennifer, and Bonnie Lashewicz. 2018. 'Quirky Kids: Fathers' Stories of Embracing Diversity and Dismantling Expectations for Normative Play with their Children with Autism Spectrum Disorder', *Disability & Society*, 33: 1120-137, https://doi.org/10.1080/09687599.2018.1474087

Moore, Sarah A., et al. 2021. 'Adverse Effects of the Covid-19 Pandemic on Movement and Play Behaviours of Children and Youth Living with Disabilities: Findings from the National Physical Activity Measurement (NPAM) Study', *International Journal of Environmental Research and Public Health*, 18: 12950, https://doi.org/10.3390/ijerph182412950

Nicholson, Simon. 1971. 'How Not to Cheat Children: The Theory of Loose Parts', *Landscape Architecture*, 62: 30–34

Office for National Statistics. 2022. *Updated Estimates of Coronavirus (COVID-19) Related Deaths by Disability Status, England: 24 January 2020 to 9 March 2022*, file:///C:/Users/Editor/Downloads/Updated%20estimates%20of%20coronavirus%20(COVID-19)%20related%20deaths%20by%20disability%20status,%20England%2024%20January%202020%20to%209%20March%202022.pdf

Oliver, Michael. 1990. *The Politics of Disablement* (Basingstoke: Palgrave Macmillan)

Organisation for Economic Cooperation and Development. 2001. *Understanding the Digital Divide*, OECD Digital Economy Papers, 49 (Paris: OECD), https://doi.org/10.1787/236405667766

Porter, Maggie L., Maria Hernandez-Reif, and Peggy Jessee. 2008. 'Play Therapy: A Review', *Early Child Development and Care*, 179: 1025–040, https://doi.org/10.1080/03004430701731613

Prout, Alan, and Allison James. 1997. 'A New Paradigm for the Sociology of Childhood', in *Constructing and Reconstructing Childhood*, ed. by Allison James, 2nd edn (London: Falmer Press), pp. 7–33

Public Health England. 2020. *Deaths of People Identified as Having Learning Disabilities with Covid-19 in England in the Spring of 2020*, https://assets.publishing.service.gov.uk/government/uploads/system/uploads/attachment_data/file/933612/COVID-19__learning_disabilities_mortality_report.pdf

Public Health Scotland. 2021. *The Impact of Covid-19 on Children and Young People in Scotland: 10–17 Year-Olds* (Edinburgh: Public Health Scotland), https://www.publichealthscotland.scot/media/2999/the-impact-of-covid-19-on-children-and-young-people-in-scotland-10-to-17-year-olds_full-report.pdf

Reeve, Donna. 2012. 'Psycho-emotional Disablism: The Missing Link?' in *The Routledge Handbook of Disability Studies*, ed. by Nick Watson, Alan Roulstone and Carol Thomas (London: Routledge), pp. 78-92

Ripat, Jacquie, and Pam Becker. 2012. 'Playground Usability: What Do Playground Users Say?' *Occupational Therapy International*, 19: 144-53, https://doi.org/10.1002/oti.1331

Rose, David H., and Anne Meyer. 2002. *Teaching Every Student in the Digital Age: Universal Design for Learning* (Alexandria, VA: ASCD)

Sabatello, Maya, Scott D. Landes, and Katherine E. McDonald. 2020. 'People with Disabilities and Covid-19: Fixing Our Priorities', *American Journal of Bioethics*, 20: 187-90, https://doi.org/10.1080/15265161.2020.1779396

Shah, Sonali. 2007. 'Special or Mainstream? The Views of Disabled Students', *Research Papers in Education*, 22: 425–42, https://doi.org/10.1080/02671520701651128

Slee, Roger. 2007. 'Inclusive Schooling as a Means and End of Education?' in *The SAGE Handbook of Special Education*, ed. by Lani Florian, (London: SAGE), pp. 161-70, https://dx.doi.org/10.4135/9781848607989.n13

Stillianesis, Samantha, et al. 2021. 'Parents' Perspectives on Managing Risk in Play for Children with Developmental Disabilities', *Disability & Society*, 37: 1272-292, https://doi.org/10.1080/09687599.2021.1874298

Sutherland, Rebecca Joy, and Tom Isherwood. 2016. 'The Evidence for Easy-Read for People With Intellectual Disabilities: A Systematic Literature Review', *Journal of Policy and Practice in Intellectual Disabilities*, 13: 297-310, https://doi.org/10.1111/jppi.12201

Swain, John, and Sally French. 2000. 'Towards an Affirmation Model of Disability', *Disability & Society*, 15: 569-82, https://doi.org/10.1080/09687590050058189

Thomas, Carol. 2007. *Sociologies of Disability, 'Impairment', and Chronic Illness: Ideas in Disability Studies and Medical Sociology* (London: Macmillan Education)

Tonkin, Alison, and Julia Whitaker. 2021. 'Play and Playfulness for Health and Wellbeing: A Panacea for Mitigating the Impact of Coronavirus (Covid 19)', *Social Sciences & Humanities Open*, 4: 100142, https://doi.org/10.1016/j.ssaho.2021.100142

UNESCO. 2020a. *Covid-19. A Global Crisis for Teaching and Learning*, https://unesdoc.unesco.org/ark:/48223/pf0000373233/PDF/373233eng.pdf.multi

——. 2020b. *Inclusive School Reopening: Supporting the Most Marginalized Children to go to School*, https://en.unesco.org/sites/default/files/inclusive_school_reopening_-_supporting_marginalised_children_during_school_re._.pdf

——. 2021. Understanding the Impact of Covid-19 on the Education of Persons with Disabilities: Challenges and Opportunities of Distance Education: Policy Brief, https://unesdoc.unesco.org/ark:/48223/pf0000378404.locale=en

UNICEF. 2020. *Children with Disabilities: Ensuring their Inclusion in Covid-19 Response Strategies and Evidence Generation*, https://data.unicef.org/wp-content/uploads/2020/12/Children-with-disabilities-COVID19-response-report-English_2020.pdf

——. n.d. 'How We Protect Children's Rights with the UN Convention on the Rights of the Child', https://www.unicef.org.uk/what-we-do/un-convention-child-rights/

United Nations 1948. *Universal Declaration of Human Rights*, https://www.un.org/en/about-us/universal-declaration-of-human-rights

——. 1959. *Declaration of the Rights of the Child*, https://digitallibrary.un.org/record/195831?ln=en

——. 1989. *Convention on the Rights of the Child*, https://www.unicef.org.uk/wp-content/uploads/2016/08/unicef-convention-rights-child-uncrc.pdf

——. 2006. *The United Nations Convention on the Rights of Persons with Disabilities*, https://www.un.org/disabilities/documents/convention/convention_accessible_pdf.pdf

——. 2013. *General Comment No. 17 on the Right of the Child to Rest, Leisure, Play, Recreational Activities, Cultural Life, and the Arts (art. 31)* (Committee on the Rights of the Child), https://www.refworld.org/docid/51ef9bcc4.html

Wenger, Ines, et al. 2021. 'Children's Perceptions of Playing on Inclusive Playgrounds: A Qualitative Study', *Scandinavian Journal of Occupational Therapy*, 28: 136-46, https://doi.org/10.1080/11038128.2020.1810768

Wright, Hannah, and Mitchell Reardon. 2021. 'Covid-19: A Chance to Reallocate Street Space to the Benefit of Children's Health?' *Cities & Health*, 11 May, https://doi.org/10.1080/23748834.2021.1912571

Zarzycka, Ewelina, et al. 2021. 'Distance Learning during the Covid-19 Pandemic: Students' Communication and Collaboration and the Role of Social Media', *Cogent Arts & Humanities*, 8: 1953228, https://doi.org/10.1080/23311983.2021.1953228

11. Play and Vulnerability in Scotland during the Covid-19 Pandemic

Nicolas Le Bigre

Introduction

When the UK Government announced on 23 March 2020 that the population would be under effective 'lockdown' due to risks from the coronavirus, the general feeling in Scotland seemed grim but resilient. There was uncertainty for the future but clarity on how we should act in the face of this danger. Soon stoicism gave way to hope. Rainbow images started to fill windows; playful messages to neighbours and loved ones appeared in public places; those privileged enough to have stable internet access embraced online interactions of various kinds; eventually new and familiar street games were carefully and creatively marked down in chalk; original forms of public-facing community interventions appeared—all of these enticing us to find togetherness, joy, strength and hope for the future. But just as quickly as we learned the promising possibilities of play within the (ever-changing) rules of our new lockdown lives, the pressures of resilience and the growing stakes of a world of growing inequities and real mortal danger led to disappointment, and eventually to new, more cynical forms of play, perhaps better attuned to the realities of a multi-year pandemic that has led to almost fifteen thousand deaths in Scotland, 178,000 in the UK as a whole, and almost fifteen million direct and indirect excess

 https://doi.org/10.11647/OBP.0326.11

deaths worldwide (National Records of Scotland 2022; World Health Organization 2022). But though forms of play during the pandemic have shifted, they have not disappeared, in line with the belief of folklorist W. F. H. Nicolaisen that 'what keeps people going most of the time is not the heavy tear of weeping but our eyes awash with tears of laughter' (1992: 39).

In this chapter I use examples from contributions to the Lockdown Lore Collection Project at the University of Aberdeen to examine pandemic play through the lens of vulnerability, within the contexts of my disciplines of ethnology and folklore. Though play can protect players by necessitating singular focus, play in any context also exposes the vulnerability of the players (Goldstein 2004: 5; Lindgren 2017: 162). This vulnerability can hint at the reasons why we play, how we play, why we need to play, and how changes in play and wider societal contexts go hand in hand. The selected examples of play highlight several themes that can be gathered under a broader category of vulnerability, including a fear of the ephemerality of community, apprehension at physical vulnerability to the virus, distress caused by societal pressures to come together, intergenerational differences and difficulties, lack of technological adeptness, loss of physical contact, fear of an unknowable future, and externally imposed limitations. It examines pandemic play in the widest sense within overlapping Scottish contexts, considering play amongst communities, children, families and adults, and even in the contexts of ethnography and ethnographers.

Though Scotland is at the heart of the text, it is impossible to ignore the wider UK context and the fact that this pandemic has been a global one. Despite having experienced great solitude, many people have also been more digitally, and thus globally, connected than ever before. Interpretation of play in Scotland cannot and should not therefore be limited to Scotland and doubtless at any given wakeful moment there are people in Scotland who are playing with friends, family and strangers from around the world. In looking at a wide range of examples from across these groups and contexts, this chapter considers how play has changed according to the vicissitudes of the pandemic and the political and societal contexts enfolded in it. It considers physical play and virtual play, and the various physical and virtual hybridities that exist amongst them, all while keeping the concept of vulnerability at the forefront.

Methodology, Ethics and Reflexivity

The Lockdown Lore Collection Project,[1] which is the source for all of the data herein, was launched in April 2020, and is part of the Elphinstone Institute Archives at the University of Aberdeen (Le Bigre 2020). It came about when, living in Leith in the north of Edinburgh at the onset of the pandemic, I was suddenly isolated from my students and colleagues in Aberdeen where I had, until then, commuted weekly. Unable to travel, I was curious to know if other parts of Scotland were also starting to be dotted with rainbows and other creative responses to the pandemic. In online discussions with colleagues, I proposed an idea for a public call-out for photos from around the country, following the model of a smaller project I had coordinated documenting signs from the Scottish Independence Referendum in 2014. As a folklorist, I was naturally curious as to what other forms of creative responses might exist so I added more overarching categories for creative forms including writing, songs and tunes. My colleague Simon Gall sagely suggested we document online initiatives developed during the pandemic so we added that to the mix. Thankfully contributors ignored this narrow initial list of categories and submitted wide-ranging creative responses that I could never have predicted. Finally, I realized the potential for using online platforms to conduct semi-structured interviews and, as personal experience narratives are at the core of most of my research, I thought it important to speak to people about their lives during the pandemic while we were all living through it, following Carl Lindahl's belief that 'shared experience seem[s] to make the story easier to tell' (2018: 231). The goal of the project was, and is, two-fold: to document for the long term Scotland's creative responses to the coronavirus pandemic, all while gaining an understanding of people's everyday routines, as well as thoughts, feelings, fears and hopes.

---

1   All mentions of the project must include thanks to my wife, Jodi Le Bigre, and my colleagues at the Elphinstone Institute, University of Aberdeen, Simon Gall, Alison Sharman, Carley Williams, Sheila Young, Frances Wilkins and Thomas A. McKean. Special thanks are due to the dedicated volunteer interviewers: Emma Barclay, Richard Bennett, Natalie Brown, Siân Burke, Mary Cane, David Francis, Claire Needler, Vera Nikitina, Laurie Robertson, Mara Shea, Eleanor Telfer and Ryo Yamasaki.

Helping me in this task (and, indeed, conducting most of the interviews) were twelve volunteer interviewers who were either past or current students and, in one case, a sociologist colleague. In total, the project has resulted in over three thousand submissions and seventy interviews, with further follow-up interviews scheduled for the near future. Because the online component—both through the contribution form and the interviews—is innate to the project, those without steady online access or a certain level of digital literacy will not have been able to participate easily. In this sense, although the project could not have existed offline during the lockdown context, it also means that the participants represent a narrower portion of society than I would have liked, the online context unintentionally excluding many of those dealing with pandemic vulnerabilities on multiple intersectional levels. We did not directly collect demographic data for contributions to the project as it was seen as an archival rather than a research project, and such questions can dissuade contributions more than encourage them. Interviewees have been self-selecting in that they contact me through an online form if they want to be interviewed, meaning they 1) have to be interested in the project and 2) have to have time to participate, both of which have presumably further narrowed the pool of contributors. But the contributions we have received have been deeply valuable. Participants have mostly been in their thirties to seventies and represent people who are single, married, without children, parents, in a variety of occupations and from various ethnic backgrounds (though principally white), representing several different levels of education.

All fieldwork was conducted diligently and ethically, with each interviewee completing a detailed consent form. Contributors submitting items to the project consented to their use covering all the possible outputs of the project, while also ensuring that any submitted photos, writings, songs and tunes were their own creation. I took a large number of photos as part of the project, and I always ensured that photos in public places—for example of window rainbows—were taken ethically, with only the item in question being the focus of the photo. All of the examples of public forms of play described below are from my own fieldwork.[2] What is described in this chapter reflects only a

---

2   These can be accessed by contacting the Elphinstone Institute Archives (email: elphinstone@abdn.ac.uk).

miniscule proportion of the total collection (which has yet to be fully catalogued) but the items have been selected to illustrate points on play and vulnerability. Play was never an explicit focus of the project or the interviews but its presence is inescapable in the responses. Contributors' names have only been used with their consent. In one instance I conducted online research into an anti-vaccination group. I have decided not to name this group. Reflexively, I must admit to being wary of boosting what I believe to be misinformation, and this group's social media posts indicate that it is eager to be searchable and mentioned in writing. I have only generally referenced posts from the organization's online channels that were publicly accessible and targeting a wide audience.

Finally, in a chapter about play, and while thinking reflexively, it would be remiss of me to neglect mentioning that, for ethnographers, play can sometimes be at the heart of our own fieldwork. Though perhaps one should not admit to it, there is a certain thrill at documenting new forms of creativity, of 'collecting' as many examples as possible, of finding synchronicity in the words of others. When listening back to some of the interviews conducted by the project interviewers—who in a few cases interviewed each other—I noticed subtle forms of play in their interviews, sometimes in light-hearted references to the project or their roles as interviewers, or to the long-term archival goals of the project. There were also hints of vulnerability in their own comments, for example, joking and worrying about my reactions to sound quality or other similar remarks. In this sense, it is important to realize that we fieldworkers are not separate from the people we interview; we are one and the same, and play has sustained us in our lives and work just as it has for others.

Vulnerability in Pandemic Play

When the UK Prime Minister, Boris Johnson, announced on 23 March 2020 that a lockdown would be imposed across England, Northern Ireland, Scotland and Wales, he listed the limited purposes for which people would be allowed to leave their homes. In addition to unavoidable travel and shopping for basic necessities, Johnson mentioned that UK residents were allowed 'one form of exercise a day—for example a run, walk, or cycle—alone or with members of your household' (Prime Minister's Office 2020). Though this clause was meant to limit the amount of time people spent outdoors, in many cases the government's 'daily exercise' allowance encouraged people who might not usually exercise to do so (Harding 2020). With playgrounds closed (in Scotland these closures continued until June 2020), this combination of staying at home with concentrated moments of outdoor living, resulted in forms of public play that concentrated in a few specific areas: windows, driveways, streets and public paths and, of course, virtual contexts as well.

By the end of March 2020, rainbows had suddenly become a symbol of hope and community resistance against the virus in the UK. Though the origins of the rainbow are unclear—apparently inspired either by a public call out by a National Health Service (NHS) nurse or a mother in Newcastle (Kleinman 2020; Marlborough 2020)—soon rainbows appeared as part of window displays, on public walls and paths and, in one case I documented, colouring each step of the outer stairs of a house in Edinburgh's Restalrig neighbourhood. The rainbows were often created by children and their families, a form of hopeful play during a difficult, vulnerable time, often with accompanying messages in support of key workers. Though most rainbows were simply individual expressions of creativity, reaching out to the wider community in theme if not by other direct means, in some cases rainbows playfully 'spoke' to their neighbours. These communal expressions of hope could be found across Edinburgh, though they often varied depending on neighbourhood, residence type, and the social demographics of each area, as can be seen in the following examples. On a middle-class, terraced street in Leith, one window rainbow in the shape of a heart was preceded by the text 'We LOVE your rainbow Number 42', addressing the neighbours across the street who had a brightly painted rainbow on paper in their own window. In a reference to hope, local pride and possibly rainbows, residents at the nearby 'Banana Flats', a well-known block of council flats that curves like a banana, regularly set up a large speaker system across residences to play the beloved Proclaimers song, 'Sunshine on Leith' (1988), at high volume. Residents in that building and other nearby buildings, all featuring window rainbows, would sing along, allowing for aural community building and play. Just west of Leith, in the well-to-do neighbourhood of Trinity, community play amongst neighbours was on full display, with the windows across four storeys of a traditional sandstone tenement featuring parts of four enormous rainbows, spanning the entire building. This concerted effort would have taken a great deal of coordination but its impressive, unmissable message of hope and communal resistance in the face of a deadly virus was clear.

These reflections of community feeling and purpose were confirmed in many of the interviews conducted as part of the Lockdown Lore Collection Project, as seen in this quotation from an Aberdeen-based librarian in her forties in an interview conducted by interviewer Natalie Brown:

> And so I think it's maybe brought out a sense of community that isn't always apparent, especially when you live in a city. You know, it's maybe a bit more different when you live in a smaller place but, in a city, you don't really have that proper community feel. But I would definitely say that, roundabout where we are just now, everybody is pulling together and just watching out for each other, which is a positive and hopefully that will continue afterwards. (Anonymous 2020)

These words aptly describe the discovery and creation of community that many felt at the beginning of the pandemic. Such descriptions of newfound community also seemed to inspire—at least in my everyday contexts and observations—discussions of a post-pandemic 'new normal'. Indeed, Policy Scotland and Scotland's Third Sector Research Forum hosted an online seminar in which I participated called 'Priorities for the "New Normal": Lessons in Lockdown Research' in August 2020. Communal play, quieter streets, and rising awareness of societal inequities showed a path to a future of communality, climate justice and social equity, though the subtext of this was an awareness of the inherent fragility and potential fleeting nature of this coming together, the unspoken fear that communal acts would not last and that they were just part of a game people played to distract themselves during a time of acute vulnerability.

Beyond this existential susceptibility, play in the community also indicated other forms of vulnerability. Not all forms of community play were coordinated amongst neighbours or large groups of people. In early April 2020, on the paths along the Water of Leith in Edinburgh, my wife and I came across a series of coloured signs tacked to adjacent trees with painted messages like 'Don't worry be happy', with 'happy' represented by a golden sparkly smiley face (Figure 11.1).

Figure 11.1 'Colourful Sign on Water of Leith Path, Edinburgh', 4 April 2020

Underneath one of the signs was a note by a grandparent saying that their five-year-old granddaughter had wanted to 'make everybody smile'. The notes also asked passers-by not to remove the images—vulnerable to a passer-by's touch—but instead to take a photo to post on Facebook, demonstrating the hybrid physical/online nature of much of the play during the pandemic, in which corporations mediate the existence and presentation of play in online spaces (Gillis 2011: 167). On the other side of the path, in a small recess in a stone wall, the same grandparent-granddaughter team had placed two boxes. One held toys and the other held books and DVDs, with a message saying: 'I have cleaned these with antibacterial wipes! Please take one and feel free to leave one of yours the next time you pass'. A small note in different coloured ink contained the response 'Thank you! Made our toddler very happy! xxx'. Here the reference to disinfection reveals the vulnerable contexts in which play was being conducted. Even the original note implicitly reveals the stringent rules of the early lockdown, during which there was ambiguity as to how many members of a household were allowed to exercise together, thus one grandparent and their granddaughter creating the trail of images and gifts. The granddaughter's reference to 'worry' also gives insight into the experiences, fears and hopes of young children during the period and their concern for the wellbeing of others.

Some forms of community play made the virus a central part of their message. On the door of their house in Leith, one family put up an image of a dog with a humorous note saying 'BEWARE OF THE DOG (HE'S SELF ISOLATING)' (Figure 11.2). There is no skirting around the virus in this creation but in its satirical play on traditional 'beware of the dog' signs, the sign simultaneously creates fun while highlighting the oft-unspoken dangers otherwise represented by rainbows and other signs of hope.

Figure 11.2 'Humorous Beware of Dog Sign, Leith, Edinburgh', 25 March 2020
Photo © Nicolas Le Bigre, 2023, all rights reserved

Likewise, in early April 2020, at an allotment garden in the north of Edinburgh, I photographed a fashion-forward scarecrow featuring eye-catching green and black stockings and matching scarf, a conspicuous black-and-white dress, a hat and, most notably for this discussion, a pair of goggles and a mask (Figure 11.3). Had the mannequin-turned-scarecrow featured hands, it no doubt would have been wearing gloves. Sure to scare away peckish birds, the scarecrow was also certain to attract the attention of neighbours passing by, provoking a laugh while also perfectly manifesting the grave danger of the virus. That it was created at a time preceding any UK or Scottish government policy or advice on mask-wearing reflects the awareness of global responses to the pandemic at the time, with some other countries having already adopted mask mandates. In this sense, the scarecrow can be seen both as a form of humorous community-building play and an awareness-raising measure, highlighting different physical vulnerabilities and corresponding ways of staying safe during the pandemic. For any local residents aware that the nearby park, Leith Links, had been used as an isolation area and mass grave for plague victims in 1645, the message would have been even more poignant (Robertson 1862, cited in Oram 2007).

Figure 11.3 'Masked Scarecrow, Leith, Edinburgh', 5 April 2020
Photo © Nicolas Le Bigre, 2023, all rights reserved

I discovered similar examples across the Edinburgh area, first with a droll example in the Water of Leith in which the standing nude statue of the artist Anthony Gormley had been modified after someone waded into the river and added a mask as its only item of clothing. Later I came across a public statue in Musselburgh, 'The Musselburgh Archer', which had been adorned with mask, gloves, scarf and hoodie, and holding in his hand not a bow but a bottle of hand sanitizer. This form of play seemed not only meant to provoke laughter, but further offered a public service of free disinfectant for any passers-by who required it.

Not all community play existed in the physical realm, of course. This early period of the pandemic also saw a rise in online group activities, such as through the use of newly developed community WhatsApp groups, as mentioned by numerous interviewees. Many families took to Zoom meetings, as well, with family quiz nights proving popular. In an interview conducted by Richard Bennett in June 2020, fifty-year-old Aberdeenshire-based former journalist and business owner, Kay Drummond, describes her own family's quiz night:

> We've set up since lockdown—my brothers and all their families—we have a weekly quiz. We have the Drummond family quiz. [...] My sister-in-law and I, in Edinburgh, she and I talked about it first and we thought it'd be a good idea. [...] It's good fun. So 8:15. What we do is, do the Clap for Carers at eight o'clock and at 8:15 settle down with a drink and some nibbles and have a laugh with the family. (Drummond 2020)

Of particular interest here is the connection between Clap for Carers and the family's quiz nights on Zoom. The former was a UK-wide campaign to publicly applaud the sacrifice of key workers, society's most visibly vulnerable members, on Thursday nights during the first few months of the pandemic. The Clap for Carers campaign has been described as a government-approved attempt to 'strengthen community cohesion and civic duty across different segments of British society' (Farris, Yuval-Davis, and Rottenberg 2021: 285). This community cohesion was enhanced, not just cynically through official rhetoric but earnestly through vernacular play as well, with different households adding their own playful twist to the practice, whether through bagpipes, and pots and pans (Hall 2020) or, as witnessed in front of my block of flats in Leith, with a bubble wand, signs and whistles. In the quotation above, Drummond describes an intriguing concurrence of national, local and familial community building through play, with the national/local Clap for Carers segueing into a family quiz night, giving Thursday evenings a distinctive connotation of play and community bonding. In this way, one could consider that Clap for Carers functioned as a kind of government-sanctioned period of communal play, encouraging Kay's family to extend that period to a full evening, with the online context allowing for different households in different parts of the country to come together and bond.

Other transitions between in-person play and online play were not always without friction. In an interview with Siân Burke, forty-two-year-old Kincardineshire-based educator Charlie Barrow and his daughter Olivia discussed difficulty in choosing between her inclinations for play through crafts and online play with her friends.

> Charlie   I think you've had that battle between being with your friends and speaking to your friends and using technology and then having time to kind of do the crafty stuff. And it seems that there's not conflict, but there's a bit of a battle because when you want to do crafty things, you're also aware that people are having a chat on Snapchat and you want to join that. Do you think you're doing more crafty things or more things on technology since lockdown?
>
> Olivia   I think I do more things on technology because I want to, like, I know that if I'd done the craft and I can call them later or something and tell them about what I've done. But sometimes I just really want to see my friends. (Barrow and Barrow 2020)

Though Charlie and Olivia agree that she very much enjoys creating crafts—and in the interview she describes making necklaces and charm bracelets amongst other creative outputs—she also mentions increasingly using various apps like Snapchat, Zoom and Messenger to see, speak to, and play with her friends in diverse ways, a phenomenon well-documented by Jackie Marsh (2014). The impossibility of physically being able to visit her friends places a greater emphasis on technological means of staying in contact, whether through special birthday Zoom quiz nights, as Olivia mentions at one point in the interview, or simply using Zoom to tell friends about new crafts she has created.

At the same time, some felt vulnerable to the stresses of community-building online events, resulting in a weariness with pressurized socializing and a world more and more dependent on online interaction. When discussing technology from his own perspective, Charlie states:

I think after a couple of weeks, after the novelty of using technology to stay in touch started to wear off, I really kind of got that Zoom fatigue. I really felt like I was spending a few hours a day looking at four-inch-tall portraits on the screen. And, you know, you have to focus on... quite an intense way. And I'd finish work and I'd just feel pretty drained. And then, 'hey, we're going to have a quiz with our friends at seven o'clock!' And it just started to be not much fun. [...] And if people start talking over the top of each other, it's really, really, really difficult. So I've kind of stopped socializing as much as I did when we first went into lockdown and resorted to maybe phoning people a bit more rather than doing the video calls. (Barrow and Barrow 2020)

The beginning of lockdown brought not only governmental, community and familial pressure to socialize with others but pressure to socialize in particular ways through particular channels, such as through the Clap for Carers or via online means. Charlie's switching to using the phone rather than using video calls reflects an apparent frustration with online technical issues, such as lag, that inhibit sociability, and also a reluctance to have to focus both visually and aurally via screen. In essence, play that seemed like a novel way of circumventing some of the physical limitations of lockdown became a chore. It lost its sense of fun. Charlie, as the player, became susceptible to social pressures, technological pressures and fatigue.

Charlie implies later in the conversation that this is maybe a generational difference, with his daughter seemingly able to play an online video game, watch television streaming services and speak to her friends on the phone all at the same time. Indeed, Olivia expands on this by discussing at some length how she plays and creates video games with her friends via an online platform, all while talking to them over the phone. She further explains that using the phone is faster than typing via the platform itself, allowing her and her friends a greater facility to focus on the game and conversation at the same time. Interestingly, this generational difference in online play is reflected in an interview by Mara Shea with fifty-two-year-old former small-business owner, Victoria Round:

I'll be very glad to see the back of family Zoom calls. (*Sighs*) Where there's so many people and so many squares and everybody either doesn't talk or... oh, it's just so unnatural. To be in a room and have an ordinary conversation will be wonderful with family members. [...] But my son who's a gamer says we should be using Discord [...] because they're much more intuitive because they don't have delays [...] Gamers have obviously been having conversations online for years, so they've got different technologies and it's a much more natural conversation. (Round 2021)

Victoria's revealing comments reinforce the idea that a generational technological gap significantly impacts the extent to which some people have been able to enjoy online play during the pandemic. In both Charlie's and Victoria's cases, the parent is aware of technologies that make online play more natural and sociable but there is a clear, if implicit, lack of enthusiasm to adopt them. As people playing in online contexts, they are vulnerable to the whims of technology and changing fashions that do not always suit them or conform to their personal interests or needs.

This gap has not existed across all forms of play, however, as discussed above with the intergenerational trail of affirmative signs on the Water of Leith. In some cases, play amongst one age group has been mirrored in another, with play amongst children inspiring adult play and vice versa. While online contexts proved to be less than fun for some participants, the classic creative practice of putting chalk to pavement thrived during the lockdowns. One early message I saw, written in chalk in front of someone's doorway, simply said, 'LOVE FROM NANA', using a common nickname for 'grandmother'. No doubt the grandmother who left the enormous chalk message could have phoned or maybe even used a video service to see her grandchild(ren) but evidently leaving a physical note had some importance for her. We can imagine that for the grandchild(ren), seeing a note in chalk, not far from other chalk drawings, might allow them to understand and enjoy the message in the context of their own chalk play. It also allowed the grandmother to put a physical marker at their door, to say 'I was here and I love you', even if she could not actually stay and see her grandchild(ren) due to lockdown restrictions. And it allowed her to leave a note that would greet the child(ren) every time they went out, presumably for their daily exercise. This longer-lasting, though still ephemeral, message, works temporally and spatially in a way that a Zoom quiz or Facetime call would have difficulty matching. As a public marker, it shows the poignant vulnerability of a grandmother who is both playing and lamenting at the same time.

Some chalk messages had a more general public in mind for their audience, as seemed to be the case for a series of chalk writings I came across in my walks. One example, found on a seaside walking path near the breakwater in the Granton area of Edinburgh, was a chalk message with the words 'DANISH SCURVYGRASS' (Figure 11.4) and an arrow pointing to an almost imperceptibly small plant with tiny white flowers growing out of the concrete.

Figure 11.4 'Botanical Chalking, Granton, Edinburgh', 13 April 2020
Photo © Nicolas Le Bigre, 2023, all rights reserved

During lockdown, when significantly fewer cars were on the road and many interviewees expressed a renewed awareness of the outdoors and the climate crisis, this small example of playful botanical education seemed particularly likely to have a receptive audience. Beyond audiences, the act of playfully naming and sharing knowledge has a personal benefit too. In an article on such botanical messages, *The*

Guardian quoted a chalker (rendered anonymous due to the apparent illegality of chalking on pavements in the UK) saying,

> Botanical chalking gives a quick blast of nature connection, as the words encourage you to look up and notice the tree above you, the leaves, the bark, the insects, the sky. And that's all good for mental health. None of us can manage that much—living through a global pandemic is quite enough to be getting on with. But it's brought me a great amount of joy. (Morss 2020)

During a period of susceptibility, not only to the coronavirus but also to climate change, using the tools of children's schoolyard games to creatively disseminate information and change people's perceptions of place and otherwise largely unnoticed plant life, brings joy to the chalker and potentially to those who come across it. This vulnerable lockdown period created a perfect moment for this kind of play to flourish and I saw several examples in different areas. This public identification of plants was roughly mirrored by a child in Leith Links who wrote, in large, carefully drawn lower-case letters in white chalk, the word *craobh* ('tree' in Gaelic) on the pavement in front of a large tree. We might imagine a child learning Gaelic using this familiar writing implement as a way of marking and remembering new vocabulary but also perhaps using it to share this Gaelic word with others. The appearance of the friendly letters offered not only the opportunity to smile—much needed during the lockdowns—but also educated non-Gaelic speakers like me.

Other chalk messages invoked a need to let go and find exuberance during what was a tough time for children and adults alike. Importantly, the play encouraged by these creations was always individual as opposed to group play, reflecting one of the more serious changes for children during the pandemic. Doug Haywood, a forty-six-year-old Aberdeen teacher, in an interview with David Francis, describes a colleague who was teaching at a hub for key workers' children early in the pandemic:

> And it's tricky, you know, trying to get kids—constantly reminding them to socially isolate. She was describing four girls that had been playing together. And, you know, she's saying to them, 'Remember, you've got to stay two metres apart, come on, you can do this'. And literally thirty seconds later she's saying the

same thing to the same girls again because, you know, they want to play. (D. Haywood 2020)

There is a difficult balance here between the children's natural urge to play together and the very serious dangers of the virus to students and teachers alike. In the chalk drawings I came across, though, children came up with creative solutions that allowed them to have fun while playing in a distanced way, thus minimizing susceptibility to a viscerally difficult-to-understand invisible virus of which they had been taught to be wary. One of my favourite examples of such a chalk creation—in the Leith Fort area of Edinburgh—was a small colourful circle with sun rays extending out on all sides and four stick figures inside, with the invocation, 'STEP INSIDE AND WIGGLE'. The circle was big enough for one person but anyone standing beyond the rays would be roughly far enough to be properly distanced. Many chalk drawings like this provoked physical play of some kind, as with the well-known hopping game known as, among other things, Peevers or Hopscotch (Ritchie 1968; Opie and Opie 1997; Roud 2011). The craving for physical play and bodily expression—whether through wiggling (and no doubt giggling) or through hopping—was evident across the streets of Scotland during the lockdowns. One hopscotch creation I witnessed in the northern section of Starbank Park in Newhaven, Edinburgh, perilously ran the length of a steep and curving walking path from the top of a hill all the way to the bottom. Its successful completion seemed an impossibility but part of the fun must have been in creating an unachievable challenge, seemingly an unintentional metaphor for our susceptibility to the limits imposed upon us during lockdowns and our efforts to redefine those limits.

Creating challenges during the lockdown was not only the recourse of children, and their creation and attempts at succeeding at them seemed to both adults and children an important way to keep mental awareness and energy levels up while also implicitly helping to cope with the restrictions. Kay Drummond sent in several videos of the garden races and rainy-day singing contests (among many other challenges) that she set up for her two enthusiastic sons. Looking back on that first summer of the pandemic during the following winter, she told Richard Bennett:

So I would say that it's as much about setting yourselves little
goals, and I feel... I know what we did in the summer was set a
lot of goals and feel that we were out in the garden achieving this,
that and the next thing, and getting the boys, you know, keeping
the boys' energy levels up as well as being active. (Drummond
2021)

The implicit challenge for Kay here is being a parent and having to come
up with and follow through on different games, contests and tactics
to keep her children engaged, healthy and content. There is also an
important element of bonding between parent, child and siblings during
a potentially very frightening period for everyone. Charlie Barrow and
his daughter Olivia also responded to the crisis by creating challenges
for themselves, in their case by sending different videos every week to
distant family members demonstrating knot-tying techniques. As the
weeks went by and the lockdown continued, the videos took a more
playful, but darker, tone, culminating in an impressively unnerving
homage to David Lynch's television series, *Twin Peaks* (Barrow 2020).
Whereas earlier videos demonstrated knot tying—a simple challenge
with a clear outcome—the latter film spookily turned this innocent
activity on its head, with an ambiguous, uneasy and unresolved
conclusion. This seemingly reflected a pandemic with no clear end
point or solution in sight, highlighting our collective vulnerability in the
context of an unknowable future.

For playful adults, limit-testing challenges in lockdown contexts
often manifested themselves through trepidatious but thrilling rule-
breaking trickery, real or imagined. One interviewee in her seventies,
whom I have left unnamed, describes three different instances of rule
breaking: one in which she meets a friend at the gate of a cemetery
'quite by chance' which does her 'so much good. Just to see another
person'. In the second instance, she describes rehearsing the story she
will tell police if she is stopped while illegally walking her dog at the
beach. In her words, 'If you're going to break one rule you're going to
break another one, aren't you?' Here she seems to be almost playfully
challenging the police more than herself. In the third instance, she
recounts the law-skirting of a friend of hers:

> I spoke to a dear, dear friend the other day. I've known her for so long. She's 93 and she said, 'Oh my darling, I'm breaking all the rules. All my friends come round once a week for cocktail parties'. And she said, 'What can old women do but break some rules?' (*Laughs*) I thought it was lovely.

The anxiety in the interviewer's voice is palpable, and she exclaims 'Oh, no!' and nervously asks, 'So they actually do come round?', only for the interviewee to quickly confirm, 'Yes, they come round to her flat and they have cocktail parties!' Nevertheless, the interviewer senses the excitement her contributor feels and at one point asks, 'And the breaking the rules, did it make you feel a little bit *Famous Five*-ish?', in reference to the British children's adventure novels. The answer comes quickly: 'Super! You just felt so bad!' There is clear playfulness in her descriptions of her mischievous forays and those of her friends. When describing an instance of getting closer than two metres to a friend of hers, she sarcastically exclaims, 'Oh, gosh, we came a bit too close then!' Vulnerability, both legally and in terms of the virus, seems to be the source of the fun here, allowing her to push herself beyond acceptable limits and play the trickster in the face of authority. Beyond fun and playfulness, though, she indicates that breaking the rules is necessary for her mental and physical wellbeing. Though she is vulnerable in the wider world, whether to authority or the virus, the vulnerability that comes with solitude and isolation is pointed, and play and trickery allow her to overcome at least one form of vulnerability during the pandemic.

As Kay Drummond says while reflecting on the garden contests described above and the realities of a snowy winter and renewed lockdown:

> This time I think it's as much about just making sure that everybody is, you know, handling it emotionally and because you haven't got the same outlets as you had before. (Drummond 2021)

Without those outlets—whether achieved in one's garden with family or through playful rule-breaking in the wider world—it is clear that many people felt increasingly vulnerable to discomfort and restlessness as the pandemic continued. Accompanying those feelings of anxiety was growing awareness of the seeming hypocrisies in the UK government's management of the pandemic. Towards the end of spring 2020, newspapers began reporting that Dominic Cummings, then Chief Advisor to the Prime Minister, broke lockdown rules by driving to his parents' farm in Durham, all while suffering from COVID-19. On his return trip to London, he and his family drove to the tourist attraction, Barnard Castle, purportedly so that he could test his eyesight and ensure that he was well enough to drive (Fancourt, Steptoe, and Wright 2020). In addition to this, perhaps ironically, being an example of bureaucratic rule-breaking and play (Martin et al. 2013: 569), this resulted in a number of angry and mocking examples of street art, indicating that cynicism and frustration were manifesting themselves in playful forms in the public sphere as well. One example, wheat-pasted onto a wall of a building on Leith Walk, was designed like an optician's eyechart— playing with Cummings' excuse of testing his vision. With words running into each other and each line getting progressively smaller, the text read, 'I went to Barnard Castle and all I got was this lousy eyechart' (Figure 11.5).

Figure 11.5 'Sardonic Eyechart, Leith, Edinburgh', 10 June 2020

As the general mood started to change in Scotland, and seemingly the UK more generally, many examples of play began to take a more cynical air. This temporal and contextual shift is neatly summarised by Victoria Round, who breaks down the pandemic while reflecting on its various stages:

> It's sort of a gritting your teeth stage now, isn't it? It's not novel. It's not... We had the novelty. We had the 'all pulling together' and feeling of community. Then we had everyone sort of desperate and turning on each other, and now it's just gritting your teeth, getting on with it. (Round 2021)

The 'turning on each other' stage seemingly refers to this period a few months in, with government scandals and people phoning the police on their neighbours to report lockdown breaches of various kinds. Round's description of 'gritting your teeth' complements Drummond's testimony above, from an interview made in the same month, that 'handling it emotionally' was key in that winter period.

Others were cynical, at least of government responses, from an earlier stage. Charity worker Myshele Haywood, in response to a query from interviewer Claire Needler about making rainbows and other 'light-hearted' things, says:

> Oh Jesus, no. Haven't done the rainbow thing. Haven't clapped for the NHS because that's just such bullshit. I will work for NHS workers to get decent pay, thank you very much. They don't need my applause. They need my activism. They need me to not vote Tory. [...] What else? Fun things. I am somebody that doesn't really do fun very well. (*Laughter*) I tend to try to do things with a purpose. Well, I crocheted a rainbow tea cosy for my husband because he was joking [...] 'Oh, I need a tea cosy'. I was like, 'Oh, do you want me to crochet you a rainbow tea cosy?' He was like 'Yeah, yeah, I do, I do', so. Okay, Google how to make a tea cosy. So that was a fun thing. (M. Haywood 2020)

But despite profound cynicism towards some of the communal displays of support for key workers, who Myshele identifies as being vulnerable to destructive government policies towards the NHS, it is important to keep aware of the nuance in Myshele's descriptions. People have had layered interactions with the pandemic, with multiple feelings co-existing concurrently. Here, Myshele's early cynicism is accompanied by an earnest expression of play in a marital context, play which is possible due to time afforded by the lockdown context. That this moment of play is facilitated by learning online how to crochet a tea cosy also perfectly reflects the continuous strands of heightened physical-online hybridity that have existed from the beginning of the pandemic. Though we might legitimately consider the pandemic and its play temporally through various stages of changing public attitudes, it is also important to remember that individuals' own responses to the pandemic and resultant susceptibilities were not necessarily limited to prevailing sentiments at any one stage.

Group responses did, however, tend to follow more obvious stages, as seen by rainbows and the Clap for Carers, public cynicism at government scandals and lockdown breaches, and eventually varying responses to vaccines and related mandates. By the second summer of the pandemic, I was living in Aberdeen, where I began documenting stickers decrying the arrival of vaccinations. Some of these stickers were carefully designed, making playful references to mid-century American advertising imagery. They featured healthy white faces—the kind that erstwhile would have hawked cigarettes through misleading statements—with the implication that the government, the media and the vaccine producers were trying to promote false hope to line their pockets or even poison the populace. There were a number of such stickers, mostly sourced from one online group, whereby individuals could download designs and print them out using label machines. Surprisingly to me, online posts on the group's public social media channels indicated a genuine sense of play and challenge in encouraging new people to join and photograph their stickers in notable locations.

Others, aware of how susceptible people can be when confronted with misinformation, and frustrated by the brazenness of the stickers, equally responded through play. One sticker, promoting a website with various discussions of conspiracy theories, pandemic-related or otherwise, was modified with the addition of another sticker placed directly in its centre, simply stating 'citation needed' (Figure 11.6).

Figure 11.6 'Ironic Sticker Request, Aberdeen', 26 March 2021
Photo © Nicolas Le Bigre, 2023, all rights reserved

In a time of division along political lines and myriad beliefs relating to personal and public health, these street sticker battles reflect serious vulnerabilities of everyday life, whether through fear of government-imposed mandates or concern for the effects of misinformation. Importantly, play allows the players to both express these vulnerabilities and deftly navigate around them.

Conclusion

This intentional or unintentional effect of play, in which players both express vulnerability and help soften or circumvent it, is at the heart of the examples described above. Play, whether online or offline, shows the vulnerability of its players. We can see above that for some, play reveals a fear of the potentially ephemeral nature of newfound community, while for others there is frustration with community that is imposed upon them. There is a lament for the loss of physical contact and regret for generational disadvantages in online contexts. Some demonstrate a fear of an unknown future, while others demonstrate exasperation with the limits placed upon them. But while in each of these cases players use play to delineate the boundaries of their vulnerabilities, they also use play to better protect those points of susceptibility. Whether through clapping, crocheting, film making, chalking, gift giving, sticker sticking, video game playing, educating, sign making, statue decorating or other novel or well-practised forms of play, players are able to understand their limitations while also slowly expanding their possibilities. And if for me this project and this chapter were forms of play, of collecting interesting items and arranging them for display, they also helped demarcate the limits of my work, pointing to vulnerabilities which the project did not clearly pick up on. One of the most poignant pandemic-related sights I encountered was when my wife and I moved back to Aberdeen mid-pandemic. Spray-painted on the wall adjacent to our home were the words, 'FUCK LIFE COVID 19 WANTED'. This served as an inescapable reminder of the enormous societal inequities amplified during the pandemic, whether due to mental and physical health difficulties, lack of green space, inability to access the internet, domestic abuse, ableism and racism on individual and structural levels, and so on. Though many of these themes were picked up on in contributions and discussed in interviews, the very nature of a university-based, online archival project meant that the voices of those most vulnerable were largely not included. By giving a number of examples of vulnerability and play during the pandemic, and by presenting the words of some of the players themselves, however, I hope to give valuable ground-level understandings to the notion that vulnerability and play are intertwined. Like all forms of folklore, people's fears, hopes, anxieties, dreams, values and levels of privilege have shaped what and how they have played and to what extent they have been able to play. Vulnerable play is simply play in its most honest form, and play—whether communal, individual, ethnographic, earnest, mischievous, or cynical—has sustained us during the pandemic. However the pandemic finishes, we can rest assured that play and its inherent vulnerabilities will accompany it till the very end.

Works Cited

Anonymous. 2020. Interviewed by Natalie Brown, 13 May, Lockdown Lore Collection Project, Elphinstone Institute Archives, University of Aberdeen

Barrow, Charlie. 2020. Personal communication. 4 May

Barrow, Charlie, and Olivia Barrow. 2020. Interviewed by Siân Burke, 19 May, Lockdown Lore Collection Project, Elphinstone Institute Archives, University of Aberdeen

Drummond, Kay. 2020. Interviewed by Richard Bennett, 8 June, Lockdown Lore Collection Project, Elphinstone Institute Archives, University of Aberdeen

——. 2021. Interviewed by Richard Bennett, 2 February, Lockdown Lore Collection Project, Elphinstone Institute Archives, University of Aberdeen

Fancourt, Daisy, Andrew Steptoe, and Liam Wright. 2020. 'The Cummings Effect: Politics, Trust, and Behaviours during the COVID-19 Pandemic', *Lancet*, 6 August, https://doi.org/10.1016/S0140-6736(20)31690-1

Farris, Sara, Nira Yuval-Davis, and Catherine Rottenberg. 2021. 'The Frontline as Performative Frame: An Analysis of the UK Covid Crisis', *State Crime*, 10: 284–303, https://doi.org/10.13169/statecrime.10.2.0284

Gillis, Ben. 2011. 'An Unexpected Font of Folklore: Online Gaming as Occupational Lore', *Western Folklore*, 70: 147–70

Goldstein, Diane. 2004. *Once upon a Virus: AIDS Legends and Vernacular Risk Perception* (Logan: Utah State University Press)

Hall, Jamie. 2020. 'Clap for our Carers: North-East Residents Pay Tribute to NHS Staff', *Press and Journal* [*Aberdeen*], 10 April, https://www.pressandjournal.co.uk/fp/news/aberdeen-aberdeenshire/2138533/clap-for-our-carers-north-east-residents-pay-tribute-to-nhs-staff/

Harding, Sarah. 2020. 'Daily Exercise Rules Got People Moving During Lockdown—Here's What the Government Needs to Do Next', *The Conversation*, 5 August, https://theconversation.com/daily-exercise-rules-got-people-moving-during-lockdown-heres-what-the-government-needs-to-do-next-143773

Haywood, Doug. 2020. Interviewed by David Francis, 13 May, Lockdown Lore Collection Project, Elphinstone Institute Archives, University of Aberdeen

Haywood, Myshele. 2020. Interviewed by Claire Needler, 12 June, Lockdown Lore Collection Project, Elphinstone Institute Archives, University of Aberdeen

Le Bigre, Nicolas. 2020. 'Documenting Creative Responses to the Pandemic', *FLS News*, 91: 15–16

Lindahl, Carl. 2018. 'Dream Some More: Storytelling as Therapy', *Folklore*: 221–36, https://doi.org/10.1080/0015587X.2018.1473109

Lindgren, Anne-Li. 2017. 'Materializing Fiction: Teachers as Creators of Play and Children as Embodied Entrants in Early Childhood Education', *International Journal of Play*, 6: 150–65, https://doi.org/10.1080/21594937.2017.1348317

Marsh, Jackie. 2014. 'The Relationship between Online and Offline Play: Friendship and Exclusion', in *Children's Games in the New Media Age: Childlore, Media, and the Playground*, ed. by Andrew Burn and Chris Richards (Farnham: Ashgate), pp. 109–32

Martin, Andrew W., et al. 2013. 'Against the Rules: Synthesizing Types and Processes of Bureaucratic Rule-Breaking', *Academy of Management Review*, 38: 550–74, https://doi.org/10.5465/amr.2011.0223

Morss, Alex. 2020. '"Not Just Weeds": How Rebel Botanists Are Using Graffiti to Name Forgotten Flora', *The Guardian*, 1 May, https://www.theguardian.com/environment/2020/may/01/not-just-weeds-how-rebel-botanists-are-using-graffiti-to-name-forgotten-flora-aoe

Nicolaisen, W. F. H. 1992. 'Humour in Traditional Ballads (Mainly Scottish)', *Folklore*, 103: 27–39, https://doi.org/10.1080/0015587X.1992.9715827

National Records of Scotland. 2022. 'Deaths Involving Coronavirus (COVID-19) in Scotland', https://www.nrscotland.gov.uk/statistics-and-data/statistics/statistics-by-theme/vital-events/general-publications/weekly-and-monthly-data-on-births-and-deaths/deaths-involving-coronavirus-covid-19-in-scotland

Opie, Iona, and Peter Opie. 1997. *Children's Games with Things* (Oxford: Oxford University Press)

Oram, Richard. 2007. '"It cannot be decernit quha are clean and quha are foulle": Responses to Epidemic Disease in Sixteenth- and Seventeenth-Century Scotland', *Renaissance and Reformation*, 30.4: 13–39

Prime Minister's Office. 2020. 'Prime Minister's Statement on Coronavirus (COVID-19): 23 March 2020', https://www.gov.uk/government/speeches/pm-address-to-the-nation-on-coronavirus-23-march-2020

Ritchie, James T. R.. 1965. *Golden City* (London: Oliver and Boyd)

Round, Victoria. 2021. Interviewed by Mara Shea, 30 January, Lockdown Lore Collection Project, Elphinstone Institute Archives, University of Aberdeen

Robertson, D. H. 1862. 'Notes of the "Visitation of the Pestilence" from the Parish Records of South Leith, A.D. 1645, in Connexion with the Exaction of Large Masses of Human Bone during Drainage Operations at Wellington Place, Leith Links, A.D. 1861–2', *Proceedings of the Society of Antiquaries of Scotland*, 4, 392–95, https://doi.org/10.9750/PSAS.004.392.400

Roud, Steve. 2011. *The Lore of the Playground: The Children's World, Then and Now* (London: Arrow)

World Health Organization. 2022. '14.9 Million Excess Deaths Associated with the COVID-19 Pandemic in 2020 and 2021', https://www.who.int/news/item/05-05-2022-14.9-million-excess-deaths-were-associated-with-the-covid-19-pandemic-in-2020-and-2021

12. How Young Children Played during the Covid-19 Lockdown in 2020 in Ireland:
Findings from the Play and Learning in the Early Years (PLEY) Covid-19 Study

Suzanne M. Egan, Jennifer Pope, Chloé Beatty, and Clara Hoyne

Introduction

The Covid-19 measures put in place by governments around the world to restrict the movement of people and limit the spread of the virus have also impacted on children's play. The importance of play in children's lives has been well documented and research shows that it plays a role in all aspects of development including physical, cognitive and socio-emotional development (e.g. Ginsburg 2007: 182, Fisher et al. 2008: 306, Howard and McInnes 2013: 738). Different types of play have been classified, as have the different ways that children can learn and develop through play (e.g. Parten 1932: 249, Whitebread et al. 2012: 31). This chapter will examine some key findings on changes in young children's

 https://doi.org/10.11647/OBP.0326.12

play in an Irish context based on parental responses gathered during the first Covid-19 lockdown in spring 2020.

The evidence on children's play during the pandemic to date suggests that globally there have been a number of changes (e.g. Barron et al. 2021: 372; Moore et al. 2021: 4). New research is still emerging but it seems that commonalities across countries during lockdowns included increases in time spent on screens and on indoor play, and decreases in physical activity and outdoor play. A cross-country comparative study of children's indoor play during the lockdown indicated many similar impacts on play behaviours and activities, irrespective of country, specific cultural factors or restrictions in place (Barron et al. 2021: 375). Children's development and how they play does not operate in a vacuum as children are influenced by the world around them and often use play to make sense of their experiences (e.g. Hirsh-Pasek, Singer, and Golinkoff 2006: 39; Hayes, O'Toole, and Halpenny 2017: 88).

According to an article on the World Economic Forum, ninety-nine percent of the world's children have lived with restrictions on movement and interactions because of Covid-19 (Fore and Hijazi 2020). The pandemic disrupted every aspect of children's lives, including their health, development, learning and behaviour, their families' economic security, their protection from violence and abuse, and their mental health. Recent research studies have also borne this out (e.g. Almeida et al. 2021: 413; Egan et al. 2021: 925; López-Aymes et al. 2021: 1, Thorell et al. 2021: 649; Thorn and Vincent-Lancrin 2022: 383). Under Article 31 of the United Nations Convention on the Rights of the Child (UNICEF 1989), children have the right to play, although this is often a neglected right (Shakel 2015: 48).

Covid-19 Restrictions in Ireland in 2020

In the Irish context, on 12 March 2020 the Government announced with one day's notice the closure of all schools, preschools, crèches, colleges and universities. This was extremely disruptive to all parents, children and families—with national restrictions announced later that month impacting all citizens. The Irish government directed everyone to stay at home except in specific circumstances (e.g. travel to and from essential work, shopping for food, attendance at medical appointments), and to practise social distancing (i.e. stay two metres apart in all public spaces). This resulted in the closure of all non-essential businesses.

During the lockdown, schools turned to online learning as much as possible. However, there was significant variation in access to digital home schooling and to electronic devices (e.g. Egan and Beatty 2021: 8). Many parents were faced with the care and education of their young children, while juggling working from home. These effects were felt globally, with the lives of young children changing considerably during this time. Playgrounds were also initially closed in Ireland. Adults and children could leave their homes only for brief physical exercise, only within two kilometres of their home, and households were not permitted to mix (RTÉ News 2020). Most television and radio coverage had extensive reporting of the crisis as effects of the restrictions and lockdown impacted on children and adults. Non-essential travel in Ireland was extended to five kilometres on 1 May and to twenty kilometres on 8 June.

In order to explore the effects of the lockdown on children's play, learning and development during this difficult time, we designed and ran an online survey to capture the experiences of families with young children aged between birth and ten years old. This built on the findings of a previous, similar survey conducted by members of the Cognitive, Development and Learning Research Lab in Mary Immaculate College, Ireland, during 2019 (Egan, Hoyne, and Beatty 2021: 224). The Play and Learning in the Early Years (PLEY) Covid-19 survey was open to parents during late May and early June 2020, approximately two months into the lockdown in Ireland. To facilitate comparison, many questions on the survey (e.g. regarding daily and weekly frequencies of various play activities) were drawn directly from the national birth cohort study *Growing Up in Ireland* (McCrory et al. 2013: 2; Williams et al. 2019: 10) and previous research (e.g. developmental scales; Goodman 1997: 582). Some questions were also adapted from previous research while others were developed specifically for the PLEY Covid-19 survey (e.g. questions relating to the impact of the COVID-19 restrictions). The survey questions and procedures were approved by the Mary Immaculate College Ethics Committee.

The Play and Learning in the Early Years (PLEY) COVID-19 Survey

The recruitment phase for the survey lasted two weeks, from 21 May through June 2020, during which time the online Play and Learning in the Early Years (PLEY) Covid-19 survey was open to participants. Parents with young children were recruited through newspaper advertisements and also through social media platforms, including via Twitter and Facebook. Information about the study, including a link to the survey, was shared with parenting networks, early years organizations and centres, schools and parents of young children who are active on social media, who in turn shared this information with their contact networks by retweeting, posting or forwarding information. Information about the survey and a link to it was also available on the Government of Ireland's Parents Centre webpage while the survey was open and it was also shared on social media by the Government of Ireland's Department of Children and Youth Affairs. All materials and procedures were approved by the institutional ethics committee.

In total, 564 parents responded to the survey. However, forty-seven responses were excluded from the analysis of the data because they only completed the initial demographic questions, while a further eleven participants had children outside of the target age range of ten years or younger. The final sample consisted of 506 participants (92.9% mothers, 5.9% fathers, 1.2% other) with a mean age of 40.36 years (SD = 4.81). The participants' children had an average age of 6.41 years (SD = 2.44), ranging from 1 to 10 years (49.8% male, 49.6% female and 0.6% unspecified). Most children had siblings (82.8%) and were breastfed (71.3%).

The majority of participants (95.8%) were from Ireland, with the remaining participants being from the United Kingdom (2%) or other parts of the world (1.2%). Most parents worked full time (61.1%) or part time (22.1%), with others looking after family or on leave (14.7%). Most parents (85.7%) indicated that, because of the Covid-19 crisis, they had changed to working from home (71.7%) or were temporarily not working due to business closure (11.8%). The majority of the sample were well-educated with 84.4% holding a college-level degree or postgraduate qualification. All participants completed the PLEY

Covid-19 survey via Qualtrics software. After expressing initial interest in the survey by clicking on the advertised link, participants were provided with additional detailed information about the survey and what was involved before giving their informed consent to take part.

The survey took approximately twenty minutes to complete and consisted of three sections asking parents about their children's play, learning and development. The first section of the survey explored the impact of the Covid-19 restrictions on children's play and learning. Parents were asked to indicate approximately how much time their child spent on an average weekday and an average weekend day over the previous two months playing with toys and games, reading and story time, outdoor play, and on screens. The final question in this section asked parents if their child had brought information about the virus or restrictions into their play (e.g. Doctors and Nurses) and particularly if they had brought it into chasing games (e.g. Tag/Tig). Responses to this section of the survey are the focus of the results reported below.

The second section of the survey measured aspects of children's cognitive and socio-emotional development using standardized scales. These included the Attentional Focusing subscale from the Children's Behaviour Questionnaire (Rothbart et al. 2001: 1396) and the Strengths and Difficulties Questionnaire (Goodman 1997: 581). The third and final section asked parents about the physical and social factors that influence their child's play and learning activities (e.g. play resources at home; parents' beliefs about playtime experiences (Fogle and Mendez 2006: 509), influences of siblings, peers and parents; supports and barriers to play; experiences in the child's home). This section also recorded information about the weekly frequency of various play activities (e.g. playing with blocks or with puzzles) and some of this information is also reported below. Parents completed most of the demographic questions first, followed by the questions about the impact of Covid-19 on play and learning. Subsequently, they completed the measures of child development and finally, the more detailed questions about influences on play, other than the Covid-19 restrictions (e.g. play resources in the home).

The Home Play Environment in Ireland
during Lockdown

The findings of the survey shed light on the types and amounts of play that young Irish children engaged in during the first lockdown. As Figure 12.1 below shows, most children engaged in up to an hour of reading/story time each day and spent more than one hour playing with toys and games, playing outdoors or on screens. The figure also shows some changes in the amount of time spent in various play activities between weekdays and weekends, with children on average spending more time in each type of play at the weekends than on a weekday. This is particularly evident for outdoor play where 38.8% of children were spending over three hours per day on this type of play at the weekend, compared with 28.2% on a weekday.

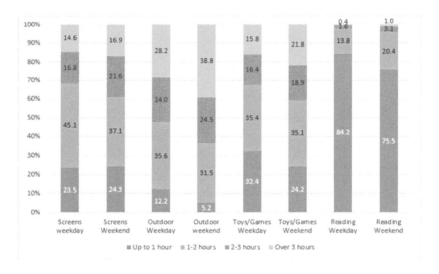

Figure 12.1 Percentage of children in each time category for each activity on a typical weekday and weekend day

Created by Egan et al. 2022, CC BY-NC 4.0

Figure 12.1 also shows that over two thirds of children played with toys or games for over an hour per day, both on weekdays (67.6%) and weekends (75.8%). Another question on the survey sheds light on the types of toys and games the children engaged with and how often. Figure

12.2 below suggests that over half of the children in the sample engaged in construction and creative play multiple times per week (three to six days per week or every day), using blocks, LEGO or building materials (52.3%) or with Play-Doh, slime, painting or drawing (53.5%). Pretend and make-believe play was also very popular with 73.9% of children, who engaged in this activity at least three days per week.

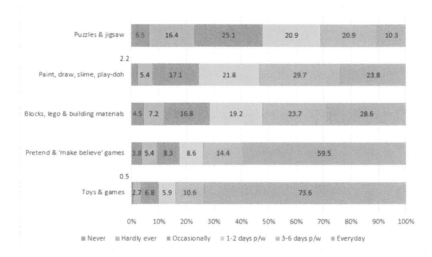

Figure 12.2 Percentage of children engaged in various play activities during the first two months of lockdown in 2020 in Ireland
Created by Egan et al. 2022, CC BY-NC 4.0

However, the rates of engagement in various play activities were influenced by the age of the child. As Figure 12.3 shows, older children aged from seven to ten years were less likely to engage in each of the various activities on a daily basis, compared with those aged from one to three years or from four to six years. For example, nearly all of the children under seven years of age played with toys and games every day during lockdown, while only fifty-seven percent of children aged seven years or older engaged in this type of play daily. Additionally, approximately seventy-seven percent of the under sevens engaged in pretend or make-believe play every day, in comparison to forty-five percent of children aged seven years or older.

	Age 1-3 years	Age 4-6 years	Age 7-10 years
Toys and games	100	90.6	57.4
Pretend or 'make believe'	77.8	77.2	44.9
Blocks, Lego, building materials	38.1	34.5	22.9
Paint, draw, slime, Play-Doh	23.8	36.5	16.7
Puzzles and jigsaws	28.1	10.9	5.3

Figure 12.3 Percentage of children engaged in various activities 'every day' by age group
Created by Egan et al. 2022, CC BY-NC 4.0

Parental Beliefs about Play and Engagement in Play Activities

Parents were asked to indicate their level of agreement with various statements regarding their beliefs about play. Nearly all parents indicated that there were plenty of toys, pictures and music (96.5%) in their home for their child, as well as plenty of books (96.6%), with ninety-one percent indicating their child had over twenty books (80.4% indicated they had over thirty children's books). Most parents also somewhat agreed or strongly agreed with statements that there were lots of creative activities going on in the home (75.7%), that it was an interesting place for their child (86.7%) and that activities were provided that were just right for their child (77.2%), suggesting most parents viewed their home as a rich play environment.

Parents also indicated that they valued play for socio-emotional and cognitive development, with most agreeing that play can help their child develop social skills (97%), improve their language and communication skills (98.6%) and help develop better thinking abilities (96.5%). Furthermore, 95.5% of parents indicated that playing together helps build a good relationship with their child. Parents also indicated that playing was fun, with most agreeing that play is a fun activity for their child (97.7%), they have a lot of fun when they play with their child

(90.5%), their child has fun when they play together (95.3%) and that it is important for them to participate in play with their child (85.1%).

Figure 12.4 below shows the frequency with which parents reported playing with their child during various activities, with thirty-three percent playing with toys and games with their child every day. The findings indicate that for the various activities listed, approximately half of parents engaged in these activities with their child on at least a weekly basis, while the other half 'never', 'hardly ever' or only 'occasionally' engaged in these activities. There was little difference in how often the parents engaged in the different types of activities whether it involved play with blocks, Play-Doh or jigsaws. The most frequent type of daily play parents engaged in was with toys and games (thirty-three percent of parents did this everyday) followed by pretend or make-believe play (twenty percent of parents did this every day).

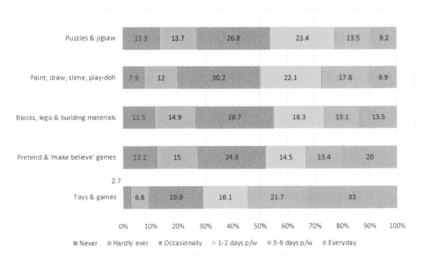

Figure 12.4 Percentage of parents who engaged with their child in various play activities during the first two months of lockdown in 2020 in Ireland
Created by Egan et al. 2022, CC BY-NC 4.0

Inclusion of the Virus and Restrictions in Play

Approximately one third of parents (34%) indicated that their child had included information about Covid-19 in their play, with reference to the restrictions, social distancing or hygiene measures present at all ages and across multiple types of play including outdoor play (e.g. 'corona chasing'), construction play (e.g. building LEGO hospital wards) and pretend play (e.g. playing Doctors and Nurses). For example, in relation to pretend play, one parent of a seven-year-old girl stated that 'she created a shop and used chalk to draw lines for social distancing and hand sanitizer at her shop stall', while another parent of a seven-year-old noted that their child was 'playing dead, playing doctors, pretend washing hands, pretend teach enforcing social distancing'. Regarding construction play, a parent of a five-year-old said, 'She made bunk beds for Lego people that were sick & placed them far away from one another & only one person allowed in the bunk to social distance', while a parent of a nine-year-old said their child 'made a hospital with patients, ventilator and test centre with Lego'.

In addition to asking parents if their child had included information about the virus or restrictions in their play, parents were also specifically asked if they were aware of their child or other children playing a version of chasing related to the virus. Approximately eight percent of parents answered yes (39 responses out of 506), with over half of the responses indicating that it took place in their child's school before closure (twenty-two of the thirty-nine responses, or fifty-six percent of responses about corona tag). All schools in Ireland closed on 13 March 2020 and did not reopen until September 2020. Those that described Covid-19 tag in another setting mainly mentioned that their child played it at home with a sibling. One parent also described the following:

> My brother in Dublin has watched children playing 'Corona', which involves the person being 'on' calling 'corona' and the others have to get up on something as 'quarantine' as quickly as possible. There were other calls, hand washing, and points of some sort involved.

Other parents' descriptions of the game were similar, with the person who was 'on' having 'Covid' and the children who were caught 'catching Covid'. A parent of a seven-year-old described a 'chase game with person on having germs!', while another parent of a seven-year-old said, 'He created a game of tig called coronavirus. He was trying to catch his sister pretending he had the virus and saying she'd catch it from him if he caught her'. The notion of Covid being deadly also featured in some of the games, with a parent of a nine-year-old mentioning 'Tag, where child caught was said to die as they had the coronavirus'. A parent of a four-year-old noted that her daughter was 'recently playing ghost tag with neighbour's child'.

Implications of the Findings of the PLEY Covid-19 Survey

The findings of the Play and Learning in the Early Years Covid-19 survey provide important insights into children's play at home in Ireland during the early stages of the Covid-19 pandemic. Given the timeframe of survey distribution, these findings provide valuable information regarding this unprecedented time for families in their home environments. The findings also highlight the value parents place on children's play and the resources available to Irish children in the home play environment during the first lockdown of 2020.

While children and their parents globally have suffered many negative effects as a consequence of the pandemic and the resulting restrictions, the findings of the current study suggest that most children spent a considerable amount of time engaged in various types of play during lockdown. A wealth of research supports the developmental benefits of play (Kane 2016: 290, Schmitt et al. 2018: 181), as well as the therapeutic benefits of play in times of crisis (Chatterjee 2018: 119). Therefore, it is positive to note that for many children in Ireland the pandemic did not reduce the amount of time spent in various types of play.

As has been reported in other countries (e.g. Bergmann et al. 2022: 4; Moore et al. 2021: 6), the current findings indicate many children also spent a considerable time on screens during lockdown, with over seventy-five percent of children spending over an hour a day on screens. However, it is important to note that the findings reported above suggest that time on screens did not displace time for other types of play for children in Ireland, such as playing outdoors. Drawing on data from the same sample, Egan and Beatty (2021: 6) previously noted that most parents reported that their child was spending less time on schoolwork than before the pandemic. Therefore, the time for most children afforded to screen use may have been at the expense of time spent on schoolwork, rather than time spent on playful activities, as time spent playing with toys and games and playing outdoors was also high. The majority of children spent at least an hour a day on these activities.

However, that is not to say that the time spent on screens or on other types of play was not educational or beneficial in other developmental ways. For example, Egan and Beatty (2021: 7) reported that more than half of school-age children in the same sample used screens for schoolwork, to play educational games or watch educational television and videos on at least a weekly basis, with up to a quarter of participants engaged in some of these activities every day. Other research also highlights the benefits of screen use for maintaining social connections between children and their friends, and also their early years settings and schools (Bigras et al. 2021: 784), given the restrictions in place during 2020. Many researchers stress the need for a broader perspective to recognize both the positive and negative impacts of technology for children (e.g. Barron et al. 2021: 268; Beatty and Egan 2020: 26) and to consider the importance of play in digital spaces (Cowan 2020: 3; Colvert 2021: 7).

While there are some similarities between the findings of the current study and international findings (e.g. Moore et al. 2021: 4), there are also differences. For example, unlike research from Canada (Moore et al. 2021: 6), which showed a decrease in outdoor play in children aged from five to seventeen years, and research from China (Xiang, Zhang, and Kuwahara 2020: 531) that showed a decrease in physical activity in children aged from six to seventeen years, the findings from the current study suggest children in Ireland, aged from one to ten years, had high levels of outdoor play during lockdown. The World Health Organization recommends that children should engage in at least sixty minutes of physical activity per day (Bull et al. 2020: 1455), and the current study shows that during the first two months of lockdown in Ireland, eighty-eight percent of children engaged in this amount of outdoor play on a weekday, with ninety-five percent at the weekend. Factors that may have facilitated this increase in outdoor play relate to both the increased time at home, as well as the exceptionally sunny and warm weather Ireland experienced during this time in 2020. Additionally, children in Ireland have almost universal access to private outdoor space as the majority of housing stock in the country consists of houses with private gardens.

The changes in the amount of time spent in outdoor play are also evident when considered in light of data gathered in 2019, also using the Play and Learning in the Early Years Survey (Egan, Hoyne, and Beatty 2021: 224). These data were gathered between June and October 2019 and the findings showed that on a weekday, twenty-six percent of children spent less than an hour in outdoor play, with seventeen percent spending this amount of time on a weekend. In contrast, during lockdown these figures were twelve percent and five percent for a weekday and weekend respectively. Similarly, in 2019, thirty-seven percent spent over two hours in outdoor play on a weekday, whereas during lockdown in 2020 this figure was fifty-three percent. It seems that the amount of time spent in outdoor play was higher in 2020 than in 2019, particularly on a weekday.

It is evident also from the findings that most parents valued playing with their child, with nearly all parents indicating that they had a lot of fun when they played with their child and that it was important for them to do so. Parents also clearly valued play for supporting their child's development, with nearly all parents agreeing that it supported cognitive, socio-emotional, language and communication skills. These beliefs about the value of play for their child, and the benefit in terms of building a good relationship with their child, was also borne out through their behaviour in playing with their child and the play resources provided by the parent in the home. For example, over half of the parents played with toys and games with their child multiple days per week while a third played pretend or make-believe games with them multiple days per week.

Encouragingly, the majority of parents reported that their home was a rich play environment for their young child. Nearly all parents indicated there were plenty of play resources in the home such as toys, pictures, books, music and materials for creative play. Given the closure of schools, early years settings and public playgrounds, as well as the two-kilometre travel-from-home restriction, this is particularly heartening to note. The findings from the current study highlight the rich home play environments available to children during the lockdown, both in terms of physical play resources as well as the play interactions between parent and child. These interactions will have been particularly important given that children were restricted to the home and missed out on interactions and playing with friends and other peers in early years and school settings (Egan et al. 2021: 928).

The Importance of Contextual Factors for Young Children's Play

These findings highlight the importance of considering many factors when examining play during the pandemic, such as play resources in the home, parental beliefs about play, parental engagement in play, child's age, local conditions related to lockdown restrictions and also the extent of school and playground closures. Bronfenbrenner's (1979: 3, 2005: 4) bioecological model can provide a useful framework in which to make sense of these findings and further international research (Egan and Pope 2022: 15). How children played and who they played with were impacted at different system levels, from the microsystem environment of the home, through to the wider macrosystem environment incorporating cultural factors and government restrictions.

For example, decisions made on a macrosystem level by the government, such as business and school closures, had direct impacts on children and families at a microsystem level in the home. Barron et al. (2021: 375) reported that there was a high percentage of parental presence in the home during the Covid-19 lockdown (75.2%) but that this figure varied markedly across the four countries in their cross-cultural comparison. Ireland had the highest percentage of parents at home (86.9%) with rates considerably lower in the UK (69.2%), Italy (52.6%), and the United States (52.9%). They found that parents being present in the home was associated with higher rates of indoor play activities and cooperative play with parents across multiple activities, such as for playing board games, playing with toys, reading and doing arts and crafts. In previous studies, lack of time has been identified as a factor affecting how parents play with their children (Shah, Gustafson, and Atkins 2019: 606) combined with family structure (Fallesen and Gähler 2020: 361). Cultural factors in Ireland, such as a high level of access to private outdoor space (a garden), also influenced how children played in the microsystem of the home play environment with high levels of outdoor play present.

The high levels of play seen in this study are encouraging both from a developmental perspective as well as a potentially therapeutic perspective (e.g. Chatterjee 2018: 119). Approximately a third of parents in the PLEY Covid-19 study reported that their child had brought information about the virus or restrictions into their play, highlighting their awareness of the situation. This was apparent across multiple types of play (e.g. outdoor, pretend play, play with objects, etc.) and across multiple ages in early childhood. It was evident that children actively reproduce and reinvent societal information rather than passively internalizing what is happening around them. Similarly, Barron et al. (2021: 372) gathered data from parents and children, including photo images of play. They suggest that indoor play in the home environment, including using technology, may have helped as a coping mechanism and to build resilience.

While many of the findings regarding the time spent in play in this study are positive, with many children spending a lot of time playing, this was not the case for all children. For example, a number of children never or hardly ever engaged in some of the different types of play activities, such as playing with puzzles and jigsaws or with blocks and building materials, as Figure 12.2 illustrates. Additionally, across the various types of play, the findings suggest that a minority of parents never or hardly ever play with their child, at least in some of the activities measured in this survey. As might be expected, the findings highlight differences in family experiences during the pandemic with multiple positive and negative effects potentially being experienced by any one family. When interpreting the findings, it is therefore important that the limitations of the study are borne in mind.

For example, the sample has a high proportion of highly educated families who volunteered to participate in the study. While Ireland has one of the highest rates of adults with third-level education in Europe (Wilson 2021), future research should aim to include a more diverse sample of families from other educational and socioeconomic backgrounds. The recruitment method of parents through online means permitted all families to participate in the research and the links to the survey were widely shared by a variety of organizations and individuals. Given that the country was in lockdown at the time, with a two-kilometre limit of movements from home imposed on citizens, it was not possible to contact a diversity of families directly to invite them to participate. Therefore, access to a computer, smartphone or the internet, along with the time needed to participate, may have acted as a barrier to some parents in participating. Future research should consider in-person methods when recruiting for other studies on this topic.

It is also important that children with a range of intellectual and cognitive abilities are included in future research. Neurodiverse children may engage in different types of play in different ways (although it is important to recognize the individual nature of each child within their ecological systems rather than make generalizations). Children with additional learning needs, chronic illness or mobility considerations may play in certain ways specific to them which may also be shaped by their environment and the interactions they have, both directly and indirectly.

It is also imperative that future research involves young children directly to ascertain their views on the impact on their play and activities, in addition to the evidence provided through parental reports. While parental reports are useful, and were the most feasible measure during this initial lockdown period for children in this young age group, investigating young children's views directly is also important. On a positive note, the data was collected directly during this unprecedented time rather than retrospectively, and therefore the risk of parental recall bias was minimized as completing the questionnaire during this timeframe did not require reflection or recall and was entirely anonymous.

Conclusion

The findings reported in this chapter represent the play experiences of families living in Ireland during this unprecedented time in their lives, the first Covid-19 lockdown in 2020. The literature highlights the important role of play for children in terms of coping with adversity and building resilience. It is therefore heartening to see that overall, many of the findings with regards to play were positive. Young children in Ireland spent a considerable amount of time in multiple types of play, in rich home play environments with parents who valued and facilitated their play both in terms of the physical resources they provided and the social support they engaged in while playing with their child. It is apparent based on the international research emerging that similar experiences were observed globally. However, it must be noted that there are also differences at the country as well as family level. Despite the child's right to play, not every child had the resources available, environments conducive to play, siblings, peers or supportive adults with whom to play. Interpreting these results and other international research through a bioecological lens offers a good approach to make sense of and learn from these findings so that appropriate supports for families can be put in place, whatever their circumstances and wherever they live.

Works Cited

Almeida, Vandaet al. 2021. 'The Impact of COVID-19 on Households' Income in the EU', *Journal of Economic Inequality*, 19: 413-31, https://doi.org/10.1007/s10888-021-09485-8

Barron, Carol, et al. 2021. 'Indoor Play during a Global Pandemic: Commonalities and Diversities during a Unique Snapshot in Time', *International Journal of Play*, 10: 365-86, https://doi.org/10.1080/21594937.2021.2005396

Beatty, Chloé, and Suzanne M. Egan. 2020. 'Screen Time in Early Childhood: A Review of Prevalence, Evidence and Guidelines', *An Leanbh Óg*, 13: 17-31

Bergmann, Christina, et al. 2022. 'Young Children's Screen Time during the First COVID-19 Lockdown in 12 Countries', *Scientific Reports*, 12: 1-15, https://doi.org/10.1038/s41598-022-05840-5

Bigras, Nathalie, et al. 2021. 'Early Childhood Educators' Perceptions of their Emotional State, Relationships with Parents, Challenges, and Opportunities during the Early Stage of the Pandemic', *Early Childhood Education Journal*, 49: 775-87, https://doi.org/10.1007/s10643-021-01224-y

Bronfenbrenner, Urie. 1979. *The Ecology of Human Development: Experiments by Nature and Design* (Cambridge, MA: Harvard University Press)

—— (ed.). 2005. *Making Human Beings Human: Bioecological Perspectives on Human Development* (Thousand Oaks, CA: Sage)

Bull, Fiona C., et al. 2020. 'World Health Organization 2020 Guidelines on Physical Activity and Sedentary Behaviour', *British Journal of Sports Medicine*, 54: 1451-462, http://dx.doi.org/10.1136/bjsports-2020-102955

Chatterjee, Sudeshna. 2018. 'Children's Coping, Adaptation and Resilience through Play in Situations of Crisis', *Children, Youth and Environments*, 28: 119–45, https://doi.org/10.7721/chilyoutenvi.28.2.0119

Colvert, Angela. 2021. *The Kaleidoscope of Play in a Digital World: A Literature Review* (London: Digital Futures Commission 5Rights Foundation), https://digitalfuturescommission.org.uk/wp-content/uploads/2021/06/DFC-Digital-Play-Literature-Review.pdf

Cowan, Kate. 2020. *A Panorama of Play: A Literature Review* (London: Digital Futures Commission 5Rights Foundation) https://digitalfuturescommission. org.uk/wp-content/uploads/2022/02/A-Panorama-of-Play-A-Literature-Review.pdf

Egan, Suzanne M., and Chloé Beatty, 2021. 'To School through the Screens: The Use of Screen Devices to Support Young Children's Education and Learning during the COVID-19 Pandemic', *Irish Educational Studies*, 40: 275-83, https:// doi.org/10.1080/03323315.2021.1932551

Egan, Suzanne M., Clara Hoyne, and Chloé Beatty. 2021. 'The Home Play Environment: The Play and Learning in Early Years (PLEY) Study', in *Perspectives on Childhood*, ed. by Aisling Leavy and Margaret Nohilly (Newcastle upon Tyne: Cambridge Scholar Publishing)

Egan, Suzanne M., and Jennifer Pope. 2022. 'A Bioecological Systems Approach to Understanding the Impact of the COVID-19 Pandemic: Implications for the Education and Care of Young Children', in *The COVID-19 Pandemic: Effects on Early Childhood Education and Care: International Perspectives, Challenges, and Responses*, ed. by Jyotsna Pattnaik and Mary Renck Jalongo, Educating the Young Child, 18 (Cham, Switzerland: Springer), pp. 15-31, https://doi. org/10.1007/978-3-030-96977-6_2

Egan, Suzanne M., et al. 2021. 'Missing Early Education and Care during the Pandemic: The Socio-emotional Impact of the COVID-19 Crisis on Young Children', *Early Childhood Education Journal*, 49: 925-34, https://doi. org/10.1007/s10643-021-01193-2

Fallesen, Peter, and Michael Gähler. 2020. 'Family Type and Parents' Time with Children: Longitudinal Evidence for Denmark', *Acta Sociologica*, 63: 361-80, https://doi.org/10.1177/0001699319868522

Fisher, Kelly R., et al. 2008. 'Conceptual Split? Parents' and Experts' Perceptions of Play in the 21st Century', *Journal of Applied Developmental Psychology*, 29: 305-16, https://doi.org/10.1016/j.appdev.2008.04.006

Fogle, Livy M., and Julia L. Mendez. 2006. 'Assessing the Play Beliefs of African American Mothers with Preschool Children', *Early Childhood Research Quarterly*, 21: 507-18, https://doi.org/10.1016/j.ecresq.2006.08.002

Fore, Henrietta H., and Zeinab Hijazi. 2020. 'COVID-19 Is Hurting Children's Mental Health: Here Are 3 Ways We Can Help', *World Economic Forum*, 1 May, https://www.weforum.org/agenda/2020/05/ covid-19-is-hurting-childrens-mental-health/

Ginsburg, Kenneth R. 2007. 'The Importance of Play in Promoting Healthy Child Development and Maintaining Strong Parent-Child Bonds', *Pediatrics*, 119: 182-91, https://doi.org/10.1542/peds.2006-2697

Goodman, Robert. 1997. 'The Strengths and Difficulties Questionnaire: A Research Note', *Journal of Child Psychology and Psychiatry*, 38: 581-86

Hayes, Nóirín, Leah O'Toole, and Ann Marie Halpenny. 2017. *Introducing Bronfenbrenner: A Guide for Practitioners and Students in Early Years Education* (New York: Routledge)

Hirsh-Pasek Kathy, Dorothy G. Singer, and Roberta M. Golinkoff. 2006. *Play = Learning: How Play Motivates and Enhances Children's Cognitive and Social-emotional Growth* (Oxford: Oxford University Press)

Howard, Justine, and Karen McInnes. 2013. 'The Impact of Children's Perception of an Activity as Play Rather Than Not Play on Emotional Well-being', *Child: Care, Health & Development*, 39: 737-42, https://doi.org/10.1111/j.1365-2214.2012.01405.x

Kane, Nazneen. 2016. 'The Play-Learning Binary: US Parents' Perceptions on Preschool Play in a Neoliberal Age', *Children & Society*, 30: 290-301, https://doi.org/10.1111/chso.12140

López-Aymes, Gabriela, et al. 2021. 'A Mixed Methods Research Study of Parental Perception of Physical Activity and Quality of Life of Children under Home Lockdown in the COVID-19 Pandemic', *Frontiers in Psychology*, 12, 649481 https://doi.org/10.3389/fpsyg.2021.649481

McCrory, Cathal, et al. 2013. *Growing Up in Ireland: Design, Instrumentation and Procedures for the Infant Cohort at Wave Two (3 Years)*, Technical Report, 3 (Dublin: Department of Children and Youth Affairs), https://www.growingup.ie/pubs/BKMNEXT253.pdf

Moore, Sarah A., et al. 2020. 'Impact of the COVID-19 Virus Outbreak on Movement and Play Behaviours of Canadian Children and Youth: A National Survey', *International Journal of Behavioral Nutrition and Physical Activity*, 17: 1-11, https://doi.org/10.1186/s12966-020-00987-8

Parten, Mildred B. 1932. 'Social Participation among Pre-school Children', *Journal of Abnormal and Social Psychology*, 27: 243-69, https://doi.org/10.1037/h0074524

Rothbart, Mary K., et al. 2001. 'Investigations of Temperament at Three to Seven Years: The Children's Behavior Questionnaire', *Child Development*, 72: 1394-408, https://doi.org/10.1111/1467-8624.00355

RTÉ [Raidió Teilifís Éireann] News. 2020. 'Timeline: Six Months of Covid-19', 1 July, https://www.rte.ie/news/newslens/2020/0701/1150824-coronavirus/

Schmitt, Sara A., et al. 2018. 'Using Block Play to Enhance Preschool Children's Mathematics and Executive Functioning: A Randomized Controlled Trial', *Early Childhood Research Quarterly*, 44: 181-91, https://doi.org/10.1016/j.ecresq.2018.04.006

Shah, Reshma, Erika Gustafson, and Marc Atkins. 2019. 'Parental Attitudes and Beliefs Surrounding Play among Predominantly Low-income Urban Families: A Qualitative Study', *Journal of Developmental and Behavioral Pediatrics*, 40: 606-12, https://doi.org/10.1097/DBP.0000000000000708

Shakel, Rita. 2015. 'The Child's Right to Play. Laying the Building Blocks for Optimal Health and Well-Being', in *Enhancing Children's Rights. Connecting Research, Policy and Practice* ed. by Anne B. Smith (London: Palgrave Macmillan), pp. 48-61

Thorell, Lisa B., et al. 2021. 'Parental Experiences of Homeschooling during the COVID-19 Pandemic: Differences between Seven European Countries and between Children with and without Mental Health Conditions', *European Child & Adolescent Psychiatry*, 1-13, https://doi.org/10.1007/s00787-020-01706-1

Thorn, William, and Stéphan Vincent-Lancrin. 2022. 'Education in the Time of COVID-19 in France, Ireland, the United Kingdom and the United States: The Nature and Impact of Remote Learning', *Primary and Secondary Education During Covid-19: Disruptions to Educational Opportunity During a Pandemic*, ed. by Fenando M. Reimers (Cham, Switzerland: Springer), pp. 383-420, https://doi.org/10.1007/978-3-030-81500-4_15

UNICEF. 1989. *Convention on the Rights of the Child*, https://www.unicef.org/child-rights-convention

Whitebread, David, et al. 2012. *The Importance of Play* (Brussels: Toy Industries of Europe)

Williams, James, et al. 2019. *Growing Up in Ireland: Design, Instrumentation and Procedures for Cohort '08 at Wave Three (5 Years)*, Technical Series, 2019–2 (Dublin: Department of Children and Youth Affairs), https://www.growingup.ie/pubs/20190404-Cohort-08-at-5years-design-instrumentation-and-procedures.pdf

Wilson, Jade. 2021. 'Ireland Has Higher Rates of Third Level Education than EU Average, Data Shows', *Irish Times*, 29 November, https://www.irishtimes.com/news/education/ireland-has-higher-rates-of-third-level-education-than-eu-average-data-shows-1.4741763

Xiang, Mi, Zhiruo Zhang, and Keisuke Kuwahara. 2020. 'Impact of COVID-19 Pandemic on Children and Adolescents' Lifestyle Behavior Larger than Expected', *Progress in Cardiovascular Diseases*, 63(4): 531-32, https://doi.org/10.1016/j.pcad.2020.04.013

13. Children's Emerging Play and Experience in the Covid-19 Era: Educational Endeavours and Changes in South Korea

Pool Ip Dong

Covid-19 and Early Childhood Education and Care in South Korea

The coronavirus (Covid-19) pandemic has produced dramatic changes in the lives of adults and children globally. As one of the countries affected by Covid-19, South Korea decided to lock down schools and keep people at home in February 2020. Interestingly, South Korea was one of the countries that rapidly controlled Covid-19 transmission and had less severe national social distancing policies than other countries (Dighe et al. 2020). Indeed, most daycare centres and kindergartens operated full-time classes in the early days of the Covid-19 outbreak.[1] As

---

1   Early childhood education and care in South Korea can be divided into two categories: daycare centres and kindergartens. Under the Ministry of Health and Welfare, daycare centres serve children up to five years old. Meanwhile, kindergartens serve three- to five-year-olds and are similar to preschools in the United States (Byun and Slavin 2020). Sometimes, the word 'preschool' can be used to help readers understand, but I will use the word 'kindergarten' in this chapter.

    https://doi.org/10.11647/OBP.0326.13

the pandemic worsened in South Korea, however, the Korean Ministry of Education (MoE) and the Ministry of Health and Welfare (MHW) announced substantial safety measures. Only a few daycare centres and kindergartens provided childcare services for working parents in urgent need of family care, called '(at school) emergency childcare services', while most centres and kindergartens stopped physical attendance in response to the Korean government's health policies. Considering Korea's high level of education fever (Lee 2005), the decision to implement a school lockdown in South Korea was not an easy one.

Unlike in other countries, schools in South Korea start a new semester on 2 March. The MoE delayed the beginning of the new school year five times and kindergartens and daycare centres opened for classes on 27 May 2020, which was three months later than the usual beginning of the school year. In the meantime, young children stayed at home with their parents, who were working remotely, while the MoE, daycare centres and kindergartens tried to provide young Korean children with diverse opportunities for learning and play through distance education.

This chapter will explain how young Korean children engaged in emerging play experiences, as well as efforts made by Korean parents, teachers and policymakers to offer several playful and educational opportunities for young children in early childhood education and care (ECEC) settings during the Covid-19 pandemic, especially in 2020 and 2021. Recently, studies have increasingly shown the effects on and changes to people's daily lives due to Covid-19 globally (e.g. Rogers 2022). This chapter will give an insight into diverse forms of educational resilience and the (un)expected educational changes brought about by the Covid-19 pandemic.

Educational Attempts for Young Children's Play during Covid-19

'A Package for Play': A Home-based Play Kit

A national-level, child-centred, play-based curriculum, called the Nuri Curriculum, is available for all children aged three to five years old in South Korea. The Nuri Curriculum is planned and provided free of charge to guarantee equivalent high-quality opportunities for all children (Dong 2022a). Early childhood teachers, recognizing the importance of play for childhood development and learning in children's lives, employed a range of opportunities and strategies for play at home when schools closed during the Covid-19 pandemic. One example is a home-based play kit called 'A Package for Play'. This package, prepared by metropolitan and provincial education offices across South Korea, consisted of toys and other materials and was sent to homes when children could not attend kindergartens (Figure 13.1). Some daycare centres and kindergartens independently prepared and sent their own 'Package for Play' to children. As a form of home support, early childhood teachers encouraged children to play with the kit and guided parents in using it with children at home (Dong 2022a).

Figure 13.1 'A Package for Play' (including face masks, coloured paper, Play-Doh, balloons, wooden puzzles, paper puzzles, and some snacks), 23 October 2020
https://www.kjilbo.co.kr/news/articleView.html?idxno=91070

When first using 'A Package for Play', most parents and children found it difficult to play with the contents at home. Many parents were embarrassed and confused about how to effectively explain and use the materials in a playful mode with their children. As a result, teachers then sent parents notices and shared diverse and creative methods, guidelines, and tips for enjoyable and productive play with young children.

'A Package for Play' was normally sent to children once a week but this schedule occasionally varied, depending on each school's situation. Many ECEC teachers considered the kit an effective and economical distance education strategy during the pandemic because it promoted parents' participation and improved their understanding of their children and ECEC (Park, Kim, and Shin 2021). Moreover, some daycare centres and kindergartens lent educational materials and toys to parents to promote children's play at home.

Many ECEC teachers felt that 'A Package for Play' effectively offered children hands-on, play-based activities. They also viewed it as a beneficial way for children and parents to interact through play (Park, Kim, and Shin 2021). Furthermore, some teachers creatively stimulated play participation within families by sharing home-play photos or holding competitions for pictures and videos of play on their class website. This helped children, parents and teachers to interact with each other during the pandemic. Some kindergartens and daycare centres in Korea still actively employ 'A Package for Play' to improve home-school partnerships. Furthermore, many parents welcomed the package because it gives them interesting ideas and information for promoting children's play at home.

Education Portals: Online Spaces for Sharing Play Information

Along with the above initiatives, the MoE, MHW and the Korea Institute of Child Care and Education provided families with information about various modes of play through websites related to Korean ECEC, such as i-Nuri (http://i-nuri.go.kr) and Play On (https://more.goe.go.kr/kids-love). These websites offer home-based play videos and pictures with guidelines for playing with toys, bodies and materials (such as stones, water, paint, clay and paper). For instance, the i-Nuri web portal was made by the MoE to provide informative educational content for South Korean parents and teachers. This content consists of language play, physical play, dramatic play, art play, science play, safety guidelines and so on. Due to the lack of physical activities and social interaction for children during Covid-19 (Hwang and Jeong 2022), many videos and photos of play were uploaded and shared to develop children's gross motor, fine motor, and social-emotional skills by promoting prosocial behaviour and physical activity at home.

Figure 13.2 A screen capture from the i-Nuri portal (http://i-nuri.go.kr), 2022
Image © Korea Institute of Child Care and Education, 2023, all rights reserved

Another example of online support can be found in an education platform called Play On. This platform was designed by the Office of Education in Gyeonggi Province to promote a child- and play-centred ECEC curriculum and to prevent losses in children's learning during the pandemic. The play content on the platform was developed by early childhood teachers and educators, making it different from other education platforms. The contents on the website were made for children, teachers and parents living in Gyeonggi Province, and provided them with various play videos and guidebooks, as well as useful educational information.

The video content on the website consisted of 148 videos (about two to three minutes long each) covering twenty-nine themes. These videos explained how to play with coloured paper, how to engage in sensory play with flour, how to play with a plastic bottle, and how to explore newspapers. Nam and Choi (2022) analyzed the video content on the Play On platform, arguing that most videos promoted open-ended play and encouraged young children to actively participate in it through cheerful music, narration and subtitles for young children.

Distance Education with Media: Real-time Interactive Learning and Content-based Learning

Due to the prolonged nature of Covid-19, various methods of distance education were explored and conducted in Korean ECEC settings. Two types of distance education in ECEC were considered: real-time interactive learning (via live-streaming platforms) and content-based learning (via broadcasts or videos) (Korean Educational Development Institute 2020). Interactive online classes for young children had never been trialled in South Korea before the pandemic. At the peak of Covid-19 transmission, daycare centres and kindergartens increasingly started to employ interactive online classes using digital technology. At first, many teachers encountered chaos because they had little experience in or infrastructure for delivering online classes. Nevertheless, the MoE actively supported ECEC teachers who were interested in online classes by providing training, and some schools independently prepared online classes for young children.

According to Cho (2021), many children and teachers met and played together via webinar software platforms (such as Zoom) to sustain and strengthen their relationships. After greetings, they shared play experiences for approximately fifteen to twenty minutes. For instance, a scavenger hunt game was played at home with video cameras displaying children as they searched for and found items (Dong 2022a). Such activities enabled adults and children to interact in a worthwhile manner. However, these play meetings were hard to conduct frequently because parents needed to set up digital devices for them. Thus, the distance education approach was mostly employed in 2020 and 2021.

Recently, despite all daycare centres and kindergartens resuming in-person classes, a few kindergartens still held annual events (e.g. family day) via Zoom because of Covid-19 measures. When many children and parents could not come together, the schools with experience of online distance education provided online spaces for students and their families to participate by providing them with playful activities (Dong 2022a). The Covid-19 pandemic led ECEC teachers to start to use webinar software platforms, and now the method is broadly applied to meet teachers' various educational aims and needs in South Korea.

Interestingly, the pandemic sometimes forced early childhood teachers to produce their own play videos to demonstrate how children and adults could play with certain materials. Teachers familiar with computers, digital cameras and smartphones made play videos in their classrooms or at home using video editing software programmes or applications, such as Windows Movie Maker and KineMaster. ECEC teachers themselves played in the videos and introduced certain games and music. Some teachers uploaded their play videos on to YouTube and shared them with children and parents in their class. The children then enjoyed these play videos, participated in the suggested activities, and thus played in different ways (Dong 2022a). For instance, when ECEC teachers introduced a play routine with paper cups, young children and parents followed along. In the process, teachers also encouraged young children to play differently with paper cups and to share their play methods with other children in the class. Parents then shared their children's paper cup play activities through photos posted on their class websites (Figure 13.3). Teachers supported children and their parents by replying to their play activity photos and providing educational suggestions (Dong 2022a).

Figure 13.3 Photos on a class website showing children's play with paper cups at home, 12 November 2020

Moreover, as an alternative way to support children's play and learning in the context of Covid-19, some early childhood teachers used broadcasting programmes and online play videos (Cho 2021; Nam and Choi 2022). For example, a special programme called 'My Home Kindergarten' on the Korea Educational Broadcasting System (EBS), a Korean public educational broadcasting company, was made specifically for young children who could not attend kindergartens and daycare centres, thus supporting their play and care at home in 2020. This programme supported many children who did not have digital devices or did not participate in online classes. Initially, the programme was intended to be broadcast for seven weeks (from 13 April to 28 May 2020). However, it was so popular among children and parents that its broadcasting run was extended. The thirty-minute programme was broadcast every morning from Monday to Thursday until December 2022. Based on the child- and play-centred curriculum, this programme emphasized various physical activities, music, and health and safety information for young children.

Educational Changes from Covid-19 in South Korea

The Covid-19 pandemic has brought many challenges and changes into the lives of young children, their parents and teachers. Above all, the unexpected situation gave rise to different perspectives among Korean teachers and parents on teaching methods and digital media-based learning in ECEC settings. Before the pandemic, the use of digital devices to interact was rare and limited (Kim et al. 2020). However, Covid-19 prevented people from connecting physically and led Korean teachers and parents to find methods to encourage children's play and social interactions through digital media.

This situation resulted in a dramatic change in people's perspectives regarding young children's use of digital media. Before Covid-19, many Korean parents and teachers expressed strong negative attitudes toward children's play with digital media (Erdogan et al. 2019; Dong 2018). However, as they experienced the reality of digital media play, they became more accepting of it and found effective ways for children to harness digital media. In this sense, more and more research was focused on young Korean children's (in)formal learning via YouTube videos and other forms of digital media at home during Covid-19 (Dong and Henward 2021). Furthermore, many Korean ECEC scholars and teachers started to critically analyse the conservative discourses on digital media in South Korean cultural contexts (Dong 2022b), and actively explored digital media's opening up of new possibilities and capabilities for teachers, or what has been termed 'digital technology knowledge and skills' (Cho 2021).

In addition, owing to Covid-19, Korean teachers began to reconsider their teaching methods, teaching materials and their beliefs about children's play, all of which had previously been taken for granted in ECEC settings. By trying new strategies to deal with pandemic-related difficulties (such as the 'Package for Play' initiatives and distance learning via Zoom and play videos), many teachers were forced to rethink their educational strategies and resilience. For ECEC teachers, the Covid-19 pandemic created chaos and confusion, but it also provided a meaningful opportunity to rethink educational flexibility, develop new teaching competencies, and overcome challenges related to children's play in ECEC.

Furthermore, the Covid-19 pandemic enabled young Korean children and parents to understand the importance of their relationships with each other. Recent studies focusing on young Korean children's views on Covid-19 and play showed that many young Korean children realized the value of their friends (Jo and Park 2021; Yang 2022; Hwang and Jeong 2022). As daycare centres and kindergartens were locked down and most children stayed at home throughout Covid-19 in 2020 and 2021, they could not play and interact with their friends freely. Some measures from the MoE and MHW to prevent coronavirus transmission in classrooms, such as the mandatory wearing of face masks and the imposition of physical distancing measures, forced many children to play alone or to engage in parallel play at a distance under their teacher's surveillance to prevent the spread of the virus (Jo and Park 2021). This situation made young children recognize the value of their playful connections with others, especially regarding their physical, emotional and social interactions with friends through play. For young children, play involves more than playful activities and learning tools. Play is a central part of children's lives and a way of understanding and engaging with one's world. In this sense, the ongoing presence of friends has been crucial for young children to make sense of their everyday play throughout the pandemic.

Moreover, Covid-19 gave some Korean parents an unexpected chance to channel their anxiety and pressure into an improved understanding of their children through play at home. As mentioned earlier, parents had a hard time caring for their children while working from home. Korean parents were required to support their child's online learning by playing with the 'Package for Play' or preparing for online classes. In the process, many parents had more time than before the pandemic to interact with their children. They were also able to experience (directly or indirectly) ECEC teachers' online classes and consult the information regarding play available via online platforms (Kim, Cho, and Oh 2021). These opportunities helped parents to better understand their children and ECEC (Jo and Park 2021).

However, the Covid-19 pandemic in South Korea has not created exclusively positive experiences or (unexpected) benefits in ECEC. Some challenges and worries also arose among parents and teachers regarding children's development, mental health, and families' socio-economic status (Byun and Slavin 2020; Yang 2022). Some teachers revealed that many children had anxiety or fear of being infected with Covid-19 (Yang 2022). Moreover, as distance education became more common, most schools had access to digital devices and did not face problems; however, some children from low-income families or with working parents could not access distance education via digital media. Thus, the MoE, schools and local governments sought to lend digital devices to those children who needed them for distance learning and employed educational television programmes such as 'My Home Kindergarten' by EBS to ensure educational equity.

In addition, the Korean government has enforced a mandatory mask-wearing rule. Although the outdoor mask mandate has been lifted and individual choice on wearing face masks outdoors is now stressed, the indoor mask-wearing mandate is still strictly imposed (Ministry of Health and Welfare 2022). Under the strict face mask mandate, Korean children and teachers must wear face masks all day at school, except when eating snacks and lunch. Accordingly, an increasing number of researchers have conducted studies on Korean children's language, physical or cognitive development and their perceptions of mask-wearing (Kwon, Jang, and Wang 2022).

At the time of writing, the Covid-19 pandemic has not ended in South Korea. However, all Korean kindergartens and daycare centres have resumed in-person care and education. As part of the new normal created by the Covid-19 pandemic, many ECEC teachers have emphasized the impact of education on children's health and safety. Also, compared to before Covid-19, more children engage in hospital roleplay in ECEC settings (Jo and Park 2021), which might reveal some changed practices among children as a result Covid-19.

Endless Resilience, Attempts and Collaborations for Children's Play in the Covid-19 era

The pandemic changed children's play and everyday practices in Korean ECEC settings. Teachers are still trying to provide young children with sufficient time and opportunities for play despite various constraints. Furthermore, many schools urge children's families to play together to stay connected. The pandemic made it necessary for Korean ECEC teachers and organizations to create ways for children to interact and play with their families to promote children's learning and development. As a result, Korean teachers and families have co-constructed methods for fostering children's education and play.

Given the challenges of the pandemic, Korean scholars have cited a need for an ecological transformation of education in South Korea (Back, Lee, and Park 2020; Dong 2022a). Reacting to new questions and needs, Korean ECEC actors, including teachers, parents, researchers and policymakers, are eagerly exploring and studying a new perspective for accepting and understanding children's emerging play culture and educational ecology. Throughout the pandemic, the value of children's play will not change and may even be enhanced, even if the forms of play are different (Dong 2022a). Thus, new patterns of home-school-community relationships, children's play around analogue and digital media, and peer cultures should be considered through a novel ecological lens to better understand children's emerging play in these fast-changing times. By exploring Korean educational responses to the Covid-19 pandemic, I anticipate that this chapter has given an insightful perspective into diverse education resilience, educational possibilities and implications, and an opportunity to rethink teaching and learning in ECEC settings in the Covid-19 era.

Works Cited

Back, Byoungbu, Soo-kwang Lee, and Bok-seon Park. 2020. *COVID-19 and Education: Implications for the Transformation of the Educational System*. (Suwon: Gyeonggi Institute of Education)

Byun, Sooyeon, and Robert E. Slavin. 2020. 'Educational Responses to the COVID-19 Outbreak in South Korea', *Best Evidence in Chinese Education*, 5: 665-80, http://dx.doi.org/10.2139/ssrn.3652607

Cho, Woon Ju. 2021. 'The Use of Digital Technology and Distance Education in Early Childhood Education', *Korea Institute of Child Care and Education*, 69: 7-14, https://repo.kicce.re.kr/handle/2019.oak/5179

Chung, Jae-chun. 2020. 'Jeollanam-do Office of Education Overcomes the Crisis of Education Gap through Distance Education', *Gwangju Jeonnam Daily*, 23 October, https://www.kjilbo.co.kr/news/articleView.html?idxno=91070

Dighe, Ami, et al. 2020. 'Response to COVID-19 in South Korea and Implications for Lifting Stringent Interventions', *BMC Medicine*, 18, https://doi.org/10.1186/s12916-020-01791-8

Dong, Pool Ip. 2018. 'Exploring Korean Parents' Meanings of Digital Play for Young Children', *Global Studies of Childhood*, 8: 238-51, https://doi.org/10.1177/2043610618798931

——. 2022a. 'Young Korean Children's Emerging Play Experiences and Educational Attempts during the COVID-19 Pandemic', *International Journal of Play*, 11: 77-80, https://doi.org/10.1080/21594937.2022.2042934

——. 2022b. 'Do Media Really Harm Young Children? Examining Young Children and Media Discourses in Korean Cultural Contexts', *Korean Journal of Early Childhood Education*, 42.5: 29-51, http://dx.doi.org/10.18023/kjece.2022.42.5.002

Dong, Pool Ip, and Henward, Allison S. 2021. 'Examining Korean Preschoolers' Learning with YouTube Videos: A Multimodal and Multiliteracy Approach', *International Journal of Early Childhood Education*, 27: 93-114, http://dx.doi.org/10.18023/ijece.2021.27.1.005

Erdogan, Nesrin I., et al. 2019. 'Do Parents Prefer Digital Play? Examination of Parental Preferences and Beliefs in Four Nations', *Early Childhood Education Journal*, 47: 131-42, https://doi.org/10.1007/s10643-018-0901-2

Hwang, Ji Young, and Mi Rae Jeong. 2022. 'Image Analysis of Children's Play: For 5-year-old Children Who Have Experienced the COVID-19 Pandemic', *Journal of Learner-Centered Curriculum and Instruction*, 22: 385-400, https://doi.org/10.22251/jlcci.2022.22.15.385

Jo, So Dam, and Su Kyung Park. 2021. 'Exploring Children's Awareness of the COVID-19 Situation through Picture Representation Activities', *Journal of Eco Early Childhood Education & Care*, 20.4: 23-46, http://doi.org/10.30761/ecoece.2021.20.4.23

Korean Educational Development Institute. 2020. 'Distance Learning in Korea in Response to COVID-19', *Covid-19 Special Issue*, 1, https://www.kedi.re.kr/eng/kedi/cmmn/file/fileDown.do?menuNo=200017&atchFileId=FILE_000000000001164&fileSn=2&bbsId=B0000008

Kim, Eun-mi, Boo-kyung Cho, and Chai-sun Oh. 2021. 'Kindergarten Teachers' Experiences of Distance Learning: The Aspects of "Connections" and Educational Meanings of the "Connections"', *Korean Journal of Early Childhood Education Research*, 23: 134-70, http://doi.org/10.15409/riece.2021.23.2.6

Kim, Min-jeong, et al. 2020. 'Exploring Kindergarten Teachers' Perceptions of Distance Education for Young Children', *Korean Journal of Early Childhood Education*, 22: 201–29, https://doi.org/10.15409/riece.2020.22.3.10

Kwon, Miji, Jang, Eun-mi, and Yang, Wonyoung, 'Mask-wearing perception of preschool children in Korea during the COVID-19 pandemic: A cross-sectional study', *International Journal of Environmental Research and Public Health*, 19, 18 (2022), 11443, https://doi.org/10.3390/ijerph191811443

Lee, Chong Jae. 2005. 'Korean Education Fever and Private Tutoring', *KEDI Journal of Educational Policy,* 2: 99-107, https://www.kedi.re.kr/eng/kedi/cmmn/file/fileDown.do?menuNo=200067&atchFileId=FILE_000000000003358&fileSn=1&bbsId=

Ministry of Health & Welfare. 2022. 'Outdoor Mask Mandate Adjusted Starting May 2', *News & Welfare Services*, 4 May, https://www.mohw.go.kr/eng/nw/nw0101vw.jsp?PAR_MENU_ID=1007&MENU_ID=100701&page=1&CONT_SEQ=371406

Nam, Ki-won, and Jung-hee Choi. 2022. 'A Study on the Content Analysis of Remote Classes according to COVID-19: Focusing on Kindergarten [Play On]', *Journal of the Convergence on Culture Technology*, 8: 69-75, http://dx.doi.org/10.17703/JCCT.2022.8.2.69

Park, Yeong-suk, Nak-heung Kim, and Mi-young Shin. 2021. 'A Study on the Current State According to Class by Age of Distance Education in Kindergartens due to COVID-19', *Early Childhood Education Research & Review*, 25: 225-49, https://doi.org/10.32349/ECERR.2021.2.25.1.225

Rogers, Sue. 2022. 'Play in the Time of Pandemic: Children's Agency and Lost Learning', *Education 3-13*, 50: 494-505, https://doi.org/10.1080/03004279.2022.2052235

Yang, Suyoung. 2022. 'Exploring Young Children's Perception of the COVID-19 Situation', *Journal of Learner-Centered Curriculum and Instruction*, 22: 563-76, https://doi.org/10.22251/jlcci.2022.22.2.563

14. The Observatory of Children's Play Experiences during Covid-19:
A Photo Essay[1]

John Potter and Michelle Cannon

Introduction

The Play Observatory was a study of children's play experiences during the pandemic, conducted almost wholly online over a seventeen-month period between October 2020 and March 2022. It was funded in the UK by the Economic and Social Research Council (ESRC) as part of the UK Research Institute (UKRI) Rapid Response to COVID-19, and was a collaboration between researchers at the IOE, University College London's Faculty of Education and Society, the School of Education at the University of Sheffield, and the University College London Centre for Advanced Spatial Analysis (UCL CASA). A key aim of the project was to collect, analyze and preserve for future generations material from children and adults in the form of text, images, moving images and more which represented their play experiences during such a challenging and difficult time, but which also demonstrated the function of play in their lives in terms of well-being and resourcefulness.

The online survey and collection tool, through which most of the contributions to the project were uploaded, was carefully designed to be

---

1   With thanks and acknowledgements to the other members of the Play Observatory team: Catherine Bannister, Julia Bishop, Kate Cowan, Yinka Olusoga and Valerio Signorelli. We would like to thank all contributors to the Play Observatory for sending us their examples of play during Covid-19.

a child- and carer-friendly submission area by the University of Sheffield team members, Yinka Olusoga, Julia Bishop and Catherine Bannister, with Valerio Signorelli from UCL CASA. This was linked from the main project website and was a welcoming and informative space. Contributors encountered detailed information about the project's ethical stance, the importance of informed consent and, where requested, the preservation of anonymity. It also contained clear guidance through the submission process and prompts for memories of play in pandemic times.

For this chapter, we have selected examples of twelve image submissions to the Play Observatory to take the form of a 'photo essay'. The selection process involves us in processes which are akin to academic thematic analysis but arguably closer to personal curation, allowing space for interpretation and representing an invitation for readers to do work on the images, to see connections and traces through them, rather than fixing precise meanings. The act of curating these has, of course, been conducted simultaneously with the more systematic and research-bound elements in the study whilst at the same time admitting a space for playful interpretation, in the spirit of provisionality and 'possibility thinking' which are themselves characteristics of 'play'.

Readers may have encountered some of what follows already in an online exhibition which we have taken part in with the Young V&A (Young V&A, Episod Studio, and Play Observatory 2022). However, we have resisted the categories employed in that larger selection, preferring instead to leave this open to the reader. We have also limited our captions to initial framing comments, these being the signposts we were initially guided by when we first saw the submissions. The majority of the images we have chosen come from UK sources but three of the twelve are from outside the UK. This is slightly higher than the overall proportion of non-UK vs UK submissions to the observatory as a whole, which is closer to fifteen percent.

We hope that readers will enjoy 'reading' these images in the same way we first did, with curiosity and without too much pre-judgement, but inevitably informed by their own experience of the pandemic, its lockdowns and restrictions. We offer these images to this volume as important visual reminders of our collective pandemic experience and to express our gratitude to the contributors for the privilege of bearing witness to intimate and familial play experiences at such a sensitive time. By bringing their own memories and thoughts to the 'pact of interpretation' (Bhabha 1994), our contributors' mediated voices are heard and valued in this essay, enabling rich, multiple and enduring readings of play in the pandemic.

A Note on Photo Essays

Before getting to the images, and because this will necessarily be different in nature to most of the other chapters, it is perhaps worth considering the purposes of a photo essay and maybe even to begin by asking what a photo essay is, or can be, in this context. Marín and Roldán (2010: 10-11), for example, distinguish between two different kinds of 'photo series' when defining a photo essay for educational research purposes. They argue that the first of these represents an organization of images into a congruent sequence, representing multiple, transforming versions of the *same* subjects or motifs. They present the second archetype as a set of congruent, sampled images 'in which the same [...] *phenomenon* is presented through a number of single cases'. Our version of the photo essay in this chapter is closer to the first idea of a 'series' but adds some of the features of photo essays used for a specific, ideological intervention around, for example, race, gender or critical pedagogy (Grimwood, Arthurs and Vogel 2015; Sensoy 2011). Our stance is one of underlining the importance of play for children and young people and its *potential* benefits in times of crisis, whilst at the same time refusing a simplistic equation of play and positive experience.

One of our stated aims in the project has been to find ways to represent the experience of lockdown for children which refuses some of the simple binaries, such as 'screens are bad, play offscreen is good', or the prevailing discourse of 'learning loss' as the only consequence that mattered for children in lockdown during the pandemic. Thus, this is not to pretend that the photographs have set out without any organizing principle. We have in fact sought to represent our belief that play, of all kinds, is central to children's lives and that we need to think how best to capture the experience of children and young people at this moment in history and how to archive it for future generations to explore.

Much of the literature of the photo essay assumes a sole author who takes the images and arranges them in order to carry out these functions. Our own role is different because we are not presenting material which we have ourselves created and uploaded (although for full disclosure, we should acknowledge that two of the images were submitted by team members).

Rather than acting as photo essay authors, and presenting our own images, we are curators of other people's contributions, of other people's images. As researchers of media, we may also have in mind other photo essays in which this is employed as a strategy, such as that which opens Lev Manovich's *Language of New Media* (2001), in which a series of black and white images set out a view of analogue versus digital media. These do more than simply establish a context. They invite interpretation from those who are already perhaps thinking about the worldview of Manovich; they understand that the work will exist somewhere between photography, technology, platform studies and cultural studies. Readers of this book will range from those interested in play theory, health and well-being, archival and folklore studies. All of these interests will sit within the context of a global pandemic and what it has meant for play, and these will also produce particular kinds of interpretations and generate relevant questions which could be asked of the images.

To return to Marín and Roldán (2010), we have an intention to represent the project in some way, to curate a small, congruent photo series which demonstrates something of the life of the project but also of what John Law (2004) calls the 'mess' of human experience. We see here examples of the 'mess' and the variety of organization of people, spaces and things which came into the Play Observatory. In being honest about our curatorial activity, we must declare that these examples are partial, restricted and the tip of a metaphorical iceberg of emotion and affect in children's play, and adult responses to it, during the pandemic. There is much more to be said about this, and the team is preparing dissemination in many different forms to accompany what has already been exhibited, said and written about this project online and in print (Cowan et al. 2021).

In what follows we have included some of the text which accompanied the deposit of the image, mostly from the adult contributor, except where indicated, along with a small amount of further contextual detail on the games and on-screen environments shown in the images, where applicable.

We would like to note, however, that the images refuse absolute fixity of interpretation. They are moments in time, in which the subjects of the image are often lost in the experiential flow of play. They are, of course, only a subset of some of the forms of play we have seen in the submissions which are themselves a subset of the wider human experience of the pandemic. We are under no illusion that these contributions represent people who answered the call and who had the time, ability and resources to upload these images. We are very grateful that they did so, mostly in the UK but also in Europe and, in one case, far beyond. We know that there were others we were not able to reach during the relatively short time we were collecting instances of pandemic play. Our hope is that these images will reach out beyond the Play Observatory and inspire others to seek out images and to think about submitting them when next we open the doors of the observatory. We certainly hope to be able to do that again, one day, and to extend our reach to communities whose voices are often absent in research.

For now, we invite you, the reader, to look through the images and seek connections to your own experiences, or those of friends and family. How would *you* categorize them and analyze them? What can you say about these human experiences and the meanings that are being made within the images which have been submitted?

Figure 14.1 'Child and chalked rainbow', Sheffield, UK, 2020-21
Play Observatory PL38A1/S001/p1, https://doi.org/10.15131/shef.data.21198142
CC BY-NC-ND 4.0

Observed in Meersbrook Park—big murals on the floor of the car park by the hall. Colourful pictures, messages of positivity and specially constructed trails. (Parent)

Additional note: Rainbows in a variety of media appeared during the pandemic in many countries, including the UK, and were used as both private and public displays of hope. The origin is unclear, but they had wide appeal and as early as April 2020 an article on the BBC Global website reported their deep connection to wider cultures as symbols of 'thank you, hope and solidarity' (Vince 2020). They appeared in many sizes and different locations. Here, the child is right at the centre of a large rainbow made in a car park.

Figure 14.2 'Child doing Cosmic Yoga', Kusterdingen, Germany, 2020
Play Observatory PL65A1/S007/p1, https://doi.org/10.15131/shef.data.21198142
CC BY-NC-ND 4.0

Cosmic kids yoga[.] My 4-year-old got really into doing cosmic kids yoga on YouTube. At the peak of his interest he was doing it everyday! Sometimes I did it with him, sometimes he did it alone. Occasionally he did it along with a friend online—we set up a zoom meeting, one child shared his screen, and they did a yoga session together.' (Parent)

Additional note: With the loss of amenity and access to outdoor spaces in the strictest of lockdowns, exercise at home became a feature of daily life in many locations. In this image there is a playful interaction between a child and a YouTube yoga channel for children (Cosmic Kids Yoga n.d.) with the child attempting to mirror the pose on-screen. UNICEF reported positively on the uses of screens which were emerging during lockdown, including for playful exercise (Winther 2020).

Figure 14.3 'Masked and socially distanced small toys', Singapore, 2020-21Play Observatory PL175A1/S001/p2, https://doi.org/10.15131/shef.data.21198142
CC BY-NC-ND 4.0

My daughter likes to play pretend with her collection of TY soft toys. During the pandemic, [this] pretend play takes on medical/pandemic related themes. For example, the soft toys will be wearing [expired] masks we have at home and attending school—much like her own experience of having to wear masks at school. She has mentioned that she dislikes doing so and including this in her pretend play could be a way to make sense of the situation. (Parent)

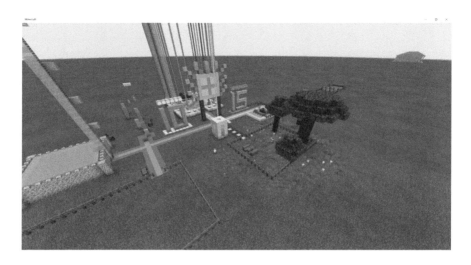

Figure 14.4 'Joint birthday party in Minecraft', Sheffield, UK, May 2021
Play Observatory PL170A1/S007/p2, https://doi.org/10.15131/shef.
data.21198142

Play in *Minecraft* '[...] organised by my eldest son [...] to mark his 15th birthday in 2021 and his younger brother's 10th birthday. He said: 'On May 11th we held a birthday festival-type celebration for me and [my brother] near Breadburg (Bread Empire capital). First we had a disco and ate cake and cookies. Then we played some minigames (parkour, trampoline, and one [a friend] designed where you have to complete an obstacle course and die at the end) [...]' (Parent and child)

Additional note: Microsoft, which owns *Minecraft*, provided its educational worlds for free use during the pandemic to support parents and children. *Minecraft* has previously been written about by researchers as supportive of a broad range of social and cultural developments as well as of media literacy education (see, for example, Dezuanni 2018).

Figure 14.5 'Homemade den showing exterior and interior with child', Nicosia, Cyprus, April 2020
Play Observatory PL72A1/S003/p1, https://doi.org/10.15131/shef.data.21198142
CC BY-NC-ND 4.0

We built this tent house on the balcony once and he asked to do it again a lot of times [...] My son seemed to have strong intentions and determination on building it and choosing and putting stuff in it. It was nice and it engaged us for quite some time, though it made me feel a bit sad. I felt like he needed 'some other place' to be when we couldn't go anywhere. (Parent)

Additional note: The two images were uploaded to the Play Observatory as a single submission to show the exterior and interior of the den. Children's uses of dens and safe spaces in which to play and build their own worlds, both indoors and outdoors, has been written about and researched extensively, including by children themselves (see, for example, Burke 2007; Sobel 2001). With so much strangeness and uncertainty during lockdown, these forms of den building during the pandemic were, arguably, attempts by children to take control of their immediate environment and create a safe place in which to be.

Figure 14.6 'Child drawing with chalk outside the house', Leeds, UK, April 2020
Play Observatory PL34C1/S001/p1, https://doi.org/10.15131/shef.data.21198142
CC BY-NC-ND 4.0

I did chalk drawings on the drive in front of my house. I was playing by myself, and my mum was sitting on a chair by the front door, doing her work on her iPad. I didn't really like people and because of COVID I didn't want people to come near the house and act like COVID doesn't exist. So, I did chalk drawings of things like a ghost, a bottle of poison, a skull and crossbones and I wrote Keep Out. Later my sister came out and we drew a creeper from Minecraft as well. I called this pandemic panic drawing. (Child)

Figure 14.7 'Children watching cardboard cinema screen outside', Sheffield, UK, March 2021
Play Observatory PL79A1/S001/p1, https://doi.org/10.15131/shef.data.21198142
CC BY-NC-ND 4.0

'Outdoor cinema'. My nieces are aged 3 and 4 1/2 and like most children today they love screen time. On a sunny day (and when their mum was trying to clean the house) she told them to play outside instead of on their iPads in the house. Before they could throw a tantrum, my sister helped make some cardboard boxes into a tv screen. It was the girls' idea to make chairs to sit and watch the frozen 'frozen' on the screen.' (Aunt)

Figure 14.8 '*HomeCool Kids* magazine cover' Birmingham, UK, May 2020
Play Observatory PL158A1/S001/p8

Setting up HomeCool Kids gave the children an opportunity to interact with their friends and the magazine has actually been the highlight of our other pandemic experiences. For us the Pandemic has actually been enjoyable as we have spent more time together. However, we have also missed out on seeing our extended family back in India. Our summer holidays have always been spent in India with family and that the children definitely miss—not being able to visit their grandparents but also the play and socialising aspect of the community. In India, X1 and X2 would spend most of their time outdoors playing with their cousins and other children from the neighbourhood. That is something that they definitely miss. (Parent)

Figure 14.9 'Intergenerational LEGO play and sorting', Nottingham, UK, 2020-21
Play Observatory PL78C1/S005/p2, https://doi.org/10.15131/shef.data.21198142
CC BY-NC-ND 4.0

Not exactly playing—but we took the time to sort out all of my
Lego and rebuild everything!

Took over the front room! Mum and dad helped.

It was fun to start with, then got boring, then was go[o]d once
we'd rebuilt everything! (Child)

Additional note: A recurring theme for us in the Play Observatory
has been the changing nature of play within families, particularly in
situations where siblings separated in age by more than a few years were
forced to play with each other, when they did not normally. The same
situation occurred where adults who had one child joined in more with
activities which might previously have been undertaken with friends in
the peer group. The LEGO construction activity shown in Figure 14.9
clearly levelled the playing field between parents and child and was
quite complex, with lots of sorting, shared endeavour and concentration
in evidence. The accompanying comment, in the child's own words, is
particularly interesting for what it says about collaborations and shared
purpose in play.

Figure 14.10 'Children playing in a stream with their dog', North Anston, UK,
March-June 2020
Play Observatory PL80A1/S002/p1, https://doi.org/10.15131/shef.data.21198142
CC BY-NC-ND 4.0

We live near a common access space called the Anston Stones, which comprises open grassland, woods and a stream that runs the length of [a] low valley this long series of fields and woods follow. Mostly it would be me taking the children out with the dog [...] The walks grew in length as we got to know more routes in the Stones and as the weather got warmer and we learned to take things like wellies to paddle in the stream. E was 2 at this time, so the off-roader buggy meant we could carry equipment and snacks underneath the seat and extend the range of activities we did beyond just walking. We also played 'pooh sticks' at the two bridges across the stream and threw sticks in for the dog to get. [It was] relaxing and fun, especially for the older child, for whom it was a break from the schoolwork. I think we also felt joy at the freedom of being outside our house and garden, as there were no other places the children could go in that time period. (Parent)

Figure 14.11 'Child pointing at spider in a plastic tank', Sheffield, UK, 2020-21
Play Observatory PL172C1/S001/p2, https://doi.org/10.15131/shef.
data.21198142
CC BY-NC-ND 4.0

I used to go for walks in lockdown[.] I used to do my homeschool[.]
My Grampa and gramma did storytime on zoom[.] We went on
nature walks and did tree rubbings[.] We set up a spider tank and
caught a spider from the garden[.]

[On lockdown] I felt like [it] could have been easier but also
could have been harder. I felt like I were alone, lonely[.] I did like
some bits, like the fun bits, but I wanted to see my friends and
play. I feel like this [is] what must [most?] people would say as
well (Child)

Figure 14.12 'Children in a tyre', Ipswich, UK, June 2020
Play Observatory PL48A1/S009/p1, https://doi.org/10.15131/shef.data.21198142
CC BY-NC-ND 4.0

Playing with a tractor tyre, jumping, hiding[.] Sisters and brother N, i and E on a daily walk [...] early evening around our local rugby field. The players had left out tractor tyres to train with and the children enjoyed climbing on equipment on them, jumping across the gap and hiding inside. [Their mood was] relaxed, happy, inventive. (Parent)

Additional note: This image typifies the results of exploratory walks close to home and the use of found materials in the environment in which to play, which chimes both with den building and thinking concerning outdoor play more generally (Whitebread et al. 2017). Its selection for inclusion by the parent also makes a statement about the relationships between the siblings, close in age and encircled within their own play space.

Final Note

This photo essay is a small, curated selection of twelve items from hundreds of images submitted to the Play Observatory. There has been some attempt, as you will probably have noticed, to be representative of some of the many different forms of play which have come into the survey. We have also tried to convey different emotions in the still images collected, as well as to show play by individual children, in family groups, and with and without adults. The hope is that seeing the images and reading them alongside the intertextual clues in the segments of chosen captions will pique interest and will drive readers to explore the project website more closely (https://play-observatory. com/), with its blogposts from the team, from children and from guests who have been undertaking similar work, in much the same way as you can when browsing this edited collection. It will also, perhaps, give you the opportunity to reflect on your own experiences of pandemic play and to share them with others.

Much of the public discourse has been focused on 'learning loss' as the key experience of the pandemic for children. Whilst the impact on schooling has been significant, the Play Observatory has attempted to shine a light instead on the impact on *play* as a key aspect of human behaviour during the pandemic, essential to our understanding of the world, of each other and how we can live together in times of crisis.

Works Cited

Bhabha, Homi K. 1994. *The Location of Culture* (London: Routledge)

Burke, Catherine. 2007. 'Play in Focus: Children Researching their Own Spaces and Places for Play', *Children, Youth and Environments*, 15: 27-53, https:// www.jstor.org/stable/10.7721/chilyoutenvi.15.1.0027

Cosmic Kids Yoga. n.d. *Yoga, Mindfulness, Relaxation...For Kids!* https://www. youtube.com/c/CosmicKidsYoga

Cowan, Kate, et al. 2021. 'Children's Digital Play during the COVID-19 Pandemic: Insights from the Play Observatory', *Journal of e-Learning and Knowledge Society*, 17.3: 8-17, https://doi.org/10.20368/1971-8829/1135590

Dezuanni, Michael. 2018. 'Minecraft and Children's Digital Making: Implications for Media Literacy Education', *Learning, Media and Technology*, 43: 236-49, https://doi.org/10.1080/17439884.2018.1472607

Grimwood, Bryan S. R., Whitney Arthurs, and Tristin Vogel. 2015. 'Photo Essays for Experiential Learning: Toward a Critical Pedagogy of Place in Tourism Education', *Journal of Teaching in Travel & Tourism*, 15: 362-81, https://doi.org/10.1080/15313220.2015.1073574

Law, John. 2004. *After Method: Mess in Social Science Research* (London: Routledge)

Manovich, Lev. 2001. *The Language of New Media* (Cambridge, MA: MIT Press)

Manovich, Lev. 2017. *Instagram and Contemporary Image*, http://manovich.net/index.php/projects/instagram-and-contemporary-image

Marín, Ricardo, and Joaquin Roldán. 2010. 'Photo Essays and Photographs in Visual Arts-based Educational Research', *International Journal of Education through Art*, 6: 7-23, https://doi.org/10.1386/eta.6.1.7_1

Sensoy, Özlem. 2011. 'Oppression: Seventh Graders' Photo Essays on Racism, Classism, and Sexism', *International Journal of Qualitative Studies in Education*, 24: 323-42, https://doi.org/10.1080/09518398.2011.561817

Sobel, David. 2001. *Children's Special Places: Exploring the Role of Forts, Dens, and Bush Houses in Middle Childhood* (Detroit: Wayne State University Press)

Vince, Gaia. 2020. *Rainbows as Signs of Thank You, Hope and Solidarity* (BBC Global), https://www.bbc.com/culture/article/20200409-rainbows-as-signs-of-thank-you-hope-and-solidarity

Whitebread, David, et al. 2017. *The Role of Play in Children's Development: A Review of the Evidence* (*research summary*) (LEGO Foundation), https://cms.learningthroughplay.com/media/esriqz2x/role-of-play-in-childrens-development-review_web.pdf

Winther, Daniel K. 2020. 'Rethinking Screen-time in the Time of COVID-19', UNICEF, https://www.unicef.org/globalinsight/stories/rethinking-screen-time-time-covid-19

Young V&A, Episod Studio, and Play Observatory. 2022. *Play in the Pandemic* [online exhibition], https://playinthepandemic.play-observatory.com

SHIFTING FRAMES

'Pandemic walk peephole'
Photo by iStock.com/Tatyana Tomsickova
https://www.istockphoto.com/photo/little-toddler-child-boy-wearing-medical-
mask-while-on-little-walk-during-the-covid-gm1365551359-436374234?

15. Happy Yardi Gras! Playing with Carnival in New Orleans during the Covid-19 Pandemic[1]

Martha Radice

Introduction

This chapter shows how people in New Orleans, Louisiana, played with the form of carnival to create a novel festive phenomenon, the 'house float', in 2021. During that year carnival parades, with their conventional moving floats, were banned because of the Covid-19 pandemic and specifically the heightened risk of transmission of the SARS-CoV-2 virus in crowds. The chapter focuses on adults' play, rather than children's. Following scholarship on play primarily by anthropologists and geographers (James 1998; Malaby 2009; Malbon 1999; Stevens 2007;

---

1   I would like to thank Maddie Fussell, Ryan Hodgson-Rigsbee, Rachel Lyons, Alastair Parsons, Helen Regis, and Stephen Young for assisting me with this study of house floats. I am grateful to everyone who has taught me about carnival, especially, for this piece, Rob Cambre, Karen Eberle, Brett Evans, Thom Karamus, Jen Pagan and the contributors to Stephen Young's website. I presented drafts of this paper in 2021 to the annual conference of the Canadian Anthropology Society and the joint conference on Creativity and Covid-19 of the Royal Anthropological Institute and Folklore Society. Alastair Parsons' research assistance was funded by the Faculty of Arts and Social Sciences, Dalhousie University. My research has been funded by the Social Sciences and Humanities Research Council of Canada and the New Orleans Jazz and Heritage Festival Archive. Many of the interviews I have conducted on carnival will form a public archive at the T. Harry Williams Center for Oral History at Louisiana State University Libraries.

https://doi.org/10.11647/OBP.0326.15

Woodyer 2012), I conceive of play not only as 'fundamental to human experience across the life course' (Woodyer 2012: 322), but also as enmeshed in everyday, routinized life rather than separate from it, as coexisting with rather than counterpoised to activities labelled as non-play. I also think of play as improvisational, embodied and contingent rather than circumscribed within a certain set of times, spaces or rules. Play has transformative potential because it contributes intense, affectively charged experiences to people's lives. While experiences of play may themselves be fleeting, they are context- and situation-dependent, shaped by the historical moment, place and society in which they emerge.

In this sense, carnival in New Orleans generates many kinds of play that are bound up with living in the city. After the Covid-19 pandemic broke out soon after Mardi Gras day in 2020, people wondered what carnival would look like in 2021. House floats turned out to be one of the answers to this question. This chapter begins by explaining what carnival consists of in New Orleans and presents five overlapping ways in which carnival is playful. It then describes how Covid-19 unfolded in the city and affected its carnival. My discussion of the house float phenomenon explores how house floats were like and unlike regular carnival, in their material and organizational structure, topics, sociality, insertion in urban space and relation to time. The conclusion pushes the comparison further by returning to the themes of play in carnival. I argue that because carnival is re-made every year through improvisation and contingency, resourcefulness is built into its social structure and this is what enabled its playful reconfiguration.

Play in Carnival

Carnival season in New Orleans, Louisiana, is a very playful time. A great deal of carnival activity revolves around the parades organized by voluntary social clubs known as 'krewes'. Carnival season opens on 6 January, Twelfth Night, when a few parades take place, and then there is a lull until three weeks before Mardi Gras, when parades pick up again at weekends. During the final week, several parades roll every single day. The season culminates in Mardi Gras, Fat Tuesday, which always falls forty-seven days before Easter Sunday. It is a public holiday in Louisiana, marked in New Orleans by general revelry in the streets (including the looser costumed 'rambles' of some carnival societies), parties in public and private spaces, the big float parades of the Krewe of Rex and the Krewe of Zulu, and the homespun 'truck parades' that follow them. The calendar for the 2022 carnival season lists forty-seven official parades in the City of New Orleans, though diverse other informal parades are not listed. Parades need audiences, and many New Orleanians plan social activities around spectatorship, arranging to meet friends or family and attending or hosting parties on the parade routes. Carnival parades in New Orleans are also uniquely interactive, in that krewe members hand out trinkets called 'throws' to clamouring spectators—most commonly plastic beads but also plush toys, blinking LED gadgets, go-cups, aluminium 'doubloons', and coveted, one-of-a-kind hand-decorated items ('signature' throws).

Since they are organized by voluntary social clubs, carnival practices in New Orleans reflect the social stratification and relative racial segregation of society at large. Among the parading krewes, there are men's krewes, women's krewes and mixed ones; a few 'old line' krewes represent the white male elite and require an invitation to join; other krewes are less exclusive but still expensive to join; still others have more affordable membership dues. There are krewes that are mostly white, mostly African American, or deliberately diverse. Distinct African American carnival traditions include the Black Masking Indians or Mardi Gras Indians (Becker 2013; Lipsitz 1988), whose elaborate beaded, feathered suits pay homage to the Native Americans who sheltered Black people escaping slavery, and the Baby Dolls, whose exquisite fancy short dresses, bonnets and parasols speak to Black women's power (Vaz-Deville 2018). These groups come out in their neighbourhoods on Mardi Gras day and do not follow published routes as they seek out and meet each other.

My ongoing ethnographic research focuses on what I call the new wave of carnival krewes, which emerged from the counterculture of the 1960s and 1970s, and proliferated as the city recovered from the floods caused by levee breaks after Hurricane Katrina. Mainstream krewes ride on big floats pulled by tractors uptown along broad St Charles Avenue, hire professional float-building and costume design companies, and outsource throw production to factories in China or elsewhere. In contrast, new-wave krewes parade mainly on foot, with small mule-drawn or people-powered floats, through the narrow streets of the neighbourhoods of Bywater, Marigny and the French Quarter, and typically make their own costumes, floats and throws. Their politics tend to be progressive and their parades often feature carnivalesque themes of satire or the grotesque body. They are also influenced by parading practices not associated with carnival, like the annual second lines of New Orleans' African American Social Aid and Pleasure Clubs (Regis 1999), and they spill over into other seasons, since some new-wave krewes parade at Halloween or in the Gay Easter Parade. Despite their differences, the various social worlds of carnival overlap, not only because individuals may participate in several different krewes or scenes, but also because their practices can be 'intertextual' (Lazar 2015), referencing and riffing off each other in their themes and symbols.

All these carnival activities provide opportunities for kinds of play. First, krewe members play with words and ideas as they come up with themes for their parades, floats, throws and costumes, engaging in what sociologists call 'interactional humour' and creating 'joking cultures' (Fine and Soucey 2005; Wise 2016). For instance, Krewe du Vieux's theme for 2006, the first carnival after Hurricane Katrina, was 'C'est Levee', shrugging off the levee breaks with a play on *c'est la vie*—that's life. The Krewe of 'tit Rǝx (from *petit* or little Rex), a group of artistically-inclined adults who have taken the local children's tradition of making floats from shoeboxes out of the classroom and into the streets, complete with a parade permit and police escort, always make puns on smallness for their parade themes—for example, Too Little Too Late (2011), Wee the People (2014), No Big Deal (2016), That's a Little Much (2020). The Krewe of Zulu, a big African American krewe that has been poking fun at stereotypes of Black people since 1909, gives out hand-decorated coconuts as its most coveted throw—so 'tit Rǝx, being miniature, gives out hand-painted pecans. The Krewe du Jieux (pronounced *Jew*), founded in 1996 by Jew-ish (emphasis on the 'ish') people wanting to carve out their own niche in this Catholic holiday, takes inspiration from Zulu to give out decorated bagels. Many krewes have 'royal courts', appointing kings, queens and other officers for the year. Zulu has a Big Shot and a Witch Doctor in their court—so Krewe du Jieux has a Big Macher (a Yiddish term for an influential person) and a Rich Doctor (Vogt 2010). Part of the play of carnival is thus making and getting such jokes which have varying degrees of insideness and often require some decoding.

Carnival participants, especially members of new-wave carnival krewes, engage in a second kind of play as they make their floats, costumes and throws—playing with materials. Anthropologist Tim Ingold (2013) argues that rather than having an image of what they want to create in their mind and then shaping materials in that image, craftspeople enter into 'correspondence' with their materials, tuning into the properties of the substance(s) so that the object they make will have unanticipated qualities. Carnival crafting often calls for this kind of experimentation. Members of the Krewe of Red Beans (a beloved local dish) glue dried legumes onto clothes to make intricate patterned suits; as they do so, they learn how much space to leave between beans to keep the cloth flexible and wearable. Similarly, I made five hundred tiny crystal balls as throws for the 2022 title float of 'tit Rǝx, 'Little Did We Know', by sticking marbles to a polymer clay base. Figuring out how to shape the base was part of the process (a coil worked best). Over the longer term, krewe members learn from each other and develop their crafting skills. Karen Eberle, who has rolled with C.R.U.D.E. (the Committee to Revive Urban Decadent Entertainment), a sub-krewe of Krewe du Vieux, for over twenty years, characterized the phases of their knowhow. At first, they were 'like children', needing to be told exactly how to make the krewe costumes, then they became more confident and quicker to figure it out, and now many of them have the skills to embellish the basic costume as they desire. The pleasure that human beings find in making, building and decorating (Dissanayake 1995) runs through much of carnival.

Carnival is also a stage for play in the sense of performance—dramatic or role play—as people adopt personas and tell stories through their costumes. Again, this is often comedic or satirical. For instance, the informal Krewe of Karens recently emerged from a group of friends dressing up to perform the American stereotype of the Karen, a fussy, entitled suburban white woman who uses her privilege to complain about what she perceives to be poor service or to challenge the activities of people of colour (Nagesh 2020). On Lundi Gras (the day before Mardi Gras) 2022, the Karens, suitably bewigged, paraded around bars in the French Quarter demanding to 'see the manager'—in order to compliment the staff, enacting the trope only to flip it. Similarly, the costumes that people make for Mardi Gras day often involve a character as well as clothing. The first Mardi Gras after Hurricane Katrina was especially ripe with comedic, cathartic performances. Jen Pagan, who I interviewed in 2020, costumed as a FEMA Fairy, writing magical cheques in the amount people wished for from the Federal Emergency Management Agency. Rob Cambre, a member of 'tit Rəx, was Stop Man, a superhero in the form of a four-way stop sign (which was how traffic was managed for months in a city with no working traffic lights). He regularly stopped foot traffic in all directions throughout the day. The fun of costuming is thus enhanced by acting out the costume, not just wearing it.

Carnival is also playful because it offers sensory thrills, the kind of intensification of embodied experience that Malbon (1999) has called 'playful vitality'. The anticipation among krewe members in the days and hours leading up to a parade—or 'funxiety' as poet Brett Evans, a member of 'tit Rəx, calls it—is visceral, and especially powerful as the parade lines up, preparing to roll. Most parades' walking or dancing rhythms are driven by brass band music: big high school, college and military marching bands play between floats in the mainstream parades; smaller professional jazz brass bands accompany the smaller walking parades. Their music moves people emotionally and physically (see Sakakeeny and Birch 2013). Parades are saturated visual experiences with the colours and lights of floats and costumes and vivid kinaesthetic experiences for anyone walking or dancing. Carnival participants are generous with food—sharing boxes of king cake or fried chicken when they are out and about, and pots of red beans and rice or jambalaya at parties—and there is always plenty to drink or otherwise consume in pursuit of an altered state of mind. Although carnival is deeply embedded in everyday life in New Orleans, it offers playful sensory experiences that surpass routine and that thrum with excitement and a sense of being alive in the moment.

Most of all, and encompassing all these dimensions of play, carnival is playful because it is sociable. Krewe members banter and bounce ideas around together, make the artifacts of carnival side by side and perform for each other's entertainment. They form krewes with friends and watch other krewes' parades with them. They make group costumes for Mardi Gras day. They learn crafting skills from each other (Kelly 2022). Paraders and spectators play the game of throws, the fun of which is often less about acquisition than about making eye contact with the float rider or parader to request and receive something. As carnival-makers craft, parade, dance or ramble, they experience the pleasure of being in sync with other people (Dissanayake 1995; Finnegan 2005; Gaunt 2006). Carnival play and creativity are thus thoroughly socially embedded, and I argue that it is precisely this social embeddedness and improvisational responsiveness that enabled the reconfiguration of carnival in 2021, in the midst of the Covid-19 pandemic.

Covid-19 in New Orleans

The early phase of the coronavirus pandemic hit New Orleans very hard. The first case of Covid-19 in the city was confirmed on 9 March, fourteen days after Mardi Gras (25 February in 2020). Cases spiralled from seventy-four cases and two confirmed deaths by 15 March to 1834 cases and 101 deaths by 31 March. It transpired that the parades and parties of carnival 2020 had been superspreading events (Zeller et al. 2021), and Mayor LaToya Cantrell was challenged on CNN television news for not cancelling carnival parades, even though no American cities were restricting large gatherings at that time. The New Orleanians I learn from resisted the carnival-shaming narrative, countering that it was not carnival but the city's entrenched social inequality—including dependence on tourism and service-sector jobs with low wages and inadequate benefits, systemic racism, unaffordable/overcrowded housing, and privatized, inaccessible healthcare—that made it structurally vulnerable to the Covid-19 pandemic (Adams and Johnson 2020; Losh and Plyer 2020; Radice 2020).

Unlike many cities in the American South, New Orleans' municipal government, with support from the Louisiana state governor, Democrat John Bel Edwards, generally acted swiftly and firmly to curb transmission of the virus, imposing or relaxing stay-at-home orders, gathering and capacity limits, mask mandates and proof-of-vaccination checks as indicated by epidemiological analyses (see https://ready.nola.gov/home/). Moreover, recognizable themes and figures from carnival were recruited into the public health campaigns mounted by NOLA Ready, the city's Office for Homeland Security and Emergency Preparedness. As a socially embedded collective cultural practice, carnival arguably provided the imaginative bridge from the individual to the collective that was needed to tackle a major public health crisis like Covid-19

(Radice 2021). Still, it was clear that carnival 2021 was going to be very different from carnival 2020.

Given the city's reliance on tourism, the mayor was reluctant to call off carnival parades but many krewes took the initiative to cancel their parades themselves before the official ban came on 17 November (MacCash and Calder 2020). This was only the fourteenth time since their inception in 1857 that formal float parades were cancelled, for reasons including wars, white supremacist violence, and a police strike, as well as two other pandemics—yellow fever in 1879 and flu in 1919 (Dunn and Perkins 2020). Accordingly, New Orleanians began thinking about other ways to mark carnival season. Several new-wave krewes organized alternative celebrations, such as drive-by *tableaux vivants* (Krewe of Joan of Arc), scavenger hunts (Intergalactic Krewe of Chewbacchus), and art installations (Krewe du Vieux) (Clapp, Poche, and Ravits 2020). But without a doubt, the safely distanced celebration that most captured the imagination of carnival-loving New Orleanians was accidentally launched on 17 November 2020 with a joke made on Twitter: 'It's decided. We're doing this. Turn your house into a float and throw all the beads from your attic at your neighbors walking by. #mardigras2021'. The tweet went viral, and the tweeter, Megan Boudreaux, a member of the Krewe of Leijorettes—adult majorettes who dress as Star Wars character Princess Leia and march in the Intergalactic Krewe of Chewbacchus—soon declared herself the 'Admiral' of the Krewe of House Floats.

Traditional New Orleans houses, which are typically single- or two-storey and have generous porches, are architecturally well-suited to this idea, so people could easily imagine how house floats would work. Ground rules were debated and set through a Facebook group and Boudreaux recruited other people to help lead the krewe, including captains for each of thirty-eight neighbourhood sub-krewes that soon formed (plus one of 'Expats' that included the entire rest of the world). A separate Krewe of House Floats website with a series of FAQs and a statement of participation was set up (https://www.kreweofhousefloats. org/). It was clear from posts in the main Facebook group that one of the biggest challenges for the leaders of this new krewe was handling the sheer volume of inquiries. By Mardi Gras day, three months later, over three thousand house floats were officially registered and mapped, though many more households missed the deadline to register so their floats did not appear on the map. Maps went live on 1 February, Mardi Gras day was 16 February and participants were expected to take their decorations down by 1 March.

The rest of this chapter focuses on the house float phenomenon. As I was not in New Orleans when it happened, it draws on digital ethnography (participant observation on social media and analysis of the copious coverage of house floats in online local and national news media), interviews conducted by phone or Zoom, and some in-person fieldwork conducted by collaborators in New Orleans. I also rely on the work of two photographers: Ryan Hodgson-Rigsbee (http://rhrphoto. com), who has been photographing carnival in New Orleans for a decade and with whom I already work, and Stephen Young, whose website of 360-degree photos of house floats (http://HouseFloatsTour. com) captured my attention while I was researching the trend. A marketing photographer in his day job, Young told me in an interview that he volunteered to document the house floats in what was a quiet period for him, and it was his very first contribution to carnival. He photographed 188 house floats, seventy-three of which feature short texts written by their creators in response to questions that Stephen asked them. Hodgson-Rigsbee is an avid documentarian of New Orleans' public culture who works with many non-profit and cultural organizations in the city. He published a book on carnival 2021 featuring many house floats (Hodgson-Rigsbee 2022). Both photographers' work has been crucial in developing my analysis, which is also embedded in my long-term ethnographic study of new-wave carnival.[2]

Playing with Carnival: House Floats on Parade

In thinking through how the house float phenomenon was like and unlike regular carnival, or at least the parading practices of carnival, five themes stand out: their material and organizational structure; the topics they represented; their sociality (who made them, using what connections); their unique spatiality compared to the usual urban

---

2   This study has undergone initial and annual review by Dalhousie University's Research Ethics Board.

activities of carnival; and finally, their temporality in relation to a specific historical conjuncture.

Like regular carnival floats and props, the qualities of the house floats reflected differential access to money, materials and know-how. My local fieldwork collaborator Maddie Fussell, who visited many house floats, suggested a three-tier classification system. Bottom-tier house floats were decorated with tinsel, lights and swagging in carnival colours (purple, gold and green) and dollar-store decorations (masks, beads) in the fashion that some New Orleanians decorate their houses every carnival season. In that sense, they did not have a theme besides 'carnival time'. Top-tier floats were the most elaborate, made by professionals. Wealthier people rented props from float-building companies or hired float designers or artists to make their house floats. However, not all professional house floats were constructed at the homes of the rich: first, because artists themselves put a lot of effort into their own house floats or helped their friends for free, and second, because of a Covid-19 relief initiative called Hire a Mardi Gras Artist (HAMGA), founded by float designer Caroline Thomas and Devin DeWulf, captain of the Krewe of Red Beans, which undertook several aid initiatives during the pandemic (Radice 2021). HAMGA raised money to employ workers in the float-building industry during what would otherwise have been a jobless season. They invited people to donate to a fund and each time it reached $15,000, they drew one name out of all the donors whose house was then decorated to professional float design standards (Figure 15.1). This creative response to precarious labour raised $330,000, employed thirty-two Mardi Gras artists, and produced twenty-three house floats (https://www.kreweofredbeans.org/projects-2). It also raised the profile of professional carnival artists and the studios that employed them; people then sought them out to make things or teach them how to make things for their house floats. The middle-tier floats were those apparently constructed by amateurs—probably by the residents themselves. They often made creative use of common materials, twisting pool noodles into spirals to make fat, flat lollipops, for instance. These types of house floats are the most interesting to me because, like the new-wave krewes I study, they are homemade and emerge through the creativity and experimentation of the people who are closest to them.

Figure 15.1 The first house float by the Hire a Mardi Gras Artist initiative, 'The Night Tripper', a tribute to the late New Orleans musician Dr John, is installed on Toledano Street, New Orleans, December 2020 (centre, with right arm outstretched, is Caroline Thomas, cofounder of HAMGA)

Photo by Ryan Hodgson-Rigsbee, CC BY-NC-ND 4.0

The Krewe of House Floats was organizationally structured in a similar way to regular carnival parading krewes. Every krewe typically chooses a theme for its annual parade, with each float representing a different take on the theme. Similarly, each neighbourhood sub-krewe of the Krewe of House Floats—which emerged via Facebook—chose its own theme to inspire their members, though no one was obliged to stick with their neighbourhood's theme. The Irish Channel neighbourhood chose 'Channel Surfing', so there were plays on TV shows, including a nod to *Gilligan's Island* and an interactive version of the TV game show *Jeopardy*, whose host, Alex Trebek, had died in 2020. The sub-krewe of St Roch chose 'St Roch and Roll', spawning floats like 'Do you Remember Roch and Roll Radio?' which commemorated boom-boxes and local music venues that had closed during the pandemic. Riffing on the popular song recorded by Marvin Gaye in 1964 and James Taylor in 1975, the Bayou Saint John and Fairgrounds sub-krewe chose 'How Sweet It Is to Be Loved Bayou', and many of their house floats featured alligators (Hart 2021).

These sub-krewe and float themes demonstrate some of the word play that is part of carnival. However, the play of satire was strikingly absent. One exception was a house float by a persistent water mains leak, entitled 'Underwater World of Annunciation St'. It lampooned the New Orleans Sewage and Water Board, often satirized in carnival for its notorious mismanagement: boil water advisories, leaks, blockages, flooding and overcharging. Political satire featured in a few house floats that commented on national politics, with Bernie Sanders in his mittens or Trump in a dumpster fire. Krewe du Vieux kept up its ribald satirical style in its art installations, under the overall theme 'Krewe du Vieux has no taste'. The Krewe of C.R.U.D.E., for example, created an anatomically explicit 'covidgina' accompanied by a poem about the complications of having casual sex during the pandemic. But among the house floats, there were surprisingly few direct satirical references to Covid-19. The oblique ones generally referred to the shared experience of lockdown rather than the virus or public health responses to it. For instance, 'Snacking in Place' (Figure 15.2) pokes fun at the comfort eating people indulged in as they stayed home. In Algiers Point, where the neighbourhood theme was 'Staycation', some house floats played with ideas of escape and boredom ('Covid Island Castaway', '"Bored" Games: Covidland'). The lack of satire can be partly explained by the temporal and spatial structure of the Krewe of House Floats. A carnival parade is mobile and passes in a matter of hours. Krewe members are masked and cannot be personally identified or singled out for any outrageous behaviour. Houses, though, stay in place, and they are occupied by identifiable people. To plaster your private home publicly with satire might be impolitic, especially at a time of both heightened political polarization and local pressure to pull together as a community.

Rather than satire, house float builders embraced sincerity and nostalgia, in the form of the tribute. Many people chose to depict a feature of carnival that they loved. Particular krewes—Endymion, Iris, Muses, and Chewbacchus, among others—were honoured, as were general features of carnival, like Mardi Gras beads and throws, the thrones on which krewe royalty sit, and even parade spectators. Jen Pagan's float, 'If Ever I Cease to Masque', honoured defunct women's carnival krewes, like the Krewe of Venus, which was pelted with rotten vegetables when it was the first female krewe to parade in 1941. Other house floats depicted something their creators loved about New Orleans or Louisiana as a whole. There were many tributes to New Orleans jazz and funk music and musicians, and to local food such as the crawfish boil. An 'Ode to the Oyster' emphasized how crucial this humble bivalve is to the ecosystem of the Gulf Coast. A house on Fortin Street, right by the Fairgrounds where the fifty-year-old New Orleans Jazz and Heritage Festival is held every April and May, was transformed into 'Forever Festin'' (Figure 15.3). The Festival, which had been postponed, then cancelled in 2020, and would be cancelled again in 2021, has an iconic visual culture, made up of the map of the stages, signs for the food and drink booths, the 'cubes' or music schedule, and the logo, so this house float was instantly recognizable. It even featured Jazz Fest producer Quint Davis driving a tractor (because mainstream carnival parade floats are pulled by tractors). Several house floats made references to pop culture beyond New Orleans, including two takes on the TV series Schitt's Creek which, as one creator wrote for photographer Young, 'brings joy to so many and has helped so many of us find a smile and laugh during a challenging year'.

Figure 15.2 'Snacking in Place', Fern Street, New Orleans, February 2021
Photo by Ryan Hodgson-Rigsbee, CC BY-NC-ND 4.0

Figure 15.3 'Forever Festin'', Fortin Street, New Orleans, February 2021
Photo by Ryan Hodgson-Rigsbee, CC BY-NC-ND 4.0

Tributes to New Orleanian and Louisianan culture and, to a lesser degree, broader popular culture feature in regular carnival. What does not, but did among house floats, are personal themes. A regular carnival float is by nature not personal: it is made by a collective, as part of a collective performance, and is embedded in the ethos and history of a certain microculture. In contrast, house floats could just represent something that just the household loved. One family honoured their pets, past and present. Another, 'Born on the Bayou', celebrated 'the birth of the homeowners' son nine months after the 2020 Bacchus parade' (Hart 2021). One creator wrote on Young's website that she realized the way to get her husband to help build their house float was to make it a fishing boat because he is passionate about sport fishing. The personal themes of some house floats reflect the relocation of carnival from public space and public sociability to domestic space and intimate social networks.

This brings us to the sociality of the house floats. Who made them, and what social ties did they mobilize in the making? These were not questions that Young asked, so there are few creators named on his website. Most of the texts are written by an unspecified 'we', which seems to refer to the household, often a family, perhaps housemates. Some people mention neighbours or friends or relatives who may not live with them. Others credit artists, though it is impossible to tell whether they were working voluntarily or for pay. This is consonant with the culture of discretion around money and employment in New Orleans, where it is a point of pride that conversations at parties rarely revolve around jobs and people can be friends for decades before they learn what each does for a living. That said, compared to mainstream carnival floats, which are built by professional design studios, and new-wave carnival floats, which are usually built by sub-krewes in rented warehouse spaces, the scale of production of house floats did shift to the domestic unit—a new cottage industry.

Many house floats seem to have been built, or at least directed, by women. Almost all the posts in the Facebook groups were made by people apparently gendered female, and most of the Krewe of House Floats officers' and sub-krewe captains' names were similarly gendered female. While this might be related to their domestic scale, it more likely reflects something that has been rising to carnival consciousness since the turn of the twenty-first century—that 'ladies make parades', as one new-wave carnival captain, Ann Marie Coviello, likes to put it. Not only have massive mainstream all-women krewes like the Krewe of Muses risen to outshine men's parading krewes along the uptown parade route, but women are the driving forces behind many, if not most, of the new-wave krewes or sub-krewes—though the gendered division of labour in mixed krewes often remains unacknowledged. As is typical of heteronormative households, so it was with house floats: even if men did some practical work, women seemed to undertake most of the project management and logistics, including communications—posting on Facebook, talking to journalists, responding to Stephen Young's questions.

It also seems that most participants in the Krewe of House Floats were white, like most carnival krewes in non-pandemic times. As mentioned earlier, African American New Orleanians have their own carnival traditions but they were historically excluded from formal carnival float parades except as torchbearers, mule or tractor drivers, or streetcleaners (Gill 1997). There are some important Black krewes, like Zulu and NOMTOC, and some quite mixed krewes among the float parades. Black women have recently founded a new sub-krewe in the Intergalactic Krewe of Chewbacchus, Women of Wakanda. However, beside such notable exceptions, most mainstream and new-wave carnival krewes remain majority white. Now, unlike regular carnival krewes, the 'members' of house floats were not often visible in documentation. This means it is hard to tell who made or commissioned what, particularly among the middle-tier, handmade floats. But of the house float creators on Young's site who supplied photos of themselves, nearly all were white.

Moreover, at least in the documentation I have analyzed where authorship is discernible, Black creators in particular set their house floats up as sites to pay homage. Four of the five Black participants in Young's website (as ascertained from the creator-supplied photos) had made floats that were explicit celebrations of African American contributions to New Orleans culture—famous African American women or Black jazz musicians, for instance—rather than, say, jokey or personal themes. Similarly, city council member Jay H. Banks commissioned a professionally made house float as a homage to his beloved Krewe of Zulu, over which he had reigned as King in 2016. This reflects the point made by Black scholars Isaac Julien and Kobena Mercer that Black cultural artifacts are 'burdened with an inordinate pressure to be "representative", and to act, as a delegate does, as a statement that "speaks" for the black communities as a whole' (Julien and Mercer 1996 [1988]: 455). While some white folks' floats paid similar homage, the sincerity of these house floats, which firmly asserted the importance of African American culture, contrasted with the overall whimsicality of the phenomenon.

As creators figured out how to make their house floats, they mobilized their social networks in similar ways to new-wave carnival participants. They turned to the Facebook groups to exchange advice on techniques and materials. Experienced carnival artists held workshops on how to work in papier-mâché or how to make the beautiful painted cardstock flowers that are an iconic carnival float decoration. People learned from each other and from YouTube, often by trial and error as they went along, in correspondence with their materials. The two neighbours who made 'Forever Festin'' experimented with posterboard, glue and wire to make their float elements, and used yacht varnish to protect them from the rain. Jen Pagan re-purposed election signs to make giant doubloons for 'If Ever I Cease to Masque'. Thom Karamus, who had made a shoebox float as a guest artist for 'tit Rəx in 2019, jumped scales to turn his house into a float in 2021. Although he had never worked in papier-mâché before, he decided to use it for his float. When I interviewed him about it, he told me he said to himself, '"How hard can it be?" And I looked at a YouTube video, I'm like, "Oh, little kids do it". Yeah, well, it's easy if you're doing something eight inches big'. Thom's piece, though, was a caterpillar's head to hang on the front of his house that was six feet high, four feet wide, and eighteen inches deep. It used nine rolls of paper towels, seven pounds of flour, half a gallon of glue, one and a half pounds of glitter, 'and a LOT of coffee', as he wrote on Instagram (@ thomofnola).

Thom's house float was part of a remarkable group project: five households on his block made house floats on the theme of *Alice in Wonderland*: the Cheshire Cat, the Queen of Hearts, the Mad Hatter, a Wonderland featuring the White Rabbit and Thom's Blue Caterpillar with the hookah (Figure 15.4). The joint effort emerged from a newfound neighbourly sociability. Before the pandemic, Thom told me, he knew his neighbours 'in kind of a regular know-your-neighbours kind of way, where you wave and say hi, and you look after each other if a storm comes, you check on your neighbour, make sure they have water'. But early in the pandemic, when most people were working from home, if at all, and bars were closed, they decided to socially distance together:

> We ended up having a root beer float party in someone's driveway. And I guess it was May or June, it was pretty hot, and we all decided we kind of liked each other, and we laughed and got along. And then, 'Okay, let's do this again'. And we'd have a pizza party, and we would play some kind of game, and it just kind of grew from there.

In mid-December, the first Hire a Mardi Gras Artist house float, 'The Night Tripper', a homage to New Orleans musician Dr John, went up near Thom's house (Figure 15.4), and the neighbours decided to make their own house floats. The theme of *Alice in Wonderland*, Thom said, 'plays very well into Mardi Gras, the whole little bottle, "Drink me", and the cake, "Eat me", and some of the more trippy, dreamlike imagery. And just the idea of Alice having this adventure and experiencing things she had never experienced before. I think it's very Mardi Gras'. Because 'The

Night Tripper' was heavily publicized, Thom's street got a lot of visitors and he enjoyed watching them realize that the other nearby house floats shared a theme. He and his neighbours even decided to celebrate Mardi Gras day together with a 'Mad Hatter's Tea Party':

> We all dressed up and we had little foods based on ideas from *Alice in Wonderland*, and we made a pot of tea. And we had a really great time. Just thinking about it now, I'm smiling. It's definitely going to go down as one of my absolute favourite Mardi Gras. And there were no super krewes, there were no parades going down St Charles, there were no masquerade balls. The city was very, very quiet. And yet we celebrated in the most wonderful way. We did not feel lacking for anything.

The pandemic and the house floats project brought Thom and his neighbours together as a community—'now we're very comfortable and we spend time in each other's homes and drive each other to the airport and go grocery shopping together and celebrate birthdays'. While their closeness might be exceptional, their joint project illustrates well the spatial shift that the house floats represent.

Figure 15.4 Thom Karamus in front of his house float, Dryades Street, New Orleans, February 2021

Photo by Ryan Hodgson-Rigsbee, CC BY-NC-ND 4.0

Indeed, the most obvious way that the house floats differ from regular carnival is spatial, turning Mardi Gras into 'Yardi Gras', as people soon called it. Symbolically, I think they echoed the 'open house' party invitations that many New Orleanians extend to friends, friends of friends and almost-total-strangers during carnival season, when private homes—especially those near parade routes—become more public than usual. In 2021, the party invitations were not to enter particular homes but to visit homes in general—at a safe distance. This, of course, was their whole reason for being. The house floats were designed to disperse rather than concentrate human bodies and their viruses. The Krewe of House Floats' statement of participation, which people had to agree with to join officially, emphasized compliance with Covid-19 regulations. It stated, 'All Krewe activities will be carried out in such a way as to avoid attracting crowds'. Dotted as they were throughout the city, the house floats reversed the centralization that has been one of the dominant trends of carnival in the last two decades, whereby nearly all mainstream float parades in the Parish of New Orleans roll along the uptown, St Charles Avenue route. The Krewe of Mid-City, for example, no longer rolls in the neighbourhood called Mid-City where it started out. The pressure to centralize comes from the municipal government which is keen to have a single route to police and clean up. Yet New Orleanians speak with nostalgia of old neighbourhood-based carnival celebrations, and they saw the house floats as a way to regain that atmosphere.

Because of this relocation to neighbourhoods, I expected to find traces of tensions between neighbours on the house float social media discussions but there were none. Anxieties surfaced occasionally about unmasked crowds forming outside the most popular houses but that was a tension between residents and sightseers, not neighbours and neighbours. There were, of course, people with whom the idea just did not resonate. Some were put off by the intense debates around 'rules' that sprang up in the house float Facebook groups as people established parameters for this novel practice. Others thought the dispersion of house floats diluted the fun: an isolated house float was hardly equivalent to the critical mass of a big parade. A few people grumbled about house floats staying up too long after Ash Wednesday. For others, 2021 represented a chance to take a year off from making things for carnival. Still other people would have liked to participate but lacked the necessary time, money or materials, or were not allowed to modify their house. I noted one case on Facebook where a woman had started making a house float only to have her landlord rescind his initial agreement. Fortunately, she found someone else to take the decorations she had begun to make.

Overall, New Orleanians regarded house floats as a blessing rather than a nuisance. At first, poet Brett Evans feared the house floats were going to be 'sadmirable'—a term he coined for the efforts made during the pandemic to lift people's spirits that fell flat, like drive-by graduation congratulations—but when he saw 'the level of gusto people were doing it with', he realized the house float phenomenon could be a 'bonus, not a consolation'. According to Brett, carnival gives New Orleanians an irrepressible impulse to 'more-it', to be extra creative and flamboyant. House floats were clearly an expression of this impulse.

Lastly, house floats were the product of a unique temporal conjuncture. Thom Karamus' commitment to the serious play of papier-mâché was only possible because his regular work, in film production, had been put on hold due to the pandemic, as had his usual conduits for carnival creativity—helping friends make throws or floats and, in some years, parading with 'tit Rəx. The success of house floats was specifically bound up with the circumstances of the pandemic in early 2021, which left many people with more time on their hands than usual. This was made plain in 2022 when the easing of Covid-19 regulations meant the regular activities of carnival could resume. Although the Krewe of House Floats relaunched, far fewer people participated, because everyone was caught up in the familiar hectic rhythms of making mobile carnival parades and costumes alongside their jobs and other commitments. Some house floats of 2021 were re-used in 2022, a practice that is rare in regular carnival where people generally do not use the same costume two years in a row and floats are redesigned and repainted every single year. The re-use of house floats reinforces the sense that they were made during an unusual time. When the ban on parades was lifted for carnival season 2022, New Orleanian carnival-makers were happy to put their energies back into their usual celebrations.

Conclusion

House floats were an unanticipated and hugely successful response to the pandemic-related restrictions placed on carnival in New Orleans in 2021. They resembled regular carnival krewes in their material variety and the ways people improvised and made the floats, in some of their themes, and in the gender and race of most of their makers. They departed from familiar carnival in their lack of satire, their mobilization of households and micro-local social networks, and their spatial shift to neighbourhoods. Thematically, the house floats often represented things people loved, in their city and their lives, and things they felt nostalgic for during the pandemic. Yardi Gras was an exceptional iteration of the annual ritual calendar, emerging from an exceptional time.

The very creativity and playfulness of carnival was what made Yardi Gras possible. The idea of house floats emerged from a joke, a play on the image of a carnival float that made it domestic and hygienic. The themes of house floats showed that people played with words and ideas as they usually do in carnival, even if there was not as much satire as usual. Making the house floats gave people an opportunity to play with materials. The plays of performance and pleasure, in contrast, were far less possible in Yardi Gras than in Mardi Gras. Performance needs an audience, and while house floats could physically resemble stages, they were not supposed to invite crowds. Besides, it was the houses, not their residents, that were in costume, playing different roles from usual. Similarly, the sensory intensity of carnival was thoroughly diluted in Yardi Gras. The house floats offered a visual spectacle, and some even gave musical ones in the form of porch concerts, but these had to be kept small. Although New Orleanians could pursue their own pleasures in small groups as they enjoyed the house floats, the excitement of moving in sync with a parade, interacting with strangers in a crowd, or thronging the streets in costume was impossible to reproduce.

That said, the house floats phenomenon was still playfully social. A contagious idea for the pandemic times, it captured New Orleanians' imaginations, allowing them to collectively and creatively declare their love for the city and its culture and to assert that flattening the curve did not have to completely flatten carnival. Playful improvisation and contingency are built into the social structure and creative practices of

Mardi Gras in New Orleans. New Orleanians re-make carnival every year, in dialogue with materials, traditions, current events, and each other. It is precisely this resourcefulness and collective creativity that enabled the playful reconfiguration of carnival during Covid-19.

Works Cited

Adams, Thomas J., and Cedric Johnson. 2020. 'Austerity Is Fueling the COVID-19 Pandemic in New Orleans, Not Mardi Gras Culture', *Jacobin*, 2 April, https://jacobinmag.com/2020/2004/new-orleans-coronavirus-crisis-health-care-privatization

Becker, Cynthia. 2013. 'New Orleans Mardi Gras Indians: Mediating Racial Politics from the Backstreets to Main Street', *African Arts*, 46.2: 36-49, https://doi.org/10.1162/AFAR_a_00064

Clapp, Jake, Kaylee Poche, and Sarah Ravits. 2020. 'Don't Do Watcha Wanna: From the Spanish Flu to the App Store, New Orleans Relearns How to Mardi Gras', *Gambit*, 1 December, pp. 13-17, https://www.nola.com/gambit/mardi_gras/article_cea3668e-2e91-11eb-a84d-efd6d94e6333.html

Dissanayake, Ellen. 1995. 'The Pleasure and Meaning of Making', *American Craft*, 55.2: 40-45

Dunn, Katherine Jolliff, and Emily Perkins. 2020. 'Carnival Canceled? 14 Years in History When Parades Didn't Roll', *First Draft: Stories from the Historic New Orleans Collection*, 17 November (New Orleans: The Historic New Orleans Collection), https://www.hnoc.org/publications/first-draft/carnival-canceled-14-years-history-when-parades-didnt-roll

Fine, Gary Alan, and Michaela de Soucey. 2005. 'Joking Cultures: Humor Themes as Social Regulation in Group Life', *Humor: International Journal of Humor Research*, 18: 1-22, https://doi.org/doi:10.1515/humr.2005.18.1.1

Finnegan, Ruth. 2005. 'Tactile Communication', in *The Book of Touch*, ed. by Constance Classen (Oxford: Berg Publishers), pp. 18-25

Gaunt, Kyra. 2006. *The Games Black Girls Play: Learning the Ropes from Double-Dutch to Hip-Hop* (New York: New York University Press)

Gill, James. 1997. *Lords of Misrule: Mardi Gras and the Politics of Race in New Orleans* (Jackson: University Press of Mississippi)

Hart, Katherine. 2021. 'Yardi Gras Stories: From Sun to Sun, They Have Big Fun on the Bayou', *Mid-City Messenger*, 4 February, https://midcitymessenger.com/2021/02/04/yardi-gras-stories-from-sun-to-sun-they-have-big-fun-on-the-bayou/

Hodgson-Rigsbee, Ryan. 2022. *Do You Know What It Means… Carnival Season 2021* (New Orleans: rhrphoto.com)

Ingold, Tim. 2013. *Making: Anthropology, Archaeology, Art and Architecture* (London: Routledge), https://doi.org/10.4324/9780203559055

James, Allison. 1998. 'Play in Childhood: An Anthropological Perspective,' *Child Psychology and Psychiatry Review*, 3: 104-109, https://doi.org/10.1111/1475-3588.00224

Julien, Isaac, and Kobena Mercer. 1996 [1988]. *'De Margin and De Centre'*, in *Stuart Hall: Critical Dialogues in Cultural Studies*, ed. by Kuan-Hsing Chen and David Morley (London: Routledge), pp. 452-67

Kelly, Briana A. 2022. 'Making Meaning: Material Culture in New Orleans' Carnival', unpublished MA thesis, Dalhousie University, http://hdl.handle.net/10222/81573

Lazar, Sian. 2015. '"This Is Not a Parade, It's a Protest March": Intertextuality, Citation, and Political Action on the Streets of Bolivia and Argentina', *American Anthropologist*, 117: 242-56, https://doi.org/10.1111/aman.12227

Lipsitz, George. 1988. 'Mardi Gras Indians: Carnival and Counter-Narrative in Black New Orleans', *Cultural Critique* 10: 99-121, https://doi.org/10.2307/1354109

Losh, Jenna, and Allison Plyer. 2020. *Demographics of New Orleans and Early COVID-19 Hot Spots in the U.S.* (New Orleans: The Data Center), https://www.datacenterresearch.org/covid-19-data-and-information/demographic-data/

MacCash, Doug, and Chad Calder. 2020. 'No Mardi Gras Season Parades in New Orleans in 2021; Krewes React to "Hard Moment"', *The Times-Picayune*, 17 November, https://www.nola.com/entertainment_life/mardi_gras/article_e5b0dd08-28dc-11eb-b8b2-939bf975bd79.html

Malaby, Thomas M. 2009. 'Anthropology and Play: The Contours of Playful Experience', *New Literary History*, 40: 205-218, http://www.jstor.org/stable/20533141

Malbon, Ben. 1999. *Clubbing: Dancing, Ecstasy, Vitality* (London: Routledge)

Nagesh, Ashitha. 2020. 'What Exactly Is a 'Karen' and Where Did the Meme Come from?' *BBC News*, 31 July, https://www.bbc.com/news/world-53588201

Radice, Martha. 2020. 'Doing/Undoing/Redoing Carnival in New Orleans in the Time of COVID-19', *Culture*, 14(1), https://cascacultureblog.wordpress.com/2020/04/20/doing-undoing-redoing-carnival-in-new-orleans-in-the-time-of-covid-19/

——. 2021. 'Creativity, Sociability, Solidarity: New-Wave Carnival Krewes' Responses to COVID-19 in New Orleans', *Anthropologica*, 63: 1-27, https://doi.org/10.18357/anthropologica6312021230

Regis, Helen A. 1999. 'Second Lines, Minstrelsy, and the Contested Landscapes of New Orleans Afro-Creole Festivals', *Cultural Anthropology*, 14: 472-504, https://doi.org/10.1525/can.1999.14.4.472

Sakakeeny, Matt, and Willie Birch. 2013. *Roll with It: Brass Bands in the Streets of New Orleans* (Durham, NC: Duke University Press)

Stevens, Quentin. 2007. *The Ludic City: Exploring the Potential of Public Spaces* (London: Routledge)

Vaz-Deville, Kim (ed.). 2018. *Walking Raddy: The Baby Dolls of New Orleans* (Jackson: University Press of Mississippi)

Vogt, Justin. 2010. 'The Krewes and the Jews', *Tablet*, 16 February, https://www.tabletmag.com/sections/news/articles/the-krewes-and-the-jews

Wise, Amanda. 2016. 'Convivial Labour and the "Joking Relationship": Humour and Everyday Multiculturalism at Work', *Journal of Intercultural Studies*, 37: 481-500, https://doi.org/10.1080/07256868.2016.1211628

Woodyer, Tara. 2012. 'Ludic Geographies: Not Merely Child's Play', *Geography Compass*, 6: 313-26. https://doi.org/doi:10.1111/j.1749-8198.2012.00477.x

Zeller, Mark, et al. 2021. 'Emergence of an Early SARS-CoV-2 Epidemic in the United States', *Cell*, 184: 4939-52.e15, https://doi.org/https://doi.org/10.1016/j.cell.2021.07.030

16. 'We Stayed Home and Found New Ways to Play': A Study of Playfulness, Creativity and Resilience in Australian Children during the Covid-19 Pandemic

Judy McKinty, Ruth Hazleton, and Danni von der Borch

Introduction

This chapter explores the way children in Australia responded to the Covid-19 pandemic through their play during lockdown in 2020. Descriptions of play activities were collected for the Pandemic Play Project ('the project'), an independent study of Australian children's play during the pandemic. The project was conducted and self-funded by Ruth Hazleton and Judy McKinty, independent play researchers based in Melbourne, Victoria. We had the support of a group of eminent Australian academics and researchers from three states,[1] who have been collecting, studying and writing about folklore and children's play over many decades (Pandemic Play Project 2020). Because of Covid-19 restrictions, the project was carried out almost entirely online, and

---

[1]   Dr June Factor, Dr Gwenda Davey, AM, Emeritus Professor Graham Seal, AM, Rob Willis, OAM and Ollie Willis.

    https://doi.org/10.11647/OBP.0326.16

under one of the longest and strictest lockdowns in the world (Fernando 2020; Mannix 2020).

The aim of the project was to find out:

- how children have taken the coronavirus into their play repertoire
- how they stayed playful at home during lockdown, and
- how the pandemic affected the way they play with their friends at school.

The project began because of our personal and professional interest, as folklorists, in children's traditional games and the play culture of the schoolyard. We wanted to find out if the coronavirus had found its way into school playgrounds in the form of games, rhymes or other traces in the children's play. However, during the course of our research we extended the scope to include younger children and a wider range of activities. This was necessary because, in 2020, children in Victoria spent more time with their families in lockdown than they did at school.

The main portal for the project was a Facebook page which connected to a website (https://pandemicplayproject.com) and email address. This allowed people to submit their contributions as various media: images, video and audio files, short text messages and longer emails. The written submissions were mostly from adults, with descriptions and lists of their children's games and activities, sometimes with images, personal comments or observations. The audio and video submissions were mostly games, rhymes and songs in the children's own voices.

The project was launched in June 2020, at a time when most countries, including Australia, had already experienced lockdowns at a local or national level (BBC News 2020). A devastating 'second wave' of the pandemic in July 2020 effectively isolated the state of Victoria from the rest of Australia, with borders closed and movement severely restricted in Melbourne, the capital city, where the project was based. While other children went back to school to play with their friends, children in Victoria were placed in lockdown for a further sixteen weeks (Boaz 2021). In a special report, released on World Mental Health Day 2021, Save the Children (2021b) analyzed the long-term effects of the Covid-19 lockdowns on children globally. The analysis revealed that 'on average Australian children spent 60 days in lockdown', although 'the figure varies dramatically across states and territories. Children in Melbourne have spent 251 days in lockdown since the start of the pandemic'.

Victoria's severe Covid-19 outbreak and extended restrictions forced the project online, which had advantages as well as constraints. With no geographical boundaries, submissions were received from every Australian state and territory except South Australia and the Northern Territory. Most of the information about play in lockdown came from families in Victoria, as the rest of the country had already moved on to a somewhat 'Covid-normal' life at that stage.

There were three key findings arising from our review of the submissions:

- the important role of adults in helping children stay playful during lockdown

- the creativity, imagination and resourcefulness of children in their play

- the importance of children's own culture and play traditions in terms of expression and responses to Covid.

In this chapter we give examples of play in relation to our key findings, discuss the relationship between digital play and children's own culture and play traditions, and present a case study of how playworkers at The Venny Inc. supervised adventure playground used a determinedly playful approach to support the well-being of local children living in high-rise public housing during the trauma of multiple lockdowns.

The descriptions of games and other play activities in this chapter, and quotes other than those directly referenced, come from submissions to the Pandemic Play Project[2] and our own observations of children at play during lockdown. Contributors were personally contacted and written permission was obtained from informants and parents before public use of the material submitted to the project. Some of the information in this chapter has previously been published in the *International Journal of Play*, and has been reprinted with permission (McKinty and Hazleton 2022: 12-33).

---

2 Descriptions from the Pandemic Play Project are anonymous to protect the identities of our informants. Quotations, names and other project references are used with permission.

Play in Times of Crisis

The role of play as a fundamental element in children's lives has long been acknowledged in academic and clinical research, as Brown states: 'Neuroscientists, developmental biologists, psychologists, social scientists, and researchers from every point of the scientific compass now know that play is a profound biological process'. He goes on to say that 'Play is the vital essence of life. It is what makes life lovely' (2010: 5, 12). Playing is how children form friendships, navigate social relationships and learn about their own culture through their games and play activities. Through play, children connect with each other and gain understanding of the world around them, a subtle process that takes time. Play Wales (2014: 2), one of the United Kingdom's foremost advocates for children's right to play, affirms the importance of play in this process:

> Making sense of the world is an enormous task for young children. They are constantly at risk of being overwhelmed by events or feelings. By re-enacting and repeating events, and by playing out their own feelings and fantasies, children come to terms with them and achieve a sense of mastery.

In a crisis like the Covid-19 pandemic, when their world is changing rapidly, play can also help children to build emotional strength. It is 'the foundation stone of resilience in children, no matter what life may throw at them' (Shooter 2015: 4). To many Australian children, 2020 became 'the year they closed the schools'. As SARS-CoV-2 infections spread, end-of-term holidays came early in some places, with car trips and plane flights banned, playgrounds out-of-bounds and 'stay-at-home' restrictions keeping families in their homes most of the time. Lockdowns forced families into prolonged close contact, and the only way to see friends was on-screen, using Zoom, Skype, FaceTime or other video conferencing programmes (McKinty 2020).

Children with access to digital technology could play with friends remotely. At its simplest, this meant sharing a Skype game of chess using two boards, one at each end; more complex engagement involved meeting a friend's avatar in a *Minecraft* world, or one of many online multi-player games. The activity children were not able to do was the thing they missed most—to play freely with their friends, a yearning shared by children around the world and captured in reports, articles and children's own descriptions of life during the pandemic (Henry Dodd 2020; Save the Children 2020; Stoecklin et al. 2021; Tucci, Mitchell, and Thomas 2020: 3, 12).

Three Key Findings

1. The Important Role of Adults in Helping Children Stay Playful during Lockdown

Coronavirus entered Australia in January 2020. During the pandemic, intermittent lockdowns were implemented as a way of reducing the spread of the virus. In addition to initial public health measures, such as hand hygiene and social distancing, lockdown restrictions included:

- 'stay-at-home' orders—only leave home for essential work; health, safety and caregiving; buying essential provisions; and permitted exercise within a specified travel radius

- a 'work from home' directive for office workers

- closure of 'non-essential' businesses, including retail, travel, recreation, entertainment and hospitality; cafes and restaurants supplying take-away food only

- 'remote learning'—attending on-screen classes from home— for primary, secondary and tertiary students

- mandated mask-wearing—initially for everyone from twelve years of age; later for everyone eight years and over.

During Victoria's second, extended lockdown, harsher restrictions in metropolitan Melbourne also included a nightly curfew from 8 p.m. to 5 a.m. (SBS News 2020).

The lockdowns significantly affected the lives of children and families. In addition to the anxiety and fear of infection, upheaval in their daily lives and loss of personal contact with friends and extended family, children and adults were forced into an artificial situation— spending all day, every day, together: no weekend activities, every day was the same. It was 'blursday, when your days are blurry because you've been in your house for too long'—the blended word submitted to the Pandemic Play Project by an eight-year-old girl, and featured in the Oxford Dictionary's list of defining words for 2020 (Oxner 2020). For families living in Melbourne through winter and spring of 2020, this extraordinary living arrangement lasted four months.

In June 2020, after Australia's first lockdown and prior to Victoria's second, extended lockdown, the Australian Childhood Foundation and the Royal Children's Hospital Melbourne each undertook a national survey into the effects of Covid-19 on families. Survey respondents were parents or carers of children mostly aged from three to seventeen years. The reports reflected variations in the parameters of each study but both were consistent in several of their findings, including the pandemic's negative effects on children's mental health and well-being, a significant increase in children's screen time, and an overwhelming number of children (eight out of ten) who missed their friends. While family experiences in lockdown were not all positive, the majority of parents in both studies felt their relationship with their children had become closer and they valued the extra time spent with them—more time 'reading, playing games and eating meals together' than before the pandemic (Royal Children's Hospital 2020: 7; Tucci, Mitchell, and Thomas 2020).

Many children also valued the extra time spent with their parents, as revealed in studies from several countries (Gray 2020; Holt and Murray 2021; Smith et al. 2022; Stoecklin et al. 2021). 'I spent more time with Mummy and Daddy' was one of the activities listed by an eight-year-old girl in her submission to the Pandemic Play Project, along with others like reading, learning magic tricks, having an 'Easter egg treasure hunt with clues' and going for 'lots of very, very boring walks'. Playing board and card games, doing puzzles and craftwork, cooking, singing silly songs, watching TV or movies and sharing jokes and riddles at mealtimes were some of the ways families came together during lockdown. As one child wrote: 'We stayed home and found new ways to play'.

Lockdown also changed the way some parents perceive play. Living so closely as a family gave parents a unique opportunity to observe how children interact with each other and their environment in play, and to sometimes be allowed to join in their games. One father described how his nine-year-old daughter introduced him to *Minecraft*, 'When remote work and remote school had finished for the day',

> the first thing she would ask is, 'Dad, is your iPad upstairs?' With the game loaded up on our iPads and connected to the same household LAN, we could see each other as a 'Friend'. She created a [...] peaceful 'Dad Learning' world on my device and was able to join me in the game to show me how to find the menu with all the different materials and objects available, and how to create a building with windows, open and close doors and even fly! She also created other worlds on her device and built houses for us to share while we explored and created all kinds of wonderful things together. Sharing screen time in this manner [...] has been a lot of fun and has enabled me to spend time playing with her in a very different environment compared with the card and board games we have been utilizing up until now.

Cohen and Bamberger (2021: 6-12) recount Israeli parents' spontaneous descriptions of the way their children, aged three to nine years, played during the pandemic, with parents commenting on developmental changes or adaptations to play, and the way the children expressed their feelings and understanding of Covid through their play activities.

Conversely, having adults around all the time can inhibit play. Children need time, space and freedom to play in their own way. 'The role of adults', according to Dodd and Gill (2020), 'is to provide physical and psychological space, and resources that support the child's play. They should only join in or interfere with the play if the child asks them to'. With adults working from home and children studying and playing at home, space often had to be negotiated. In unit blocks and apartments, the close and continual proximity of adults to children, who are usually at school all day, sometimes provoked disputes over the use of shared spaces (Foster 2020). Play Australia underlines the importance of separate playing spaces: 'Allowing children to create a space of their own where they can retreat to and indulge in play, is an important step in them reclaiming some power and control over their environment' (Miller 2022: 2).

A widespread response to lockdown in Australia was the relaxing of the usual household rules by parents. In contrast to a common family hierarchy where 'Adults generally define the purpose and use of space and time [and] children usually find ways to play that appear within the cracks of this adult order' (Lester and Russell 2010: ix), there seemed to be an early acceptance by many parents that play was important for their children, and that adjustments needed to be made to their usual way of living. Save the Children (2021a) offered sage advice about what was to come:

> Be prepared for your days to be messy. There may be days when the home becomes a messy play area, or working parents rely on TV more than usual. While lockdown continues for the next few weeks or months, a little chaos is to be expected.

Bending the rules allowed children to wear their roller blades inside the house; eat snacks on the trampoline; take over whole rooms to build cubbies and box forts; move cushions, mats and furniture to make obstacle courses; and lay long, wobbly trails indoors for a game of 'The Floor is Lava'. In this game, players make their way along the trail, trying to reach the end without overbalancing and stepping into the 'lava'. The game becomes more exciting when there is a 'Lava Monster' ready to disrupt play by displacing the trail or unbalancing someone into the 'lava'.

Children's experiences of lockdown, and their opportunities for play, depended on where they lived, and to a greater extent on their socio-economic situation. Families living in poverty do not have the extra income to order board games, puzzles and other resources online. Lockdown intensified already-existing inequalities for children and families, particularly in metropolitan Melbourne. For children living in high-rise public housing towers these included access to digital resources, play materials and safe outside playing spaces. Lockdown was a test of their resilience and perseverance against sometimes overwhelming odds. Large families, cramped living conditions and lack of access to the outdoors made lockdown unbearably challenging for children and families living in the flats.

The following is a personal narrative by Danni von der Borch, a senior playworker at The Venny Inc., one of five staffed adventure playgrounds in Australia and, in 'normal' times, the communal backyard for children living in nearby public housing towers. The towers are home to residents on low incomes and people of culturally and linguistically diverse backgrounds, including refugees who have escaped war and conflict overseas. Local community languages, apart from English, include Amharic, Tigrinya, Arabic, Oromo, Somali, Vietnamese and Mandarin.

The Venny's Response to Lockdown: A Case Study

In March, 2020, when Australia's first lockdown was imminent, we spent time with the children we work with, practising what it might be like to be distant but still together; preparing them, and ourselves, for something unknown which was about to unfold. We danced in separate parts of the yard—dancing alone and separate but still connected. It was autumn and the fading afternoon sun gave us warmth and a glow; the music was loud and we danced. We were preparing for when we would have to be apart from each other and for when The Venny would have to close. We practised 'self-hugs', feeling the presence of each other but not being together. Adults and kids sharing the same unknown future.

Moving to online sessions seemed like something from a nightmare—being in a virtual world with each other, not in a relational experience but one mediated via technology and a computer screen. We all felt acutely the weight of responsibility, asking, 'How will we continue to play?' 'How can we connect with The Venny children and provide the goodness we know they get from playing?' We just had to get creative and find the ways. And we did. Throughout every lockdown in 2020–21, The Venny provided three online play sessions a week.

Children and families across Melbourne had to adjust to online remote learning, and the demands of this left kids feeling drained. We felt awful asking them to show up for yet more screen time—play sessions with us. This led us to wonder about points of connection and how we could 'stay in touch', particularly with kids who don't have their own phone or access to devices and unlimited data. How could we extend our presence, our reach, whilst still complying with lockdown rules? The answers came in several forms:

Play Packs

From the first lockdown we recognized the need for children to have things to do and a focus for play, during their many hours indoors. We put together and delivered weekly Play Packs to children living in local public housing in Kensington, North Melbourne and Flemington. We wanted to make sure everyone had the resources they needed to join in with our online sessions. Each pack came in a hand-folded origami newspaper bag—this inspiration came early to avoid plastic bags. The origami bag served a dual purpose—when unfolded the newspaper became a working surface for doing messy art/clay/craft activities. Win-win! My aunty took on the task of regularly folding bundles for us to use, relying on friends to donate their newspapers. We were so grateful.

Our first pack was for making 'Grass Head Creatures', so children had something to tend to, watching it change and grow over the days and weeks ahead. We often made 'how to' videos connected to the Play Packs, so children could do the activity when it suited them and away from the screen. These videos, photos and messages were posted on our social media platforms, Facebook and Instagram. We also used WhatsApp chat groups with residents to share information and keep in touch.

The 'Hard Lockdown'

On 4 July, 2020, about three thousand people in nine local public housing towers were placed under an immediate, police-enforced 'hard lockdown'. No-one was allowed into the towers and no-one was allowed out (McKinty and Hazleton 2022: 4). After five days, eight of the towers were released—people living in the ninth tower were kept inside their homes for a further two weeks, 'unable to attend work, visit the supermarket or, for the most part, access fresh air and outdoor exercise'. Almost half were children under eighteen years (Glass 2020: 12, 36).

Through our local connections and deep relationships, The Venny played a crucial role in providing sensory play and art activity packs for children experiencing the hard lockdown. Within days of the 4 July directive, The Venny was overwhelmed with donations of play and art/craft materials, books and toys, as well as financial donations to help support our ongoing work. Within the week we were able to mobilise volunteers and, with the support of Artists for Kids Culture, pack 220 bags for delivery to the towers. Already embedded on the ground at the North Melbourne incident control site, and with support from the City of Melbourne, The Venny staff were able to manoeuvre our way into the delivery schedule, to make sure the Play Packs were delivered to children within the towers. This contact remained once the hard lockdown was lifted, with direct deliveries to children and young people continuing.

Letter Boxes

During the first week of lockdown, a young girl was outside The Venny, leaning on the shipping container. We saw each other and she said to me:

> I'm lonely.
> There's no one to play with.
> I come here every day. I give The Venny a hug and say 'I hope you get well'.
> It's so awful,
> Mum's in her room,
> My brother is out,
> I'm on my own.
> I wrote a letter to you, but I didn't know how to post it to you.

We began thinking about how old-fashioned letter-writing and posting was another way to connect. The children could post a letter to us and we could leave replies or treasures in the boxes for them to find. And yes, there were discussions about what sort of surfaces or objects might be Covid carriers and if we needed to do infection control cleans and processes around what went into the letter boxes.

Quite by chance, on the last, anxious day before lockdown, I saw a man working in his garage making toys from scrap wood. I stopped, feeling unsure if my lingering would be welcomed or not, but he was so warm, so friendly, and reminded me of my own dad. He showed me what he called 'snappy boxes'—essentially a hinged box with eyes, and when you opened it, inside were teeth. I immediately thought these would make perfect letter boxes. He agreed to make us a few and refused to accept any payment. We attached the letter boxes to posts in the bushes outside The Venny fence—secret boxes that would inspire play and connection to the physical site of The Venny, and also allow for communication that was not digital but in the form of magical trinkets, chalk, high bounce balls, pictures, drawings, postcards and poems.

Using Zoom for Online Play: What We Did and How We Played

Moving to Zoom, one of the core questions for us as playworkers was how to continue to allow kids to 'lead the play'; and if we were the content creators, providing the play packs and activities, how would that influence children's play? From the outset we thought a lot about the Zoom platform and its functions. We discussed the power of the 'Host' role and the 'mute' button—the total inverse of the child-led and shared power situation we most want to encourage in the face-to-face play environment. Rather than simply taking that power as the Host to mute participants, we developed a hand signal, waggling our fingers, that the children would mirror, so there was a moment of shared participation and forewarning before muting. It was a small thing but one that allowed us to collaborate and share the power together.

We considered the child safety protocols of using online: the Zoom ID was disseminated directly to children we knew via a verified contact—it was never shared on social media or the website. For the sessions we set up a separate 'welcome room', where two staff verified the identities of kids entering the Zoom session. Once welcomed, they were sent through to 'the yard' where all the other staff were and where the action happened.

In the first weeks of lockdown children were exhausted by too much screen time—with remote online learning and then more online programmes. They often began a session with low energy, looking drained and sad, so we quickly realized that we needed to get them active, discharging and expressing emotions. One session was a giant pillow fight to some fun music, and at the end kids were lively, chatty, being funny, playful and relaxed. We included dancing in most sessions and invited kids to offer a song for the play list. This brought joy and happiness to the session.

We wanted to encourage 'soft attention' at times—not always having to look at the screen but rather to focus on their own activity, i.e. drawing and painting together and then sharing whenever they wanted to. The focus was often sensory, creative play and art-making, but also silly and irreverent fun, jokes and quizzes and sharing stories. We often invited kids to use their voices—be vocal, sigh loudly, beat their chests, make sound, be loud—just to feel the release of this. We would often pull faces, stick our tongues out and invite silliness—no performance required here—no 'be good' and attend.

Clay was always popular, creating creatures or landscapes and objects. A 'corona-free cubby' was an invitation that led to the creation of places beyond the world of corona—several islands were made, lots of water and swimming, a boat with a hammock, an elephant, a turtle, a whole world with everything you need (even a Venny!). Our creatures and characters met each other, and stories were developed and shared. Watered-down clay was made into mud to paint our faces.

Figure 16.1 'Mud on our Face', Children playing 'together apart' during The Venny's 'Mud on our Face' online play session over Zoom, 2020

Screen image by Danni von der Borch, courtesy of The Venny Inc., CC BY-NC-ND 4.0

One session we put a torch, cellophane, rubber bands and sticky tape in the Play Pack and played around in the dark. We used the newspaper bag to make a lantern cover for the torch, cutting shapes in the bag and covering them with coloured cellophane. Kids went crazy!! They hid in wardrobes and cupboards, shut themselves in bathrooms, hung blankets over bunk beds, went under beds and made cosy blanket cubbies. They danced and swung their lights around in a frenzy of frenetic dancing at the disco. They also played with their own video screens a lot—watching the weird distortions of light and shadow on their faces—making scary faces at each other. It was a happy riot.

Another time we gave extra newspaper, coloured paper and masking tape, and used this to make wearable 'statement pieces', and the creative energy was wonderful—hats, boots, shoes, headdresses, a lantern, wigs and crowns. One child made a crown that let her teleport herself straight to where she needed to go—home, The Venny, supermarket, school, movies and home again—in that order.

Sand Trays

Sand trays formed part of The Venny's considered play approach for children in lockdown. These could be used in the corridors of public high-rise buildings or in the living room. Sand is a sensory play experience that allows children to build worlds in the sand and to tell stories from this place. We sourced, assembled and delivered 110 sand trays during the lockdown period, including sand and small objects to play with. Venny staff interacted with children via online sessions to support their play and storytelling. The worlds the children created through their sand trays varied, from escape fantasy to confinement and lonely worlds. The response from parents was one of immense gratitude that their kids were able to lose themselves in playing for lengthy periods of time, and it was something that siblings could do together.

Respite Visits to The Venny

Small respite visits were held outdoors on-site during the end of lockdown in 2020 and again in 2021 when regulations and compliance allowed. These were limited to children who were deemed at greater risk due to demonstrated and deteriorating mental and emotional health, or who were in environments where the health and well-being of the adults they lived with had an adverse impact. This included children in environments where aggression was escalating. Using play as the primary tool, these children were supported to find their way back from traumatic experiences and make sense of their world again. This was empowering for these children and helped them to rebuild confidence and self-esteem, and regain a sense of control.

In one session a family of three children, aged eight, six and five years, took me and found a rope, tied my hands together and sat me on a chair. They used milk crates to build a wall around me, trapping me in. When I asked, 'Are you closing me in?' the response was fast and firm—'Yes, you've been so bad'. I am in prison. The children's roles in this game are police, security and a lawyer.

One of them brings a clock over and tells me that when it is six in the morning I will die. I ask, 'What will happen?' He says, 'I will shoot you and you'll go ahhhh, and then the police will throw you in the water'. The 'lawyer' finds a high stool and places it where she can watch from a high vantage point. The 'security guard' makes a point of squinting his eyes to look mean, puffing up his chest and saying, 'I am so strong'. They set up a phone on the chair so I can speak with the 'lawyer'. I am required to plead to all sorts of crimes, including murder. This game continues the next time they visit and when they want to go off and explore other things, they set up a 'security surveillance camera', switching it on and telling me it's connected to a 'wristwatch' that one of them is wearing, so they would 'always know'. This deep play continued over several consecutive sessions and became a vital part of these children's processing of experiences endured.

We have attempted to find connection, play and creativity with all the children of The Venny community. We welcomed many new kids and families during and after the hard lockdown and did outreach with these kids to ensure they were included and welcomed. We found a way to exchange energy, to play and bounce off each other, to encourage kids to lead and to open their imagination and for a small time lose themselves in play.

2. Children's Creativity, Imagination and Resourcefulness

In 2020, almost all children in Australia experienced being in lockdown. The patterns of their lives at this time were similar to those of children in other parts of the world (Graber et al. 2020; Holt and Murray 2021; Stoecklin et al. 2021). Freed from the pressures of time-driven daily living, children found they could explore new options for extended play. This influenced outdoor play, and included the appropriation of public spaces. In local parks, neighbourhood streets and on remarkably car-free roads, traces of play were seemingly everywhere as children found creative and sometimes unusual ways to stay playful and resilient. While enjoying, or enduring, daily exercise outings with their parents, Melbourne children explored their local streets—young children rode bikes and scooters along the footpaths, stopping at the kerb to let the adults catch up. Free-wheeling groups of older children, mainly boys, often met at their local parks to ride their bikes, climb trees and play.

One of these meeting places was an early 1900s Melbourne suburban public garden, with an open, grassed sports oval at one end and thirteen acres (five hectares) of shady tree-lined avenues with shrubs, planted gardens and grassed areas at the other. There, in the tree area ('the park') away from the sports ground, four boys, aged nine to ten years, began meeting on weekday afternoons after remote schooling. Initially they simply rode their bikes in the park, along the gravelled walkways or across the loose earth around the park's perimeter. Then, with growing confidence, they decided to make 'jumps' by piling mounds of loose earth in the park nearest the streets where they lived. This created an informal bike track. The word spread rapidly along the children's grapevine and soon others were riding their bikes to the park more often. Pioneers and newcomers banded together to form a flexible cohort of between ten and twenty boys aged around eight to eleven years.

The bike track was extended around the park perimeter, with jumps at intervals. On weekends, and during school holidays-at-home, children gathered under a large, shady tree, with bikes strewn on the ground, to plan the day's riding. Someone usually brought a small shovel to repair the jumps. On days when the park was busy a few parents, some also on bikes, went along to keep a benevolent eye on the interaction between riders and walkers. The parents seemed somewhat bemused by their children's intense and prolonged engagement with this activity. The bike tracks were used by any child on wheels, including scooters: they added risk, challenge and fun to the day's outing, with opportunities for extended play. The park was their chosen place to play; in creating the bike tracks the boys shared their play experience with other children. Their appropriation of space around the margins of the park had inadvertently added the word 'play' to the list of reasons to leave home during lockdown.

At any other time, this subversive activity would not be tolerated. Public parks are designed by adults with adults in mind, and children are usually relegated to the swing sets and climbing equipment in designated playing areas. Occasionally traces of play can be found among the shrubs but these are usually quite small, personal and ephemeral. The fact that the bike-track boys could openly claim their territory and alter the space to play in their own way, within a public park, was intrinsically connected to the lockdown. The tolerant attitude of adults in the park was a reflection of the relaxed approach to play found in family homes during this time.

Perhaps a clue to the mindset, and exceptional tolerance, of the council in charge of the 'bike-track' park can be found in the playful wording of a temporary sign placed beside the oval, a popular place to exercise dogs:

ATTENTION ALL DOGS
This is the Central Park oval and the designated **dog off-leash** area.
Ask your human to let you off-leash here so you can go for a run and explore!
Please remember you are only allowed to be off-leash if you promise to be a good dog and listen to your human. And, remember you must be on your leash in all other areas of Central Park.
Have fun, good dog !

Unfortunately, the lifespan of other informal bike tracks depended on the attitude of local councils. The bike track and jumps described above remained (and were maintained by the children) for most of the long, second Melbourne lockdown, which lasted for four months. In another large Victorian regional city, a smaller bike track, with a few jumps, was quickly removed by council workers. This conflict between children attempting to make their own play spaces and the authorities in charge of public parklands is vividly described by Sleight (2013: 61), who evokes the streets and open spaces of nineteenth- and early twentieth-century Melbourne, and describes 'the most concerted attempts by the city's youngsters to refashion the landscape to suit their purposes, attempts that met with determined efforts by trustees to prevent damage'.

Figure 16.2 'Spoonville, Glen Iris (2020)', one of the many 'Spoonvilles' created by children in local parks and neighbourhoods during lockdown
Photo by Judy McKinty, CC BY-NC-ND 4.0

Another example of children appropriating public space was the emergence of 'Spoonvilles', groups or 'villages' of mainly wooden spoons, decorated with coloured markers and craft materials like beads, pipe cleaners, googly eyes and fabric scraps to look like people (Boseley 2020). 'Spoonvilles' were omnipresent, appearing on nature strips (grass strips alongside footpaths), in front gardens and—a particularly favoured place—at the base of trees in public parks. Children made their spoon people at home and carried them to the local park, placing them upright beside characters made by other people. This gave children a sense of connection and a chance to display their craft work in public. Like the bike track above, 'Spoonvilles' were tolerated by local authorities and remained largely undisturbed during lockdown. In one park, a playfully contrary group of children responded to this global craze by creating a 'Forkville' on the other side of the tree.

Children chalked rainbows, colourful patterns and messages on footpaths, driveways and in the middle of the road ('Careful of Kids'). The appearance of hopscotches on public walkways turned local streets into community play spaces, where everyone could join in. One nine-year-old girl drew hopscotch patterns on the footpath and wrote how to play on papers she pinned to a tree. Among the patterns were 'Stepping Stones'—a line of shapes for people to walk along—and 'Dog Scotch', where the shapes were paw prints, for dogs to play.

The International Play Association (2017:14), in supporting children's right to play, states:

> An optimum play environment is [...] a trusted space where children feel free to play in their own way, on their own terms. Children's spaces should include chances for wonder, excitement and the unexpected and, most of all, opportunities that are not overly ordered and controlled by adults. These spaces are crucial for children's own culture and for their sense of place and belonging.

3. The Importance of Children's Own Culture and Play Traditions in terms of Expression and Responses to Covid

Traditional Play and Technology During the Pandemic

When children are old enough to socialize meaningfully with their peers, they become immersed in their own unique culture. Thriving largely beneath the gaze of adults, childhood culture is at once structured, grounded in tradition and innately embedded in the experience of childhood itself and simultaneously adaptable, constantly evolving, responsive and connected to the immediate world in which we live (Seal 1998: 92).

Children's play culture passes from child to child and includes verbal lore (such as jokes, rhymes, subversive humour and chants) and games (imaginative games, dress-ups and role play, physical challenges, and schoolyard games like Hide and Seek, and Chasey). Children's traditional play has roots in ancient culture and is enthusiastically adopted by children worldwide regardless of cultural, geographic, historical and socioeconomic boundaries (Opie and Opie 1977: 22-23). One of the most significant findings from our project has centred around the relationship between technology and traditional play in the lives of children during lockdown. At a time when children were separated from their peers and suffering ongoing uncertainty, they quickly and masterfully adapted the digital realm and technology to maintain their own play culture.

Figure 16.3 'Pin the Mask on the Virus game (2021)', a Covid-19 adaptation of the traditional blindfold game Pin the Tail on the Donkey, created by two children, aged eleven and nine, for a birthday party

Photo by Kate Fagan, CC BY-NC-ND 4.0

Having to endure prolonged periods of lockdown inflicted many families with a profound sense of loss in terms of physical space and social connectivity. Adults not considered 'essential workers' were required to work from home, while children and older students navigated online classes, sometimes all within the same space. The household became an environment in which separate spheres of life suddenly collided. Requiring access to multiple devices and familiarity with new platforms, digital technology became integral to day-to-day life—a situation previously unimaginable to most households. Families from disadvantaged backgrounds were loaned basic digital resources for use at home; access to reliable internet became essential, but inconsistent network connections and sub-standard devices meant that inequities became increasingly apparent. At the other end of the socio-economic spectrum, sales of gaming consoles rose almost three hundred percent in the space of one fortnight in March 2020 as life in lockdown commenced (Dring 2020).

Extended screen time became unavoidable. Not only were children exposed to significantly increased screen usage for education, they also relied more on technology to entertain themselves and maintain their social lives and friendships. For Australian parents and caregivers, this was not easy to accept, due to dominant cultural narratives around the negative impacts of 'screen time' on children's health, fitness, socialization, safety, cognitive development and mental health (Walmsley 2014). Anticipating that increased use of technology during the pandemic would exacerbate these fears, UNICEF published an article urging adults to re-think their attitudes toward the household use of devices and acknowledge the benefits of online connectivity for children (Kardefelt, Winther and Byrne 2020). Basically, we were required to re-think the common assumption that 'proper' play belongs only within the sphere of the physical playground.

Our findings have mirrored those of other studies in concluding that digital play is not separate from, but rather an extension of, traditional physical play and that traditional forms of play feature regularly in the digital realm (Mavoa and Carter 2020: 2-3). We observed this within three distinct contexts: verbal play, hybrid play and in the digital playground itself. We also identified one key factor, not in common use prior to the pandemic, that allowed play to flourish as brilliantly as it did—the use of Voice over Internet Protocol (VoIP) platforms such as Zoom, Kids Messenger and Discord.

Once a platform for business, international communications and serious gaming communities, video-conferencing became a common tool for facilitating regular interaction between friends and family during lockdown (Cowan et al. 2021: 12). Many parents admit to being completely unaware, before the pandemic, of the available platforms allowing real-time conversation for children, other than FaceTime, Zoom, Microsoft Teams or Skype. Navigating the creation of email and platform accounts, and negotiating access guidelines and security settings for their children, proved a very steep learning curve for many parents. The initial stages of enabling these networks was a source of great challenge and frustration for some.

Eventually, previous generations' experience of a knock on the door followed by 'Can you play?' was signalled during lockdowns by the sound of a device alert. The sound of children's voices once again filled isolated households—this time virtually instead of physically. Children's traditional play is very much a transactional experience. The glee in the telling of a naughty joke or rhyme is greatly reduced if there is nobody present to appreciate the deliciousness of the subversive humour (and adults often just do not 'get it'). Without access to peers, a vast pool of play becomes less meaningful or simply disappears. Being able to communicate in the moment, embrace spontaneity and engage with the natural ebb and flow of play decisions is fundamental to traditional play in childhood, and VoIP platforms proved to be the perfect conduit. In utilizing these, play became more immediate, cooperative and fluid (McKinty and Hazleton 2022: 14). In terms of verbal play, the use of VoIP platforms allowed children to interact as they might in the playground. Not only could they now relish their sayings, jokes, rhymes, insults and slang in real-time, they could explore their experiences of the pandemic together in an almost in-person way.

Living 3,700 kilometres (2,300 miles) and three time zones apart in Melbourne, Victoria and Geraldton, Western Australia, Charlie and Lola (both aged ten) developed an almost daily friendship that included using tablets and smartphones. Together they conducted physical jumping competitions, cooked, and carved Halloween pumpkins together. They took photos and videos of each other, added effects using downloaded applications and relished the joys of playing with silly and distorted images. Other children used video conferencing to host and attend 'playdates', 'crafternoons', birthday parties and 'game dates'. Such occasions became regular and much-anticipated moments of personal contact, mimicking pre-pandemic life in a virtual context.

From Sydney, New South Wales, one mother described her daughter and friends playing a spontaneous game of online Hide and Seek. The person who was 'hiding' would either describe the furniture in various rooms or give the group a visual tour of rooms nearby. They would all then take turns guessing where the imaginary hiding place was until one child guessed correctly and became the next person to 'hide'. In another example, a four-and-a-half-year-old girl from regional Victoria displayed her inherent talent for imaginative play when she placed her grandparents (who were online from the UK via tablet) into a cardboard box and 'flew' them through the air. In the video submission, she is dragging the box across the floor and pretending they are all flying in an aeroplane.

In all of these activities we see examples of 'hybrid' play, where play is initiated in the physical world while simultaneously utilizing video and audio communications technologies (Cowan 2021). In the digital realm, VoIP platforms enabled a much deeper cooperative play experience, particularly within immersive games like *Minecraft* and *Roblox*. As distinguished from single-player games and games dependent on structured progress and narratives, games like Minecraft and Roblox are essentially virtual playgrounds. Considered 'sandbox games', players have infinite control over their virtual environments in terms of building and shaping their own worlds and gameplay.

The nature of sandbox games does not limit the use of human imagination. In engaging with this kind of play,

> the intangibility of children's imagination is not only laid over inert but compelling material, it is also delegated to machinic analogues. This process by no means replaces human imagination, as the critics of digital play might have it; it extends and augments it—rendering it poorer in some aspects but opening all sorts of new games and meta-games. (Giddings 2014:127)

Access to VoIP platforms has enabled sandbox games to become the perfect emergent spaces for combined play and socialization (Rospigliosi 2022: 2). Game rules and protocols can be negotiated and developed spontaneously, game objectives identified, and cooperative strategies can be debated and agreed upon in real-time. In games like Roblox and *Minecraft*, where players can build and create their own games and 'clubs', the theme of Covid was an immediately discernible feature of the virtual playground. Hospitals and anti-virus armies were created in response to the pandemic. Quests and missions designed to hide from Covid were plentiful and, interestingly, avatars wore masks and attire reflecting common anxieties about the pandemic.

In the context of pandemic play, these avatars (or online identities) have been used in a very simple and similar way to the age-old game of 'dress-ups'. Within our submissions, we documented masks on Barbie dolls and a real-life dress-up character, 'Captain Covid', alongside a cohort of digital figures wearing masks and Covid t-shirts in the virtual playground. The simultaneous curatorship of individual and group digital identities is a remarkable illustration of how children flipped the frameworks of traditional play and responded to the pandemic in a very powerful way.

Despite the confines of lockdowns, access to technology enabled children to continue to engage with their own traditional play culture, also allowing them to develop a sense of agency against the unknown and do so collectively—*with* their peers and beyond the boundaries of the family home and local streets. We would also argue that the use of VoIP platforms has fundamentally and permanently changed the play landscape for many children growing up in the pandemic, adding new dimensions of connectivity and opportunity that will still be in popular use after the pandemic has passed on.

Conclusion

Children's experiences of play in lockdown were influenced by a very broad range of variables including their age, where they lived, who they lived with, their access to play resources including digital equipment and the internet, their socio-economic situation, support from adults, and connection to friends. Rules were relaxed to support playfulness at home and in the streets and parks of local neighbourhoods.

Yet the critically important role of play in times of crisis was fully revealed in the warm, caring, mindful and supportive relationship between local playworkers and some of the most disadvantaged and traumatized children in the city—those who live in cramped flats in Melbourne's high-rise public housing towers. This is the true power of play.

Works Cited

BBC News. 2020. 'Coronavirus: The World in Lockdown in Graphs and Charts', https://www.bbc.com/news/world-52103747

Boaz, Judd. 2021. 'Melbourne Passes Buenos Aires' World Record for Time Spent in COVID-19 lockdown', *ABC News*, https://www.abc.net.au/news/2021-10-03/melbourne-longest-lockdown/100510710

Boseley, Matilda. 2020. '"A Form of Connection": Spoonville Craze Revives Community Spirit in Australia', *The Guardian*, https://www.theguardian.com/australia-news/2020/sep/02/a-form-of-connection-spoonville-craze-revives-community-spirit-in-australia

Brown, Stuart. 2010. *Play: How It Shapes the Brain, Opens the Imagination, and Invigorates the Soul* (New York: Avery Books)

Cohen, Esther, and Esther Bamberger. 2021. '"Stranger-Danger": Israeli Children Playing with the Concept of "Corona" and Its Impact during the COVID-19 Pandemic', *International Journal of Play*, 10, https://doi.org/10.1080/21594937.2021.2005398

Cowan, Kate. 2021. 'Play Apart Together: Digital Play During the Pandemic', https://play-observatory.com/blog/play-apart-together-digital-play-during-the-pandemic

Cowan, Kate, et al. 2021. 'Children's Digital Play during the COVID-19 Pandemic: insights from the Play Observatory', *Journal of e-Learning and Knowledge Society*, 17: 8-17 https://doi.org/10.20368/1971-8829/1135583

Dodd, Helen, and Tim Gill. 2020. 'Coronavirus: Just Letting Children Play Will Help Them, and their Parents, Cope', *The Conversation*, https://theconversation.com/coronavirus-just-letting-children-play-will-help-them-and-their-parents-cope-134480

Dodd, Henry. 2020. 'I Can't Believe I Am Going to Say This, but I Would Rather Be at School', *The New York Times*, 14 April, https://www.nytimes.com/2020/04/14/us/school-at-home-students-coronavirus.html

Dring, Christopher. 2020. 'What Is Happening with Video Game Sales during Coronavirus?' *GamesIndustry.biz*, https://www.gamesindustry.biz/what-is-happening-with-video-game-sales-during-coronavirus

Fernando, Gavin. 2020. 'Is Melbourne's Coronavirus Lockdown Really the Longest in the World? Here's How Other Countries Stack Up', *SBS News*, https://www.sbs.com.au/news/is-melbourne-s-coronavirus-lockdown-really-the-longest-in-the-world-here-s-how-other-countries-stack-up

Foster, Sophie. 2020. 'Coronavirus: Kids Playing, Riding Bicycles Spark Building Disputes', *realestate.com.au*, 28 April, https://www.realestate.com.au/news/coronavirus-kids-playing-riding-bicycles-spark-building-disputes/

Giddings, Seth. 2014. *Gameworlds: Virtual Media and Children's Everyday Play* (New York: Bloomsbury Academic), https://doi.org/10.5040/9781501300233

Glass, Deborah. 2020. 'Investigation into the Detention and Treatment of Public Housing Residents Arising from a COVID-19 "Hard Lockdown" in July 2020' (Victorian Ombudsman), https://www.ombudsman.vic.gov.au/our-impact/investigation-reports/investigation-into-the-detention-and-treatment-of-public-housing-residents-arising-from-a-covid-19-hard-lockdown-in-july-2020/

Graber, Kelsey, et al. 2020. 'A Rapid Review of the Impact of Quarantine and Restricted Environments on Children's Play and Health Outcomes', *PsyArXiv Preprints*, https://doi.org/10.31234/osf.io/p6qxt

Gray, Peter. 2020. 'How Children Coped in the First Months of the Pandemic Lockdown: Free Time, Play, Family Togetherness, and Helping Out at Home', *American Journal of Play*, 13, https://www.museumofplay.org/journalofplay/issues/volume-13-number-1/

Holt, Louise, and Lesley Murray. 2022. 'Children and Covid-19 in the UK', *Children's Geographies*, 20: 487-94, https://doi.org/10.1080/14733285.2021.1921699

International Play Association. 2017. 'Access to Play in Crisis Toolkit', *Play: Rights and Practice: A Toolkit for Staff, Managers and Policy Makers*, https://ipaworld.org/resources/

Kardefelt Winther, Daniel and Jasmina Byrne. 2020. 'Rethinking Screen-time in the Time of COVID-19', UNICEF, 7 April, https://www.unicef.org/globalinsight/stories/rethinking-screen-time-time-covid-19

Lester, Stuart, and Wendy Russell. 2010. 'Children's Right to Play: An Examination of the Importance of Play in the Lives of Children Worldwide' (International Play Association), https://ipaworld.org/ipa-working-paper-on-childs-right-to-play/

McKinty, Judy. 2020. 'Pandemic Play Project: Project Background', https://pandemicplayproject.com/About/

McKinty, Judy and Ruth Hazleton. 2022. 'The Pandemic Play Project— Documenting Kids' Culture during COVID-19', *International Journal of Play*, 11: 12-33, https://doi.org/10.1080/21594937.2022.2042940

Mannix, Liam. 2020. 'The World's Longest COVID-19 Lockdowns: How Victoria Compares', *The Age*, https://www.theage.com.au/national/victoria/

the-world-s-longest-covid-19-lockdowns-how-victoria-compares-20200907-p55t7q.html

Mavoa, Jane and Marcus Carter. 2020. 'Child's play in the time of COVID: Screen games are still "real" play', *The Conversation*, https://theconversation.com/childs-play-in-the-time-of-covid-screen-games-are-still-real-play-145382

Miller, Robyn Monro. 2022. *Children, Play and Crisis: A Guide for Parents and Carers* (Play Australia), https://www.playaustralia.org.au/category/resource-type/pdf-document-download

Opie, Iona, and Peter Opie. 1977. *The Lore and Language of Schoolchildren* (London: Granada)

Oxner, Reese. 2020. 'Oxford's Defining Words of 2020: "Blursday", "Systemic Racism" and yes, "Pandemic"', National Public Radio (NPR), https://www.npr.org/2020/11/23/938187229/oxfords-defining-words-of-2020-blursday-systemic-racism-and-yes-pandemic

Pandemic Play Project. 2020. 'About/The Project/Who We Are', https://pandemicplayproject.com/About/

Play Wales. 2014. *What Is Play and Why Is it Important?* https://www.playwales.org.uk/eng/publications/informationsheets

Rospigliosi, Pericles 'asher'. 2022. 'Metaverse or Simulacra? Roblox, Minecraft, Meta and the Turn to Virtual Reality for Education, Socialisation and Work', *Interactive Learning Environments*, 30: 1-3, https://doi.org/10.1080/10494820.2022.2022899

Royal Children's Hospital Melbourne, 2020. *RCH National Child Health Poll 18. Covid-19 Pandemic: Effects on the Lives of Australian Children and Families* (Melbourne: Royal Children's Hospital), https://www.rchpoll.org.au/polls/covid-19-pandemic-effects-on-the-lives-of-australian-children-and-families/

Save the Children. 2020. 'Life During Coronavirus: Missing School, Missing Friends', https://www.savethechildren.net/blog/life-during-coronavirus-missing-school-missing-friends

Save the Children. 2021a. 'Surviving and Enjoying Lockdown with Kids', https://www.savethechildren.org.au/our-stories/surviving-and-enjoying-lockdown-with-kids

Save the Children. 2021b. 'COVID-19: Children Globally Struggling after Lockdowns Averaging Six Months', https://www.savethechildren.org.au/media/media-releases/children-globally-struggling-after-lockddown

SBS News. 2020. 'Melburnians Spend First Night under Strict Curfew as Major Changes to Workplace Restrictions Expected', https://www.sbs.com.au/news/article/melburnians-spend-first-night-under-strict-curfew-as-major-changes-to-workplace-restrictions-expected/6ga1nnd57

Seal, Graham. 1998. *The Hidden Culture: Folklore in Australian Society* (Perth: Black Swan Press)

Shooter, Mike. 2015. *Building Resilience: The Importance of Playing* (Play Wales), https://www.playwales.org.uk/eng/publications/informationsheets

Sleight, Simon. 2013. *Young People and the Shaping of Public Space in Melbourne, 1870-1914* (Surrey: Ashgate)

Smith, Melody, et al. 2022. 'Children's Perceptions of their Neighbourhoods during COVID-19 Lockdown in Aotearoa New Zealand', *Children's Geographies*, https://doi.org/10.1080/14733285.2022.2026887

Stoecklin, Daniel, and others. 2021. 'Lockdown and Children's Well-Being: Experiences of Children in Switzerland, Canada and Estonia', *Childhood Vulnerability*, 3: 41–59, https://doi.org/10.1007/s41255-021-00015-2

Tucci, Joe, Janise Mitchell, and Lauren Thomas. 2020. *A Lasting Legacy: The Impact of COVID-19 on Children and Parents* (Melbourne: Australian Childhood Foundation), https://www.childhood.org.au/covid-impact-welfare-children-parents/

Walmsley, Angela. 2014. 'Backtalk: Unplug the kids' *The Phi Delta Kappan*, 95(6): 80, https://www.jstor.org/stable/24374523

17. Techno-Mischief: Negotiating Exaggeration Online in Quarantine[1]

Anna Beresin

Zoom playdates became a thing during lockdown, along with Zoom sleepovers, Zoom show and tell, and Zoom birthday parties. In Philadelphia, Pennsylvania, this author studied children's folklore during 2020-2021, opening a window into online toy play, online games and the complexity of arranging and sustaining children's relationships (see also Beresin, Chapter 8 in this volume). How did children's culture emerge in the tightly designed adult commercial world online? How do children make their online world within online worlds more flexible, given the limitations of quarantine? This chapter suggests that children's folklore, its songs, jokes, games and even physical play forms, is alive and well during online Zoom playdates, and that hybrid online play has served as a container for children's mischief during the pandemic. Focusing on a video transcript, we will micro-analyze the text in three different ways: as folklore through a cultural lens, as negotiation through a sociolinguistic lens and as exaggeration through the lens of mischief.

Two families shared this forty-eight-minute Zoom playdate, recorded with familial permission by one of the parents in December 2020. Participants include one mother and her three children, an eleven-year-old boy, his techno-savvy seven-year-old brother, and their

---

[1] Thank you to the families who generously shared this video. Whenever I hear the *Iron Man* theme song, I will think of you.

  https://doi.org/10.11647/OBP.0326.17

four-year-old, kitten-loving sister. Their playdate is with two brothers across the street, ages eleven and seven years, and their kittens from the same litter. Schools were completely online at this point due to the pandemic. In a prior interview, also on Zoom, one of the mothers described the challenges of doing anything social during the pandemic and how the idea of a pod was unappealing given the age range of her children. Fortunately,

> In March, there is one family, one family that we almost consider relatives, we have known them for eleven years and have raised our children together, and they ended up moving across the street from us. The family 'like family'? They have two boys the same age as our two boys. My kids are very close to kids on the block and some of them they've known their whole lives. We've only lived here for three years and some of them just happen to live here now, and there's friends that live here now and new friends that live here now. So, there's definitely a block scene going on. We have a few other friends that the kids would reach out to regularly before and we can't really do it now because they've got their block things going on too, and they have different rules than ours and again, it's like negotiating so many rules all the time.
>
> The boys, they do more video time but they do all these online games where they interact with their friends. *Fortnite* (the online game) is really big, especially with the more middle school age group, but my younger son plays it because it's social, and he gets to play with his friends *Minecraft*, where they make all these worlds. So, like, reaching out, connecting through that way, sometimes the little boys will play LEGOs while on Zoom, or on Facetime. So, they set up their Facetime screens and make like LEGO creatures together.

Covid is not the subject of this video, although the children express amazement at the amount of time they have in this situation and are playing within its framework. Covid serves as the container for their socialization on Zoom, just as Zoom has served as the container for their parents' work during the pandemic. The method of choice comes from video microanalysis, a qualitative methodology rooted in both conversation analysis and animal study (Beresin 2010; Birdwhistell 1970;

Burghardt 2005; Meyerhoff 2006; Streeck 2008; Tannen 2007). When significant, gestures are described and attention paid to prominent motifs within frames. It can be said that all cultural and psychological study comes down to the analysis of motifs, those small units of language and art linked at their roots to the word 'motive' and 'motivation'.

The entire transcript that follows is intentionally included in order to preserve the subtleties of the play forms and the humour in the interaction. Segmented into two acts and several scenes, each subset has a definitive starting and ending point, although the motifs and themes are repeated throughout the session. Sociologist Erving Goffman described social analysis as dramaturgy and his colleague, anthropologist Ray Birdwhistell, utilized the term 'scene' in his microstudies of videotaped gestures. In this case, Act 1 includes moments of introduction, shifting power dynamics, displays of technology and purchasing power, along with attempts at joking and rapping by both young humans and a virtual AI assistant. Act 2 has even more sophisticated technology use, with looping references to earlier parts of Act 1. The content contains classic echoes of children's folklore: taboo speech, potty humour, teasing and also inventiveness, accomplishment and cooperation.

The Transcript Key

In addition to acts and scenes being marked in **bold** for easier reading, so too are any references to children's folklore genres that have appeared in the canon by Iona and Peter Opie or Brian Sutton-Smith, from fartlore to jokes to songs (Opie and Opie 1959; Sutton-Smith 1981, 1997). This is intended to show connection to the childlore of previous generations. Secondly, on the left side are also codes made after the transcript was written, each utterance marked. In order to address changing culture, digital or technical toy displays are marked by **TD**. **NTD** signals non-technical or non-digital playthings, like the showing off of cats or food. Thirdly, following this author's previous study of exaggeration at play based on the animal play literature, moments of exaggeration (**E**) and negotiation (**N**) were also labelled (Beresin 2018; Burghardt 2005). Animal play research is an underutilized tool in the study of human play although there is a growing interest in similarities across species in the study of emotion, conflict and conflict resolution (de Waal 2009,

2019). Picture the transcript with layers of code like onion skins, or a clickable portrait made three dimensional in print. Instead, we embolden the font and add code, sometimes several in one utterance. We have looping phrases of culture, social negotiation and some mischievous exaggeration.

The transcript is best read aloud, complete with sound effects.

Act 1 Scene 1

00.00

    Noises. No images.

    (*Mom sets up Zoom in two rooms.*)

06:27

    Older boy:

E N   Hey Mom. Mom mom mom. Can you hear meee?

    (**Spoken in singsong**)

    Repeats Momomomomomom. Momomomom.

E N   Momomom, can you hear meeeee?

    (*Spoken in exaggerated monotone*)

    (*Little sister sits next to him.*)

    (*Younger brother imitates his sound off screen*)

E   Little sister: MMMMMmmmmmmommom.

E   *Two brothers sing*: Mommmmomomom.

06:44

N   Mom says: Can you stop that? That's very irritating.

NTD   (*They each open small chip bags*)

TDEN   7-year-old sings: Where did *Iron Man* tell me to go?

E   11-year-old sings back: **In my butt crack, yeah, yeah, yo!**

    (*43 seconds of crunching chips and logging on*)

E   Older boy declares: Oh, so this is what playdates have come down to.

    (*They both giggle*)

N   Friend asks: Should I put the camera that way?

N   Sure.

TD	Pin my video and I pinned yours,
	so we really don't have to deal with my mom.
NTD	(*Crunches*)
TD	7-year-old Brother: **He's level 100 now.**
	I'm actually at 80. Only 80.
	(*They are talking about Pokémon*)
E	(*The 7-year-old goes behind his brother and lifts his shirt to show off his belly*)
	Other boy online: Guys we still have like a MONTH.
TD	11-year-old boy: I'm like at 79.
N	Brother: You're 78 or 79, last time I checked 79. I'm 80.
NE	Older Boy: (*wiggles head*) I'm 79.
	And actually, if I don't get to 100, I don't really care.
TDE	Younger boy: I promised little sister I'd get her Baby Brogu.
	I don't know why, but I'm challenging myself.
N	(*2.5 minutes of negotiating with Mom edited*)

Act 1 Scene 2

(*While bigger brother is off screen, 7-year-old take over the bouncy ball seat in front of the computer. There is side talk about **showing off their kittens***)

E	7-year-old sings and bounces: LeBron. . . LeBron.
	(*He references LeBron James the **basketball player***)
TD	You guys are muted.
NTDE	(*7-year-old smiles and takes off shirt*)
E	He states: It's 25 degrees outside. 25.
	And it feels like way below zero, pretty sure.
11:07	

(*Cat show and tell from the other screen*)

NTD	They were going to eat the LEGOs. We had to put them in the bathroom
N	Friends on screen: Hey can I screen share?
N	Brother asks: Why?
TD E	Someone sings: **Disabling**. . .
NTD	Little brother: I can't wait until it's 4:00!
	Little sister: Hi!
	Hi!
E	*She singsongs about her half-naked brother:* **He's a tough ma-an.**
	He's a tough ma-an.
NE	(*Other guys giggle on screen*) Are you a tough, are you a tough man?
	Are you a tough man?
E	He replies: If I can get my sister to the ground without using my hands, then yes.
	Are you a tough man, though?
N E	**My sister is punching m**e.
E	Oh, my brother is not a tough man.
NTD	This looks like you. [We can't see it]
12:32	
TD NE	(*7-year-old tentatively points an* **invisible gun** *at screen*)
	Wanna know something?
N	What?
N	He says: Why does Lexa and Oren in the *Fortnite*, in *Fortnite* have the **same symbol**?
	Alexa has it on her shoulder and Oren has it on his chest?
N	Other child on screen answers: Cause they're brother and sister!
	Cause they're brother and sister.
N	He says: Yeah. But they're robots.
N	They're not robots, they're animes. Anime.
NTDE	(*7-year-old* **bounces on bouncy ball**)

Act 1 Scene 3

13.00

> (*Big brother comes into the screen*)

N	D?
N	Yeah,
TD	You know that car that I really wanna buy? That Z has?
N	Yeah?
TD	I thought it was like 400 dollars. Turns out it's only 150 dollars.
	I'm gonna buy it, as soon as my mom lets me.
N	Sister: You're gonna buy a real car?
TD	No, an **RC car** [remote-control car].
N	Brother: Don't do *Iron Man*.
TD	Friend: I'm gonna share my screen.
N	What was that?
N	Can I share my screen?
NE	No. (*Singsong*)
N	Why not?
TDE	(*In background* 'Yo, *Iron Man* coming through')
TDE	They chorus: 'Welcome to Altec'.
TD	11-year-old: So, well anyways, I'm going to buy this because. . .
N	Wait, what's that powering on?
TD	'Welcome to Altec'.
N	What?
TD	It's a speaker.
N	Cool.
TD	Now, you're talking through this.
TD	He counters: Hey Echo. Hey Alexa!
TD E	Sibling shouts: Echo!
TD	Order the iPhone, Amazon!
TDE	11-year-old continues: Hey Siri, **Tell me a joke**.
E N	Sibling calls: Siri, **What's a name for pee?**

TD	11-year-old: Hey O. Listen to my Alexa
14:33	
ETDN	Siri, tell me a joke
	(*Siri uses a British accent*)
E	My friend was changing a tyre, dropped a tyre on his foot.
	Now he needs a **tow**
	(*Nobody laughs*)
	(*Child reads joke aloud*)
E	My friend was changing a tyre dropped a tyre on his foot.
	Now he needs a **toe.** Ha ha. (*Little sister giggles*)
TD	Friend on screen says aloud: He has 4 controller, back
	pedals. Can you see this?
N	I think you can. What are those? What ARE those?
TD	PS 4 back controllers
N	OHHH cool.
15:19	
TD	They go on the back and they're back buttons.
N	7-year-old asks: How many people are on this meeting?
N	Three. Three.

Act 1 Scene 4

TDNE	(*Five minutes edited of starting and stopping of beat boxing to a metronome app: Thwa, Thwa, Thwa, Thwa, 123, 123, 1234, 1234, Bumpadeepee, Bumpadeepee, Bphf,* **Bphf, Bphf, Bphf**)
18:20	
N	Hey! Your mom is on this meeting, too.
N	(*Softly*) I know.
E N	**Fart, Fart, Fart, Fart** (*Sung in the background*)
	(*Brother warns quietly 'not to change my name'*)
E NTD	My boyfriend yeah. 'Philly State of Mind'.

TD	7-year-old: I wish we were recording that. Oh yeah! We are.
NTD	(*20:43 to 25:53 The two older ones attempt to rap, mumbling lyrics read online. There is an attempt at singing explicit lyrics by Scholito and Og Afroman*)
E	(*Younger brother parodies*) **I need to eat your body. I need to eat your face.**
	Need to eat your wiener so I get another face.
25:53	
N	11-year-old: Hey, both of you, quiet, it's my turn. It's my turn.
NTD	Friend continues: Yeah, yeah, I'm Philly Strong.
NE	11-year-old: Stop singing this *Hamilton* song!
N	It's not a *Hamilton* song!
N	I don't care, it's as long as a *Hamilton* song! Give me a turn; give me a turn.
E	I'll show you real music.
E	This one's explicit so. . . (*he stops*)
NTD	(*Brother inaudbily sings in background*)
TDE	11-year-old: Hey Siri, sing me a rap.
N	Friend: Hey, listen, listen to this.
N TD E	11-year-old: Hey Siri, Siri. Sing me a rap.
TD E	Siri offers (*in a British accent*):
	One, two, three and to the four.
	Siri's to the mic to answer what you ask for.
	Ready to make an entrance, so here's my claim,
	This assistant wrote the rules to the game.
	Drop me a 'Hey Siri' and I'll do my best not to stumble.
	Assisting you is my thing, you, you know I won't grumble.
	It's nothing but a Siri thing, baby.
	Maps, tunes and weather coming daily.
	Helping you is just why they made me.
	Hey, I guess that all rhymed. . .vaguely.

	Helping you is why they made me
	I guess that all rhymed, vaguely.
28:06	
EN	Siri. Sing me a good rap.
TDE	Okay, if you insist:
	I could while away the hours
	Conversing with the flowers
NTD	(*Little sister comes on another screen*) Hey, can you hear me?
E NTD TD	(*7-year-old brother is tossing a large soft Pikachu* Pokémon *in circles*)
TDE	Waltzing with the rain
	And my head I would be scratching
	While my thoughts were busy hatching
	If I only had a. . .
N E	(*45 seconds edited of mom disapproving of a* **'tushy'** **shaking** *display and*
TD	*curiosity expressed about lighting for 'gamers'*)

Act 2 Scene 1

29:16	
NTDE	(*More* **Kitten Show and Tell, pretend farting, sibling rivalry**)
	(*The friend gestures* **rubbing a nose booger on finger** *to keep little brother away*)
E	'It's Instant Child Away'.
35:59	
N	Great.
	(*Younger brother smiles*)
TD	I, I assigned you to a breakout room.
N	I can't see it. Mute him.
N	Big brother: Hey. Don't mute me again. I don't like that.

N	Do you really wanna find out what the consequences of muting me are?
	(*He replies in singsong*)
E N	Noooh, but I do wanna figure out what your strategy is.
N E	I have **spies** on the inside.
	(*Giggles*)
N	Brother's friend: Do not do that again.
N	I'm telling mom.
E	You're gonna get in trouble!
TD	Hey, can you make the chat not private anymore?
N	I don't know how to do that.
N	Oh man. I wanna share my screen.

Act 2 Scene 2

37: 28

E	(*7-year-old smiles. Mouthing the letters **P O O P**. Giggles*)
N	I'll try.
TD N	7-year-old: I'm gonna share my screen.
N	Wait. What?
E N	Why is your name Poop?
	(*Giggles*)
E N	Who knows why?
N	Did you rename him?
	(*Giggles*)
N	**Don't tell him.**
	How do you rename people?
E N	Rename me the **Butt Crack**.
	(*Giggles*)
N	Okay
	(*Giggles*)
E	(*Whispers*) When my Nanny goes on Zoom, she will be renamed the Butt Crack.

	(*They giggle*)
N	How do you change names?
TD	**I'm changing your name right now**.
N	How do you change your name?
TD	If you go to- there's going to be two people and there's going to be a three there.
E	You gotta click on that to rename yourself.
E N	How do you **spell b-u-tt**? How do you spell butt?
N	I wanna rename.
N	I don't know how to rename you.
N	Never mind I got it.
NTD	(*5 minutes edited of cookie display, Mom inviting Lego play as an alternative activity, and more peer instruction about*
TD E	*renaming and the spelling of poop-related names. Mom is asked for spelling advice and when they misspell on purpose, she*
E NTD	*retorts, 'Oh, you pesky boys'.*
	This is followed by wrestling on screen)
45:55	

Act 2 Scene 3

N E	Mom: You can close the **Poop** screen if you want. (*She giggles*)
N	What are you trying to do?
TD	He's trying to make me co-host
E	Mom. Gosh. You're like an expert on Zoom! (*7-year-old grins*)
	You know more than Nana! (*He claps above his head in victory*)
E TD N	Poop is co-host, can you make US co-host?
	Yeah, you have to make Cindy a co-host, not Poop.
	(*He smiles and concentrates*)
E	His older friend offers: Hey, you are a genius on this.

E TD	(*He laughs*) I sure am. I do it every day.
N	The two friends: No, no, no, no, stop, stop it stop
	(*He pushes the younger one off*)
N	Can you get your big brother?
TD E	**Muted! Muted!**
TD	Everybody see my screen.
	(*It has the Mom's work up, an encyclopaedia entry in her field for her students*)
N	Yes.
	Friend's big brother: I can see your screen.
N	Hey, can you get your brother?
N	No
E	He's mad at me for **farting in his face**.
	(*Giggles*)
TD E	(***He sings Iron Man theme***)
N	Just yell, yell his name
N	Can you just yell, Yo, come here?
NTDE	(*Mom offers LEGOs again*)
N	Remember I couldn't find 'em?
	(*He stays at computer*)
TD	I'm going to do a different screen, okay.
NTDE	(*Friend's **brother hits him gently in head with stuffed bear or dog***)
N	7-year-old: Ready?
47:23	
N TD E	Friend: Do you see my screen? Stop it!
	(*He shouts at brother who has hit him again with the stuffy*)
N E TD	('Philly State of Mind' *comes on screen*) (*Sex and drug references*)
N	I can see your screen.
N	Mom: Turn down your volume so dad doesn't hear your screaming.
	Yes.
TDE	(*Screen is now PS4 controller back paddles*)

(*Items on screen range from $19.99 to $139.99*)

N	Hey, Mom Can you get the older brother?
N	Mom, Yeah.
N	What are you drawing?
TD	(*7-year-old is doing a line drawing on the computer*)
NE	A peanut?
E	(*He scribbles overlapping angular unrecognizable shapes, giggling.*
TD	I'm drawing something!
48:01	
END	

Folklore on Zoom

'Oh, so this is what playdates have come down to'. This playdate is different, yet strikingly familiar—songs, jokes, displays and more displays, body parts, toys and high-status items, not unlike this author's earlier studies of children's folklore on concrete playgrounds. There the teachers saw the playground as pandemonium, a waste of time (Beresin 2010, 2014, 2019) and here the parents saw this session as 'chaos'. How to make sense of this seemingly chaotic blend of cultural motifs and phrases?

In a sense, this online play date was a condensed playground event. The grotesquery of nose boogers or noxious touch and taboo rhymes can be found in every large collection of folk games from nineteenth-century Newell to twentieth-century Sutton-Smith (Newell 1883; Sutton-Smith 1981). The seemingly unique online pranks such as disabling or muting are really versions of Tag or Keep Away. Joel Schneir, in the book *Hybrid Play*, suggests that online play 'offers opportunities to observe a "playground" space as the site of hybridized social, gamic and digital literacies/realities', and Sara Grimes notes elsewhere that the politics and rhetorics associated with physical playgrounds can be also found online (Schneir 2020: 203; Grimes 2021). It is interesting that in this Zoom playdate there is no game per se and it looks like there is no sustained play, no established superhero enactment, no doll or world-building play, no ball games. There are three major folk play genres here—bodylore and its control (Young 1993), pop culture name dropping (Opie and Opie 1959) and technological display (Sutton-Smith 1986), a sort of collector's gallery of the exaggeration of culture.

Bodylore	Pop Culture	Tech Display
butt crack joke	*Iron Man*	disabling
naked belly showing	*Pokémon*	remote control car
tough man teasing	LeBron James	Altec
pee joke	*Fortnite*	Echo
fart sounds	Anime	Alexa joke
eat your body song	Beat boxing	Siri rap
tushy shaking	*'Philly State of Mind'*	renaming
booger play	*Hamilton*	muting
poop naming	LEGO	PS 4 controllers
rough and tumble	*Wizard of Oz*	

Whole treatises have been written about the cheekiness of fartlore (Blank 2018) and children often play a kind of Hide and Seek with parental figures when approaching taboo subjects. Mom is played with, 'Momomomomom', and teased indirectly, her presence acknowledged by the older boys even when not directly present. She joins in with the now classic parental line: 'You can close the Poop screen if you want'. Shira Chess calls our attention to the expansion and contraction of the body in relation to hybrid play forms: while online we have a wider access, the visual field contracts (Chess 2020). If we look at the overall transcript structurally, we see that the first and last scenes have the most parental presence, and the second and second-to-last scenes have direct body references. In several moments the focus is on the intersection of all three—bodylore, pop culture, and technological display—with online rapping about the body and an invitation extended for Siri, the virtual assistant, to have a turn.

Since the 1970s, folkloric and anthropological research shifted from genre or object study, whether that involved songs, narratives or material culture, to the study of cultural stylization as a performance narrative.

With the increasing availability of tape recorders and video cameras, the goal was not to merely address the geographic or historical framing of things but to capture interactions as samples of the larger culture and their repeated variations. To understand the complexity of this video on Zoom, we too shift from the cultural bits to the focus on the role of these bits in motion, a semi-staged performance of looping cultural motifs with the screen as curtain, a puppet theatre of techno toys in action. Tech display emerges as a form of folk dialogue in performance, an extension of a gestural language of exchange. Here toys and the skill to toy with technology have cultural capital, a form of wealth potential that crosses over between child cultures and adult cultures, particularly among middle-class children (Pugh 2009; Lareau 2003). The children juggle the many motifs of culture in a time of great pressure and limitation, all the while appearing to be doing nothing other than hanging out with technology (Ito 2020; Sutton-Smith 1986). Says the seven-year-old, 'I do it every day'.

As the tension builds, the older children mumble rap variants of 'Philly State of Mind', a remix of the sorrowful Scholito 2019 version, which echoes the cheerfully nostalgic 'ILL State of Mind' by Neeko and Deana Marie that sings of Philadelphia's charms, which in turn riffs off of Jay Z and Alicia Keys' iconic 'Empire State of Mind', both from 2009. They in turn are borrowing from Nas' 'N. Y. State of Mind' from 1994, which was a hip hop take on the bluesy Billy Joel hit 'New York State of Mind' from 1976. This looping of motifs and phrases contrasts with Siri's inability to rap well or joke well, offering status to the children who are proud of their possessions and their city. They are victorious in their skill compared to the brainless Siri as they toy with the technology, tolerating the AI like a friendly but clueless uncle.

The Sociolinguistics of Play

In Katie Salen's *The Ecology of Games*, Reed Stevens, Tom Satwicz and Laurie McCarthy advise us to pay attention to 'in-game, in-room, in-world' modes simultaneously to understand the complexity of online play (2008). If we were to do so purely on a sound level, we would hear:

Scene 1.1 begins with non-technical display and singsong teasing
Scene 1.2 begins with non-technical display and singsong teasing

Scene 1.3 begins with negotiation and technical display, adding
    AI voices
Scene 1.4 begins with tech infused beatboxing
Scene 2.1 introduces intentional muting
Scene 2.2 highlights renaming as mischief
Scene 2.3 concludes with praising, screaming and quiet
    distraction online

This exaggerated soundscape and increasing display of goods function as a power signal system, as games themselves can be described as models of power (Sutton-Smith 1981b). Picture the downward dog of the panting puppy at play; there is a lot of starting and playful offering going on. Exaggeration begins the video and appears in each new scene as a sound-filled attention grabber. Yet there are complex, indirect attention-seeking strategies here. Anthropologist Arjun Appadurai describes display as a form of gifting, of potential power exchange, and so the moments highlighted in this transcript of nontechnical display of cats and snacks (NTD) as well as the technical display of high-status technology like Siri (TD) are indirect future offerings (Appadurai 2013). I show this to you to show off my status and to invite you to join me or exchange with me. One can see interactions in all talk and play as a form of expansion and contraction of attention (Derber 1979; Tannen 1990, 1998, 2006), akin to the courtship dances of birds, a choreography of power and exchange (Burghardt 2005; Graham 1991; Horosko 2002). Like sound, the displays of technology serve as bait.

If we code all of the children's folklore goofiness as a form of cultural *exaggeration* at play and we reduce all of the non-technical display (NTD) and technical display (TD) as *negotiation* à la Appadurai, *then every utterance here by a human participant can be seen as negotiation, or exaggeration, or both* in the transcript. Utterances were coded as exaggerations if they were marked by humour via laughter, by tone via singsong, or by consistency with classic folklore genres of play as in rough and tumble or toy use. Utterances were coded as negotiations if marked by questions, implied questions or a series of back-and-forth dialogue around a specific topic. Some utterances were coded as *both*, as in 'Mom, mom, mom. Can you hear meee?' with its repetition of Mom and extended sound of 'meee' in question form. The rhetorical question of 'Are you a tough man?' deserves a label of both exaggeration and negotiation as it is offered in singsong by the four-year-old sister. Even Siri was involved in exaggerated negotiation, 'Siri. Sing me a good rap', although the creators of 'her' algorithm need lessons in hip hop rhythm. Some folklore genres embody this combination of exaggeration and negotiation: the set-up of a joke, the move and counter move of wrestling. Musical layering, whether through remixing, call-and-response singing or harmony itself all offer exaggeration and negotiation to varying degrees. What surprises this author is the ubiquity of both exaggeration and negotiation on Zoom given the parental ambivalence about screen time and looming parental presence nearby.

Slight conflict erupts in Act 2, Scene 1 and all types of exaggeration are reduced dramatically within this scene. What the transcript does not reveal is the power display of bullying by children, the mere primacy of exaggeration over negotiation, but instead presents a dance of indirect, negotiated expansion of status within play. As Jean Piaget called the turn-taking at play and games the root of democracy itself, the practice of exaggerated negotiation is hardly trivial (Piaget 1965). Different children at different moments conducted the interaction (Kendon 1990) and although much is displayed, very little is actually exchanged. The constant presence of negotiated display is not unique to Covid times, nor unique to online play, but it does reflect a level of playful engagement online that contradicts the stereotype of isolated online passivity in pre-pandemic times. The sociolinguistic study of the unfolding and signaling of social play may shed light on how we stay social as our lives remain hybrid. What elements stop play in its tracks? How can play be extended and deepened, given its long developmental history as an essential part of human culture and childhood?

Techno-Mischief

A classic strategy in children's folklore study is to follow the trail of individual acts of mischief, those culturally marked bits of sneakiness that subtly follow rules while subverting them. One of our young players singsongs, 'I want to know what your strategy is', as his brother counters that he is watching him for signs of trouble. 'I have spies on the inside'. The children toy with each other indirectly, and with mom, and with technology, and with their new life on Zoom, to figure out what their exaggerated strategies might be while attempting to negotiate the absurdity of being locked inside with the world in front of them on the screen. Note the small inserted label in the top right corner of the screenshot below. 'Oh, you pesky boys'.

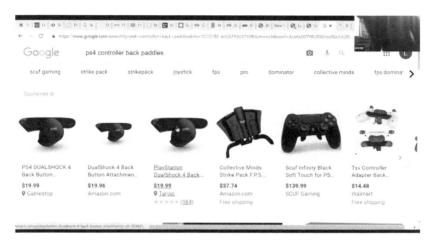

Figure 17.1 'Online Play Session', 2 March 2021

Like the munching kids here, drooling over toys and toying with each other,

> The trickster myth derives creative intelligence from appetite. It begins with a being whose main concern is getting fed and it ends with the same being grown mentally swift, adept at creating and unmasking deceit, proficient at hiding his tracks and at seeing through the devices used by others to hide theirs. Trickster starts out hungry, but before long he is master of the kind of creative deception that, according to a long tradition, is a prerequisite of art. (Hyde 1998: 17)

Whether found in traditional tales of coyote, raven or monkey, or in art pieces by the Dadaists or by Banksy, tricksters offer micro-exaggerations of the world they live in, while revealing our own patterns of culture (Nauman 1997). The role of the trickster also offers hybrid victory in the face of loss (Levell 2021; Sutton-Smith 1997). Consider the constraints the children are working under—lack of privacy, lack of movement opportunity, lack of face-to-face encounter and the powerlessness felt by all during the pandemic. One would expect increased trickery in such times although mostly what has been documented has been increased mental health suffering, suggesting that children need more opportunities for complex power reversal in pandemic times. It is no accident that younger ones played tricks on the older ones here, reversing the hierarchy.

Mischief is kept in check by our relationships with each other, and it is the wise parent or innovative school that makes space for exaggeration, particularly during adversity. Although Nicola Levell was writing about art and politics, Levell's words apply here as well, 'Rather than perceiving mischief as a deviant and even harmful mode of behaviour [...] it is embraced as a means of empowerment to trouble, tease and tickle, and open up a space for engagement where new possibilities and understandings can unfold' (Levell 2021: 13).

The trickster embodies the ludic form through exaggeration in order to enliven interaction. Yet such things are not typically valued. One early reader of this chapter suggested removing the 'naughty bits'. Besides the naughty bits being the most entertaining ones, the transcript shows there is more here than simple fun or ambiguity in such mischief (Sharp and Thomas 2019; Sutton-Smith 1997). As my own trickster teacher Brian Sutton-Smith wrote, 'The true trickster is so frivolous he can invert frivolity' (1997: 211).

Like the view of muddy water under a microscope, we see through microanalysis that the transcript pulses with life, a welcome image during a deadening pandemic. Some would say this Zoom playdate does not speak well of our larger culture but it does speak well of play, as the children show off hacking as a life skill during the pandemic. They remind us that hybrid play is more than the overlapping of virtual reality and real life. Children's folklore, the expressive cultures of childhood, more than a catalogue of historical references or shifting game genres. Our social worlds are now significantly online and the hybridity of children's techno-mischief reveals techno-play at the intersection of pop culture, bodylore, power struggle, economics and the pandemic frame. Play emerges as offered or sustained cultural exaggeration and fundamentally social, even when no obvious game is being played and the players are quarantined in separate buildings.

Perhaps the greatest challenge is the unknown stress of such speed in this condensed playground event and the bombardment of so many images and sound bites on young minds. Shuman Basar, Douglas Coupland and Hans Ulrich Obrist, authors of *The Extreme Self*, caution that 'we're not built for so much change so quickly. Technology has outrun our ability to absorb it' (2021: 59). Given the power differential, this may be particularly true for children. Ideally, young people would have as much time to digest as to consume, and they deserve more credit than they get for their attempts to play at such speeds online.

It would be easy to point out how the many corporations listed in this transcript are taking advantage of young potential consumers stuck inside. Not only are wallets tested but there is a training ground here of brand name loyalty and the gathering of data at the children's fingertips (Mäyrä 2020; Zuboff 2019). Yet, the children are not passive consumers of culture here. *Iron Man* knows about butt cracks. The computer has a poop screen. Siri is terrible at rapping. It's only fair, you may be muted.

Works Cited

Appadurai, Arjun. 2013. *The Social Life of Things: Commodities in Cultural Perspective* (Cambridge: Cambridge University Press)

Basar, Shuman, Douglas Coupland, and Hans Ulrich Obrist. 2021. *The Extreme Self* (Walter and Franz König)

Beresin, Anna R. 2010. *Recess Battles: Playing, Fighting, and Storytelling* (Jackson, MS: University of Mississippi Press)

——. 2018. 'Play Signals, Play Moves: A Gorilla Critique of Play Theory', *International Journal of Play*, 7: 322-37, https://doi.org/10.1080/21594937.20 18.1532681

——. 2019. *The Character of Play* (Washington, DC: Council for Spiritual and Ethical Education)

Birdwhistell, Ray. 1970. *Kinesics and Context: Essays on Body Motion Communication* (Philadelphia: University of Pennsylvania Press)

Blank, Trevor. 2010. 'Cheeky Behavior: The Meaning and Function of "Fartlore" in Childhood and Adolescence', *Children's Folklore Review*, 32: 61-85

Burghardt, Gordon. 2005. *The Genesis of Animal Play: Testing the Limits* (Cambridge, MA: MIT Press)

Chess, Shira. 2010. 'Casual Bodies Are Hybrid Bodies', in *Hybrid Play: Crossing Boundaries in Game Design, Player Identities and Play Spaces*, ed. by Adriana de Souza e Silva and Ragan Glover-Rijkse (London: Routledge), pp. 98-111

Derber, Charles. 1979. *The Pursuit of Attention: Power and Ego in Everyday Life* (Boston: G. K. Hall)

Goffman, Erving. 1959. *The Presentation of Self in Everyday Life* (Garden City, NY: Anchor Press)

Graham, Martha. 1991. *Blood Memory* (New York: Doubleday)

Grimes, Sara. 2021. *Digital Playgrounds: The Hidden Politics of Children's Online Play Spaces, Virtual Worlds, and Connected Games* (Toronto: University of Toronto Press)

Horosko, Marian. 2002. *Martha Graham: The Evolution of Her Dance Theory and Training* (Gainesville: University of Florida Press)

Hyde, Lewis. 1998. *Trickster Makes This World* (New York: Farrar, Straus and Giroux)

Ito, Mizuko. 2020. *Hanging Out, Messing Around, Geeking Out: Kids Living and Learning with New Media* (Cambridge, MA: MIT Press)

Kendon, Adam. 1990. *Conducting Interaction: Patterns of Behaviour in Focused Encounters* (Cambridge, Cambridge University Press)

Knapp, Mary and Herbert Knapp. 1976. *One Potato, Two Potato: The Folklore of American Children* (New York: Norton)

Lareau, Annette. 2003. *Unequal Childhoods: Class, Race, and Family Life* (Berkeley: University of California Press)

Levell, Nicola. 2021. *Mischief Making: Michael Nicoll Yahgulanaas, Art and the Seriousness of Play* (Vancouver: UBC Press)

Mäyrä, Frans. 2020. 'The Hybrid Agency of Hybrid Play', in *Hybrid Play: Crossing Boundaries in Game Design, Player Identities and Play Spaces*, ed. by Adriana de Souza e Silva and Ragan Glover-Rijkse (London: Routledge), pp. 81-97

Meyerhoff, Miriam. 2006. Introducing Sociolinguistics (London: Routledge)

Nauman, Francis M., and Beth Benn. 1996. *Making Mischief: Dada Invades New York* (New York: Whitney Museum of American Art)

Newell, William Wells. 1963 [1883]. *Games and Songs of American Children* (New York: Dover)

Opie, Iona, and Peter Opie. 1959. *The Lore and Language of Schoolchildren* (Oxford: Clarendon Press)

——. 1969. *Children's Games in Street and Playground* (Oxford: Oxford University Press)

Piaget, Jean. 1965. *The Moral Judgement of the Child* (New York: Macmillan)

Pugh, Alison. 2009. *Longing and Belonging: Parents, Children, and Consumer Culture* (Oakland: University of California Press)

Schneier, Joel. 2020. '"You Broke Minecraft": Hybrid Play and the Materialisation of Game Spaces through Mobile Minecraft', in *Hybrid Play: Crossing Boundaries in Game Design, Player Identities and Play Spaces*, ed. by Adriana de Souza e Silva and Ragan Glover-Rijkse (London: Routledge), pp. 199-216

Sharp, John, and David Thomas. 2019. *Fun, Taste & Games: An Aesthetic of the Idle, Unproductive, and Otherwise Playful* (Cambridge, MA: MIT Press)

de Souza e Silva, Adriana, and Ragan Glover-Rijkse. 2010. 'Introduction: Understanding Hybrid Play', in *Hybrid Play: Crossing Boundaries in Game Design, Player Identities and Play Spaces*, ed. by Adriana de Souza e Silva and Ragan Glover-Rijkse (Routledge, London), pp. 1-12

Stevens, Reed, Tom Satwicz, and Laurie McCarthy. 2008. 'In-Game, In-Room, In-World: Reconnecting Video Game Play to the Rest of Kids' Lives', in *The Ecology of Games: Connecting Youth, Games, and Learning*, ed. by Katie Salen (Cambridge, MA: MIT Press), pp. 41-66

Streeck, Jürgen. 2008. *Gesturecraft: The Manu-facture of Meaning* (Amsterdam: John Benjamins)

Sutton-Smith, Brian. 1981. *A History of Children's Play: The New Zealand Playground 1840-1950* (Philadelphia: University of Pennsylvania Press)

——. 1981b. 'Games as Models of Power', unpublished paper, conference on the Content of Culture in Honour of John M. Roberts, Claremont, California, 30 November-1 December

——. 1986. *Toys as Culture* (New York: Gardner Press)

——. 1997. *The Ambiguity of Play* (Cambridge, MA: Harvard University Press)

Tannen, Deborah. 1990. *You Just Don't Understand: Women and Men in Conversation* (New York: Morrow)

——. 1998. *The Argument Culture: Moving from Debate to Dialogue* (New York: Random House)

——. 2006. *You're Wearing That? Understanding Mothers and Daughters in Conversation* (New York: Random House)

——. 2007. *Talking Voices: Repetition, Dialogue, and Imagery in Conversational Discourse* (Cambridge: Cambridge University Press)

de Waal, Frans. 2009. *Age of Empathy: Nature's Lessons for a Kinder Society* (New York: Crown)

——. 2019. *Mama's Last Hug: Animal Emotions and What They Tell Us About Ourselves* (New York: Norton)

Young, Katherine. 1993. *Bodylore* (Nashville: University of Tennessee Press)

Zuboff, Shoshana. 2018. *The Age of Surveillance Capitalism* (London: Profile Books)

18. What's behind the Mask? Family, Fandoms and Playful Caring around Children's Masks during the Covid-19 Pandemic

Yinka Olusoga and Catherine Bannister

Introduction

Recognition of Covid-19 as an airborne respiratory virus introduced mask wearing suddenly, and potentially disruptively, into the everyday lives of many children and young people in the UK. Guidance, and later regulations, requiring mask wearing for older children in communal spaces, and the uptake in families of masks for younger children despite age-related exemptions, meant that many families, including our own, swiftly began developing habitual practices around mask wearing. This chapter goes 'behind the mask' as a physical, material object representative of the pandemic, and mask wearing as a focal pandemic practice, to explore mask-related practices within extended families. These practices began reframing masks for children and young people as playful personal items, seeking to make the strange familiar and even fun, to reassure children during a difficult period and to offer outlets for expressing children's identities and interests.

This chapter draws mainly on auto-ethnographic observations within our families based in the UK, where public mask wearing as a means of infection control was not a broad societal norm prior to the pandemic. It considers mask design, and the giving and receiving of masks within extended families, as both an extension and expression of caring, protective, intergenerational relationships. We explore children's own agency in mask design and how children drew on their own fandoms and digital/literary/media interests, such as the *Harry Potter*, *Star Wars* and *Marvel* franchises. We also consider how masks were even presented to children as a gift or treat, drawing on celebratory tradition. The chapter demonstrates how the underlying relationships within families behind these practices address narratives of children as vulnerable and lacking agency during the pandemic.

Before discussing the role(s) of face masks in our children's own lives, some scene setting is necessary to summarize the complexities of the UK's approach to children's face masks during the global Covid-19 pandemic. As the pandemic became a reality for the UK in early 2020, the government began introducing policy 'at a speed and scale only seen during wartime' (Cairney 2021: 90). Earliest measures prior to the UK's first national lockdown, announced on 23 March 2020, promoted personal behavioural changes: effective hand washing, social distancing when out and about, and self-isolation for anyone showing possible symptoms (Cairney 2021: 100), and these practices continued to be emphasized for much of the pandemic period.

One area of 'uncertainty' early in the pandemic, however, concerned the usefulness of face coverings to impede the spread of the virus (Panovska-Griffiths et al. 2021: 1), particularly for children. The UK government had at first indicated that face coverings were not required, 'despite prior reports in April 2020 at the height of the pandemic suggesting that they might be useful when used in a risk-based way' (Heald et al. 2021: 2). In June 2020 the World Health Organization (WHO) recommended the wearing of cloth, non-medical face coverings in 'enclosed spaces' (Heald et al. 2021: 2). That same month, in the UK, compulsory mask wearing was introduced on public transport, and in shops in July, alongside a slight reduction in social distancing to boost the retail economy (Heald et al. 20201: 2). In September, a campaign from the Department of Health and Social Care unveiled the slogan 'Hands, Face, Space', placing wearing a face covering on a par with hand washing or sanitizing and social distancing (cf. Warren and Lofstedt 2021).

The WHO recommendations mentioned above only applied, however, to those over twelve years old 'on the basis that younger children may have lower susceptibility and potentially lower transmissibility than adults' (Panovska-Griffiths et al. 2021: 3). In the UK, those belonging to groups defined as 'less able to wear face coverings' included children under eleven, with an accompanying recommendation from the UK Health Security Agency that children under three should not wear face coverings for health and safety reasons. When primary and secondary schools reopened to some year groups in June and July 2020, as the first national lockdown began to ease, guidance was provided restricting social mixing with class 'bubbles', 'distancing, hand hygiene, enhanced cleaning and isolation of symptomatic individuals' (Sundaram et al. 2021: 273). Mask wearing, however, was not instigated among primary school children, although in secondary schools 'the government permitted schools to encourage mask wearing in communal areas' (Panovska-Griffiths et al. 2021). Mask wearing in secondary schools persisted until the end of January 2022, by which time 'all mask requirements in schools had been dropped and masks were actively discouraged' (Williams et al. 2022).

The UK's approach towards mask wearing among school-aged children, alongside measures such as vaccination programmes for primary school-aged children, can be contrasted with that of other countries, such as Australia and Aotearoa New Zealand, say Williams et al. (2022). They write that 'whereas messages around facemasks in the UK, including in schools, have been confusing, other countries have provided a clear and consistent message around their value, for example the United States'. Instead, concerns were expressed around younger children's welfare if required to wear masks that could potentially affect facial recognition, communication and 'block signaling between teacher and learner' (Spitzer 2020).

Multiple discourses could also potentially be at play here, notably the construction of children as vulnerable victims of the pandemic, suffering from learning loss and social isolation, with concerns also expressed over very young children's social and psychological development in a mask-wearing world (Cabrera 2021; Twele, Thierry, and Mondloch 2022). Moreover, the wearing of medical-style or cloth face coverings in public to prevent the spread of respiratory viruses is not a habitual practice in the UK, unlike in some Asian countries such as Japan (Burgess and Horii 2012) and China, making the shift to a (temporary) 'new normal' of public mask wearing during the coronavirus pandemic a stark visual signifier and reminder of the pandemic situation. Feng et al. also call attention to the 'societal and cultural paradigms of mask usage', observing that the disparity 'between face mask use as a hygienic practice (i.e., in many Asian countries), or as something only people who are unwell do (i.e., in European and North American countries), has induced stigmatization and racial aggravations' (2020: 436).

Even putting mask wearing aside, we can recognize that types of head or face covering in the UK has become an issue fuelled by relatively recent moral panics (Cohen 2002) around perceived threats from both 'outside' and 'within' the dominant culture: fears of fundamentalism purportedly in the name of Islam (which further 'othered' Muslims in the UK) and of the 'hoodie' (a pejorative term directed at some young people, deriving from hooded sweatshirts that, with the hood raised, could somewhat conceal its wearer's identity). British Muslim women choosing to wear headscarves or to wear a veil can experience 'hostility' (Phoenix 2019: 1633) while the 'hoodie' was portrayed as 'an assumed indicator of moral decline among youth in contemporary Britain' (Hier et al. 2011: 260). Yet Belton argues that attire such as hooded tops and baseball caps are a response on the part of young people to our surveillance society, whereby 'groups (mainly of young people) develop a determination to minimise the extent they can be spied upon by often invisible observers' (2009: 133).

Ike et al. (2020: 994) point out that throughout history masks have held 'the power to communicate and signify a wide range of individual and culturally held beliefs'. If face covering was contentious before the pandemic, then during it mask wearing became further politicised via the concepts of communal responsibilities pitted against individual freedoms. During Covid-19, mask wearing became ideologically framed and, say Ike et al., writing from a United States perspective, 'divisive' along Democrat and Republican lines: 'In one sphere, the mask communicates a belief in medical science and a desire to protect one's neighbor from contagion. In the other sphere, the mask communicates oppression, government overreach, and a scepticism toward established scientific principles' (2020: 994).

Family and Digital Autoethnography in a Covid Frame

Adams and Manning describe autoethnography 'as a method that combines tenets and techniques of ethnography and autobiography' (2015: 351). Ellis, Adams, and Bochner state that, like ethnography and autobiography, 'autoethnography is both process and product', something the researcher 'does' and a written record that is the product of that activity (2011: 273). They argue that autoethnography is 'an approach to research and writing that seeks to describe and systematically analyse (graphy) personal experience (auto) in order to understand cultural experience (ethno)' (2011: 273). They claim it as an approach to the social sciences that 'attempts to disrupt the binary of science and art' (2011: 283), bringing together and storying the personal and the social, whilst maintaining a commitment to being rigorous and analytical, theoretical but also value-centred. Kennedy and Romo (2013), citing Gergen and Gergen (2000: 1028), position autoethnography as a 'historically, culturally, and personally situated' methodology. This makes it particularly apposite for research carried out in Covid times and about personal and familial responses to the pandemic as an unfolding historical and cultural event, experienced as a personal and situated phenomenon, the end of which was (and is) not clear and predictable. Adams and Manning (2015) propose four qualities of autoethnography that make it an approach particularly suited to conducting family research. Firstly, it facilitates the study of the everyday. Secondly, it also enables study of the unexpected and of how families respond to challenging circumstances (of which the Covid pandemic is clearly an example). Thirdly, autoethnography seeks to situate and contextualize the personal against existing bodies of research and knowledge, and fourthly, it seeks to do so in ways that are accessible to wider non-academic audiences.

Within autoethnographic research, different approaches exist. Interpretive-humanistic and critical ethnographies are the approaches that have informed our thinking in this case. Both focus on thick descriptions from the field which are unpacked and analyzed against the wider cultural contexts. Neither type emphasizes systematic collection, triangulation or coding of data but both can include observation, collection of artefacts (including images), conducting formal interviews and/or informal conversations, and employing provocations to elicit discussion of memory (Adams and Manning 2015). Writing about her work on transnational family ethnography in the digital age, Winarnita states that 'social media and electronic communication are critical parts of contemporary ethnographic methodologies' (2019: 105). She argues that digital technologies not only sustain and preserve family networks interrupted by distance, they are part of an intergenerational connecting social and cultural context in which self and family identities are created, shared and discussed. Winarnita's research is a pre-Covid transnational study, examining the experiences of female migrant workers in Australia and the role of digital technologies in maintaining their familial relationships in Indonesia. The circumstances of the pandemic make this work relevant to our study of family mask wearing practices during Covid in the UK when various degrees of lockdown restricted the physical gathering of families across households and saw a proliferation of use of digital platforms for familial communication.

Interpretive-humanistic autoethnographies, Adams and Manning argue, 'use personal experiences as a way to describe, and facilitate an understanding of, cultural expectations and experiences' (2015: 353). This has clear resonances with our focus here on how children and families navigated new, unfamiliar and fluctuating expectations of behaviour related to the wearing of face masks during the pandemic. Critical autoethnographies use personal experiences to help identify and challenge oppressive, harmful or unjust 'values, practices and experiences' and to uncover and bring attention to 'silent or suppressed experiences' normally absent from, or under-represented in, research and in popular discourse (Adams and Manning 2015: 353). This critical approach is present in Gingrich-Philbrook's rejection of any framing of autoethnography as a method or 'procedure' (2005: 298). He argues instead that autoethnography is better understood as an orientation towards inquiry—one that foregrounds a Foucauldian notion of 'subjugated knowledge' which can be understood as 'ways of knowing, lost arts, and records of encounters with power' (2005: 298) that run counter to dominant societal orthodoxies.

Children have been persistently framed as 'other' during the pandemic. They have been declared, on one hand, an outlier group, unlikely to suffer health consequences from the virus and, on the other hand, have been labelled 'potential "vectors" for the disease'

(Cortés-Morales et al. 2022). In relation to mask wearing, different and seemingly quite arbitrary age-related expectations have been placed on children in different parts of the world. The framing of children as a whole, and sub-groups such as neurodivergent and dis/abled children as vulnerable, has intersected with competing discourses that position the wearing of face masks both as their salvation and as a form of abuse that could cost their lives. What little research has been done into children's use of face masks has predominantly focused on assessing their efficacy in reducing virus transmission, strategies to support children (including specific groups of neurodivergent or dis/abledchildren) to tolerate mask wearing, and worries about the potential role of masks in causing or exacerbating social and language barriers that could impact negatively on development (Eberhart, Orthaber, and Kerbl 2021; Sivaraman, Virues-Ortega and Roeyers 2021; Pourret and Saillet 2020; Singh, Tan and Quinn 2021). Children's use of different technical types of masks has been researched, based on adult preferences and requirements of Covid measures (Halbur et al. 2021). However, there has been a lack of focus on children's mask choices, on masks as a canvas for children's identity expression and on family masking practices, and a lack of family autoethnographic work that could shed critical light on this subjugated knowledge from the perspectives of children and families. Our chapter seeks to address this gap.

As authors of this chapter, we might best be described as accidental ethnographers. Guy and Arthur (2020) found that for many women in academia, the already fuzzy boundaries between work life and home life became further blurred and impossible to maintain as Covid measures brought work roles and homeschooling roles into the home on an unprecedented scale. I (Yinka) sometimes felt that, rather than working from home, I was now living at work. Our shared academic focus is on childhood and play, mine from a historical perspective and Cath's from a folkloristic one. We are also both parents and proud members of neurodivergent families with interests in identity and fandoms. Separately, and from our own individual impulses (which we discuss below), each of us was informally collecting and analyzing our family practices around children and face masks from early in the pandemic. This became a shared research project in retrospect when, via an online and interactive series of video meetings, we began to share stories and images with each other and to revisit family texts and

WhatsApp messages. We began to make connections across our families and beyond to wider national and global contexts, relevant concepts from our respective academic disciplines and the emerging research in the new academic field of Covid Studies.[1] Nash, O'Malley and Patterson (2021) warn that in family autoethnography decisions have to be made in writing about focusing on families or on themes. They write that 'in one approach, the families got lost, while in the other, the themes got lost' (2021: 105). Ellis, Adams and Bochner remind us, 'when researchers write autoethnographies, they seek to produce aesthetic and evocative thick descriptions of personal and interpersonal experience' (2011: 277). They describe the use of 'layered accounts' where data and analysis intertwine, aided by the use of 'vignettes, reflexivity, multiple voices, and introspection' (2011: 278-79). Drawing this advice together, we have chosen to make use of vignettes. We have also chosen to disrupt the narrative flow, moving backwards and forwards in time as we present episodes of data, in order to explore themes that have emerged as we have collected, analyzed and reflected on our families' personal experiences and considered them within wider cultural experiences.

Pandemic Researchers/Pandemic Parents: Locating Our Researcher and Parent Selves in the Research

Yinka and the Historical Impulse

We all play roles within our family structures and one that I have claimed since childhood is that of family archivist. I record, salvage and file away traces of the present before it slips into the past. I like to think that this is a trait I inherited from my maternal grandparents who kept the top drawer of a huge mahogany chest filled with documents and artefacts from a shared family past, lined with pages from newspapers from bygone decades. Every now and then the drawer would be opened and an evening spent pulling out these items. A hand would reach in to extract the next treasure—binoculars, a pair of leather gloves for

---

1   Recognising that our experiences had the makings of a small research project, we sought ethical approval from the University of Sheffield Research Ethics Committee and consequent consent from child and adult family members before embarking on specific data gathering.

motorbike riding, diaries, letters, official records and the occasional photograph—and I would listen with rapt attention as the telling and re-telling of family stories unfolded, the comedy, tragedy, mundanity or triumph associated with each object explored.

In adulthood, I have my own drawers and boxes of similar keepsakes. However, the development of digital technology has meant that the largest proliferation of my instinctive urge to record family history is virtual rather than material. My iPhone tells me that I have over 27,000 photographs stored in the iCloud. On a single day I can take more photographs of my children than were taken of me in the entirety of my own childhood. I am drawn to take these photographs of my children's lives and activities as a mother. However, the images I see on my camera screen as I frame my shots are inevitably also viewed through my lenses as a historian of childhood and a researcher of children's play, past and present. I document my children's playful and creative activity, interested in playful processes and in the meanings (cognitive and emotional) they construct and deconstruct for themselves in their play. As well as people, I have a strong attachment to place and to recording the changing, often fleeting and ephemeral, streetscapes and landscapes that provide the context for my family's lives. In my wider family, the sharing of digital images via platforms such as WhatsApp and Facebook is also a regular occurrence. Therefore, as well as providing provocations for the telling and retelling of stories, like the physical family artefacts of my children, these images prompt an ongoing thread of family discourse, connecting images of play and childhood today with family childhoods past.

When the Covid-19 pandemic reached the UK, I viewed it from the start as a historical event. My maternal grandparents, both now deceased, had lived through the flu pandemic of 1918 but no trace of their experience remained that could have served as a reference point for making some sense of the developing crisis. Their childhood flu experiences were not part of family history, not represented in artefacts from the mahogany top drawer. I had so many questions to ask of them but no means to do so. So personally and professionally, I was determined that the first global pandemic of the digital age was something to be documented and archived to help us bear witness to it and enable future generations to understand. Many colleagues who specialize in empirical fieldwork with strangers or laboratory-based research were cut off from their research due to Covid lockdown. In contrast, I was embedded at home, the epicentre of childhood and play research in Covid times, watching it emerge before my eyes—a participant-researcher in an unfolding family autoethnography.

Cath and the Folkloristic Impulse

While the pandemic could be seen as a period of fragmentation, with social distancing measures separating us physically from work colleagues, friends, family members and even meaningful places and spaces, for me it was also a time of curious coalescence as my researcher identity merged with the roles I (Cath) inhabit in my home and my immediate family's life. As I embarked on new ways of enacting my responsibilities—home working while parenting and homeschooling my sons, then aged nine and fourteen—boundaries between what I was observing on the Play Observatory project concerning children's pandemic-related play and what I was observing my own children doing in their day-to-day lives began to blur. While gathering data online due to social distancing, I was simultaneously living 'in the field'. Furthermore, broader societal perceptions about children's well-being playing out in media and social discourses, and also being interrogated by our research team, were issues I was grappling with as a parent— issues such as popular concerns over children's increased time on digital devices, and notions that children were suffering due to social distancing measures and other preventative acts such as school and club closures. What could folklore studies as a discipline, I questioned, bring to these questions and to my own immediate situation?

Our project team had followed somewhat in the footsteps of two British folklorists, Iona and Peter Opie, in our devising of the Play Observatory survey, drawing on their now established but then groundbreaking approach of questionnaires designed for children, as we sought to centre children's voices. Consequently, our survey was as child-friendly as possible and, moreover, we took inspiration from the Opies' method of 'prompts' to encourage children to share in their own words their pandemic play experiences. We also attempted to devise a survey which allowed children to self-identify in terms of ethnicity and ability/disability (Olusoga, Bannister and Bishop 2021). These choices speak to folklore studies' potential to act as a mediator and platform for marginalized groups through its focus on, and valuing of, unofficial cultural practices shared among peers in 'folk groups' (Ben-Amos 1971: 12-13). As Fivecoate, Downs, and McGriff observe, folklorists 'acknowledge that the vernacular knowledge held by small groups of people is valued, valuable, and worthy of serious academic attention' (2021: 2).

Furthermore, folkloric expressions can be a lens through which to observe events and crises spawning, for example, beliefs and language, contemporary legends, narratives, jokes, parodies and memes, reflecting public anxieties, lived experiences, and social and political tensions (cf. Sebba-Elran 2021). Such events can also throw issues of marginalization and disadvantage into relief. With children perceived, as the above discussion has shown, as victims of the pandemic, creating an outlet to share their play practices through our Play Observatory allowed us to investigate those popular perceptions through valuing and respecting children's own experiences, including their emotional experiences.

Reflecting on my own positionality (Holmes 2020), I can see that my responses to my own children's play were informed by that same folkloristic sense of value. Both my children, made anonymous as Jeff and Frank in this chapter, are neurodivergent. Prior to the pandemic, I acknowledged their online digital play as important as a means for them to communicate with each other and friends in ways that my eldest particularly finds complex in face-to-face interactions with peers.

In regards to this chapter's specific topic of face masks and masking, folklore is concerned with material culture/material behaviour (Jones 1997) as an expression of communal identity and group traditions, with the making or crafting of artefacts, their design, practical applications and symbolic collective meanings falling within folklore's remit. Jones argues that folklore research has demonstrated that 'to understand tangible things we must investigate the circumstances that obtained before their existence, the processes by which they came into existence, and the consequences of their existence' (1997: 209).

As an example, Chomitzky (2020: 27) draws folkloric connections between Ukraine's 'national cultural history' of embroidered textiles which influenced cloth mask designs during the pandemic in both Ukraine and among the Canadian diaspora. She writes that 'through a subversion of their common purpose—to hide one's identity—masks have been used in the pandemic as an open/performative display of culture'. This perspective let me reflexively reframe my own family's mask-making practices and the choices my children made in mask design as (alongside playthings) markers of group identity and belonging (to a fandom, in my son's case, or to a *Minecraft*-located virtual world for both) and, for the mask makers, part of both family tradition and a broader tradition of making within the home (and transmission of such knowledge), which was adapted during pandemic times, in my own family's experiences, by those already occupying caregiving roles.

The Data: New Family Practices and Networks of Caring—Material and Practical

Mask Design and Identity: Fabric and Fandoms

Vignette 1: Accessorizing the Face Mask (Yinka)

It is Wednesday 3 June 2020, and I have escaped temporarily from my desk and laptop screen in the dining room and I am sitting reading on my bed. My nine-year-old son, Levi [name changed] comes in and announces that he has accessorized his new face mask. I look up to see him wearing his custom-made face mask that arrived in the post a few days earlier. Levi has always had a fascination for dressing up, particularly as characters who are the villains in the book, film and television franchises he enjoys, and he has developed an eclectic mix of interests and fandoms. These come together in his styling of his new face mask. The *Harry Potter* face mask, a white text and shield design on a black background, fits tightly over his face and nose, lying just beneath his eyes. On top of the material, above where his top lip resides beneath the fabric, he has placed a brown, stick-on moustache. He and his sister got these for Christmas and they make regular appearances in his costume designs and occasionally on random inanimate objects around the house. On Levi's finger is a large ring in the shape of a skull. He bought it on holiday the previous summer in the gothic seaside town of Whitby and liked it because it resembles the skull in the dark mark that Voldemort's followers have and that appears in the sky in *Harry Potter and the Goblet of*

Fire and in *Harry Potter and the Half Blood Prince*. On his head is a black turban, reminiscent of the one worn by Professor Quirrel in *Harry Potter and the Philosopher's Stone* to conceal the fact that Voldemort is possessing his body and his face has manifested itself on the back of Quirrel's head. Levi is very pleased with his assembled look. He has taken the *Harry Potter* mask as a starting point and 'villiainified' it with his accessories. He agrees to my taking a photograph, which I do, and says that I can share it with our family in our WhatsApp group. My sibling Ash [name changed], who made the face mask that inspired the look, replies with the tears of joy emoji.

It was via a message on 5 May 2020 that the prospect of home-made face masks was first mooted in the family WhatsApp group chat by one of my siblings, Ash. In the message, Ash self-identified as 'Guardian of the Sewing Machine', an ancient behemoth of apparatus passed down the family generations. If I (Yinka) am a family archivist, Ash is the family maker, who works in the creative industries, more recently becoming a potter and the designer and maker of last-minute costumes for school events. Attached was a photograph of them wearing their first prototype, a tight-fitting black cotton mask very much in keeping with their usual clothing aesthetic. The message stated that more material was being ordered and invited requests. I felt huge relief and much gratitude. During these early months of the pandemic I had seen a flood of information wash across my social media feeds on the topic of home-made cloth masks. Knowing that I am someone with absolutely no ability to sew, I had experimented with a version I had seen on Instagram, where a sock, a cotton filter and some hair ties could be improvised into a mask, but found it loose fitting and clearly not likely to be effective, especially for children, and I had felt a rising tide of panic. In a second WhatsApp message, Ash stated, 'I am intending to make some for everyone [...] Should get delivery of some groovy materials tomorrow [...] Place your orders folks'. Discussion followed and ideas for materials were suggested, enabling Ash to curate a selection of materials that applied to the adults in the family (for example, a deep purple slightly patterned material for our mother and me) and another selection that appealed to the children, drawing on some of their interests (such as planetary science) and fandoms. After delivery delays, ten days later another WhatsApp message arrived with a photograph of five materials and Ash asked the children in our extended family to make their selections for their first custom-made masks. I texted them my children's choices and Ash replied, 'I'll get sewing—quite looking forward to doing something different and a little less messy than pottery'. Looking at the image again in autumn of 2022, Levi remembers being 'excited' to get his first face mask. He chose the *Harry Potter* design for his first one and a *Star Wars* design for his second one. He observes, 'If I was choosing today I'd have the *Marvel* one'. We lament together that now in 2022 we do not wear the cloth masks any more. Although he chooses to mask indoors still, Levi now wears black disposable N95 masks and has never been moved to accessorize them.

Popular media franchises play a significant role in my (Cath's) immediate family's life as something all of us—me, my husband, and our sons—can enjoy together. The release of a new *Marvel* superhero movie routinely heralds a trip to the cinema or we pile onto the sofa to rewatch old favourites together at home. My sons boast a staggering collection of toy lightsabers and LEGO sets tied into both fictional worlds, while Frank loves dressing up as his favourite heroes (and villains), including Spiderman and Darth Vader. While the pandemic curtailed cinema trips, we were able to sustain our interests during social distancing, gifted as we were with increased family time together to catch up on films and spin-off series, and to play and create together around our shared media interests. The continuity of these habitual activities was comforting, as was, perhaps, the predictable but no less enjoyable narratives of good triumphing over evil these franchises provide.

When my mother-in-law, anonymized in this chapter as Brenda, began making masks for her grandchildren, she sought out fabric which reflected their own interests, including media interests, inviting (by various remote means) the children in our extended family to pick something they would be happy to wear. Jeff who turned fourteen in 2020, requested a simple blue and white mask made from cloth but reminiscent of the clinical, disposable masks worn by medical professionals, a familiar sight by that time in televised news reports on the pandemic. Frank, meanwhile, opted for home-made masks in *Star Wars* fabric, in his favourite colour of Jedi Blue. The masks seemed to me an extension of the artefacts, toys and other ephemera related to the franchise he already owned—soft toy plushies of 'baby Yoda' from *The Mandelorian* and the droid BB8, lightsabers galore, and a range of picture books and guides to the *Star Wars* universe.

Intergenerational Mask Gifting

Vignette 2: Masks and Celebration (Cath)

It's a warm summer's day during the global pandemic. For the first time in many months, some members of our wider family are together, playing catch-up on missed celebrations. It feels so familiar except some things are undeniably different. Even before we get together, there's Covid-19 tests to be taken, doors and windows are slung open, and hand gel is massaged into palms at every opportunity. We adults loiter in the garden and gingerly skirt round each other, eschewing the habitual hugs and kisses, mindful of space. The house has been decorated—this is a celebration, after all—and on the balcony a string of inscribed paper hearts documents missed family landmarks due to social distancing restrictions—birthdays and wedding anniversaries that would normally trigger family gatherings instead celebrated over the phone, through WhatsApp or on Zoom calls. What has not changed is how my children and their cousins crash back together as though never separated, laughing and chasing, checking each other's smartphones, or playing shop in the shed at the bottom of the garden.

It's a celebration for them too and, to mark it as such, Brenda, my mother-in-law, has created that traditional celebratory staple of children's party bags, each containing some sweets and a healthier snack of raisins, a balloon, some blowing bubbles, and a more recent salient material artefact, a cloth face covering. The notion of Covid-19 party bags tips me into surprised laughter at first but on reflection these paper bags encapsulate some of the discourse around children and Covid-19, subverting notions of children's isolation and mask wearing as a potentially detrimental practice for youth. The masks have been hand-made by Brenda, our family's self-appointed seamstress, in what could be interpreted as an act of care for her eight grandchildren. Furthermore, each mask reflects each child's personality, their taste or special/media interests, from dinosaurs to *Star Wars*. Placed in bags brimming with tiny treasures, these masks become reframed as treats and as playful, and my youngest niece is excited to try hers on immediately without adult prompting.

Figure 18.1 Child trying on a home-made fabric face covering, gifted in one of the party bags visible (2020)

Reflecting later on her mask-making and gift-giving, Brenda acknowledged the play potential of masks, even as our wider family had adopted mask wearing for all ages as a protective safety measure during Covid-19. Furthermore, she recognized the inclusive element in ensuring the children had masks of their own. 'They wanted to be part of it', she said, adding, 'I made them for them to play in.' She continued, 'The children didn't have to [wear masks] but I made them so they would be grown up and have their own masks. They liked them, actually. They wore them a lot'. She recalled how, when childminding her then four-year-old grandson (my nephew), he had placed masks that she had made on the cuddly toy customers to his 'café', mimicking adult behaviours in his play, but also protecting and caring for the toys.

Masks and Maker Identities

Sharing and critically reviewing our respective images and stories from our emergent family masking practices in 2020 from the vantage point of 2022 was a catalyst for another round of family conversations. We were interested in those who claimed and enacted the role of 'family maker' and the ways in which they had centred children, their interests and identities. For Ash, my (Yinka's) sibling who we encountered earlier in this chapter, making face masks for children and adults began as something aimed at family. However, from the impulse to share potentially life-saving information about mask construction, via social media, emerged a new accidental identity, 'community maker'.

Vignette 3: 'Family Maker' to 'Community Maker'
(Yinka)

It is early May 2020 and Ash has spent a great deal of time in recent weeks online, on sites such as Pinterest and Instagram, seeking sewing patterns for making cloth face masks in the home, including ones that will fit children. Having sourced a site that provides different adult- and child-sized patterns, and identified the technical types of material needed to construct safe and effective masks, Ash's attention turns to the look of the masks. Again Ash searches the internet this time for colours and patterns that will appeal aesthetically (for adults in the family) and that reference favourite fandoms (for children and adults alike!). In the meantime, Ash sets up the family sewing machine and sets about creating a first prototype.

On 5 May 2020, having finished this first mask, Ash tries it on, takes a selfie and shares it with the family via WhatsApp (as discussed earlier in this chapter). Ash then opens up Facebook and posts the link to the pattern alongside the same selfie with the caption 'Seeing as every other country on the planet is recommending the use of face masks in public [...] I thought I'd get out the sewing machine and see what I could knock up. This one has a pocket for a filter and a nose wire for a close fit. Pattern and instructions here if anyone's interested'. Within hours there are over thirty comments on the post, many of them from friends, asking if they can place orders for Ash to make masks for children and for adults. Requests are also made for masks in other fabric patterns, such as skulls, and Ash begins to realize the scale of demand that has inadvertently been uncovered. As well as being part of a creative circle of friends, via the neurodivergence in Ash's own family, their online social media community has come to include many similarly neurodivergent families whom Ash realizes they want to help. By 23 May 2020 Ash has completed making the first set of masks for family members and has also used the intervening period to devise a way of responding to this demand, and so Ash makes a new Facebook post (Figure 18.2).

Finally - first set of masks completed! These have 4 layers of material (2x100%cotton, 2x non-woven lining fabric), filter pocket, and wire pocket for shaping around the nose.

Some of you have expressed interest in them, so if you're still interested DM me. Tell me which material you want and what size (Small kids >7, Young kids 7-12, Teens/women, Men).

I'm NOT doing this as a commercial venture. It's not a side hustle. I'm making for my family but if anyone else wants that's fine. I'm not asking for money but I would ask that if you get one, you give a donation to   They're a small, local autism charity who are struggling during this crisis. They've saved my life plenty of times and I'd like to pay them back.

Figure 18.2 Ash's Facebook post offering to make bespoke face masks in exchange for donations to a charity, 2020

This marks the start of what will become something of a cottage industry for Ash in the summer months of 2020. Orders come in and requests for different materials. A downstairs room becomes the centre of operations. Against the auditory backdrop of the clattering of the sewing machine, cut-out materials ready for sewing, constructed masks ready for lacing with ties, and envelopes ready for stuffing and labelling are spread across available surfaces. Online, images of recipients wearing their custom-made masks are shared and the website of a small northern charity receives an unexpected, and much needed, stream of income.

Reflecting on this intense period of activity in autumn of 2022, Ash is clear that they did not initially set out to become a 'community maker'. However, as Ash reminiscences, the particularities of that summer of 2020 made them feel almost obliged to take on the role:

It was the beginning of the pandemic, nobody knew what the hell's going on. You couldn't just go to the shops and buy masks in the same way that you could six months later, so loads of people said, 'Ooh, can I have one? Can I have one?' [...] because it was the pandemic, because people (*pauses*) [...] it was a safety thing, and because they were friends [...] I didn't want to then charge them for it but I also, you know, it IS a lot of stuff, the material alone as well as the actual time to do it, so I was like urgh (*pulls a face*). So that's when I thought, right, ok, well, we'll do this as a fundraiser.

Ash explains to me (Yinka) how this community maker role therefore became a layered one, connecting aspects of self and parental identity and firmly locating this as an ethical as well as caring role.

So, I make the mask, so that will be my contribution to the THT [name of charity], and yours to some degree. You get a mask, they get some money, I get to feel good about a charity that I support. And it just exploded basically (*laughs*).

A sensitivity to neurodivergence and a commitment to working with and centring the child is also apparent as Ash explains the twin starting points for mask making:

Well, that was in terms of the physical construction of it, in terms of the safety, but it was, you know, they [children] need to actually be part of the process. It's always the case, particularly with children with ASD, actually with any kid, but you know particularly with children with ASD, you can't just spring stuff on them, they have to have buy-in and be part of the process, because if you just go to them and go (*claps hands*), 'Put this on! Boom!', you're not going to get anywhere.

This involvement of children takes them and their interests seriously. It also interrupts a dominant societal discourse of masks as utterly alien objects being imposed and tolerated (Halbur et al. 2021), placing them instead within the discourses and practices of fandom, play and self-expression. For one child, Ash's nine-year-old son Jakob, involvement was taken a step further as he became an eyewitness and then a participant in Ash's community making endeavours.

Vignette 4: Intergenerational Transmission of 'Family Maker' Identities (Yinka)

It is June 2020 and Jakob is being homeschooled as the closure of primary schools continues. Jakob finds himself intrigued by his mother's latest creative project, making face masks to order for family and friends and raising money for an autism charity. He has enjoyed working on creative projects involving hand sewing before but this is the first time he has seen a machine for sewing being used. The machine is big, heavy and noisy, and for safety Jakob is not allowed to touch it. He is allowed to watch, however, and to handle the sewn masks that it produces. As his interest in the way the masks are constructed is noticed and encouraged, he eventually becomes involved in the final step of mask assembly, threading ties through the masks so they can be fastened across the face. His contribution to the process is reminiscent of an apprenticeship. He is inducted into enacting a part of the process and getting to watch a skilled person enact the other steps. As the weeks progress, Jakob expresses an interest in using a machine for sewing himself and a plan is made to research sewing machines for children so that he can get one for his next birthday.

The government has already announced how the country will come out of lockdown and so, by July, Jakob and his mother know that he will be returning to school in September, after a gap of five-and-a-half months. Jakob becomes very anxious at the idea, dreading being separated from his mother during the school day. Together they embark on a sewing project to help Jakob with his anxiety over the summer and with the transition back to attending school every day in September. Ash purchases two kits to make small, handheld soft dolls. The facial features and hair for the dolls can be customized and bespoke clothing made for each doll. The Mini Me project allows Jakob to spend time with Ash making miniature versions of themselves. Together they hand sew the dolls, design the facial features and make the clothes. Attention to detail is important to him. A hoodie is designed for each doll to match clothes they wear in real life. They use a felting kit to make the hair for each doll—long curls for Jakob and shorter black hair for Ash, with a white streak at the temple. On the arm of Ash's Mini Me, a tattoo is carefully reproduced in miniature form. Finally, a blue quilted pouch is made to transport the Mini Mes inside Jakob's school bag, so that they are there with him in school, ready to be held, looked at and cuddled when he needs them.

Figure 18.3 Hand-sewn and hand-felted parent and child Mini Mes made by Jakob and Ash, 2020

For Ash and Jakob, working together on mask making facilitated an intergenerational 'master' and 'apprentice' (in inverted commas due to these being historically gendered terms) exchange of knowledge and skills, and a passing on of a claim to being a 'family maker'. Looking back on this in 2022, Ash states:

> I think the masks was a watershed, so to speak, I mean the idea of using a machine was very sort of 'Mmmm!' (*mimes placing a hand on the face as though in thought*) for him.

Jakob is now an accomplished maker with numerous projects under his belt. When I (Yinka) ask him why he chooses to make something, rather than just buying a version someone else has made from a shop, he explains that what he likes about sewing is that 'you can customize it more [...] if you can't get the shape that you want, you can just make it the shape that you want'. Customization, he continues, is complex, involving 'functionality [...] Maybe a big pocket and a side pocket [...] Sometimes it's with the material'.

Ash also explains how Jakob connected the learning of these practical skills to his digital literacies:

> We've done loads of projects together, just making things. So he's got various bags and cushions and stuff he's made, and Banarnie of course—the banana for his monkey [...] He made a production video of the making of Banarnie.

Ash reminds Jakob of the plan for the video: 'You were going to share it with your friends at school, or your teacher, to prove we were actually doing some work (*laughs*)'.

Our discussion now moves forward to 2022. Jakob has now started in middle school and has been having his first design and technology lessons. This first term the focus is on sewing and our discussion uncovers how Jakob's maker experiences of summer 2020 seem to run counter to the dominant discourse of 'learning loss' that has tended to frame discussions of children and the pandemic:

> Yinka   And now that you're in middle school, and you're doing design and technology, is it helping, the fact that you know about sewing?

Jakob	Yeah
Yinka	How does it help? Have you been having any lessons about sewing?
Jakob	(*Pauses and looks at his mum and then whispers*) I get to be smug! (*Smiles and laughs*)
Ash	(*Looking at Jakob—giggles then turns to camera*) He gets to be smug, that's how it helps him!

Brenda, now in her seventies, is the 'maker' and crafter in my (Cath's) husband's family, a role which she inherited from her own mother whose knitted jumpers and cardigans kept my children snuggly when they were small and which are still treasured items in the family, passed on to each new arrival. Brenda knits, but prefers to sew, and since retirement has taken up patchwork and quilting as a hobby, producing cushions and quilts for our whole family, sometimes for special occasions such as landmark birthdays or for new babies. When the practice of mask wearing began to become established, Brenda turned to her skills and the materials she already had in her home to make masks, in the face of a shortage of manufactured protective garb. 'When you are a patchworker, you have a "stash"', she explained. 'Everyone talks about what you've got in your stash. I didn't understand it then, but I do now'.

Brenda's stash provided some of the material for her mask making and she ordered further material online, although she struggled with a shortage of elastic to hook the masks in place. She derived the pattern for masks, meanwhile, from a crafting charity which was founded in 2020 and local to her area of North East Derbyshire. 'They made [masks] because all the care homes round here couldn't get PPE', said Brenda, 'so these ladies were tearing up sheets and aprons to make masks'. Brenda estimates that she made around thirty masks for members of her family. Brenda's gifting of masks, and other homemade items including patchwork quilts made in lockdown, was also, she revealed, an attempt to neutralise anxieties about the pandemic, and to remind her grandchildren that—while they couldn't meet—they were still present in their lives. Describing how she made some purses in *Harry Potter* fabric to post to her granddaughters living in a different city, Brenda said:

I'm hoping they [the children in our family], that with the Covid thing, the little ones didn't feel frightened, because we were playing it down, sending them barmy things to remind them that grandma and grandad are still here.

Digital Play and Virtual Masks

During the pandemic children's digital technology use increased, with 'digital play [...] actively encouraged as a measure for slowing the spread of the virus' (Cowan et al. 2021: 9). Children's social relationships, such as friendships, were also supported and sustained through technology use and were enacted in virtual settings (Quinones and Adams 2021). This, we suggest, had an impact on their own identity-constructing practices and meaning-making play in a pandemic context. Hafner writes that 'virtual worlds provide an opportunity for users to create a "second self" (Turkle 1985), with the potential to establish a "fresh" identity (or set of identities) online' (2015: 98). In relation to children's play, Marsh has observed that virtual worlds offer children opportunities to 'play with identity representation' (2010: 33). While our own children used technology and apps to maintain contact with friends and family as their real-life selves, such as WhatsApp which became a key means of communication between children/parents and grandparents, aunties and uncles in Cath's extended family, we both observed our children's tendencies towards inhabiting online spaces over more extended periods of time, and further developing their virtual/online identities as their physical spatial worlds and face-to-face play opportunities receded during periods of social distancing and lockdowns.

A favourite online game of my (Cath's) children was *Minecraft*, a virtual-world building videogame in which players can construct their own landscapes using a range of materials portrayed by blocks. Players may insert themselves into their landscapes in the form of avatars which embody players in virtual space (c.f. Marsh 2010: 33), and can customize their appearance using the tools made available to them, a feature available across a range of videogames and platforms. Hafner notes that, in designing an avatar, players may incorporate aspects of their real-life identities into their virtual selves (2015: 99).

During the pandemic this customization began to include opportunities for players to adopt face coverings for their virtual selves. McKinty and Hazleton's account of Australian children's play during the pandemic researched via their Pandemic Play Project observed a trend in online gaming during the pandemic whereby 'in many online games, players opted to join or create groups to combat Covid-19, and a wide variety of masks made by developers and players themselves were made available and worn in-game' (2022: 26). Xin Tong et al., for example, note that some adult players of the Nintendo game *Animal Crossing: New Horizons* chose to 'mirror' offline behaviours in virtual spaces, as they 'tried to embody their real-life identities in their virtual avatar' (2021: 16). This included 'putting masks on their avatars much as they did in real life to combat COVID-19'.

Not only were my children apparently content to wear cloth face masks when entering indoor physical spaces such as shops, but they began playfully adopting mask wearing in virtual spaces as well, kitting out their avatars in face coverings when playing online games. While playing *Minecraft* on a server which my sons co-developed in elaborate detail with their friends online during the pandemic, both my boys added masks available through character customization to their *Minecraft* 'skins'. Their virtual selves wore them when they were out-of-doors (in the game) battling their way across the vast, and Covid-19-free, plains of their worlds. When I asked Jeff, now sixteen, about how masks came to be a feature of his *Minecraft* play, he explained:

> Around the start of the pandemic in early 2020 *Minecraft* added a face mask cosmetic to the Bedrock Edition character creator. Me and my brother used that for a bit. Around the same time they added title screen 'splash texts' with advice such as 'don't touch your face!' and 'prepare, but don't hoard!' to encourage people to follow Covid rules.

However, as Jeff also reminded me, there was no Covid-19 in *Minecraft*. So why wear them? 'Masks are cool', Frank informed me about his choice to adopt a blue face covering for his 'skin', suggesting that, for him, the mask he sometimes wore in-game was a stylish addition to his virtual appearance rather than a practical item and preventative measure. Masks were also a free accessory within their version of the game, I was told. And with the four friends' play in *Minecraft* often taking the form of battles for territory as part of their co-created storyline, their skins often clad in armour and helmets, a mask was perhaps an exciting supplement to battle dress.

Discussion

Masks as a Means of Identity Expression Reflecting Digital/Media Interests

The above discussion demonstrates how children were able to engage with their interests including fandoms and digital play through mask wearing by selecting masks that related to their literary and media preferences, and by adopting masks in the digital realm. In a sense, we could consider fandom face masks a type of fan merchandise or 'merch', even though in these instances the 'merch' was gifted rather than purchased. Godwin observes that not only does merchandise—'mugs, t-shirts, décor, and other items'—signal fans' appreciation of a franchise, but these materials act as 'interfaces' that 'display both fan interests and aspects of a fan's identity' (2018). Describing such merchandise as 'liminal', she notes that it can function to blur the boundaries between the storyworld and the everyday. In light of this, Frank's *Star Wars* face mask can be seen as much more than simply a protective measure, due to his strong connection to the franchise and his regular immersion in its storyworld through play, reading and viewing. Wearing his homemade 'merch' connected him to his interests and also affirmed and signalled to observers his identity as a fan of the franchise, as well as perhaps offering him a foothold in a reassuring, imaginary world.

Meanwhile, masks added to videogames and apps, we suggest, contributed to normalizing mask wearing for young people during the pandemic, blurring the boundary between on and offline by reflecting this new 'irl' practice in virtual environments, thus supporting their transition to habitual mask wearers. However, in an immersive, imaginative game such as *Minecraft*, masks also potentially acquired new meanings through play—not necessarily related to the pandemic— as children performed their in-game identities.

Families as Networks of Care and Support, Assisting Transition and Providing Spaces for Children to Experiment Playfully with Mask Wearing and Identity Exploration

Mask making activity was a material expression of family networks of care. In our vignettes we have observed how family makers centred their practices both on the safety needs, but also on the identity needs, of the children. Masks were not merely viewed as medical devices or measures against disease that children should be trained to 'tolerate'. They were also positioned as vehicles for self-expression and for children's ability to claim participation in communal caring practices. The huge increase in the use of digital platforms for instant communication was a feature from the earliest days of the first 2020 lockdowns and became an important means of maintaining familial networks of care across households and generations. In the making and sharing of masks, however, there was also a contrasting slowness and a return to the physicality of the sending and receiving of letters and parcels in the post. As well as providing a mask through the post to protect a loved one, Brenda reminds us that gifts of hand-made masks were also mementos from one generation to another. The physical presence of the mask acts as a substitute for the mask giver, attempting to maintain an emotional connection during prolonged periods apart.

Innovatively Creating New Pandemic Celebrations and 'Passaging' Practices

An emergent theme in this chapter has been that of children's identities and self-expression, and the role that masks have played in that self-expression during the pandemic. Regarding identity as a process of becoming, rather than a static state of being, and furthermore identity as intrinsically social (Jenkins 2014: 18), we can consider how family and peer protective and playful practices around mask wearing supported children's status transition or 'passage' from non-mask wearers to mask wearers with agency, making their own choices about mask design and use. Brenda's comment that the children wanted to be a part of the unfolding situation, hence playing an active role rather than being bystanders excluded from actively protecting themselves and their community, demonstrates adults' willingness to take children and their pandemic experiences and identities seriously, even while acknowledging the playful affordances of masks. Framing masks as both serious and playful for children supported their adoption of masks and also supported them emotionally by doing so. Furthermore, while the pandemic prevented many families from marking special days in the way they would prefer, it also gave rise to opportunities for new or different celebrations and rituals (Imber-Blac, 2020), such as the family gathering discussed by Cath in Vignette 2 above. Transforming masks into gifts for children as a part of that celebration recognized their status socially as mask wearers, recognized their individual identities through the choice of meaningful fabric designs for each child, and encouraged even the younger children to feel more 'grown up' (a transition in itself) and included.

Conclusion

In this paper we have presented an autoethnographic account of the mask-making and gifting practices involving children in two families. In doing so, we have challenged a dominant discourse about face masks during the Covid-19 pandemic as something inherently negative that children were forced to tolerate. Furthermore, we have uncovered a subjugated discourse in which children's initiation into mask wearing was playful, child-centred and empowering. Face-mask making and wearing, as emergent material practices, made family networks of care, understanding and communication visible, linking maker and wearer as participants in both family and wider societal enactments of consideration.

The children in our families were able to choose their masks, to have masks custom-made and to receive these playful and meaningful masks as gifts that reflected their interests. This was possible because the people who had made the masks knew them and consulted them, and took children and their interests seriously. The children were also free to experiment with masks as a new form of self-expression, to accessorize them, to move beyond the mere functionality of masks and towards a concept of the mask as a canvas for self-expression and customization and thus identity. Finally, for the children in our vignettes, face masks were important transition objects as they journeyed through the liminal space of the early pandemic, navigating their way from their pre-pandemic selves and carving out for themselves their emergent pandemic identities. At the time of writing, we are in the third year of the Covid-19 pandemic and around the world expectations and requirements regarding children's use of face masks remains diverse. However, for people in different places and at different times, as the pandemic continues to unfold, a wider lesson for practice in relation to children and masks is that, whilst the mask is a medical tool, it can also be a playful cultural space upon which children can project and play with identity.

Works Cited

Adams, Tony, and Jimmie Manning. 2015. 'Autoethnography and Family Research', *Journal of Family Theory & Review*, 7: 350–66, https://doi.org/10.1111/jftr.12116

Belton, Brian. 2009. 'Here's Looking at You Kid (or the Hoodies Fight Back)', in *Developing Critical Youth Work Theory* (Leiden, The Netherlands: Brill), pp. 131-43

Ben-Amos, Dan. 1971. 'Toward a Definition of Folklore in Context', *Journal of American Folklore*, 84: 3-15

Burgess, Adam, and Mitsutoshi Horii. 2012. 'Risk, Ritual and Health Responsibilisation: Japan's "Safety Blanket" of Surgical Face Mask-Wearing', *Sociology of Health & Illness*, 34:, 1184–198, https://doi.org/10.1111/j.1467-9566.2012.01466.x

Cabrera, Elena. 2021. 'Are You Smiling under Your Face Mask? The Potential Negative Psychological Side-Effects of Covid-19 on Children That Are Going Unnoticed', *Charged Magazine*, 2 April, http://chargedmagazine.org/2021/04/are-you-smiling-under-your-face-mask/

Cairney, Paul. 2021. 'The UK Government's COVID-19 Policy: Assessing Evidence-Informed Policy Analysis in Real Time', *British Politics*, 16: 90-116, https://doi.org/10.1057/s41293-020-00150-8

Chomitzky, Katya. 2020. 'Pandemic, but Make It Fashion: Ukrainian Embroidered PPE in the Time of COVID-19', Folklorica: *Journal of the Slavic, Eastern European, and Eurasian Folklore Association*, 24: 27-50, https://doi.org/10.17161/folklorica.v24i.15689

Cohen, Stanley. 2002. *Folk Devils and Moral Panics*, 3rd edn (London: Routledge)

Coelho, Sophie G., Alicia Segovia, Samantha Anthony, et al. 2022. 'Return to School and Mask-Wearing in Class during the COVID-19 Pandemic: Student

Perspectives from a School Simulation Study', *Paediatrics & Child Health*, 27: S15-S21, https://doi.org/10.1093/pch/pxab102

Cortés-Morales, Susana, et al. 2022. 'Children Living in Pandemic Times: A Geographical, Transnational and Situated View', *Children's Geographies*, 20: 381-91, https://doi.org/10.1080/14733285.2021.1928603

Cowan, Kate, et al. 2021. 'Children's Digital Play during the COVID-19 Pandemic: Insights from the Play Observatory'. *Journal of e-Learning and Knowledge Society*, 17.3: 8-17, https://doi.org/10.20368/1971-8829/1135590

Eberhart, Martin, Stefan Orthaber, and Reinhold Kerbl. 2021. 'The Impact of Face Masks on Children: A Mini Review', *Acta Pædiatrica*, 110: 1778–783, https://doi.org/10.1111/apa.15784

Ellis, Carolyn, Tony E. Adams, and Arthur P. Bochner. 2011. 'Autoethnography: An Overview', *Historical Social Research*, 36: 273–90

Feng, Shuo, et al. 2020. 'Rational Use of Face Masks in the COVID-19 Pandemic', *Lancet Respiratory Medicine* 8: 434-36, https://doi.org/10.1016/S2213-2600(20)30134-X

Fivecoat, Jesse A., Kristina Downs, and Meredith A. E. McGriff. 2021. 'Envisioning a Future Folkloristics', in *Advancing Folkloristics*, ed. by Jesse A. Fivecoate, Kristina Downs, and Meredith A. E. McGriff (Bloomington: Indiana University Press), pp. 1-8

Gingrich-Philbrook, Craig. 2005. 'Autoethnography's Family Values: Easy Access to Compulsory Experiences', *Text and Performance Quarterly*, 25: 297-314, https://doi.org/10.1080/10462930500362445

Godwin, Victoria L. 2018. 'Hogwarts House Merchandise, Liminal Play, and Fan Identities', *Film Criticism*, 42, https://doi.org/10.3998/fc.13761232.0042.206

Guy, Batsheva, and Brittany Arthur. 2020. 'Academic Motherhood During COVID-19: Navigating Our Dual Roles as Educators and Mothers', *Gender, Work and Organization*, 27: 887-99, https://doi.org/10.1111/gwao.12493

Hafner, Christoph. A. 2015. 'Co-Constructing Identity in Virtual Worlds for Children', in *Discourse and Digital Practices: Doing Discourse Analysis in the Digital Age*, ed. by Rodney H. Jones, Alice Chik and Christoph A. Hafner (London: Routledge), pp. 97-111

Halbur, Mary, et al. 2021. 'Tolerance of Face Coverings for Children with Autism Spectrum Disorder', *Journal of Applied Behavior Analysis*, 54: 600–17, https://doi.org/10.1002/jaba.833

Heald, Adrian H., et al. 2021. 'Modelling the Impact of the Mandatory Use of Face Coverings on Public Transport and in Retail Outlets in the UK on COVID-19-Related Infections, Hospital Admissions and Mortality', *International Journal of Clinical Practice*, 75: e13768, https://doi.org/10.1111/ijcp.13768

Hier, Sean P., et al. 2011. 'Beyond Folk Devil Resistance: Linking Moral Panic and Moral Regulation', *Criminology & Criminal Justice*, 11: 259–76, https://doi.org/10.1177/1748895811401977

Holmes, Andrew Gary Darwin. 2020. 'Researcher Positionality: A Consideration of Its Influence and Place in Qualitative Research: A New Researcher Guide', *Shanlax International Journal of Education*, 8.4: 1-10, http://files.eric.ed.gov/fulltext/EJ1268044.pdf

Ike, John David, et al. 2020. 'Face Masks: Their History and the Values They Communicate', *Journal of Health Communication*, 25: 990-95, https://doi.org/10.1080/10810730.2020.1867257

Imber-Black, Evan. 2020. 'Rituals in the Time of COVID-19: Imagination, Responsiveness, and the Human Spirit', *Family Process*, 59: 912-21, https://doi.org/10.1111/famp.12581

Jenkins, Richard. 2014. *Social Identity*, 4th edn (London: Routledge)

Jones, Michael Owen. 1997. 'How Can We Apply Event Analysis to "Material Behavior," and Why Should We?' *Western Folklore*, 56: 199-214, https://doi.org/10.2307/1500274

Kennedy, Kimberley, and Harriet Romo. 2013. '"All Colors and Hues": An Autoethnography of a Multiethnic Family's Strategies for Bilingualism and Multiculturalism', *Family Relations*, 62: 109–24, https://doi.org/10.1111/j.1741-3729.2012.00742.x

Marsh, Jackie. 2010. 'Young Children's Play in Online Virtual Worlds', *Journal of Early Childhood Research*, 8: 23-39, https://doi.org/10.1177/1476718X09345406

McKinty, Judy, and Ruth Hazleton. 2022. 'The Pandemic Play Project: Documenting Kids' Culture during COVID-19', *International Journal of Play*, 11: 12-33, https://doi.org/10.1080/21594937.2022.2042940

Nash, Catriona, Lisa O'Malley, and Maurice Patterson. 2021. 'Experiencing Family Ethnography: Challenges, Practicalities and Reflections on Practice', *Qualitative Market Research: An International Journal*, 24: 97-112, https://doi.org/10.1108/QMR-03-2019-0050

Olusoga, Yinka, et al. 2022. 'Preserving the Present: Designing a Child-Centered Qualitative Survey for a National Observatory of Children's Play', *SAGE Research Methods: Doing Research Online*, https://dx.doi.org/10.4135/9781529603736

Panovska-Griffiths, J., et al. 2021. 'Modelling the Potential Impact of Mask Use in Schools and Society on COVID-19 Control in the UK', *Scientific Reports*, 11: 8747, https://doi.org/10.1038/s41598-021-88075-0

Phoenix, Aisha. 2019. 'Negotiating British Muslim Belonging: A Qualitative Longitudinal Study', *Ethnic and Racial Studies*, 42: 1632-650, https://doi.org/10.1080/01419870.2018.1532098

Pourret, Olivier, and Elodie Saillet. 2020. 'Wear Your Mask, but Think about Deaf Students', *Nature*, 586: 629–30, https://doi.org/10.1038/d41586-020-02823-2

Quinones, Gloria, and Megan Adams. 2021. 'Children's Virtual Worlds and Friendships during the COVID-19 Pandemic: Visual Technologies as a

Panacea for Social Isolation', *Video Journal of Education and Pedagogy*, 5: 1-18, https://doi.org/10.1163/23644583-bja10015

Sebba-Elran, Tsafi. 2021. 'A Pandemic of Jokes? The Israeli COVID-19 Meme and the Construction of a Collective Response to Risk', *Humor*, 34: 229-57, https://doi.org/10.1515/humor-2021-0012

Singh, Leher, Agnes Tan, and Paul C. Quinn. 2021. 'Infants Recognize Words Spoken Through Opaque Masks but Not through Clear Masks', *Developmental Science*, 24: e13117–n/a, https://doi.org//10.1111/desc.13117

Sivaraman, Maithri, Javier Virues-Ortega, and Herbert Roeyers. 2021. 'Telehealth Mask Wearing Training for Children with Autism During the COVID-19 Pandemic', *Journal of Applied Behavior Analysis*, 54: 70–86, https://doi.org/10.1002/jaba.802

Spitzer, Manfred. 2020. 'Masked Education? The Benefits and Burdens of Wearing Face Masks in Schools during the Current Corona Pandemic', *Trends in Neuroscience and Education*, 20: 100138, https://doi.org/10.1016/j.tine.2020.100138

Sundaram, Neisha, et al. 2021. 'Implementation of Preventive Measures to Prevent COVID-19: A National Study of English Primary Schools in Summer 2020', *Health Education Research*, 36: 272–85, https://doi.org/10.1093/her/cyab016

Tong, Xin, et al. 2021. 'Players' Stories and Secrets in Animal Crossing: New Horizons: Exploring Design Factors for Positive Emotions and Social Interactions in a Multiplayer Online Game', *Proceedings of the ACM on Human-Computer Interaction*, 5: 1-23, https://doi.org/10.1145/3474711

Turkle, Sherry. 1985. *The Second Self: Computers and the Human Spirit* (New York: Simon & Schuster)

Twele, Anita, Sophia M. Thierry, and Catherine J. Mondloch. 2022. 'Face Masks Have a Limited Influence on First Impressions: Evidence from Three Experiments', *Perception*, 51: 417–34, https://doi.org/10.1177/03010066221091729

Upton, Dell. 1979. 'Toward a Performance Theory of Vernacular Architecture: Early Tidewater Virginia as a Case Study', *Folklore Forum*, 12: 173-96

Warren, George W., and Ragnar Lofstedt. 2022. 'Risk Communication and COVID-19 in Europe: Lessons for Further Public Health Crises', *Journal of Risk Research*, 25: 1161-175, https://doi.org/10.1080/13669877.2021.1947874

Williams, Simon, et al. 2022. 'The UK Is an International Outlier in Its Approach to Covid in Children', *BMJ*, 376: o327, https://doi.org/10.1136/bmj.o327

Winarnita, Minkia. 2019. 'Digital Family Ethnography: Lessons from Fieldwork amongst Indonesians in Australia', *Migration, Mobility, & Displacement* 4: 105-17, https://doi.org/10.18357/mmd41201918973

19. Art in the Streets: Playful Politics in the Work of The Velvet Bandit and SudaLove

Heather Shirey

Art in the streets, and here I refer to graffiti, murals, stickers, paste-ups and other installations on walls, the pavement and signs, is uniquely positioned to respond quickly, effectively and sometimes playfully in a moment of crisis. Its placement in public space means that street art has the ability to reach a wide audience but to be effective it must be easily consumable in a single glance, speaking in a visual language that is clear and direct. In many places throughout the world, our movement in shared space was restricted due to the pandemic. In a time of social isolation, street art takes on additional significance as a form of communication and interaction.

By its nature, street art is interactive, engaging with people as they traverse the city. Art, like play, can serve to facilitate conversation and interaction. Like play, street art is frequently improvisational. Artists working in the street often approach their work in a playful manner, creating amusing and seemingly lighthearted images to capture attention. At the same time, street art is often used to express dissent in an oppressive political climate, frequently offering a critical assessment of the structural inequities and human rights issues that are exacerbated in a time of crisis (Konstantinos and Tsilimpounidi 2017; Awad and Wagoner 2017; Bloch 2020; Urban Art Mapping 2020). This critical stance may also be communicated in a playful manner, appearing lighthearted while conveying a serious political message.

This photographic essay is an examination of the work of two prolific street artists who address Covid-19 through art in the streets: The Velvet

   https://doi.org/10.11647/OBP.0326.19

Bandit, a paste-up artist in Northern California, and Assil Diab, also known as SudaLove, a muralist who was working in Khartoum, Sudan, during the early months of the pandemic. These artists bring to us perspectives from two continents: North America and Africa. These two artists were working artists prior to the pandemic but both SudaLove and The Velvet Bandit expressed a new urgency to bring their artistic practice to the streets in the context of this global crisis. SudaLove created a number of murals in a short period of time in 2020 while The Velvet Bandit has continued to produce works addressing Covid-19, often interwoven with pieces addressing other issues such as Black Lives Matter, elections and reproductive rights.

In the works investigated here, both The Velvet Bandit and SudaLove create artistic interventions in the street as a means of engaging with Covid-19 in a manner that was light and playful but also serious and political. As is typical of street art, their work is highly accessible, using simple visual language. At the same time, each piece requires deeper contextual knowledge to understand the underlying political and social significance.

The interviews referenced in this photographic essay were conducted by members of the Urban Art Mapping research team, an interdisciplinary group that created and maintains the Covid-19 Street Art Database.

The Velvet Bandit

Based in Northern California, The Velvet Bandit's artistic practice in the streets emerged in the context of the pandemic. While she always had a passion for art, it was not a full-time pursuit until spring 2020, when she was furloughed from her job in a school cafeteria. In a 27 January 2022 interview with Urban Art Mapping, The Velvet Bandit spoke to the idea that producing art can itself be both playful and an act of healing during traumatic moments: 'When the pandemic first hit, I became unemployed and my two children were suddenly homeschooled, and I had nothing but my art supplies to keep me sane, to keep my children sane' (Velvet Bandit 2022).

The Velvet Bandit creates small, original paintings on paper that are adhered to a surface with wheat paste. Each individual piece is usually referred to as a paste-up. The Velvet Bandit paints in acrylics, creating bold and colourful imagery, often accompanied by text. Typically, a paste-up artist is able to complete their work at home or in the studio, slapping it up on a wall or surface in public space quickly and covertly. The Velvet Bandit usually undertakes this work in an unauthorized manner and she makes efforts to maintain her anonymity. Whether they are painted over, removed or simply degrade over time, paste-ups always have a limited lifespan, encouraging artists working in this medium to create images that speak very directly to the moment.

Figure 19.1 The Velvet Bandit, 'Take Me To Your Leader', photographed 6 April 2020

'Take Me To Your Leader' was photographed by the artist on 6 April 2020 in Santa Rosa, California, and shared by way of the artist's Instagram account. It is quite typical for The Velvet Bandit to share her work by way of social media in order to gain wider visibility. This is particularly important because these small pieces, adhered to a surface using wheat paste, are quite ephemeral. The coronavirus is depicted as a spiky blue and turquoise sphere, reminiscent of a bouncy ball. A bright pink label on the sphere reads 'Take Me To Your Leader'. This piece is a play on the popular science fiction troupe in which an alien life form arrives on earth, presumably with hostile intentions, and asks to be taken to the leader. In science-fiction films, the leader is generally depicted as inept and unable to solve the crisis, leaving it to local heroes to save the planet. The cartoon-like rendition of the virus and playful reference to popular alien movies and cartoons makes this paste-up seem lighthearted and fun but it reflects deep frustrations with the country's leadership in spring 2020. In this case, The Velvet Bandit uses a seemingly playful paste-up to express profound disagreement with President Trump and his handling of a national crisis. Widespread lockdown policies, which were in place in many places throughout the United States at the time this piece was documented, had a disproportionate impact on working-class people. Those in power, including Donald Trump, were well insulated from the virus and protected from the negative consequences of the shutdown, while people working in industries such as hospitality and healthcare faced the realities of job loss and lack of safety. This piece reflects a very real if malicious shared hope that Donald Trump would himself be forced to confront the virus in a manner that was up close and personal while also expressing doubt that he, as a 'leader', could resolve the crisis in an effective manner.

Figure 19.2 The Velvet Bandit, 'Bring Back Ebola', photographed 11 May 2020

'Bring Back Ebola', a bright red popsicle set against a vivid blue dumpster, appears to be a light and playful reminder of a refreshing childhood treat. However, this seemingly simple image reflects on more complicated ideas about epidemics and pandemics, the containment of disease and how we face realities that were previously unthinkable. Looking closer at the popsicle, we can see text reading 'Bring Back Ebola', referencing the Ebola haemorrhagic fever outbreak that first emerged in late 2013 in Guinea and led to widespread transmission in Guinea, Liberia and Sierra Leone in 2014-2016. Ultimately seven other countries were affected, including Italy, Spain, the United Kingdom and the United States, leading to concerns that Ebola would develop into a global pandemic. The virus was successfully contained, though, due to the coordination of international public health organizations. In 2016, the World Health Organization (WHO) lifted PHEIC (Public Health Emergency of International Concern) status for Ebola (Centers for Disease Control 2019). In contrast, when the 'Bring Back Ebola' popsicle wheat paste was documented in Santa Rosa, California, on 11 May 2020, the World Health Organization had declared Covid-19 a pandemic (this happened on 11 March 2020) and on 2 May 2020, WHO had renewed its emergency declaration. Lockdowns were widespread and the US unemployment rate had just hit its worst point since the Great Depression. Many people wondered if an end was in sight for the pandemic. The death toll was quite high in the United States at this point, hitting one hundred thousand deaths less than a week after this piece was documented. In the United States, people were confused by seemingly conflicting messages that came from the Centers for Disease Control and federal, state and local governments. In retrospect, the viewer of this piece might feel a strange nostalgia for the Ebola outbreak: a time when there was much fear of a pandemic but a sense that international organizations were working cooperatively to resolve an issue of global concern. In reality, the 2014-2016 Ebola outbreak had very little actual impact on life in the United States and, while there were some travel restrictions, it necessitated no changes to daily life. Ultimately, the fatality rate with Ebola was much higher in each infected individual but the virus was more easily contained when compared to Covid-19.

Figure 19.3 The Velvet Bandit, 'Smile More', photographed 10 May 2020

'Smile More', documented on 10 May 2020 in Santa Rosa, California, uses a children's book character to reflect on the issue of street harassment. A child would easily recognize this figure as a play on the Disney illustration of Alice in Wonderland. Here Alice wears a face mask with text reading 'Smile More.' Men randomly commanding women to smile is a common form of street harassment in the United States and it sends the message that a woman has an obligation to arrange her face in a manner that conforms to a man's desires. 'Stop Telling Women to Smile' was a nationwide street art project beginning in 2012 by artist Tatyana Fazlalizadeh. Fazlalizadeh's portraits of real women were juxtaposed with text calling attention to street harassment (Fazlalizadeh n.d.). Whereas Fazlalizadeh's series focused on imposing portraits of real women juxtaposed with their own words, The Velvet Bandit takes a more playful approach by using Alice as a stand-in for the victim of harassment. At a time when the use of face coverings was widespread or even mandatory, some women felt that a mask could serve as a shield and offer a sense of privacy from strangers in the street (Maloy 2021). Others lamented the fact that the mask made it more difficult to use facial expressions to ward off harassers (Nadège 2020). In this way, a playful rendition of Alice in Wonderland serves as a critique of the patriarchy.

Figure 19.4 The Velvet Bandit, 'Wake Me Up When It's Over', photographed 17 December 2020

'Wake Me Up When It's Over' was documented in San Francisco on 17 December 2020. This wheat paste shows a child tucked in and sleeping peacefully. He is covered by a bright yellow blanket and he wears blue plaid pyjamas and a turquoise medical mask. Wearing a medical mask while sleeping alone in bed would clearly be unnecessary so we can surmise that the artist chose to include the face covering in order to emphasize Covid-19 as the subject of the work. The time on the alarm clock reads 2020 and text on the headboard reads 'Wake Me Up When It's Over'. The text playfully reflects on our ironically naïve expectation that the passing of a milestone, the turning of a new year, might bring with it new realities and that the negative events and experiences of 2020 could be somehow partitioned off and contained. There was indeed a sense of hopefulness in December 2020 as vaccines were beginning to be available to selected populations, and the United States was looking ahead to the inauguration of President Joe Biden and the hope of a new national response to the virus in January 2021, making this a playful reflection on the mood during the period after the presidential election and the inauguration.

Figure 19.5 The Velvet Bandit, 'Orange Ya Glad I'm Not Covid 19', photographed
4 March 2021

'Orange Ya Glad I'm Not Covid-19' was documented on 4 March 2021, several weeks after Donald Trump's departure from the White House. Still, the spherical orange with a single jaunty leaf shooting off to the side serves as a stand-in for a portrait of President Trump, who was often mocked for the orange tone to his skin and his dramatic swoop of hair. While playfully referencing the punchline of a familiar 'Knock knock' joke, this piece indicates how deeply politicized the pandemic became in the United States, as Donald Trump frequently expressed opinions, gave advice and supported policies that contradicted scientific facts.

SudaLove

Assil Diab, working in the streets under the name SudaLove, is a Sudanese street artist educated in graphic design at Virginia Commonwealth University and based in Doha, Qatar. (Muzawazi). She is known as the first female graffiti artist in Sudan and Qatar (Muzawazi 2017). In 2019 SudaLove undertook an important series of works memorializing political martyrs in Khartoum, Sudan, where she and her collaborators took tremendous personal risks to paint murals that honoured ordinary citizens who were killed by the state during the revolution. During the early months of the pandemic, SudaLove returned to Khartoum to spray-paint a series of murals that use large, brightly coloured, engaging imagery to address the public health crisis that Covid-19 presented. Sudan reported its first confirmed case of Covid on 13 March 2020. The infected patient had traveled to the United Arab Emirates and died on 12 March 2020 in Khartoum. SudaLove's murals relating to Covid-19 were produced in March 2020.

Figure 19.6 SudaLove with Khalid al Baih, 'Covid Explosion', photographed March 2020

The 'Covid Explosion' was a collaboration with political cartoonist Khalid al Baih. During the early part of the pandemic, many artists sought to visualize the coronavirus, transforming the invisible into something more tangible. As it is spread through invisible droplets, it is impossible to actually see the coronavirus and therefore it is perhaps easy to ignore the reality of its presence. Borrowing from an image by Khalid al Baih, SudaLove depicted a laboratory flask spewing out a green spherical form with the virus's crown-like protein spikes. Tiny green dots surrounding the flask and virus reference its spread through miniscule droplets. The image is large, colourful and engaging, and yet it also does the important work of visualizing and therefore making real the presence of Covid-19.

In an interview with Urban Art Mapping in January 2022, Diab spoke of her role as an artist educating people about public health concerns:

> There was a mandatory lockdown so I had to have permission to carry out these murals, and when I used to go out and I used to see people walking, there were lots of homeless people in the streets. They would come up close and try to touch my spray paint— and I would say 'no, this is a mural about the coronavirus and we have to stay away from each other'—but some of them didn't even know what the coronavirus is. You could tell that people had no idea what was going on and when you explained it, they didn't really care. And it is not that people don't care about their health, it's just that people went through so much before that, the pandemic was the least of their problems at that time. (Diab 2022)

To this end, SudaLove painted several murals using playful imagery to promote the proper use of face coverings as well as mandated stay-at-home orders.

Figure 19.7 SudaLove, 'Stay At Home', photographed March 2020

One example is a portrait of a man in a white hoodie with pink sunglasses. He wears a surgical face mask. Text in Arabic reads 'Stay At Home' and small renditions of the spikey coronavirus surround the text.

Figure 19.8 SudaLove, 'Face Masks', photographed March 2020

In another mural a crowd of individuals, all wearing different styles of head coverings and clothing, is created through simple black outlines. The figures are packed closely together and they are all shown in profile, as if they are engaging with each other. Each figure wears a blue surgical face mask. Diab stated in her January 2022 interview that it was rare to actually see people wearing face coverings in the street and she meant for the mural to normalize their use (Diab 2022).

Figure 19.9 SudaLove, 'Face Masks/Stay At Home', photographed March 2020

The third and most complex of these murals depicts four large, highly detailed portraits of individuals wearing different styles of head coverings. Each figure is wearing a surgical face mask with text reading 'stay at home' written in a different language. SudaLove explained:

> You're tackling issues from a very national point which is a Sudanese point of view. We have over three hundred tribes in Sudan with different religions and dialects, so even when you want to get married, people usually ask what tribe you are from. […] So the idea was to tackle the health issue and bring it from a very personal point of view, to talk about tribes. So that's why I put these different Sudanese people from different tribes all on the same wall, all saying 'stay at home' in their own dialect. […] This is a time when we need to come together to fight this one issue regardless of your tribe, your background, you are gonna get the virus. (Diab 2022)

Figure 19.10 SudaLove, 'Omar al-Bashir Virus', photographed March 2020

Finally, most overtly political of SudaLove's Covid-19 works is a depiction of deposed head of state Omar al-Bashir with a green face and two horns emerging from his head, transforming him into a spikey coronavirus. Widespread protests against al-Bashir began in December 2018 and he was ousted by a military *coup d'état* in April 2019. At the time this work was painted, al-Bashir was imprisoned and preparing to face trial for corruption charges. While the image appears playful and cartoon-like, it addressed the intertwined nature of Covid-19 and politics, specifically the need to find unity during a politically divisive moment. About this work, SudaLove stated:

> Now we have this pandemic right after we won this war, and now we have something else we've gotta take care of, and that's another issue in Sudan as well with our medical organization, just how our healthcare in Sudan is not that great. So the idea was to remind people that we got over the biggest disease that we had, which was Omar Al-Bashir, and we need to come together at this time again to fight this new health war, which is the coronavirus. To paint Omar Al-Bashir in daylight in a public place was just baffling to me because you couldn't write or say anything in public that opposed him [before the revolution]. (Diab 2022)

As the artist indicates, this simple, cartoon-like image embodies complex ideas about ongoing struggles in post-revolutionary era, made all the more complicated by the pandemic.

Seen together and in the context of the global pandemic, the work of SudaLove and The Velvet Bandit demonstrates that playful imagery can provide an avenue for responding to the pandemic in a manner that is quickly accessible to the public. In contrast to art created in private spaces, art in the streets allowed for the shared processing of the complex shared trauma of isolation, embracing playfulness while also recognizing a sense of loss and disbelief, as well as the justified feelings of anger and confusion that shaped experiences around the world.

Works Cited

Avramidis, Konstantinos, and Myrto Tsilimpounidi. 2017. Graffiti and Street Art: Reading, Writing and Representing the City (Abingdon: Routledge)

Awad, Sarah H. and Brady Wagoner (ed.). 2017. *Street Art of Resistance* (Cham, Switzerland: Springer International; Palgrave Macmillan)

Bloch, Stefano. 2020. 'COVID Graffiti', *Crime, Media, Culture*, 17: 27-35, https://doi.org/10.1177/17416590209462

Centers for Disease Control and Prevention. 2019. '2014-2016 Ebola Outbreak in West Africa', https://www.cdc.gov/vhf/ebola/history/2014-2016-outbreak/index.html

Diab, Assil. 2022. Interview with Urban Art Mapping, 27 January

Fazlalizadeh, Tatyana. n.d. 'Stop Telling Women to Smile', http://www.tlynnfaz.com/Stop-Telling-Women-to-Smile

Maloy, Ashley Fetters. 2021. 'Masks Are Off—Which Means Men Will Start Telling Women to "Smile!" Again', *Washington Post*, 22 May, https://www.washingtonpost.com/lifestyle/2021/05/22/men-telling-women-smile/

Muzawazi, Rumbie. 2017. 'Assil Diab: Being an Arab Muslim Female Painting in the Streets Is Not Always Applauded', *She.Leads.Africa*, 11 September, https://sheleadsafrica.org/tag/sudalove/

Nadège. 2020. 'We Need to Talk about Street Harassment while Wearing Masks', *Medium*, 16 July, https://medium.com/fearless-she-wrote/we-need-to-talk-about-street-harassment-while-wearing-masks-58fda4bef657

Urban Art Mapping. 2020. 'Covid-19 Street Art Archive', https://covid19streetart.omeka.net

Velvet Bandit, The. 2022. Interview with Urban Art Mapping, 27 January

Conclusion:
Covid in a Play Frame

Anna Beresin and Julia Bishop

President Biden declares 'the pandemic is over'.
(CBS *60 Minutes*, 18 September 2022)

We wondered if people would be puzzled by a book about a deadly virus and play, although those we approached understood the concept of the book intuitively. Yet, a romanticized 'Barneyesque' view of play remains primary, that play is a nicety, a simple extra. Play stays with us evolutionarily because it serves as a vessel for complex ideas, a paradoxical container for the light and the heavy, for both laughter and anguish. These portraits and landscapes of Covid play reveal not just our collective creativity and community earnestness in a time of fear and potential illness, but also something about the complexity of play itself as an essential part of what it means to be human, particularly a young human.

In an essay reprinted in his posthumous book *Play for Life: Play Theory* and *Play as Emotional Survival* (2017 [2008]) Brian Sutton-Smith called play 'dialudic', his slightly tongue-in-cheek conflation of 'ludic' (Latin for 'play') and 'dialectic', a process of attempting to find truth through conflict and disagreement. His underutilized concept of play's dualistic nature appeared throughout his writing and helps us see how play contains opposites inside our culture and inside our heads. To play is to have a symbolically loaded conversation, even if we are alone in our room when we do it, balancing as we attempt to solve complex problems, personally, socially, culturally, historically. Perhaps the tensions within such an activity play out through the pulsing dynamics of negotiated

 https://doi.org/10.11647/OBP.0326.20

exaggeration. So let us return to each chapter in *Play in a Covid Frame* and see what a dialudic lens reveals about Covid in a play frame.

Tag embodies the quintessential dialudic game—the one touched becomes the one who chases, inverting roles and shifting the narratives. Bishop's chapter on Coronavirus Tag demonstrates the paradox that this game is both unique to this time and also not unique, connecting it to other forms of Tag and noxious touch. This can be said for all play—it is both of this moment in time and built upon forms that have come before. Bishop's chapter also presents Twitter as a place for hashtagged comments relating to play, raising an implied question about where we hope to find common discursive spaces in the future. Krnjaja and Mitranić write that the pandemic has informed us about how play is pivotal for both the individual and our collective society, that programmes must balance children's needs for self-expression and also act in the child's best interest during a pandemic.

Sienkiewicz, Beideman, LeBron, Lewis, Morrison, Rivera and Faticone, and also O'Dwyer, Hannan and Neville, present the inequality of access to play spaces, both physical and virtual. Both chapters focus on the importance of cultural inclusion, in school and after school, and that play is key for pandemic mental health. In Rochester, New York, the team notes the paradox that programmes serving children need both consistency and flexibility during crises like Covid. Perhaps games are the ultimate training ground for rule-bound improvisation. O'Dwyer, Hannan and Neville make an important case for culturally specific comparative data across time.

During the pandemic, we have all had to re-examine what we feel is essential in our lives. King raises the question whether playworkers should be considered essential workers, suggesting an overall public misunderstanding of both play and play's essentially social nature. Terada, Ermilova and Shimamura describe the central paradox in playwork of interference without interference. The banner at the adventure playground in Kawasaki City reads 'No Prohibitions', yet prohibitions became necessary as the playground remained open during the height of the pandemic in order to serve the most vulnerable families. The cultural variations of health taboos during Covid within the frame of a scientific narrative of safety would be worthy of further study.

In our Portraits section, Heljakka puns with her discussion of 'bearers of hope'. Drawing on the literature that addresses paradoxes of toys, we are reminded that the toy is not only an object of solitary play. Displayed in public spaces, the bears promoted 'ludounity', intergenerational collaboration and optimism in the symbol that represents both mourning and huggability in a touchless time. Beresin contrasts play opportunities in three urban communities and notes their vast differences, their common play themes, and the complexity of world-building as a pandemic folk practice in a time of limited space. Play allowed the children to use this time to create future scenarios offering escape, demonstrating that at play we time travel. We were here and elsewhere simultaneously. Carter argues that school is fundamentally social and that face-to-face play with friends was indeed irreplaceable, although some were happy at home and some not. There was a newfound joy when lockdowns were lifted.

Renel and Thom decry the medicalization of play for disabled children and young people, and through their superhero kits sought to share positive memories of play as protection. Calling for anti-ableist resistance, they describe the unequal lifting of restrictions. The paradox here is of super resilience within spatial injustice, amplifying the importance of play for all. Le Bigre presents vulnerability as a source of fun, particularly for elderly women in their disregard of lockdown rules, noting that vulnerable play is play in its 'most honest form'. To invert power presents a deliciousness at play; it defies death as it courts death. So, we may 'clap for the carers' but we take delight in chalking signs for each other in liminal places.

Egan, Pope, Beatty and Hoyne reframe portraits through data showing that, although children over seven years of age played with toys and games during the pandemic, only fifty-seven percent of them did so daily. One third of the families included in their study mentioned children directly playing with Covid as a theme—playing dead, playing doctor, pretending to wash hands or pretending to social distance. We are again reminded of the varying degrees of access to outdoor spaces in a time where outdoor spaces were initially taboo and then celebrated as the only real safe places to gather. Dong documents families' curated photos of innovative play kits with nonspecific materials. Here digital devices connected where physical bodies could not go. Potter and Cannon's photo essay becomes an elicitation tool for each of us, presenting the paradox of a holistic partial view, a thematically varied sampler. Here we see outdoor cinemas, wild pets inside, and dens or forts as part of a global archive of this time.

Shifting frames are themselves dizzying and clarifying. Radice's study of Yardi Gras layers a new stable moving tradition, with 'sadmirable' improvisation with inside jokes and puns. Like the houses that together represented different characters in their themed house decorations of *Alice in Wonderland*, participants and researchers found ways to collaborate. Festive sensory bombardment was recast in a time of sensory deprivation, without sacrificing the inversion of anti-racist and anti-classist humor. McKinty, Hazleton and von der Borch note the paradox of children needing adults to remain playful at this time while celebrating children's own pandemic peer culture. Beresin writes of the complex cultural layers of trickster play as negotiated exaggeration while social events turned virtual during lockdown. The message here is: we did it ourselves, but we got by with a little help from our fam.

Olusoga and Bannister reveal another icon of paradox, the mask itself, as it protects, conceals and displays elements of culture and personal style. Children's agency emerged in their choice of fandom on display as they presented their hidden faces as a form of identity. We close with Shirey's photo essay of pandemic art by the Velvet Bandit and SudaLove. Off-the-wall humour on the wall, the work invites both the 'quick glance' of understanding and sustained hunting for new images in new places. One artist works satirically, the other exaggerates with scale and portraiture.

In the future, follow the online 'viral' pandemic slang, as older youth often point the way to new forms of children's folklore. The virus has been called the 'Miley Cyrus', the 'Pandemi Lovato', the 'Panjolina Jolie'. Are all human nicknames for the pandemic female? Other popular terms for Covid still in use include the 'Rona' and 'Boomer Remover'. The ageist snarkiness is perhaps understandable, given the fragile world we are passing along to future generations. A pandemic denier is a 'Covidiot'. Staying home is a 'Coronacation'. Outfits worn inside during quarantine? 'Infits'.

Covid emerged as a mobile global disease and the responses described in this book are themselves localized yet widespread, reminding us that illness and play are misrepresented if we only look at individual cases, even though each one has value. We will remember this time not just for its cycles of sickness and raw emotion but as a time of adjustment to a changing social life. We learned that one park's policies were handled differently from similar ones in another country. One public school's limitations regarding play space and play time differed from another public school within the same city. Pretend play was as varied as families' stories of resourcefulness. Games had different rules and motifs within the same thematic frame. Yet, common themes of isolation and material, temporal and spatial innovation emerged cross culturally. There was a collective sense of loss and wistful opportunity as children in different parts of the world pretended to be ill, to make each other sick and to heal each other, to re-create the daily tasks of pandemic life and to practise escape.

> *We hauled empty luggage*
> *And vaccinated our eyeballs*
> *Muzzled toys in quarantine*
>
> *And were 'not it'*
> *Or maybe had 'it'*
> *Our shuttered lives flung open*
> *By parks and internet*
>
> *And we emerged*
> *Unmasked*
> *Still caped.*

Author Biographies

Catherine Bannister, PhD, is a research associate at the University of Sheffield, exploring children's digital play and wellbeing, and was a researcher on the Play Observatory project investigating children's play during Covid-19. She also spends her time picking up LEGO, tripping over toy Minecraft weaponry and wondering what to cook for tea. Her interests include children's experiences of custom and tradition, in virtual/digital settings as well as in physical ones, and contemporary rites of passage for young people in the context of uniformed youth organizations. Cath is author of *Scouting and Guiding in Britain: The Ritual Socialisation of Young People* (2022) and co-founder of the Contemporary Folklore Research Centre at the University of Sheffield.

Chloé Beatty is currently a PhD researcher in the Department of Psychology in Mary Immaculate College (MIC), Limerick. She graduated with a BSc in applied psychology from the Institute of Art, Design, and Technology (Dún Laoghaire). Her research places a particular emphasis on early screen exposure and engagement, and its impact on socio-emotional and cognitive development in young children. She is also a member of the Cognition, Development and Learning Research Lab in MIC.

Jenn Beideman, MPA is the director of whole child advocacy at Common Ground Health in Rochester, New York. In her role, she oversees the Healthi Kids Coalition, a grassroots coalition advancing whole child health in the Finger Lakes region. Originally from Canada, and mom to an almost one-year-old, Jenn brings to the position over a decade of experience in government relations, public policy, built environment, play based learning, playful learning landscapes and health equity.

Anna Beresin, PhD, serves as professor of psychology and folklore at the University of the Arts in Philadelphia, Pennsylvania. She co-edits the *International Journal of Play* and studies children's folklore, primate physical play, language play and the connections between play, culture and art. Her books include *The Character of Play* (2019), *The Art of Play: Recess and the Practice of Invention* (2014), and *Recess Battles: Playing, Fighting, and Storytelling* (2010). She co-authored *Group Motion in Practice: Collective Creation through Dance Movement Improvisation* with Brigitta Herrmann, Manfred Fischbeck, and Elia Sinaico (2018). Visit her at www.annaberesin.com.

Julia Bishop is research associate in the School of Education, University of Sheffield, UK with a PhD in folklore from Memorial University of Newfoundland. She has documented play and social inclusion, playground games and songs in the new media age, digital play in the early years, memories and experiences of play, and play during the Covid-19 pandemic. Julia is co-chair of the British Academy research project Childhoods and Play: The Opie Archive (www.opiearchive. org), and on the editorial board of the *International Journal of Play*. Her publications include contributions to *Play Today in the Primary School Playground* (2001), *Children, Media and Playground Cultures* (2013), *Children's Games in the New Media Age* (2014), *Changing Play* (2014), and *The Lifework and Legacy of Iona and Peter Opie* (2019).

Michelle Cannon, PhD, is programme leader of the MA in Digital Media: Education at the UCL Institute in Education. She leads the moving image production module and co-facilitates the enquiry module. She is an experienced ethnographer with children and young people and makes use of participatory creative methods of enquiry having worked on two international EU-funded research programmes in collaboration with the British Film Institute and European cultural agencies. She was a co-investigator on the ESRC-funded national Play Observatory project researching instances of children's play and film-making during the pandemic. She is on the editorial board of the journal *Film Education* journal and is an executive member of the *Media Education Association*.

Caron Carter is senior lecturer in early childhood and childhood education at Sheffield Institute of Education, Sheffield Hallam University with a PhD from the University of Sheffield and a National Professional

Qualification for Headship (NPQH). Prior to joining Sheffield Hallam University, Caron was an early years teacher in a nursery infant school and a primary school for eleven years, five years as a deputy headteacher. Caron is currently researching how schools are supporting children's friendships and wellbeing during the 'new normal'. She is part of a team from her university working on funded projects focusing upon improving outcomes for children in specific areas including, friendship, wellbeing, play and transitions. Finally, Caron is also a postgraduate research tutor in education at Sheffield Hallam University and an assistant editor for the *International Journal of Pastoral Care in Education*.

Pool Ip Dong is an assistant professor of early childhood education and a director of the Center for Teaching and Learning in the Institute of Creative Convergence Education at the Changwon National University in South Korea. Her research focuses on children's play with digital media and research methods through digital media, especially digital play, popular culture, new media and art education in early childhood education. Currently, she is conducting studies about Posthumanism and New Materialism in digital play, AI and digital media in early childhood education, and children's creativity and play.

Suzanne Egan is a researcher and lecturer in the Department of Psychology, Mary Immaculate College (MIC), Limerick. She graduated with a PhD in psychology from Trinity College Dublin and also holds postgraduate qualifications in cognitive science and in statistics. Her research examines the processes involved in imagination, thinking and reasoning, and the factors that support development in young children. Suzanne is the director of the Cognition, Development and Learning Research Lab in MIC, which focuses on the impact of playful activities on early development, such as reading, screen time and outdoor play. Recently she has been involved in the evaluation of the Bookseed scheme, an infant book gifting programme in Limerick. She is currently co-chair of the Children's Research Network, an all-Ireland network which brings together researchers, practitioners and policy makers.

Mariia Ermilova, PhD, is an ecologist and environmental educator, doing biocultural diversity concept-based community design projects. She has been working as a co-manager of the Iwase Neighborhood Association in Matsudo, Japan, since 2016, cultivating native flowers and herbal gardens in the area. She is currently a postdoctoral researcher at the Graduate School of Horticulture, Chiba University, Japan.

Dina Faticone is the chief programme officer at Common Ground Health in Rochester, New York, where she has worked collaboratively with community partners to advance whole child health and play for over a decade. Dina's favourite memories of childhood play were riding bikes, playing pick-up games with neighbourhood friends and building forts by the creek in her neighbourhood. Her favourite way to play as an adult is dancing and playing with her eight-year-old son. Dina has a master's degree in sustainable development from Brandeis University.

Carmel Hannan is a lecturer in sociology at the University of Limerick, Ireland, and an expert on Irish family dynamics and child development. Her research interests and publications focus on stratification issues within the family particularly as they relate to class dynamics and she has led a number of research projects in these fields. She received her DPhil from Nuffield College, Oxford. Prior to that, she worked as a senior researcher at the Institute for Social and Economic Research at the University of Essex and at the Economic and Social Research Institute in Dublin.

Ruth Hazleton is an independent academic, oral historian and folklorist based in Melbourne, Australia, with a special interest in children's folklore and traditional play. Ruth conducted field research for *Childhood, Tradition and Change*, a four-year national study of play funded by the Australian Research Council, and has published work related to children's folklore, Australian folklife and traditional music. She has a graduate diploma in Australian Folklife Studies (Curtin) and currently works as an oral history interviewer for the National Library of Australia. Ruth is also a musician and songwriter with an extensive career in the performance of traditional and original song.

Katriina Heljakka, Doctor of Arts, MA Art History, MSc Economics, leads the Pori Laboratory of Play research group at the University of Turku in digital culture studies. Previously, she has worked on the Academy of Finland research project Ludification and Emergence of Playful Culture, and at the Centre of Excellence in Game Culture Studies, and recently as part of museum teams playifying various exhibitions.

Heljakka's academic articles on toys and play experiences have been featured in international publications by the New York University Press, Routledge, Palgrave, and Springer, as well as in multiple scientific journals, such as *American Journal of Play* and the *International Journal of Play*. Heljakka currently studies technologically driven play, playful environments, tools and techniques in playful learning and work, and the visual, material, digital and intergenerational cultures of play.

Clara Hoyne recently completed her PhD at the Department of Psychology in Mary Immaculate College, Limerick, Ireland, and is a member of the Cognition, Development and Learning Research Lab in the department. Her main research interests include early child development, the home learning environment and reading with infants and young children. Clara is also part of the evaluation team of an infant book-gifting programme, Bookseed, which was supported by the JP McManus Foundation and Children's Books Ireland.

Pete King, PhD is a senior lecturer at Swansea University, Wales, and programme director for the MA developmental and therapeutic play course. Pete is the co-editor of the two volumes of *Researching Play from a Playwork Perspective* (2018; 2022) with colleague Dr Shelly Newstead, and co-author of *The Play Cycle: Theory, Research and Application* (2020) with the late Gordon Sturrock. He has developed an observational tool, the Play Cycle Observation Method (PCOM), which records the process of play that underpins the Play Cycle. In March 2020, when the UK went into lockdown, Pete started what turned out to be an eighteen-month longitudinal study on how playwork and playworkers coped with Covid-19 and lockdown.

Živka Krnjaja is a full professor at the University of Belgrade, Serbia, in the Faculty of Philosophy, Department of Pedagogy and Andragogy. In the last six years she has been actively involved in the national reform of early childhood education in Serbia. She is one of the authors of the national curriculum framework for early childhood education, *Years of Ascent*. She is an author and co-author of numerous books and manuals for practitioners, including topics of curriculum development, project learning and pedagogical documentation in kindergarten. Her focus of research and teaching is learning in early childhood education, child's play and creativity, curriculum development and evaluation and research of practitioners.

Nicolas Le Bigre is a teaching fellow in ethnology and folklore and manages the archives at the Elphinstone Institute, University of Aberdeen. His research and teaching interests include migration, folk narrative, personal-experience narrative, memorialization, political materiality and vernacular religion. His work often involves supporting wider community projects across Aberdeen and the North-East of Scotland. He is a council member of the Folklore Society.

Beatriz LeBron is the PlayROCs project coordinator at Common Ground Health in Rochester, New York. She is responsible for executing Healthi Kids' Play ROCs campaign, developing strategies and tactics that advance play as a cornerstone of whole child health in schools and in neighborhoods. She has three children, three grandchildren and a newly adopted puppy.

Shanielia Lewis is the mother of a vibrant and creative daughter. She is a parent leader, advocate and entrepreneur. Shanielia is passionate about community work and consistently seeks out opportunities to contribute to community initiatives. Her current interests include gardening, reading and soap making. Shanielia Lewis has been an active member of the Healthi Kids Coalition in Rochester, New York, for the past five years.

Judy McKinty is an independent children's play researcher, based in Melbourne, Australia, with a special interest in children's folklore and traditional games. Her work includes the study of play in schools; string games workshops; an Aboriginal children's play oral history project with Dr June Factor and field research for *Childhood, Tradition and Change*, a four-year national study of play funded by the Australian Research Council. She has a master of cultural heritage from Deakin University and is an honorary associate of Museums Victoria and a life member of Play Australia. From mid-2020 she researched children's play during the pandemic with Ruth Hazleton.

Nevena Mitranić is a teaching assistant and PhD candidate in pedagogy in the Department of Pedagogy and Andragogy, Faculty of Philosophy, University of Belgrade. As a junior researcher at the Institute of

Pedagogy and Andragogy, she has participated in projects to pilot the preschool curriculum draft *Years of Ascent*, and inclusive early childhood education in Serbia. Her focus of research and teaching are learning in early childhood education, child's play and creativity, curriculum development and evaluation.

Emma Morrison has been active with PlayROCs since 2018 facilitating community driven days for children throughout her neighbourhood in Rochester, New York. She helps organize community play days, complete with games, food and fun activities for children in an environment that is safe for them to play. She organizes field trips to local parks and distributes books to children at her local Recreation Center. Emma hopes to get more parents involved in efforts to support play in their neighbourhoods.

Patricia Neville, PhD, is senior lecturer in social sciences at Bristol Dental School, University of Bristol, England. She is a research active sociologist who advocates for a social science perspective to health research. Her current research interests include sociology of health, gender and equality issues, and professionalism as well as a longstanding interest in contemporary Irish society.

Maria O'Dwyer, PhD, is the national coordinator of the Prevention and Early Intervention Network in Ireland, a collective of practice, advocacy and research organizations that champion timely and appropriate supports as the key to better outcomes for children and families. A sociologist, Maria's particular areas of research expertise and interest are early childhood care and education, outdoor play, child friendly cities and community development.

Yinka Olusoga, PhD, is a lecturer in education at the University of Sheffield where she co-directs the BA in Education, Culture and Childhood. She is the director of the British Academy research project Childhoods and Play: The Iona and Peter Opie Archive, and a co-investigator on the Play Observatory, a collaborative project examining children's play during the Covid-19 pandemic. Yinka's research focuses on discourses and histories of childhood, play and education and on the co-construction of environments for children's play and creative engagement. She is interested in children's digital literacies and the intergenerational co-construction of play and storytelling.

Jennifer Pope, PhD is an early childhood expert, lecturing in the Department of Reflective Pedagogy and Early Childhood Studies in Mary Immaculate College, Limerick, Ireland. She graduated with a PhD in paediatric epidemiology in 2006. Jennifer's research examines the impact of early life experiences on health and well-being. She is passionate about the importance of early childhood and the need to address inequities and promote children's well-being in the earliest years. Jennifer has a particular interest in the professional development of ECCE students and in researching how children's well-being is promoted from an ecological perspective, including the role of the outdoors, play and the early learning environment.

John Potter is professor of media in education at University College London's Faculty of Education & Society. He is director of the ReMAP (Researching Media Arts and Play) research centre and associate director (media) of the UCL Knowledge Lab. His research relates to media education, play on and offscreen, theories of curation and agency in social media, and teaching and learning in the context of digital media. He recently directed the ESRC-funded National Observatory of Children's Play Experiences during COVID-19, a collaboration with colleagues in the School of Education at the University of Sheffield and the UCL Centre for Advanced Spatial Analysis. Previously, he worked as a primary school teacher in Tower Hamlets in London's East End, as a local authority education advisor in Newham, and as a teacher educator at both Goldsmiths College and the University of East London.

Martha Radice is a social anthropologist whose work focuses on the social, spatial, and cultural dynamics of cities. Her current ethnographic research, a contribution to the anthropology of joy, explores new-wave carnival culture in New Orleans, Louisiana, especially as it relates to sociability, material culture, urban space, and the politics of race. Like her previous projects and her PhD in Urban Studies, it is funded by the Social Sciences and Humanities Research Council of Canada. Dr Radice is associate professor in the Department of Sociology and Social Anthropology at Dalhousie University, Halifax, Nova Scotia, and a past president of the Canadian Anthropology Society.

Will Renel is a practice-based researcher with a background in inclusive play. Having completed his doctorate in communication design at the Royal College of Art, Will is currently the director of research at Touretteshero CIC and a postdoctoral research associate at the Helen Hamlyn Centre for Design. Will's work is situated between the fields of critical disability studies and inclusive design and centres anti-ableist practices and non-normative ways of being, thinking and doing.

Lydia Rivera is a mom, a small business owner and a passionate advocate for kids and family voice. She is vice president of the Edgerton Neighborhood Association and a member of the Healthi Kids Coalition in Rochester, NY. Lydia advances community play by organizing days of active play for children in her neighborhood through the PlayROCS Advocacy Committee. She recruits and organizes parents to participate in other initiatives as well, such as the Parent Leadership Training Institute, efforts to beautify the community of Edgerton, and the Greater Rochester Health Foundation's learning collaborative and grant funding endeavors to support youth whole child health.

Hitoshi Shimamura is the founder and the director of the organization TOKYO PLAY. He is also the director of the Japan Playwork Association. After graduating from Sophia University, he completed the programme in playwork at Leeds Metropolitan University in the United Kingdom. He then worked at Hanegi Play Park in Tokyo and Children's Yume Park in Kawasaki. In 2005-2011, he served as the regional vice president of East Asia of the International Play Association (IPA).

Heather Shirey, PhD is a professor of art history at the University of St Thomas in Saint Paul, Minnesota, USA. Her teaching and research focus on race and identity, migrations and diasporas, and street art and its communities. Shirey is a co-director of the Urban Art Mapping research team, a multi-disciplinary group of faculty and students. The group created and manages multiple street art archives, including the Covid-19 Street Art Database (https://covid19streetart.omeka.net) and the George Floyd and Anti-Racist Street Art Database (https://georgefloydstreetart.omeka.net).

Holly Sienkiewicz is a mother to two active young boys, ages two and five, and serves as director of research at Common Ground Health, a regional health planning agency in the Finger Lakes region of New York, USA. She witnessed the effects of the Covid-19 pandemic on her own children developmentally and socially and wants to ensure that all children can continue to play, imagine, and create as the pandemic ebbs and flows. Holly loves to hike and explore new places with her family, and to read to her children daily. Her doctorate is in public health education from the University of North Carolina at Greensboro.

Mitsunari Terada (Charlie), PhD, works as a landscape planner, facilitating local governance for child-friendly communities. He is an IPA Japan board member and a senior researcher of the Information Research Center for Japan Adventure Playground Association. He is a specially appointed assistant professor in the Faculty of Regional Policy of Takasaki City University of Economics, and practically lives in a community centre as a co-manager of the Iwase Neighborhood.

Jessica Thom is an artist, writer and part-time superhero who co-founded Touretteshero CIC in 2010 as a creative response to her experience of living with Tourettes Syndrome. Jess worked for over a decade as a playworker in London and is currently the co-artistic director of Touretteshero. Jess campaigns for disability rights and social justice and is on a mission to change the world 'one tic at a time'.

Danielle von der Borch has been a playworker at the Venny since 2001. The Venny was established in 1981 in Melbourne, Australia, as a communal backyard for children in public housing and local community. Currently in the role of director of play and programmes, Danni has a deep commitment to the protection of free play and the child's right to freedom and belonging. A graduate of Victorian College of the Arts, her creative practices inform her work and she engages with a therapeutic intention while working with vulnerable children. Danni has an MA in Creative Art Therapy, MIECAT Institute, and is also a performer, previously with Rawcus Theatre, 2009-2022.

Postscript:
Suggestions for Those Who Work and Play with Children, Youth and Adults

Anna Beresin and Julia Bishop, with Chloé Beatty, Caron Carter,

Suzanne Egan, Beatriz LeBron, Ruth Hazleton, Katriina Heljakka,

Nicolas Le Bigre, Shanielia Lewis, Judy McKinty, Nevena Mitranić,

Emma Morrison, Patricia Neville, John Potter, Martha Radice,

Holly Sienkiewicz, and Danni von der Borch

We arranged to continue our cross-cultural dialogue and move it from print to Zoom and back to print again. Given play's profound connection to vitality, what have we discovered about play and Covid and about what might come next? The challenging paradox here is that play can and cannot be planned, but it certainly can be unnecessarily diminished.

The following contains suggestions for discussion and recommendations for training and practice. Eighteen researchers participated—the transcript here greatly reduced with the content chosen for relevance and edited or rearranged for clarity. The text here does not do the discussions justice given the warmth and enthusiasm of these virtual meetings. All of us were working in isolation, or in small teams, and had not met prior to these conversations. The first meeting included the editors and Chloé Beatty, Suzanne Egan, Beatriz LeBron, Shanielia Lewis, Emma Morrison, Patricia Neville, Martha Radice and Holly Sienkiewicz. The second involved the editors, Caron Carter, Katriina Heljakka, Nicolas Le Bigre, Nevena Mitranić and John Potter.

    https://doi.org/10.11647/OBP.0326.21

Much of the significance here extends well beyond the Covid pandemic, relating both to the field of play advocacy in general, and also to what might be anticipated during future pandemics. We present it as a single piece representing the two online meetings, with a written introduction by three esteemed Australian researchers for whom the meetings took place in the wee hours of the morning—Judy McKinty, Ruth Hazleton and Danni von der Borch.

What We Learned: The Australian Pandemic Play Project

Free play is fundamentally important to children of all ages and something that must be understood at a sophisticated level by government policymakers and education departments alike. In play, children can reclaim a sense of self, feel more whole and more in control. Through free play, children control the narrative themselves and learn how to explore, express and come to terms with situations they don't understand, giving them a strong sense of agency in a crisis. Opportunities for play are, and should be, a core feature of therapeutic treatment and recovery from trauma.

Research conducted throughout the pandemic has highlighted the need for all children to have easy access to safe outdoor spaces to play. This is particularly relevant to children living in high-density situations (such as multistorey apartments and high-rise public housing), and children from lower socioeconomic and disadvantaged backgrounds. The provision of secure public spaces for children to play in allows them to experience a sense of ownership and agency through play. These spaces must be made available for the exclusive use of children and young people, where they can feel safe, welcomed, and enjoy the freedom to create, make, tear down and start again.

Relevant to both school and public play contexts, these spaces should also allow children to play safely away from the constant scrutiny and intervention of adults.

Our research also highlighted the enormous inequities in the availability and provision of resources for play, particularly during lockdown, including technological equipment and access to the internet. Due to various factors (such as geographic location, socioeconomic situation and ability of schools to provide children with devices and tech resources), this requires more careful consideration with significant implications for both play and educational equality.

Based on The Pandemic Play Project (Australia), we would recommend the following:

- That access to the internet and technological equipment is reviewed at policy level and prioritized for children in educational and home settings.

- That government and non-government aid agencies incorporate the distribution of open-ended play materials and equipment as part of emergency relief packages: for example, craft supplies, paint and other construction materials, simple toys, modeling clay, skateboards or bikes

- That at a policy level, children must play a consultative role in the planning and design of play spaces, especially for children of school age. Children are, after all, the experts in play.

- That local jurisdictions be encouraged to fund play spaces designed to allow children to play more freely within a safe space.

- That qualified play workers be engaged within schools and school jurisdictions on a regular basis.

- That parents have better access to educational material about the value and importance of allowing children to play more freely, including the importance of digital and online play as well as in physical spaces.

- That coursework on the characteristics and importance of play be developed and delivered as a core subject for undergraduate students studying education, childhood, and teen development.

Voices from Canada, England, Ireland, Scotland, Finland, Serbia and the United States

Anna: Welcome. So glad you are all here.

Study Play Across the Lifespan

Martha: Am I the only one who did not study children's play? Children are involved in the kind of carnival that I studied to a certain degree, and certainly they love 'tit Rɘx shoe box parade because it's tiny, but my research highlights the importance of play for adults, especially making as play, a kind of playing with materials, because that's what people did during the pandemic carnival. I mean this is what they do anyway in carnival, but they just took it to a new, different direction in 2021. The house floats that my chapter discusses were created on a domestic scale but were also an experience shared across the city. I think it's important to think about play beyond the family unit—play in a neighbourhood and on a larger community level.

Anna: Including your work was intentional, Martha, not just because it was really fun and beautiful to see, but I think Julia and I shared a commitment to the idea that that paradoxically play is essential for children but it's also essential across the lifespan. Some of the greatest theorists of play have talked about the continuum of play rather than the uniqueness of it during childhood, even though it may be critical during childhood.

Martha: The development stuff is great but it also makes it still very instrumental, and the fun thing about looking at adult players is that one assumes that adults are more or less fully developed, although we can always learn more and develop more, but the frivolous elements of play are no bad thing, right?

Shanielia: I'm really happy Martha said this because I have a teenager and I see as she gets older—there's less intention around including play in her activities, and that concerns me because there is no less need for play outside of organized sports. I am always looking for ways to engage her and her creativity. She's really creative, and I'm finding less opportunity for that in our communities. Martha, I got really excited to hear you speak, because even as adults, like we forget how to play, and I think we train our teenagers to do that. Now you have to get serious. Now you've got to think about college, and none of that. And we wonder, like, why are they less engaged in school? They don't want to go to school any more. They don't want to learn any more, because it's no longer fun. They're not playing. And we learn more when things are fun, instead of having to, like, memorize things, which is unfortunately what our education system has become. But even for myself. I'm wondering now, I think I need more fun. How do I play either by myself or with my friends? I think I've lost track of this over time.

Anna: Can I jump in and ask you a question? You said that your teenager has opportunities for creativity, but less so for play. How do you distinguish the two?

Shanielia: She goes to a school of the arts, and I see her less excited about doing art now, because it involves a grade, and it involves being defined and monitored. And you know it has to be a certain way. And the more that happens, the less excited she is about it. She just wants to do her thing how she wants to do it. Provide her with materials and leave her alone, and it's starting to become more of like being told what art should look like and how she needs to be, and she's like 'Yeah, I don't want to do this anymore'. And it's, you know, I'm literally watching this in real time. So that's the difference to me, like play comes from you. It's like a creative spark from you that excites you, whereas you know the other stuff, it's like, 'Okay, I'm creating this container for you, and you have to operate within it'.

Holly: I'm really glad you shared that Shanielia and we haven't met in person, but I'm Holly, and we emailed and communicated while writing this chapter, but we have yet to meet in person. That's a lot of what our Healthi Kids team is trying to do is focus on unstructured play. And how do we provide more opportunities for kids to have unstructured play? Because Shanielia you're exactly right, once you put the parameters and the structure around it, it becomes innately less fun, and I feel like there's too much structure already in our children's lives.

Value Unstructured Play

Chloé: That's something that also shone through in the work we did during Covid as well during lockdowns, the level of unstructured play rose and that was commented on positively from the parents as well.

Patricia: Therein lies the rub of it, the paradox because we here are advocates for unstructured play, for that which can't be limited, that comes from within and is spontaneous, organic. And yet the conversations that we're automatically drawn into at a policy level, you know, even within educational discourse, is, we need to sort of pin it down.

Anna: Let's unpack this a bit more. Holly wrote this interesting thing in the chat, she's said, 'I would like to add that some educators remove play as a punishment for behaviour issues within school, not realizing that that is really detrimental to children's education, and has the potential to affect them negatively academically as well'. I would add, it is so negative, it can be seen as a public health issue. I know the American Academy of Pediatrics came out with a statement saying what a terrible idea it is to remove recess as a punishment, but many elementary schools in America still do. So, to link these two, I'm curious, how do we advocate for the unstructured?

Julia: Does anyone have the silver bullet?

Shanielia: I want to say just like education, a lot of things affect that space without having to be directly linked. Okay, I think I definitely had more free play growing up than my daughter does, and part of that is the expectation and the emphasis on grades and the emphasis on a certain path.

Holly: Part of working with Beatriz and working with Shanielia and our Healthi Kids team, part of it is advocating for safe place spaces, too. So many of the families in our area there's not outdoor spaces that parents are always comfortable having their kids walk to, like the neighbourhood park. They're not necessarily comfortable with that, so it's, you know, it's advocating for play, but it's also for healthy communities and advocating for these spaces to be safe for people to be out and about and accessing the resources that may already exist that may need improvement. But accessing what's there as well.

Anna: One of the things I think we can do is for us all to return copies of this book to the people that we studied, if we were affiliated with a programme or a school or a parent group, to close the loop in terms of communication.

Broaden the Vision of Play Advocacy

Martha: This question of how we advocate or how we structurally make play more important for everybody is a really good one because, for me, one of the interesting things about studying New Orleans is what we can learn from the practices of carnival that are very much embedded in the city. They are complex and have multiple purposes. So, they're put to instrumental uses as well with the place marketing and tourism promotion, and so on. But there are also these practices that give everybody the liberty of playing for a period every single year, and part of my argument is that the reason they were able to adapt carnival so well to the pandemic is that carnival is always improvisational, and it's always responding to current events.

But it's very much embedded in everyday life, so one of the questions that's always trotting round in my head is, how can you foster that structure elsewhere? How can you have license to play on an ongoing regular basis? I think it really helps that it's this one season every year. Make it regular. And then there are some quite peculiar things, like there's actually a bylaw forbidding commercialization of carnival sponsorship, so it's never the Kellogg's Carnival. It's never the ScotiaBank Carnival. It helps people feel like it belongs to them rather than to a corporate sponsor. So yeah, these are always the questions I think about in relation to the relevance of my research.

Anna: One of the things that seems so unique about New Orleans carnival is that it's not just a one-day thing, that people spend 364 days prepping for that one day. I think sometimes that special time thing for children gets translated into a commercial carnival; it comes in and sets up in the school yard. They do a play day and then it's over. What I've seen here in industrial northeast America, it becomes a one-and-done thing and kids hold their breath all year waiting for that one fun day because they're not involved in the prep. They're not involved in the tradition and the ritual. But I think you're onto something about this paradox of tradition. How do you establish new and flexible traditions around play?

Shanielia: I wanted to speak about normalizing play, those are my words. We have a museum, a play museum here in Rochester. The kids hit the door, they already know, 'I'll see you at a certain time' and they just want to tear it up for whatever period of time, and I think that's a very valued way of, like, creating intentional play spaces where we can take our families. But then comes the conversation around accessibility, right? Because there's a charge to do so. How do we create accessible safe spaces for all of us? Because some of these things do exist but there's a price tag attached. If it exists and we can't access it, then what's the point? How do we identify, then resource, the things that are already in our communities, instead of trying to reinvent the wheel?

Notice the Blending of Play in Physical and Digital Spaces

Martha: The contagion of creative ideas was interesting. The Pass the Brush videos; did you see those? Or Don't Rush challenge videos where people would make videos collectively but apart to kind of show their solidarity, and so on, very beautiful videos that were often rather fun. And then the house floats. What happened in New Orleans was that because parades were cancelled, people decided to decorate their houses as carnival floats. It all started with a Twitter joke. And then all of a sudden, there were thousands of homes in the city that got on board and decided to make this version of carnival happen. Somebody said, 'Okay, it's decided. Let's do this'. Let's decorate our houses as floats and throw beads from our attic to passersby. So, it's very unevenly distributed, right?

There are people who were working far too hard to be able to engage in these things. But then there were a lot of people who were furloughed or working from home, or who needed something to do with kids at home. Another phenomenon like this was the re-creation of artworks that people did with domestic objects that spread around the internet. I mean, you can tell that I have time to look all these things up and was not trying to corral small children into doing online school! So, yes, it was unevenly distributed, and it depended on resources and so on.

But I found it surprising that people found the time, that people took those ideas and ran with them.

Chloé: I find that actually extremely heartening to hear how something like that can happen from such a simple act like a tweet or a social media post. Because if we think back to the question that you posed earlier on, how do we get these messages out? To policymakers, to advocates, sometimes it's as simple as 'Let's just make a post on social media. Let's just have a voice'. Everyone has the power to have a voice with globalization, with social media these days.

Suzanne: One of the things that actually struck me with some of the data that I gathered and actually used, and Martha's use of the word 'contagion' put it into my mind, following on from her point, was children bringing the pandemic into their play. I think one of the things that was, oh, surprising and not surprising was just the range of ages of children, the variety of backgrounds, and the variety of locations globally, where we see a broad influence of the environment shaping children's play. But it's still slightly surprising to see that children in Ireland and England and Australia and America, they're all putting masks on their dolls. They all have their teddy bears washing their hands.

We know children often use play in response to trauma, to ill health or to war. But I don't think there's ever been such a large-scale, mass, unwanted experiment where we've seen such a large negative effect happen to pretty much every child all across the world, how many of them brought Covid into their play. So, I suppose that was one of the surprising and not surprising things for me in terms of some of the findings that we saw on our research, in Ireland and internationally as well.

Julia: I just wanted to follow on a little bit from Suzanne's point. Really, I'm not sure whether it's a coping strategy. But what really surprised me just going back to that question was the corona chasing games, the Corona Tag, using evidence that I gathered from Twitter, because it's very difficult to be in all the playgrounds of the world simultaneously. It was just amazing how much just through tweets you are able to gather just how widespread that game was and that, it just apparently sprung up pretty much overnight amongst children who could not have possibly transmitted it to each other during that time. But you know also, I was very struck by how very varied it was, and creative, and how incredibly responsive it was to what was happening in the media.

An example I have in my chapter concerns Marcus Rashford, the footballer, and how he had successfully campaigned for a voucher scheme, set up during lockdown for children in poverty who were entitled to free school meals, to be continued in the summer holidays too. And someone had reported a variation in the [Coronavirus] Tag game, and it was that if they were tagged with 'Tory', the Conservative party, they weren't allowed to eat until someone tags them with 'Rashford'. So, they had to be touched with those terms, and it was just incredible.

Another one was a Stuck in the Mud game and one of the release mechanisms after you'd been caught was you had to put out your arms like a soap dispenser or hand sanitizer and, if your arm was pressed, then you were released because you'd been 'disinfected' and you hadn't got corona anymore. Another release mechanism was the children had to sing 'Happy Birthday' twice. I just was astonished— we're talking middle childhood here, you know, the seven-to-eleven age group—just how sensitive they were, responding immediately to discourses they were hearing in adult worlds. Now whether that's a coping mechanism, I'm not sure, but I think it's a really interesting thing that perhaps we haven't really clocked sufficiently.

Provide Material Access for Play

Emma: One good thing came out of this, because I have my great grandchildren over the summer months, we were able to go to the Recreation Center because they serve lunch there. So that was a treat for them to walk down and be able to see other people. One thing I used to do there was, to keep myself separated from a lot of people, was take them down to the park and walk them around the pond, and they were able to learn about you know, fish, about the ducks about the geese that were there, and you know, just to get near the water and stuff; it's things like that I was able to do with them. Just being able to be around other people was important. And they gave us bags, you know, with free items in them, and we used them, because there's a lot of different things, different activities in there that they could learn by. And it just made me feel better about this situation.

Holly: I was just going to say for those who didn't read our chapter, part of what we talked about, and what Emma's referring to is this Play Kit distribution, so really assembling thousands of play kits. There were things like footballs, beach balls, jump ropes, chalk, colouring books, you know, just things that could be given out in a bag to families, to the children, just to help encourage play whether it was indoors or out. That was kind of one of the elements of how the Healthi Kids team tried to keep play going during the pandemic.

Anna: Thank you both for sharing that. There's some great stuff going on in the chat.

Beatriz wrote: 'Kinetic toys, balls, slime, chalk, bubbles, colouring items, too. We also did some where we partnered with our local PBS station to do some nature exploration. Many kids' card games etc., FYI on the Play Kits'.

Martha added: 'there's a community art organization in Halifax-Wonder'neath- that distributed thousands of art kits to kids in a similar way'.

Julia wrote: 'the opportunities afforded by the pandemic for play in communication are something one hopes young ones will recall in later years'.

Chloé noted: 'Emma's experience really ties in with the idea of "learning lost during lockdown," and how there were plenty of opportunities for learning, just not in the conventional sense'.

Suzanne: One of the things that really came through in the data that we gathered in May and June 2020, so it was kind of early on, it was the first lockdown. It was quite severe in Ireland, with a two-kilometre restriction on our movement, and everything was closed. All businesses, all schools. So, you know it was very much each family unit was in their own home. People weren't traveling to see families, playgrounds were closed. Everything was closed. One of the things that we spoke about, and you mentioned the subtitle of creativity, is kind of some of the ways people got creative in their play and in their adaptations to this unprecedented situation. But one of the things that really came through in our survey was how much the children were missing all of their friends, and all of the parents missing the social supports and their networks, this came through really strongly as well. So. Yes, there were some positives for play, but there were lots of negatives to both for play and for mental health.

Caron: I really had a sense from the data that the parents had got this sort of renewed value and appreciation of play and friendship. That really came across quite strongly. It may have been there before, but I think all of the parents kind of emphasized that. You know, in that absence that noticed how important friendship and play were. Also, I was just thinking about also Katriina's sort of play with objects. I wrote something a couple of years ago around how children often see these objects a bit like imaginary friends, as their friends. And I collected some data with children who had LEGO figures and actually referred to them as their friends, you know, and have them in their pockets, and had them at school with them. And it kind of afforded them perhaps some security, but also made them feel much more confident in the presence of these object friends.

Honour a Sense of Loss

Suzanne: Lots of parents talked about, you know, maybe a safe place in a daycare centre, or in the school that was no longer available. There was too much traffic in the neighbourhood, or, they couldn't let them out. Just missing out on friends, but how difficult it might be for the youngest children to keep in touch with friends online. So those young children don't have smartphones. They're not great on Zoom with maintaining conversations. So, I think that besides the isolation, missing out on those connections and those interactions, different types of playful opportunities and different types of play, it's something that kind of negatively affected the experiences at the time. I think people of all ages felt that again kind of globally, it's very much a universal experience.

Holly: I would add in and echo those thoughts. There's something like this sense of ambiguous loss where you don't really know what you've lost. But you lost something.

I'm a parent of two young kids, two and five, and the baby was born right before Covid started. So, a young family, we didn't have any support, and his aunt he met eighteen months later. I know my five-year-old now, he's starting to attend birthday parties for friends and he's like 'Well, why, haven't I ever had one?' We did it as a family, but when his birthday was, there were exposures. Families have handled Covid restrictions differently. I have seen in my own children, them not understanding it, and that's something that they're still grappling with.

Suzanne: I think it is also because children obviously develop so quickly. You know you kind of have a new child every six months. My own children were six and eight when we entered the pandemic; now they're eight and eleven. I'm kind of looking at my children exiting their childhood, you know, in the not-too-distant future. I'm kind of thinking, I thought we had another couple of years to do that thing. Sometimes it feels like forever, and other times it's gone in a blink of an eye. For a two-year-old, or a four-year-old, or a six-year-old, it is a huge chunk of their life that they have been living with these really weird circumstances. I think we won't know, for a few years to come, actually, the full effect of this, both on their play behaviours, and on all aspects of their development when the whole world shut down.

Anna: In the chat, Beatriz wrote that '[her] experience with [her] grandson who is just now getting to explore more, now that he's turning three, he has lost some social development'.

Shanielia: I want to contribute as a parent of an older child. The isolation did affect her developmentally in terms of, like, where she was. We know that right now as teens your friends are everything. And so it was really heartbreaking, like for me as a parent.

When she saw her friends out in public, I had to say, 'Remember, it's Covid', because the instinct is to run and hug your friend. And that it felt like she was being robbed, and I'm the person robbing her because I'm having to say to her, 'You know you can't do that' and it was so heartbreaking. But one thing I also do see—was how she and her friends adapted. They leaned heavily into social media and creating things that they shared so they could have, like, still a collective experience. They did lots of group calls, like I felt dragged into the virtual world, where I think the transition for them was just building, because it's a natural playground for them, right? So they used those tools to create collective experiences for themselves, until they were able to go back to school and be together physically.

Anna: Just like us right now.

Shanielia: For me, it was more work, but for them it was more play. It was another tool, and so they just transitioned into it like that. It was something they had command of, they had control of, like. They checked in with each other continuously, and where, as before, I think there would be more one-on-one interactions, it was more like a group. So there was like a group call going all the time, or something was happening, and I'm like, 'Hey? What's going on?' and just like, 'Oh, I'm here with so-and-so, and so-and-so talking', even though physically they were isolated. I don't know how it affected anybody else's family. So, in your home you're with your family and being in school you're with your friends—that separation kind of just diminished even more.

Recentre Culture and Social Life in Recommendations for Play

Nevena: What we tried to do is to connect many different actors, like students, kindergarten teachers, parents, and children as well, in something that they do together.

Anna: How would you expand that on a policy level? How would you take the idea of the importance of social life and community life, and implement it in a concrete way?

Nevena: We had this sort of agreement at the policy level as well, because our ministry puts those sorts of suggestions for kindergarten professionals as what they should do in the time of the pandemic, and we were consulted, so we told them what to do. Like not to put pressure on the content the children should go through, but just put the focus on the opportunities together, opportunities to communicate together with parents, with children. To just let them play. And the policy levels stood behind this idea and published this. It's something that's official. So, I think that meant a lot, because it was the official recommendation for the entire country.

Caron: In my chapter I talk a lot about time and space to build and just nurture friendships, particularly now post-Covid, to reconnect. There are times where children, particularly young children, haven't been able to socialize and we know that play is so integral to friendship. This has, you know, affected those relationships with some children, the idea that children hadn't been able to physically interact. You see, this sort of rough and tumble play, and this sort of hugging and wrestling, and you know that kind of thing, that there hadn't been those sorts of play, it had been missing.

I would add time to reconnect. It kind of links in with that idea of well-being, because I think for some children, they had found ways to connect, that might have been online ways to connect. It might have been through a video call. Or, some children were able to engage with imaginative play online through Zoom with friends. So, for some children it had worked quite well. But then for other children it just hadn't worked at all you know, and they felt uncomfortable in those contexts.

Nicolas: I can think of lots of examples from fieldwork and from other things where people expressed ill ease with societal pressures, especially during the pandemic, of having to gather with people like 'Oh God, it's another Zoom night with my eighteen relatives. How am I going to deal with this?'

Caron: The bubble systems that we had in schools in England meant that some children couldn't play with their friends that they usually play with. So, for some it was quite a profound loss really for them, and they kind of almost had gone through that kind of grieving process of not being able to be with and play with the children that they wanted to. So, there was a real impact on well-being for some children.

Anna: May I ask, the bubbles, we call them 'pods' here in the States, were they naturally occurring? Or were they assigned by the schools?

Caron: I mean I don't know for all schools, but it seemed to be from the parents that I interviewed that they were sort of assigned by the schools. So, schools decided locally how they were going to do that. So, for some it was classes were split up, or for some children they could only play with the children in their class. For some of the schools, it could be that they could play with the whole year group. But the children talked a lot about it. The parents in that scenario talked a lot about if they were in a particular year group, and they couldn't play with somebody who was in the other class or year group that they had previously played with and that that was a big thing. And I know for some children, they found it difficult to reconnect afterwards and to go back to those friendships, because what happened was when children were put into those bubbles, then there were lots of issues when they came back together, because some children had managed to forge new friendships, and some hadn't, you know; so it's quite complex really. Some children might have had well-established, quality relationships that were able to reconnect again, and for others, it just, it just didn't work for them and they lost friends.

Katriina: The first really artefact-based evidence that we have collected during this pandemic about the importance of physical objects and the kinds of meanings they channel, is that they are communal objects, and very important for our building of this resilience. So that's the first lesson and the second one is that, yes, the resilience aspect I already mentioned, but I'd like to think of a playful take on that term and title it "playful resilience" because I have understood that it's very much about survival by doing and doing by playing. This represents sort of a type of toy activism. It has a lot to do with human gestures, and what we saw humans doing during the pandemic through screens. And they were these very tender and affectionate gestures, like the two toys hugging each other. Third, the Teddy Challenge proved, as a hybrid form of play, that screens can be extremely important for our well-being. Teddy bears and other plush toys were displayed behind window screens captured by the camera functions, and thus screens of mobile devices and ultimately shared through social media, mainly observed and consumed through various screens on smartphones, tablets, and computers, and without the inclusion of smart devices and social media. The phenomenon could not have become viral and global, highlighting an instance of what I then have termed ludounity, playing for the common good.

Question 'Resilience'

Anna: One of the topics that came up in our parallel discussion yesterday is the love and discomfort we have with the word 'resilience'. On the one hand, the whole study of play during this time is really about this sense of survival and resilience, exactly what you were talking about, and on the other hand there's some anthropological discussion around the word which suggests that the term puts the onus on the individual to be plucky to pull themselves up by their bootstraps and just carry on individually. To tie back to Nevena's opening comment and also Caron's idea of the communal response to the pandemic, does this in a way put the burden on the child, or on the family?

Katriina: It's a very good question, and a very good point. And this is not an individual matter in the sense that a transitional object is in the traditional sense, and our understandings of the plush toy or soft animal, mainly the representing of the mother for the child. This is that maybe that discussion should be unpacked somewhere, a little more in detail. But you're absolutely right not to put the pressure on the young individual that a child is. In Finnish we have *sisu*, which is translated often to 'guts' and guts is sort of an inner power that makes you go the extra mile. And this is a very cultural thing for Finnish people who have survived the wars before, and it has a lot of historical baggage in a sense. But I happen to know a *sisu* researcher who works in the area of positive psychology, and we have talked with her about play and its relation to this *sisu*. There's a word in English called grit? Grit, yes? Does that describe what I just said?

Nicolas: Actually, I was quite interested in your discussion of resilience, and I think one way that we might consider resilience is on a scale of privilege, I guess, because I think some people are perhaps more privileged to be resilient than others are. It certainly is in the UK context.

Being a folklorist, we always talk about childlore, which is really interesting, but I think lots of people can tend to see play only through the prism of childhood. But what I saw through my article, I guess from my book chapter, is that play exists through the ethnographers who are doing the work; they are willing participants in play as well. You know, the ethnography itself can be seen through the prism of play.

But in terms of the privileges of resilience, I mean in the UK, one thing that seemed striking to me was that in lockdown, all the public parks were made inaccessible for a period of time. I had a big project called the Lockdown Collection Project, and people were sending me their creative responses to the pandemic and that's sort of the basis of my chapter. And one person was talking about all these fantastic challenges she was setting for her children in her garden and she sent fifty videos of her kids doing an obstacle course and other things like that, absolutely wonderful stuff. But I couldn't help but think of all the kids for whom traditionally their only place to do that would have been the playground where all of the swing sets were chained up and closed off. Or you know, other kids were telling me about how they were using the internet. They were, you know, using Snapchat, or whatever other exciting apps that existed to sort of converse with their friends. But then there's, you know, a larger cohort than I think most people realize, people who have no access to the internet or very unstable internet connections, particularly in rural areas in Scotland. So that was completely unavailable to those children.

In terms of public policy, it's understanding the effects of targeting and criminalizing things like using public parks because it's really easy for somebody who is making this policy who has their own garden. We had lots of situations in Scotland, and in the UK where neighbours would be calling out people in the public park. And they would say, 'Oh, there's somebody using the swings or somebody using the park right now. They're breaking lockdown rules'. And they would, you know, get a fine or whatever it is. So, if somebody is using the park in that context it's probably because they don't have access to their own garden, and most likely the person making that phone call has their own garden. So, I think that idea of being privileged enough to be resilient is something that's probably worth bearing in mind.

John: I think that resilience has a political dimension in our country as well in the sense that there was for a longtime kind of directive to schools to take up resilience guidelines and educate children for resilience at the same time as the government is imposing really draconian austerity on already very poor people. So, although I'm drawn to it in the sense of, we know of children who've been in really drastic situations—you can see examples of children's resilience sadly every night on the TV screen and coming in from Ukraine—and there is something in that. But the political use of the word resilience is to be resisted, I think.

When Julia and I and the other team members were talking, Yinka Olusoga came up with 'resourcefulness' as a kind of a word to capture more than resilience, because resourcefulness suggests the use of available resources, be they linguistic or material or spatial to play in some way. So, we've begun to use resourcefulness as well, haven't quite let go of resilience, but I have so many caveats to do with giving in to austerity as being a good idea.

Document Changing Culture

John continues: So, our concept for the chapter was to present a series of images as a photo essay. But when I was thinking about it, it drove me into the literature about what a photo essay does, and how it can be used in terms of representing a psychological state, a personal state, a creative state. So perhaps the most famous example would be the dust bowl photographs by Walker Evans that accompanied James Agee's *Let Us Now Praise Famous Men*. Beyond the gendered language from that time, it was, you know, landless farmers, and some of those images are so striking. It was an enormous kind of photo essay. I wanted to choose twelve images that represented, broadly speaking, the different kinds of things that came into the wonderful survey environment that was designed by the Sheffield team to welcome families and children in, and so the images that I selected were of that nature. They showed public art. They showed private spaces. They showed children interacting with screens. They showed things that children made on screen.

So, the light bulb moment really is to see the variety, to look at the ways in which screens were used, to remember that in the early days of the various lockdowns UNICEF said, 'Children, play with screens!' after years of saying, 'Children, don't play with screens!' Suddenly, it was okay. It was like permission had been given. So now, of course, screens are bad again. It's come back round the other way, unless it's educational software.

I was thinking about the differences between categorization and thematic analysis. So, when you're a qualitative researcher and when you're an archivist with an eye on the future and heritage, how do those two things work together? That's been in the DNA of the Play Observatory which has led to some really interesting conversations about what we do. And a complicating factor for us was that there was also an exhibition in which there's like a third layer of interpretation, which is by a kind of public-facing youth museum, called the Young V&A, formerly the Museum of Childhood, appending their own kind of categorizations to what we were looking at and how the interpretation process works. What is the audience, and how do you go through it, and how do you preserve the child's voice?

Katriina: I guess it's a matter of personal survival, to deal with this through researching it. I'm making sense out of being a playing human amidst this kind of crisis.

Nicolas: One thing that I'm curious about and have looked at a fair bit is the idea of rules, and there were various kinds of rules during the pandemic. There was, you know, the sort of physical rules imposed, given the fact that there is this virus that could kill any one of us. And then there's also governmental rules, and then there's also the embedded rules of various games that we play. One of the most interesting things for me was probably one of the funnest to read, examples of play from some of our contributors where people described when they were breaking rules, and when they were breaking lockdown rules. And the sort of glee with which they were saying it, such as this one person's talking about a ninety-three-year-old woman who holds cocktail parties in her flat. I wonder to what extent that made its way across all the other examples here, if rules came up at all, and rule breaking?

Anna: It certainly came up in my chapter on techno-mischief, the microanalysis of a Zoom play date. There was a deliciousness in subtle and selected rule breaking.

Julia: Some of the early reports of Coronavirus Tag, the chase game that seems to have been very widely disseminated during this time and seems to have just cropped up in the minds of so many children simultaneously, virtually overnight, I was able to find evidence via Twitter, which is not the most neutral source of evidence, that it was weaponized by some who didn't want kids to go back to school again, and in all sorts of tweets. There were accounts of children who actually, despite the fact that they were actually being told the rules, and the rules were literally that that they mustn't touch, they mustn't get within two metres of each other, and so on, teachers are saying they went straight out. They had the assembly. They were told the rules. They went straight out into the playground, and they began tagging each other by coughing on each other.

They absolutely seemed to be subversive, oppositional and challenging. They were playing with those rules in their own games with rules. And it really struck me that this wasn't just tabloidism. It was actually something that was happening, to some extent. Tag is just so widespread. It is iconic of children's sociability and interaction in those school settings, and this seemed to threaten the game. It has this whole metaphor of contagion and yet it paradoxically was threatening their whole sociability at the time.

Anna: Do you think it was because they felt it was so extreme? The limitations? They used this aggressive coughing as they had nothing left to interact with?

Play's Purpose Is Not to Have a Single Purpose

Suzanne: One of the things that I've learned through my own research, and lots of other people have found this as well, is that play supports multiple aspects of development, cognitive development, socio-emotional development, and physical development, and it's not just school where learning and development takes place, even academic development. So many aspects of play support academic development and I think getting that importance of play, getting that knowledge to policymakers and to a lot of educators, I think would be really valuable.

I think it ties in with Covid because there's a lot of pushing around [the idea of] learning loss, and it is important, you know—a lot of children, a lot of families have suffered to a certain extent. But I think the amount of learning loss may depend on the individual child, the family, the stage that they're at in school. In Ireland, the lockdowns went on for quite a period of time, but what we found was that actually there was a lot of play going on, and that this was supporting multiple aspects of development. So, while there might have been learning loss in school, there was a lot of learning taking place through play.

Nevena: What was most important for us was that play functions as an opportunity together. Together. So, I think that a lot of people today look at play as some sort of benefit, of course, but for individual children, that they will learn something, and children will gain some sort of cognitive skills or something else. But that's just like marginal stuff. The most important thing is the opportunity together, and to really work together on something that is different, something that is beyond the context into which we are put.

Julia: I think it surprised me how productive these discussions have been in actual fact, and how they helped us. I also like the fact that they are multivocal, you know this is collaborative with so many voices, co-produced. So, it's not actually one person's or two people's points of view. It's interesting to have this kind of thing. There's probably a word for this but I don't know what it is, but you know some sort of metaphor for all these different points, intersecting and diverging and so on. And I think that's a good way to finish.

Acknowledgements

The editors would like to acknowledge the generous financial support of the University of Sheffield and the Folklore Society (London) in the publication of this book. We also wish to thank Alessandra Tosi and colleagues at Open Book Publishers for their enthusiasm and commitment to open access publishing. Lastly, we appreciate the time and goodwill of all those who participated in this global study and wish everyone good health.

Index

About the Team

Alessandra Tosi was the managing editor for this book.

Melissa Purkiss performed the copy-editing and indexing.

Jeevanjot Kaur Nagpal designed the cover. The cover was produced in InDesign using the Fontin font.

Melissa Purkiss typeset the book in InDesign and produced the paperback and hardback editions. The text font is Tex Gyre Pagella; the heading font is Californian FB.

Cameron Craig produced the EPUB and PDF editions..

Ross Higman produced the HTML and XML editions. The conversion is performed with open source software such as pandoc (https://pandoc.org/) created by John MacFarlane and other tools freely available on our GitHub page (https://github.com/OpenBookPublishers).

This book need not end here...

Share

All our books — including the one you have just read — are free to access online so that students, researchers and members of the public who can't afford a printed edition will have access to the same ideas. This title will be accessed online by hundreds of readers each month across the globe: why not share the link so that someone you know is one of them?

This book and additional content is available at:
https://doi.org/10.11647/OBP.0326

Donate

Open Book Publishers is an award-winning, scholar-led, not-for-profit press making knowledge freely available one book at a time. We don't charge authors to publish with us: instead, our work is supported by our library members and by donations from people who believe that research shouldn't be locked behind paywalls.

Why not join them in freeing knowledge by supporting us:
https://www.openbookpublishers.com/support-us

Follow @OpenBookPublish 🐦

Read more at the Open Book Publishers **BLOG**

You may also be interested in:

Susan Isaacs
A Life Freeing the Minds of Children
Philip Graham

https://doi.org/10.11647/obp.0297

**Learning, Marginalization, and Improving
the Quality of Education in Low-income
Countries**
Daniel A. Wagner, Nathan M. Castillo and Suzanne Grant Lewis

https://doi.org/10.11647/obp.0256

Mary Warnock
Ethics, Education and Public Policy in Post-War Britain
Philip Graham

https://doi.org/10.11647/obp.0278

Milton Keynes UK
Ingram Content Group UK Ltd.
UKHW020933160324
439531UK00002B/10